FOLK-CUSTOMS
IN
TAMILNADU

FOLK-CUSTOMS
IN
TAMILNADU

G. Shanthi

SHARADA

Sharada Publishing House
Delhi

First Published : 2012

ISBN : 978-81-88934-69-0

₹ 1400

Published by
Anjana Bansal
SHARADA PUBLISHING HOUSE
111, Vidya Vihar Apartment, Sector-9
Rohini, Delhi-110 085 (INDIA)
Ph. : +91-11-3292 1560, 2755 2102
Email : bansal_sph@rediffmail.com
Website : www.sharadabooks.com

Printed at
Salasar Imaging Systems
Delhi

Contents

Acknowledgements

I am deeply thankful to my professor Dr. S. Agesthialingam, Director, Centre of Advanced Study in Linguistics, Annamalai University for his constant help, valuable suggestions during my ICSSR Post-Doctoral work.

I wish to record my thanks to Dr. V. Gomathinoyakam, Head of the Department of Sociology, Annamalai University and Dr. S. Sakthiwal, Lecturer, CAS in Linguistics, Annamalai University for their help during my ICSSR Post-Doctoral work.

I have to thank Dr. S. Suyambulingom, Department of Mathematics, Agricultural University, Coimbatore for his help while collecting date in Coimbatore. I convey my heartiest thanks to Mr. K. Somasundaram, TPTC, Chidambaram for his constant help during my data-collection in all the villages.

I am thankful to Mr. D. Palanisamy, P.G. Assistant in Botany and to Mr. Tamilmani, P.G. Assistant in Zoology of PRG Higher Secondary School, Udayarkudi for their help during my data-collection in Udayarkudi village. I am also very much thankful to Mr. Mohanram, Kannan of Thiruvendipuram for their help during my data collection in Thiruvendipuram. I am thankful to Mr. and Mrs. Pitchaimuttu and his family members, Headmaster, Valayamadavi for their constant help during my visit for data-collection in Valayamadevi.

My heartful thanks to The Director, Indian Council of Social Science Research, New Delhi for awarding me this fellowship to enable me to do this project.

I am thankful to Mr. M. Muthukumaraswamy, Librarian, Department of Linguistics, for helping me by giving books and to Mr. P. Parathasi, Department of Linguistics for typing this project work.

I am thankful to all the informants for their cooperation during my data-collection. Once again I wish to convey my thanks to all, those who helped during this project work.

Lastly, I am thankful to Mrs. Anjana Bansal, Sharada Publishing House published this project.

G. Shanthi

Introduction

"Customs and traditions are group accepted techniques of control that have become well established, that are taken for granted and that are passed along from generation to generation" (Bogardus, E.S., "Sociology").

Custom can be considered as a broad term embracing all the folkways and mores. In day-to-day life custom is used as synonymous with habit, but there are vital differences between the two. Habit is a personal phenomenon while custom is a social phenomenon. "A custom is formed on the basis of habit gaining the sanction and the influence and therefore, the social significance which is peculiar to it" (Maclver, Society).

Customs are social habits which through repetition become the basis of an order of social behaviour. They are long established habits and usages of the people. A peculiar characteristic of custom is that it exists only as a social relationship and has for the individual an external sanction. The social character of custom is revealed by those customs which cannot be practiced but collectively, for example, the various celebrations on the occasion of birth, marriage and death etc. when people come together and by participating in a common occasion stimulate the social consciousness of one another. According to Davis, Kingsley in "Human Society", the term "custom" is "closer to folkways than to mores, but it tends to convey the traditional, automatic and mass character of both of them."

Customs create habits—though custom is the result of habit,

however, there are many customs which may give rise to habits and be supported by them. Thus, customs create habits and habits create customs. Thus, the two, though distinct, are intricately related in social life. The process of custom determining the habits and the habits in turn determining customs is a significant aspect of social organization.

When the customs and habits are compared, former is a social phenomenon, socially recognised, is normative, has got great social significance, maintains social order, is inherited, has an external sanction whereas the latter is an individual phenomenon, is not socially recognised, is not normative, is more personal importance, facilitates individual activity, is learnt and has no external sanction.

A customs is traditional practice—a mode of individual or a habit of social life—that is transmitted by word of mouth or initiation, then ingrained by social pressure, common usage and parental or other authority.

"A custom may be either peculiar to a single family or it may be common to a group of families, the common bond of union being regencies in a particular locality or unity of tribe or caste or unity of creed" (Heramba Chatterjee Sastri "The social background of the forms of Marriage in Ancient India"—Volume II).

Folklife refers to the full traditional lore, behaviour and material culture of any folk group, with emphasis on the customary and material categories. Hindu customs and ceremonies are the pillars upon which the entire edifice of Hindu civilization is established. "The Hindu customs and ceremonies are as ancient as the mightily Himalayas; yet it is equally as modern as atomic era. It spirit of modernity extends from the inner man to his outer science, from his unsuspected self to the produce of his intellect and reason. In this sense, science is not the enemy of Hinduism but a preparation for it" (B.N. Banerjee, "Hindu Culture, Custom and Ceremony").

Alexander H. Krappa in his book 'The Science of Folklore' divide the body of customs and rites into three classes *viz.*, (1) rites connected with definite days and seasons of the solar year; (2) rites observed on definite occasions such as birth, marriage, death etc; and (3) special rites of aversion and avoidance.

First one is compared with the Hindu festivals, function, celebration within a year. Second one is compared with the custom, ceremonies, rituals etc. of the Hindu caste people (this project work is the same as above). Third is compared to superstitions.

Social customs have a new dignity and value to those who regard them as the expressions of the communal will and the crystallizations of the communal experience. Folk-customs are the social customs. Customs and folk-customs are one and the same, since in every Folk's life their culture, tradition etc. are reflected through their customs, habits etc. Mostly, custom includes celebrations, ceremonies and rituals connected with a human life cycle. In "Hindu" religion we can find customs far each and every moment of a life cycle.

P.V. Dagadisa Ayyar in his book "South Indian Customs" points out that "Not even a single one of the Hindu customs, however unimportant and simple, is without a religious basic or principle behind it." Therefore, the Hindus hold that their customs and usages are inviolable though they appear to be meaningless and unintelligible at the present valiant in the land are, in the opinion of the "Hindus", "as sacred as religion itself."

Caste System

India is a country containing innumerable caste people. The basic Hindu social institution is caste (B.N. Banerjee "Hindu Culture, Custom and Ceremony"—In Part-II viz., "Hindu Custom"). The division of labour in the socio-economic development came to be known as caste systems. As a result, assigning tasks to different sections of the society necessitated the recording of rules and norms for functioning of the society as harmonious group. These records also were codified and modified. The existing rituals and ceremonies prescribing new ones. This is the classical economic theory about the origin of Hindu caste system.

According to Hindu culture the "Caste system" was not to divide the Hindu society but bring about its organizational unity and human solidarity.

Moreover, India was the home of many societies with different cultural and social traditions. To preserve their separate entity, barriers were set up. Foreign tribes invaded India and settled down in the country adapting Hindu customs. These people formed a new separate caste. The number of sub-castes was produced by the inter-mixture of various castes.

The present work is divided into two parts. First part consists of Analysis of Folk-customs consisting of five chapter viz.,

1. Folk-customs—A Sociological point of view,
2. Folk-customs—An Anthropological point of view,
3. Folk-customs—Caste variation,
4. Folk-customs—Regional variation,
5. Folk-customs—Rural and Urban area differences.

Second part consists of the collection of Folk customs from various caste people. There are six chapters viz.,

1. Customs connected with child birth and childhood days;
2. Customs regarding "Sacred thread ceremony" and "Puberty Rituals";
3. Marriage customs;
4. Customs during first pregnancy;
5. "Sashtiyapthapurthi" and "Sadhabhishegam"; and
6. Death customs.

A list of folk-songs collected during the date collection and also a sample of questionnaire is attached in the appendix part.

Conclusion is also given in the end of the Part-I viz., Analysis part. An introduction is given in the beginning of the Part-II, in which the informations about the informations are given. Map are also drawn to indicate the villages from which the data are collected.

Part-I
FOLK-CUSTOMS

1

Folk Customs : A Sociological Point of View

Sociological study helps to understand the social phenomena and it centres around the society of men. Society of man poses certain qualities, some of these are as old as the society itself and some are as new as changing world around us. Due to circumstances and habits man lives in groups. Maclver and Page define "By group we mean any collection of human beings who are brought into social relationships with one another."

Social groups can be divided into two viz. (1) Primary groups and (2) Secondary groups.

Primary Groups

The primary group in the form of the family initiates into the secrets of society. Essential conditions for primary groups are closeness, smallness and continuation of the association. Closeness means a degree of physical proximity. Awareness of a group develops with the degree nearness that a particular group makes available to its members because by physical closeness or a type of physical closeness made possible by modern means of communication, an individual can most easily use the means of establishing closer ties of association. Smallness of a group facilitates full participation of its members in some common activity. It also helps in a better understanding amongst its members. These two factors are the determinant of the strength of a group. Continuation of association is necessary in primary group, duration of relationship of the members of groups strengthen them.

These main aspect viz. closeness, smallness and continuity (or) durability of association are the three inter-related essentials of a primary group.

Secondary Groups

The secondary group consists of an area of secondary contacts in which relationships are impersonal, formal and conventional. Large-scale associations of men, the impersonal organisation represent the secondary groups. Secondary groups show the characteristics (which are not explained here since they are not essential for this chapter), which remain in sharp contrast with characteristics of the primary groups. The main distinction between primary and secondary groups are as follows :

Primary groups	*Secondary groups*
(a) They are small and their membership is limited	They are large and their membership is not limited
(b) The relations among this group are spontaneous and develop unconsciously	The relations among this group are developed consciously
(c) They are informal	They are formal
(d) This group is regulated by customs, folkway and mores	This group is based on formal control viz., codes and laws
(e) They are universal and are found in every culture and society	They are not universal in nature

The folkways may be defined as those social behaviour patterns of men which are common to all and have their base deep down to the primitive animal life of man. Renter and Mart define "The folkways are simply habits of action common to the members of a group. They are ways of the folk that are somewhat standarised and have degree of tradition sanction for their persistence". Maclver and Page "The folkways are the recognised or accepted ways of behaviour in society".

Folk beliefs and manners of action (customs) are an important part of all societies, primitives as well as civilized. Though superficially folkways may not seem essential, yet, their very persistency makes them important from the sociological point of view. Many social superstitions prevalent in our society have their origin in man's primitive life, yet they influence the course of our social behaviour. Through folkways, past comes to live with present.

Society is a dynamic phenomena. It changes its forms according to geographical and cultural conditions. Culture has two main aspects viz., Material culture and Non-Material culture. Material culture is reflected in Science and technology whereas Non-Material culture is revealed in traditions, customs, folkways, mores, norms and valuations. In some societies, it is the non-material culture that predominates. On the basis of culture, society has been classified into the following categories as : (a) simple or traditional society and (b) complex or open society.

In a traditional society, people are guided more by religion and spiritual consideration. The role and status are based on the ascribed system. Social statue is based on birth and heredity. Since the traditional society is custom-bound, as such there is lack of social mobility. The main characteristic features of the traditional society is governed by traditions, customs, religion and conservation. Social life is governed by traditions and customs. Family, caste, religion and clan are the main agencies which regulate social behaviour. Social life is relatively unchanged because it is connected with the ascribed bases of social existence. The traditional society is rigid in its structure since members of such society are governed by traditions and customs. Similarly, social stratification is based on the ascribed system. Since the customs and traditions have strong control, there is less change in role and statue. People generally follow their hereditary occupations. Due to these factors mobility in a traditional society is very low.

Caste

The Indian caste system is also a unique system of social stratification. In first place caste is connected with economic differentiation. In the traditional village economy caste is an occupational group. Caste is social phenomena found in almost all human societies but at nowhere it took such a well defined and rigid form as it did in India. Caste implies an element of heredity and birth in social stratification.

Sir Risely defines "caste is a collection of families, group of families bearing a common name, claiming a common descent from a mythical ancestor, human or divines, professing to follow the same hereditary calling and regarded by those who are competent to give an opinion as forming single homogenous community."

Social norms, occupy an important place in the life of the society as well as individual. They regulate, control and influence the individuals before society and collective behaviour of the members of the society. Folkways and mores are a part of our social life. They influence the individual as well as social behaviour and that is why, they are important in our social life.

Folkways are not universal. It differs from society to society. It is so because of the conditions, the attitudes, the socio-economic conditions and cultural background of different society. Tradition as defined by Ginsburg, "By tradition is meant the sum of all the ideas, habits and customs that belong to people and are transmitted from generation to generation" (The Psychology of Society"—Morris Ginsburg").

Origin of Custom

A custom does not grew all of a sudden. It is a gradual development and takes good deal of time. In fact, it is a means to strengthen the existence and the values of the society.

Customs influence the individual behaviour as well as social behaviour. Customs occupy an important place in the society. Most of the customs among Hindus are based on religious belief. Every custom is based upon certain beliefs (mostly religious). Following are the customs pertaining to a particular social group even though there are basic customs and beliefs common to all social groups in the Hindu society.

All the customs from child birth to death (customs of a human life cycle) are collected from various social group (caste) and the particular custom pertaining to a social group are given in the following pages.

Regarding child birth, it is in custom to celebrate putting arm-rings to the children on 7th or 9th day in Brahmin (Iyer) caste. At that time they clean the roller in a pair of grinding stones and smear sandal paste, turmeric powder, *kumkum*, put flower and a new cloth on it. Then a married lady puts the roller in the cradle thrice and take it out. This custom is based on the belief that this will give a child to a childless married lady. This custom is in vogue only among this social group.

In Brahmin (iyangar) while celebrating "Naming ceremony", they write a few names on the paddy and put black (or) red thread across the paddy, place the child on the thread in the direction east to west and tie the thread in it's waist. After that, child's mother whisper the child's father's name (i.e. her husband's name) in the ears of the child and take the child from the paddy. At that time it is usual to place *kumkum* or collyrium on the forehead of the children the same day they celebrate "virai daanam" (giving seeds to some brahmins). Child's father's parents have to meet the expenditure for this function. On this occasion it is a custom to give paddy, betel leaf, nut, plantain, fruits, twenty five or fifty paise coins to some brahmins as alms. At the time of presenting these things, the brahmins who get the alms have to spread the *dhoti* around their waist and the child's father has to put these alms in the *dhoti*. These alms are compulsorily first put in a corner after the brahmins went to their houses. These people are unable to explain the belief for doing this custom. These are pertaining to this social group only.

In the same way, the Pillai group people insert margosa leaves on the front of the pial and fix a margosa stick in front of the pial where the child is born. This custom is in vogue only among this group and it is based on the belief that ghosts will not enter and take away the child from that place when there is margosa leaves, stick etc. On that day, they cook meals with seven green leaves and give it to the child's mother. An old married lady mix nine varieties of grain in the cowdung and places it on the wall. These people also give "virai daanam" on 15th day after child birth if the first child is a male. On that day they put new dresses to the child, place the child in a big plate, place pen, notebook etc. by the side of the child. Then they invite a brahmin and give him sugar, plantain, fruits, paddy, grains, coins etc. and similar gifts are given to four other persons. These are done on the belief that the child will lead a long, prosperous life.

While putting arm-rings they first tie the fibre of the white coarse plant (vellerukku nar) around the waist, the belief that the blemishes will not affect the body of the child. On this day these people celebrate an important function and give offerings to Goddess Mariyamman. They place "kalasas" before Goddess Mari, pour water inside it and place Margosa leaves in the "Kalasas". They offer a mixture of rice and jaggery at that time. When offerings are given to Goddess Mari, they tie a yellow string with a piece of turmeric root to the mother and the child. On that day, it is usual to prepare "Kaayappiti"—an edible which is made by mixing and powdering the gingely seeds and jaggery, and this powder is given a round shape by pressing it in the hands. These customs are peculiar to this social group only.

Vysya Chattiyar people also put the roller in the cradle on the day of "cradling ceremony" like Brahmin (iyer) caste people on the same belief.

Vaniya Chattier people put golden ornaments into the

measuring pot and it is shaken and a name is given to the child on the day of "naming ceremony".

When the child attains first year the Brahmin (iyer), Brahmin (iyangar) and Vysya chettiar people do a function "aayishomem". This is done on the belief that this will give long life to the child.

Cakkili (cobbler) caste people celebrate a function viz., "Sooru uttum dinam" (food giving ceremony) between first and five years old child. When we look into the customs done at the completion of fifth year, Brahmin (iyer) caste people have a peculiar custom. While the child is admitted to the school, they take betel leaf, nut, plantain, paddy full of corn-measure and a turmeric root. After going to the school they give turmeric root in the hand's of the child and make the child first to write in the paddy (in the corn measure) by the turmeric root. This is done only by this group people.

These are the peculiar features of child birth and childhood days among certain social group which are celebrated and done generation by generation.

Likewise when we look into the ceremonies, celebrations of the boys aged between ten and twenty, only Brahmin (iyer), Brahmin (iyangar), Asari (Pattar-goldsmith, taccar-carpenter) group people celebrate the "Sacred thread ceremony" (Punul kalyanam). The customs regarding this ceremony are more or less same in all the above four social groups.

Regarding the celebrations of the girls aged between ten and twenty "puberty ritual" is an important custom, which is in vogue among most of the social groups. Brahmin (iyer), Community people did not celebrate this ritual elaborately like other social groups. In other castes the basic custom is more or less same with slight differences (It is mentioned in Chapter 7, of Part II). In all social groups it is in custom to leave the girl in a separate room as soon as the girl attains her age. But in Senguzta Mutaliyar caste they build a hut made up of two millet mats and then only they leave the girl inside the hut. In cobbler group people they prepare a hut made up of green coconut leaves and leave the girl inside the hut for thirty two days.

Among Vysya chattiyar people they do "punniyadaviam" on 11th or 13th day. On that day afternoon (or) in the evening they celebrate a function viz. *tatibom* to remove the ceremonial impurity. For that they place five standing lamps in the position of a square and put five thread wicks in five faces of the lamp and light the wick. Then they connect these five lamps by five or seven threads and the girl and the other seven members sit inside it. Then they smear sandal paste and *kumkum* etc. to the girl and the other seven members give *kumkum* and turmeric (both made like a ball) to the girl. The girl decorates her leg with these balls and she does this to the other seven members with her, and throws away the balls so on to hit the wall on her back. After that she gives turmeric, *kumkum,* blouse piece to the other seven members with her. Then one among the seven cut the thread connecting the five lamps by sharp knife and after this the seven members take bath and a grand feast is arranged.

Menstruating period is considered to be ceremonially impure in Hindu society. When a girl first attains her age then in all social group they leave the girl in a separate place and only after doing "punniyadanam" i.e., the act of removing the ceremonial impurity due to attaining age, they allow the girl inside the house. Not only that is in custom, but every month at the time of menstruating period the girl is to be in a separate place or room for three days. These customs are in vogue from generation to generation. These customs are based on the belief that the ceremonial impurities are not strictly allowed in Hindu society and they has to be removed, otherwise they believe that the evil aspects will affect their family.

After these celebrations, Marriage ceremony is an important custom among all social groups. In Brahmin (iyer) and Brahmin (iyangar), they give more importance in the agreement of the horoscope than in other castes. In these castes only the bride's horoscope is to be sent to the bridegroom's house. But in all the other castes this is in other way round.

Particularly in Vysya chattiyar caste, if the bride's and bridegroom's party approve each other, the bridegroom's party go to the bride's house and discuss about the dowry etc. In this discussion itself they talk about the things for "vadugu" (punul kalyanam), about the five kind of tiffens, silver vessels, the rate for "aavani avittam", for the "first night", for Deepawali, for the ceremony in which changing the marriage badge etc. only if the rates and other things are agreed, they select an auspicious day for the engagement.

Engagement is celebrated in the bride's house. On that day itself they seat the bride and bridegroom side by side. On that day they fix up an auspicious day for the marriage. For both the parties there will be a broker and both the parties have to give a deposit amount to him. This is done for not changing their words. All the details are written in a document and given to both parties. Then the dresses from bride's to bridegroom's and from the bridegroom's to bride's party are given to the bride and bridegroom respectively. Both the bride and bridegroom wear the new dresses and they sit together in a seat. Then they show "aalam" around their head.

In Soozhiya Chettiyar caste, they send the bride to bridegroom's house immediately after engagement and only the day before marriage they invite the girl to their house.

After engagement marriage celebrations are done. Brahmin caste people instead of celebrating "puberty rituals", they celebrate a function, on the belief that "ghost will not seize the girl and any blemish will not affect her." The day before marriage day they decorate the girl, seven or nine married women place seven or nine things (like paddy, lighted lamp, grains etc.) around her. Then they place these things on the parts of her body like head, shoulder, hand, leg and take back. Usually, marriage is celebrated in the bride's house in this caste on the marriage day they celebrate a function known as "Paradesik koolam". At that time, the bridegroom has to wear nine yards *dhoti* and a towel and hold a bundle of cloth. A friend or brother-in-law of the bridegroom hold an umbrella for the bridegroom at this time and then the bridegroom undertakes "yadhradanam". After this function the bridegroom return back. Then the bride and bridegroom are seated in a swing and the aged women show the "paccaipiti" (the cooked rice mixed with turmeric powder and *kumkum* and made like a ball) around bride and bridegroom thrice in clockwise and thrice in anti-clockwise direction.

After this function the girl has to change her dress, to wear nine yards saree. It is a peculiar custom among this social group is that the girl is to be seated on her father's lap, a ploughing instrument is placed on the head of the girl and taken back. This is done in the belief that "the girl will lead her life in a fertile manner". The nine yards saree worn at the time of tying marriage badge is in a deep red or purple colour. This saree has to be worn on all the festival and ceremonial days (but now this custom is chaning). These people wear two marriage badges, one from bride's house, another from bridegroom's house. These are the main peculiar customs different from other social group.

Brahmin (iyangar) caste people do the marriage as per the above caste people but with one difference. While tying marriage badge bridegroom's father has to sit on a raised seat made up of paddy specially built up for this occasion. Bride's father has to sit below the fort. Then the bridegroom and the bride has to sit on the lap of their father respectively. Only after this bridegroom tie the marriage badge to the bride. This custom is in vogue due to prestige motive.

In Pillai caste after tying marriage badge (in all castes except in Brahmin (iyer), Brahmin (iyangar), viswakarma (goldsmith), this custom is in practice), it is in custom to tie golden plate tied in yellow string on the forehead of the bride. For this, this caste people spread rice on the floor, place a plantain leaf on it and the bride stands on it. Then her mother-in-law, sister-in-law tie the golden plate on her forehead. Likewise bridegroom's mother-in-law, sister-in-law tie the golden plate on his forehead. This is a peculiar custom among this social group.

Pattar (goldsmith), taccar (carpenter) caste people wear nine yards saree at the time of tying marriage badge. Before marriage goldsmith caste people celebrate a ceremony "kappu kattutal". On that day a new pot is bought and it is decorated by turmeric powder, *kumkum* etc. and a yellow string is tied round it. Then five married women put the paddy in that pot and pour water on the paddy, light and show the camphor. Then with that fire of the camphor they kindle fire in the hearth and the paddy is boiled and it is ground to become a rice. Then before the brick is taken to the bridegroom's house they worship and offer to their family God by cooking the above mentioned rice. These people also tie two marriage badges.

Sengunta Mutaliyar caste people wear "pottuttaali" (small round size marriage badge) and these people can marry again when a lady became a widow. This is not so in other social groups.

In cobbler caste they celebrate a ceremony viz. "puttu kumpitutal" (worshiping the ant hill) immediately after marriage. At that time the newly married couple, friends, relatives all go to the forest and worship their family God "Madurai Viran" (also called as "mada sami"). Bark of the cassia airiculate (avaram seti) is cut and erected on an ant-hill. Then goat, cock etc. are killed and offered to it (This plant's bark is used to tan leather. So, this plant is worshiped by these caste people as a God since this plant's bark helps them in their work viz., repairing the chappels etc. So, this group of people worship this first immediately after the marriage). At this time they will sing and dance. After finishing the ceremony, these people return back to their house and worship the God in the house. This particular custom is not in vogue in other social groups.

Most of the Marriage customs of vysya chattiyar are peculiar which are mentioned in the Part-II under Marriage customs (cf. Chapter 9, p. 424). These elaborate customs and beliefs are not found in other caste people.

When we look into the customs regarding marriage of Yadhavappillai caste people (konar) there is a peculiar custom done if the horoscopes of the bride and bridegroom do not agree. If the horoscopes do not agree, then they cook rice, divide them into three parts, put gold, silver, copper powder in the three parts respectively. Then they place it for the crow to take and if the crow takes the food mixed with silver powder then they proceed further in this matter.

These are the peculiar customs regarding marriage pertaining to each social group which are handed down from generation to generation. Apart from these customs there are basic customs common to all social groups.

After marriage pregnancy is an important aspect in every human life. First pregnancy is celebrated in every social group in a grand manner. Even though the basic customs resemble one another in the various group there are some peculiar customs pertaining to each social group.

In Brahmin (iyer), if a lady is pregnant they take a black saree (termed as "macakkai karuppu") on the 5th month to the pregnant lady. They celebrate "valaikappu" on 7th month (like other social groups) and "Siimandam" on 8th or 9th month in the bridegroom's house.

In Brahmin (iyangar) caste, on 9th month bride's parents prepare a sweat (appam) parcel tie it in a plantain leaf and tie that plantain leaf to the pregnant lady's belly (in that portion of the saree). Then they bring the girl to their house. These people also celebrate "valaikappu" and "siimandam" as per the above caste people.

In Pillai caste they do not celebrate "valaikappu" or "Siimandam". But the 7th month in both bride's and bride-groom's house they tie vasampu (sweet flag) in gold and tie it in the marriage badge chain.

Pattar caste people also tie vasampu (sweet flag) in gold and tie it in the marriage badge chain in 5th month. They also celebrate "valaikappu" in 7th or 9th month like other caste people.

In Vysya chattiyar, if a lady is pregnant then they celebrate some functions which are mentioned under Part II (cf. Chapter 10, part II, p. 478).

In Sozhiya chettiar in 7th month they tie vasampu (sweet flag) and celebrate "siimandam" They do not celebrate "valaikappu".

Isai Velalar caste people take new black saree (termed as "macakkai karuppu") on the 5th month. If the black is not acceptable to their family God or Goddess, they take other colour saree.

In Barber and Nadar caste people also they take black saree in the fifth month and other customs resemble the other caste people.

The above mentioned customs practiced by the social groups are in vogue from generation to generation.

Apart from this some social group celebrate "Sashtiyapthapurthi" (60th birthday) and "sadhabhishegam" (71st or 80th birth day). The customs are same for all social groups who celebrate it. Among the thirty social groups (mentioned in this work) only Brahmin (iyer), Brahmin (iyangar), Pillai, Isai velalar, Patayacci, Sengunta Mutaliyar, pattar (goldsmith), Asari (carpenter), Chettiyar (vysya), Chettiyar (sozhiya), Chettiyar (vaniya), Pillai (tuluva vellalar), Reddiar, Naidu, Thondaimandala Mutaliyar, Nadar, Dever, Udayar, Kallar (devar), Tuluva Naickar, Jankamar, Konar (yathavappillai), Vannan (washerman), Navitar (barber) cakkili (cobbler) celebrate this "Sashtiyapthapurthi". The other social groups people viz. Nayakkar (canar), Nayakkar (tatar), Muppanar, Kuravar (asmajoki) and Harijan do not celebrate this 60th birthday. Those social groups celebrate this function, celebrate this more or less in the same manner. Likewise "sadhabhishegam" is celebrated by Brahmin (iyer), Brahmin (iyangar), Pillai, isai veleler, cengunta Mutaliyar, Pattar (goldsmith), Asari (carpenter), Chattiyar (vysya), Reddiar, Thondaimandala Mutaliyar, Udyaar and Cakkili. the remaining group people do not celebrate this function. Moreover, all the social groups who celebrate this function do it more or less in the same manner.

Death is the end of the human life and at the time of death also, various social group celebrate some customs and ceremonies. The main difference between the Brahmin (iyer), Brahmin (iyangar) group people and the other group people is that Brahmins never keep the dead body for long time for any reason and they cremate the body on the same day when death occurs.

In other social groups except Brahmins there is a custom of doing a ceremony "vazhi kuutti vitutal" (showing the way to the dead body) and then only they send the news to others and weep. A peculiar custom among Pillai group people is that after doing the funeral ceremonies on the first day, they take bath and before returning to the house they give lamp, plate, tumbler etc. to a brahmin priest, as an alm (daanam). This is done in the belief that the dead persons will be lighted to reach their place. In pattar, Asari caste people they bury the dead body in a sitting posture.

In Brahmin (iyangar) group people and Naidu group people the death customs are done only after removing the "Vainava muttirai daanam", i.e., when young, brahmin priest comes and puts "muttirai" in the hands of the person and only after removing this they do all the death ceremonies. When persons with this "muttirai" die, the priest comes and burns the "muttirai" by means of fire and then do the other death customs. It is a peculiar custom among these social group people.

In Brahmin caste (iyer) on 15th day they give "maaciyam" (a ceremony for a dead person). They give the same on 27th day, 3rd month and 6th month. In Brahmin (iyangar) caste people on the day of "paal teli" they cook meals without salt and put it into the river. Then within ten days of the death of the person they have to give a *dhoti*, pot made up of white metal, spoon, lamp, coins etc. as alms to a person. Then from the 10th day to 12th day they give various type of alms to a brahmin priest (All these are mentioned in the chapter 12, Part II, p. 496). Under Death customs, Cakkili caste people do a ceremony "pezhem parapputal" on 8th day.

The other basic customs regarding death are more or less alike for the various social groups and are celebrated with slight difference. Thus, from child birth to death each social group have their own way of celebrating certain ceremonies, these customs are handed down from generation to generation and reflect the socio-economic condition of every society.

Thus we can conclude customs are formed spontaneously because of society. They are a part of social inheritance and are not formed by individuals. Customs are conservative and it is not easy to change them. Customs have capacity to influence the behaviour of the individuals more effectively and in a more comprehensive manner as compared to traditions.

From the above discussions of various folk-customs of various social group, we can say that customs provide readymade pattern of bahaviour and it simplifies the process of learning of the individual. Due to this it is easy for individual members, to establish adjustment with the social situations and meet the new social situations in an senior manner. Customs bring about the elements of uniformity in the social behaviour of the individuals as members of the society.

These customs control the behaviour of the individuals. They force them to act according to the prescribed patterns. They do not allow the individuals to go astray. Thus, these customs act as important agencies of controlling the behaviour of the individual members of the society and also collective behaviour of the society.

2

Folk-Customs : An Anthropological Point of View

Anthropology is "the science of man and his works and behaviour" Cultural Anthropology is an important branch of anthropology which studies the cultural heritage of man. Culture is a powerful force in human behaviour, in both individual and social. Human society and culture are the intimately intertwined aspects of a complex of phenomena that regularly occur only in association, whereas on the unhuman level, societies occur but there is no significant culture.

Customs are the only source to know about the unlettered peoples since they do not leave any biographies and written histories about them. So, the main thing they left us are their customs and customs are culture. In man, society and culture come so intertwined that one never occurs without the other.

There are various methods to study the culture and society, but the functional methods is the best progressive developmental method. This method is based on the assumption that every cultural element has a definite functional role. On the basis of this functional role, the culture can be easily understood. This method gives emphasis on the study of culture as a whole, rather then on the basis of its various components. According to Malinowski, the different elements of culture are related with each other. Each element satisfies human needs in a particular way. Therefore, in order to understand the culture, it is better to study the function which it performs.

The functional method is based on certain assumptions. Chief among them are :

1. Study of cause and effect relationship. According to this, the different elements are inter connected with each other. This method gives emphasis on the search of cause and effect relationship between the various parts of culture.

2. Study of relationship between the unit and the whole-culture is an integral whole. It is constituted by various elements. Functional method, therefore discovers the relationships which exist between the various components of culture.

3. Functional determinism—According to this method, the nature of each part of culture or institution is determined in accordance to its function. Therefore, in-order to understand the various units of culture, it is necessary to study the functions which they fulfill. So, this functional method is very useful in the study of culture and social institutions in the anthropological studies, therefore, it occupies a very significant place.

Every custom of human life cycle is celebrated to satisfy the human needs. When we take the life of human life cycle from birth to death, we can find a number of customs. There are handed down from generation to generation, these reflect the culture of the society. Each social group has its own way of cultural background to celebrate the functions. Even though they have their own way of cultural background, the basic functions are one and the same.

If we look into the customs of 1. Child birth, 2. childhood days, 3. Puberty rituals, 4. Sacred thread ceremony, 5. Marriage, 6. Pregnancy, 7. Sashtiyapthapurthi, sadhabhishegam, and 8. Death ceremonies etc. are inter-connected with each other even though they are different elements of culture. By means of functional method we can discover the relationships which exists between the various components (mentioned above) of culture.

Customs, traditions, thoughts, beliefs, faiths, superstitions etc. are embodied in culture. In other words, we can say whatever man posses, that is his culture. Man is a combination of biological and social elements. These two merge together in the behaviour of man. Behaviour of man is not constant and it changes in accordance to place and time. It has undergone continuous changes throughout the history of human society. New learnings and experiences always change the pattern of human behaviour of a social group. Culture being the essence of human experience, and behaviour itself changes through the efforts of human society. Culture consists of the manifestations of human behaviour. Culture is therefore man-made.

Many scholars defined culture in various ways, chief among them are as follows :

Taylor—According to Taylor "Culture is that complex whole, which includes knowledge, belief, art, morals, law, custom and other capabilities acquired by man as a member of society.

D.S. Slotkin—D.S. Slotkin, in his book "Social Anthropology" defines culture in the following words :

"A culture is the body of customs, found in a society, and anyone who acts according to these customs is a participant in culture. From biological point of view, its culture is the means by which a society generally follow the same body of customs".

General Characteristics of Culture

(1) Culture is learnt and is transmitted from one generation to the other. (2) Culture is social because it could not develop outside society, culture is that totality, which human beings posses as members of society. (3) Culture is social heritage of man—culture is not confined to any particular generation. It is rather a social heritage which is transmitted from generation to generation. It is the function of culture to pick up and nurse those experience of man which are eternal in nature. It collects the gems and discards the stones. (4) Culture satisfies human needs—culture meets the demands of mankind. The demand of reproduction, of nursing an infant during dependency etc., are met by culture from generation to generation. (5) Culture

is the product of human society. Among all the creatures only man has the capacity to create culture. No derives this capacity from culture.

Culture is social in its essence because there is no culture beyond society. Culture is not possible without society as such the factors involved in the growth of culture could be traced in the social life. Man cannot live without society. This collectivity which man has created during the long course of his evolution is known as society.

Culture is not the product of a particular period or age. It grows through ages. It is as old as the human society itself. The present stage of culture is the result of long history. There are various views regarding the growth and development of cultures; some of the thinkers are of the opinion that each culture is independent, consequently each culture has its own course of development.

In this chapter main concept of life viz. Marriage is discussed. Marriage customs reflects the culture of a social group as well as a society. In Hindu culture marriage plays an important role. Marriage as an institution, has been prevalent in primitive as well as in modern societies. The Institution of marriage has changed according to the changes in the society. There is difference in the marriage as it was prevalent in the primitive society and the marriage in a civilized society, but the basic elements of marriage remain the same. Marriage is defined by various scholars. Western Mark defines :

"Marriages as a relation of one or more men to one or more women which is recognized by custom of law and involves certain rights and duties in the case of both the parties entering the union and in the case of the children borned of it."

Gillin and Gillin defines

"Marriage is socially approved and way of establishing a family by procession".

From the definitions given by all scholars we find that marriage is an institution which grants sanction to certain relation-physical, psychological, social and economic, etc. It also determines their social relationship and lays down the norms for the recognition of children, born of their relationship by the society.

Different Forms of Marriage

Marriage, as prevalent today, has different forms. Its forms are guided by the cultural pattern of the society. The latest classification is made on the methods of acquiring the spouse or the number of spouses. Generally, following two types of marriage can be considered. (1) Monogamy, and (2) Polygamy.

1. Monogamy—In this type of marriage one woman can marry one man and vice versa. It has been defined by Piddington in the following words : "Monogamy is a form of Marriage in which no man may be married to more than one woman at one time.

This type of marriage which is prevalent in most of the civilized as well as in other societies, is based on certain factors. First cause is the Economic Co-operation. This type of marriage is guided by the spirit to maintain economic standard. Spirit of monopoly exists in almost all the societies where there is a spirit of monopoly, neither a man can tolerate his wife having more than one husband nor does a woman can tolerate her husband having more than one wife. This type of marriage is also guided by the number of man and woman.

There are advantages as well as disadvantages in Monogamy type of marriage. This type of marriage is important from economic as well as social point of view. This type of marriage brings about the stability in the family. The relationship between husband and wife is based on affection, goodwill and co-operation and that is why there is stability in the family. Secondly, in this type of marriage, the laws regarding inheritance of the property can be properly laid down. There is equality in the distribution of property. Since the earning members do not have to maintain several peranns, the standard of living is quite high. Lastly, in this type of marriage there is class relationship between husband and wife which is based on mutual respect, affection and goodwill.

Whatever the advantages or disadvantages or the defects may be, it has to be pointed out that monopoly remains with that type of marriage which is prevalent in almost all the civilized countries and societies of the world and is also respected and liked by the people. Particularly in Indian culture, specifically in Hindu Society only this type of marriage is allowed and is in vogue among all social group people.

2. ***Polygamy***—In this type of marriage, a man is permitted to have more than one wife and a wife is permitted to have more than one husband. It is divided into three categories viz. (i) Polygamy, (ii) Polyandry and (iii) Group marriage. For this chapter explanation for this categories are not necessary and so they are not mentioned here.

In this chapter the basic customs pertaining the all social groups regarding marriage are discussed. The basic customs regarding marriage are as follows :

1. Comparison of horoscope of the bride and bridegroom.
2. If they agree then each party meet in each other's house.
3. They discuss about the ornaments, dowry etc. from each other's party to the other.
4. If everything is alright the bride and bridegroom meet each other and if they approve of each other they fix the engagement.
5. Usually engagement is celebrated in the bride's house.
6. At the time of engagement the main functions in most of the social groups are : (a) bride's and bridegroom's parents exchange the plates and (b) get the written document of the engagement. Moreover, on that day itself they give atleast an ornament or any golden thing to the bride. These are all done in front of the (brahmin) priest. For this function they invite relatives and friends and arrange a grand feast.

7. After selecting an auspicious day they fix the marriage.
8. Before 3 or 5-days before marriage they build pandar for marriage and erect the first pillar for pandar in the eastern or northern east side. This pillar is erected by the priest, bridegroom, five or seven married woman. This pillar is decorated by small red cloth, turmeric, mango leaves, sandal paste, *kumkum* flowers, sometimes by margosa leaves etc.
9. It is in custom to celebrate "nalungu" to the bride in her house 3 or 5 or 7 days before marriage according to her relatives. It is usual to celebrate "nalungu" in her parent's house and then her "uncle" does this function. Then only others celebrate "nalungu" to her.
10. On the day before marriage for both bride and bridegroom, they celebrate "nalungu" in their houses respectively.
11. Nine grains are soaked in water (paaligai) 3 or 5 days before marriage mostly where the marriage is celebrated (i.e. in either bride's or bridegroom's house).
12. There is a custom of putting "punul" (sacred thread ceremony) in thread, silver and gold to the bridegroom before marriage. This is usually put by the brahmin priest.
13. On the day before marriage bride groom's procession is celebrated with bomb and show.
14. In some social groups where the marriage is celebrated in bridegroom's house they come to invite the bride to their house. At that time they bring flowers, plantain, sugar, saree, ornament etc. Few groups of people put "pariyam" to the girl and take the girl to their house. After going to their house they worship their family Goddess (or) God.
15. On the Marriage morning bride and bridegroom keep fasting. Then they tie "kankanam" (yellow string) in each other's wrist.[1]

16. After this in some (not in all social groups taken for analysis) social group it is in custom of celebrating "cikakkaay kazhittal". At that time they place oil, sikakkaay etc. on the head of the bride and bridegroom and then they take bath.
17. The other custom before tying marriage badge is that the bride and bridegroom do "puja" for the feet of their parents. This is termed as "paada puujai seytal".
18. Usually the bride wears silk saree at the time of marriage.[2]
19. Most of the social group decorate a separate marriage platform. Brahmin (iyer), Brahmin (iyangar) people place only the "siir samankal" (parents given to the bride from her house) in the marriage platform. They also place two standing lamps in the platform.
20. All the other social groups place following things in the marriage platform : "saalungaravam pot" (a big mouthed brass vessel), Kudavilakku, paaligai, peepul tree's bough, two standing lamps, other "siir samankal", one (or) two rows of "pandamuttikkaal"[3] pot each contains three or five pots.
21. In almost all social group brahmin priest (priest-pandaram in Harijan, Isai Velalar caste etc.), comes, kindles holy fire, recites holy *mantras*. He places the marriage badge in a plate where coconut, flowers, plantain, turmeric etc. gets the blessings of the elderly people.
22. Then he gives atchatai (rice mixed with turmeric powder) to the elderly people and they put the atchatai on the couple while tying marriage badge.
23. After getting the blessing of the elderly people, the priest gives the marriage badge to the bridegroom and he ties it in the neck of the bride (In some social group all the three knots are put by the bridegroom and in some other social group first knot is put by the

bridegroom and the other two are put by the sister-in-law of the bridegroom).

24. While tying marriage badge, bride's sister-in-law hold the lamp in the back of the bride and the bride's party is to put coin in the lamp. This is not in vogue in Brahmin (iyer) and Brahmin (iyangar) caste people. Only other social group people do this type of action.

25. The pot (Saalungaravam pot) is filled up by water at the time of tying marriage badge is same in social group. In other social groups it is filled up with water even when it is placed in the marriage platform. Various things like conch, milk ladle, stylus for writing, palm leaf, knife, lemon, ring etc. in the pot. While going round the marriage platform thrice the newly married couple take and put back the things in the pot.

26. After tying marriage badge the couple, bride's sister-in-law, bridegroom's brother-in-law go round the marriage platform thrice. Everytime when they completes one round bridegroom's brother-in-law puts fried rice by placing the hand of the couple on one another. Then all of them put the fried rice by placing the hand of the couple on one another. Then all of them put the fried rice in the holy fire. In the third time after putting fried rice bridegroom's brother-in-law puts ring in his finger and in return bridegroom[4] puts ring to this brother-in-law.

27. Except in few castes, in all the other castes it is a custom to tie the golden plate tied in yellow string on the forehead of the bride and bridegroom. Usually, their mother-in-law, uncle, aunt etc. tie this string on the forehead of the bride and bridegroom.

28. Then the bridegroom places the leg of the bride on the stone mortar and put ring in her toe. In some social group it is also in custom to put ring in the toe of the bridegroom before or after marriage.

29. Then the couple are invited to a separate place and their party give milk and plantain to them.
30. In some social group immediately after this they take the paaligai, peepul tree's bough etc. to the river bank or tank. Then they leave the "paaligai" in the river or tank and erect the peepul tree's bough in the bank of the river or tank. Before leaving the "paaligai" in the river they untie the yellow string in their hand and leave it in the water.
31. After this the bride fill up the water pot with water and returns from the tank or river to the house. Mostly in all social group it is a custom to break a coconut while the bride enters into the house each time.
32. Then "Nalunku" is celebrated. This is termed as "Nakavalli muhurttam", "naalam niir satanku" etc. by various social group, but the basic thing is one and the same. This "nalungu" is celebrated before leaving the "paaligai" in some social group and after leaving the "paaligai" in some social group. In few groups there is no "nalungu" at all. At the time of "nalungu" the couple play various type of games which are mentioned in the Chapter 8, Part II, p. 404).
33. If the marriage day itself is an auspicious day for celebrating "first night", they celebrate it on the same day. Otherwise they select an auspicious day, take new dresses for the couple for this function and celebrate it.
34. After everything is over the newly married couple go and come thrice to each other's house, and mingle with each other's family. Some social group people celebrate the "first night" only after this.
35. If there is any evil effect than the couple go round the peepul tree after marriage in the month of "aati" (July-August).

Regarding the basic customs these are the main concepts

of the Hindu marriage system. Moreover, within one year of the marriage bride's parents have to do some "siir" for the functions. They have to spend money for their occasion. If we come across the functions and festivals of Hindu society, they are numberless. Beginning from the month of "aati" (July-August), a newly married bride and bridegroom is to celebrate this elaborately. On the 18th of this month, the old marriage badge is untied, new one is tied, they worship the garland and worship the river Goddess and leave the garland in the river. Bride's parents have to met the expenditure for this. Likewise for Deepawali, for Pongal, for Karthikai etc. bride's parents have to do "siir". Moreover, if the bride becomes pregnant they has to do various functions.

It is not only for marriage, in Hindu culture for every aspect of human life cycle they has to celebrate it. This is in vogue even in uncivilized as well as civilized societies.

Marriage, according to Hindu philosophy is helpful in evolution and development of various instincts and faculties. When we take Marriage and family they go together. In fact family is a society while marriage is an institution. Without family, marriage is not possible and without marriage family is not possible.

Socialization is nothing but acclimatisation of the children to the society. Through language and their actions, a child is able to learn about various customs and traditions of the society. It is the family that transmits the culture to the new generation. Family is responsible for preserving culture. The culture is also transmitted from one generation to the other through the institutions of the family.

From the example of marriage customs, we can mention about the Hindu culture. The role of culture is important in our life. First of all, culture is transmitted from generation to generation, i.e. culture is not the achievement of any particular generation. In culture, additions and alternations are made by each successive generation of human beings. It is inherited by each successive generation of human beings. Culture links the past with present. It gives to each generation a better position in the struggle of life.

Culture keeps man within the bounds of society, culture alone can keep the savage in chains and keep the man within the bounds of society. A child is born into a distinct cultural environment created by the people who around him. From the very beginning, the response of a child and the behaviour of family members towards child are conditioned by cultural factors. First his parents, his family members and later the neighbourhood and then the whole society comes forward to initiate his in the culture which has filtered down to them (parents) or the society through all past generations.

Culture functions towards socialization. This role of culture which may be terminal as socializing role, is best evident in the case of marriage, basically based on the desire of procreation. But the human way of fulfillment of that desire is both limited and transformed by cultural elements. Man does not perform the reproductive function by virtue of instinct alone, rather he does it in a distinct cultural surroundings.

Culture unites the various social forces. Culture is the most unifying factor among the heard of other factors and forces which come together to form the vast complex, i.e., society, culture also provides opportunity for the fuller expression of human personality. Socially, culture provides the standard of values of life, culture makes in the judge of our own conduct and it is due to the fact that culture may be cited as the most potent means of social control.

While we look into Anthropology we have to mention about civilization. Civilization stands for those means which serve our demands. Culture and civilization are inter-active and inter-dependent. Culture is the expression of our way and mode of life. If we want to borrow the culture of the other country, we will have to change the whole way of our life. But civilization can be borrowed without remodeling our way of life. Thus, culture and civilization act as an environment. But culture is more active and powerful than environment.

According to Malinowski, culture is a means or an implement through which man fulfills his various needs. According to needs, there are different aspects of culture that are inter-dependent. Culture is not the product of a particular period or age. It grows through ages. It is as old as the human society itself.

There are different type of functions viz., 1. Social functions, 2. Traditional function of the family, and 3. Cultural functions of the family. These functions are reflected through folk-customs. From child birth to death, the celebrations and functions are the main aspect in a human society. These functions are handed down from generation to generation, and thus reflects the culture of the society.

According to the Anthropological point of view every custom, belief etc. in a human life cycle is important since they are the natural sources and a reflecting mirror of every society. It is evident that the origin of folkways generally is also unconscious, since there seems no reason why the emotions or the ethical effect enveloping a custom any action should incline more than the custom itself to spring up unconsciously.

When we compare Anthropology and Folk-custom, Anthropology is the science of man and his works and behaviour and it is a recorded and written concept, while the folk-customs, traditions, fashions etc. are unwritten. Unwritten and unrecorded traditions, culture etc. are the folk-ways and customs. Folk-ways are not universal, they differ from society to society. It is so because of the conditions, attitudes of the socio-economic conditions and the cultural background of society.

Thus in this chapter on Folk custom—An Anthropological approach, only the concept of marriage is discussed since it is the centre point of every human life cycle. Only when marriage is celebrated, the other concepts of life like pregnancy, child birth, customs connected with childhood days both for boys and girls, marriage, death can be discussed. In this chapter all these are not explained except Marriage.

All the customs, functions, ceremonies, celebrations, beliefs of human life cycle can be dealt with like marriage customs from Anthropological point of view. Only for example Marriage customs are discussed here and others are not. Thus, Folk-customs can be viewed in Sociological point of view, linguistic point of view, Anthropological point of view, psychological point of view etc. Like sociology and Folk-customs are inter-twined with each other, Anthropology and Folk-customs are also intertwined with each other. The main concept culture of Anthropology is reflected in Folk-customs. Thus, we can conclude folk-customs is a reflecting mirror of cultural, social, economical, traditional background of a society.

REFERENCES

1. In some social group brahmin priest ties the yellow string to the bridegroom and the bridegroom ties yellow string to the bride.
2. In Brahmin (Iyer), Brahmin (Iyangar) Visvakarma (Patter-goldsmith, taccar-carpenter) etc. wear nine yards saree at the time of tying marriage badge. In some social groups they wear cotton saree (Patayacci, Sengunta, Mutaliyar, Nayakkar (tatar) (yellow saree), Devar, Jankamar, Harijan caste people wear cotton saree. Reddiar caste people also wear nine yards saree at the time of tying marriage.
3. This is placed only by certain social group people.
4. Only in some social group bridegroom puts ring to his brother-in-law in return for his ring.

3

Folk-Customs : Caste Variation

Folk-customs vary from region to region and caste to caste. In this chapter the customs of various caste people are discussed. The customs from child birth to death (the customs, of a human life cycle) are taken for analysis. All the customs of child birth, Sacred thread ceremony, Puberty rituals etc. are given in this chapter by giving number to each custom under each category. Then the variation due to caste are given in tabular column and remarks are also given.

Even though the basic customs are same we find difference because of the cultural background pertaining to a society which are transmitted from one generation to the other. Moreover, a society cannot be without customs and customs cannot be without society, i.e. both customs and society are intertwined and they depend upon the cultural background.

Child Birth

Following basic customs are celebrated at the time of child birth and childhood days. Apart from these customs, some customs are pertaining to a particular caste, which are mentioned in the chapter (Folk-customs—Sociological approach).

1. Putting arm rings to the children (kaappitudal).
2. Preparing rice mixed with jaggery (kaapparisi kintudal).

3. In that day cleaning the roller in a pair of grinding stones and smearing sandal paste, turmeric powder, *kumkum*, flower and new cloth on it. Then a married lady put the roller in the cradle thrice and take it out.
4. Putting arm-rings-first margosa fibre and then in silver, gold in the hands of the children.
5. Putting into the cradle or in the cloth cradle.
6. Brahmin priest kindling holy fire and recite holy mantras.
7. Doing punniyadanam.
8. Naming ceremony.
9. Virai daanam.
10. Celebrating "Aayishoman" for the long life of the children in the first year of the child.
11. Celebrating the "Ear boring ceremony".
12. Removing the hair on the first date of birth.
13. Sending the child to the school in the 5th year by taking sweets, money etc. to the child.
14. At that time distributing sweets to the children in the school.
15. While admitting the child in the school preparing rice mixed with jaggery is in custom.

Number of customs							
	1	*2*	*3*	*4*	*5*	*6*	*7*
Brahmin (iyer)	7th or 9th day	Yes	Yes	Yes	7th or 9th day	Yes	11th day
Brahmin (iyangar)	11th	Not in custom	Not in custom	Yes custom	3rd	Yes	11th day
Pillai	7th day	Not in custom	Not in custom	Yes	15th day	Yes	15th day
Isai	16th velalar	Not in	Not in	Yes custom	15th	Yes	15th day
Patayacci	9th day	Not in custom	Not in custom	Yes	30th	Yes	12th day
Sengunta Mutaliyar	7th or 9th day	Not in custom	Not in custom	Yes	7th or 9th day	Yes	11th day
Pattar (gold-smith)	7th day	Yes	Not in custom	Yes	7th day	Yes	13th or 15th or 16th day
Asari (carpen-ter)	7th day	Yes	Not in custom	Yes	7th day	Yes	13th or 15th or 16th day
Chettiyar (vysya)	3rd or 5th or 7th day	Not in custom	Not in custom	yes	on the night of doing naming ceremony	Yes	9th or 11th or 13th day

Member of customs							
8	*9*	*10*	*11*	*12*	*13*	*14*	*15*
11th day	Not in custom	Yes	on the first date of birth	on the first date of birth	Yes	Yes	Yes
11th day	11th day	Yes	on the first date of birth	not compul-sory	Yes	Yes	Not in custom
15th day	15th day	Not in custom	on the first date of birth	on the first date of birth	Yes	Yes	Not in custom
15th day	Not in custom	Not in custom	on the first date of birth	on the first date of birth	Yes	Yes	Not in custom
3rd day	Not in custom	Not in custom	on the first date of birth	on the first date of birth	Yes	Yes	Yes
11th day	Not in custom	Not in custom	on the first date of birth	on the first date of birth	Yes	Yes	Yes
3rd or 5th month	Not in custom	Not in custom	on the first date of birth	on the first date of birth	Yes	Yes	Not in custom
3rd or 5th month	Not in custom	Not in custom	on the first date of birth	on the first date of birth	Yes	Yes	Not in custom
3rd or 5th or 7th month	Not in cusotm	Not in custom	on the first date of birth	on the first date of birth	Yes	Yes	Yes

	1	2	3	4	5	6	7
Chettiyar (Sozhiya)	7th day	Not in custom	Not in custom	Yes	7th day	Yes	11th or 13th day
Chettiyar (Vaniya)	15th day	Yes	Not in custom	Yes	15th day	Yes	13th day
Pillai (Thuluva Vellalar)	11th day	Yes	Not in custom	Yes	11th day	Yes	11th day
Reddiar	7th day	Yes	Not in custom	Yes	11th day	Yes	11th day
Naidu	3rd day	Yes	Not in custom	Yes	3rd day	Yes	16th day
Thondai-mandala mudaliyar	16th day	Yes	Not in custom	Yes	16th day	Yes	16th day
Nadar	3rd day	Yes	Not in custom	Yes	30th day	Yes	16th day
Nayakkar (canar)	15th day	Yes	Not in custom	Yes	15th day	Yes	15th day
Nayakkar (tatar)	16th day	Not in custom	Not in custom	Yes	16th	Yes	after 16th day
Muppa -nar	16th day	Yes	Not in custom	Yes	16th day	Yes	16th day

8	9	10	11	12	13	14	15
according to economic situation	Not in custom	Not in custom	on the first date of birth	on the first date of birth	Yes	Yes	Not in custom
15th day	Not in custom	Not in custom	on the first date of birth	on the first date of birth	Yes	Yes	Not in custom
11th day	Not in custom	Not in custom	on the first date of birth	on the first date of birth	Yes	Yes	Not in custom
16th day	Not in custom	Not in custom	on the first date of birth	on the first date of birth	Yes	Yes	Not in custom
16th day	Not in custom	Not in custom	2nd date of birth	2nd date of birth	Yes	Yes	Not in custom
on the first date of birth	Not in custom	Not in custom	on the first date of birth	on the first date of birth	Yes	Yes	Yes
30th day	Not in customs	Not in custom	on the first date of birth	on the first date of birth	Yes	Yes	Not in custom
5th day	Not in custom	Not in custom	on the first date of birth	on the first date of birth	Yes	Yes	Not in custom
16th day	Not in custom	Not in custom	on the 1st date of birth or 3rd or 5th year	on the first date of birth or 3rd or 5th year	Yes	Yes	Not in custom
16th day	Not in custom	Not in custom	on the first date of birth star	on the first date of birth star	Yes	Yes	Not in custom

	1	2	3	4	5	6	7
Devar	after 22nd	Not in custom	Not in custom	Yes	after 22nd day	yes	11th or 15th day
Udayar	1st day	Yes	Not in custom	Yes	16th day	Yes	16th day
Kallar (devar)	16th day	Yes	Not in custom	Yes	11th day	Yes	21st day
Tuluva Naickar	9th day	Yes	Not in custom	Yes	30th day	Yes	11th day
Jankamar	7th day	Not in custom	Not in custom	Yes	9th day	Yes	9th day
Konar (Yadhava Pillai)	7th or 30th day	Yes	Not in custom	Yes	16th day	Yes	16th day
Kuravar (Ramaj oki)	7th day	Not in custom	Not in custom	Yes	16th day	Not in custom	16th day
Vannan	7th day	Yes	Not in custom	Yes	16th day	Yes	9th day
Navitar	7th day	Yes	Not in custom	Yes	16th day	Yes	9th day
Cakkill	7th day	Yes	Not in custom	Yes	21st day	Yes (here priest is Pan-daram)	9th day
*Harijan	7th day	Yes	Not in custom	Yes	–	–	11th or 16th day

* This usually celebrated in the first date of birth. But it not compulsory to celebrate within this period. They have to celebrate it before marriage.

8	9	10	11	12	13	14	15
after 22nddays	Not in custom	Not in custom	on the first date of birth star	on the first date of birth star	Yes	Yes	Not in custom
16th day	Not in custom	Not in custom	on the first date of birth star	on the first date of birth star	Yes	Yes	Not in custom
16th day	Not in custom	Not in custom	on the first date of birth	on the first date of birth	Yes	Yes	Not in custom
not celebrated separataly	Not in custom	Not in custom	on 5th year	on the first date of birth	Yes	Yes	Not in custom
3rd month	Not in custom	Not in custom	on the first date of birth	on the first date of birth	Yes	Yes	Not in custom
16th day	Not in custom	Not in custom	on the first date of birth	Not compulsory in the first year	Yes	Yes	Not in custom
16th day	Not in custom	Not in custom	on the first date of birth	on the first date of birth	Yes	Yes	Not in custom
16th day	Not in custom	Not in custom	on the first date of birth	on the first date of birth	Yes	Yes	Not in custom
16th day	Not in custom	Not in custom	on the first date of birth	on the first date of birth	Yes	Yes	Not in custom
16th day	Not in custom	Not in custom	on the first date of birth	on the first date of birth	Yes	Yes	Not in custom
—	—	—	—	—	Yes	Yes	Not in custom

* These people send the child and it's mother to her house (i.e. to her husband's house) on 11th (or) 16th day itself since these people have to do work and earn for their daily meal. So, they do not keep the child and it's mother for long time in their house.

II. Sacred Thread Ceremony and Puberty Rituals

1. Sacred Thread Ceremony

This Sacred thread ceremony is celebrated only by some caste people. Mainly Brahmin (iyer), Brahmin (iyangar), Pattar (goldsmith), Asari (taccar) caste people celebrate this ceremony. Following are the basic customs during this celebration :

1. Age of the boy while putting sacred Thread.
2. Brahmin priest kindling the holy fire and reciting holy mantras and putting the sacred thread on the chest of the boy.
3. Placing the 'kalasam' on the rice, under which plantain leaf is spread, under which paddy is spread.
4. Anointing the boy with the water in the "kalasam".
5. While putting sacred thread the boy has to wear five fold *dhoti* (panjakaccam) and a towel around the waist.
6. Inviting relatives and friends.
7. Giving presentations to the boy.
8. Grand feast is arranged to the guests.

These customs vary from caste to caste. The variation is due to cultural heritage from generation to generation. These customs are compulsory among these caste people. The differences are indicated in the form of tabular column in the following page :

Number of Customs

	1	2	3	4	5	6	7	8
Brahmin (Iyer)	15th year	Yes	Not in custom	Not specified	Yes	Yes	Yes	Yes
Brahmin (Iyangar)	15th year	Yes	Yes	Yes	Not specified	Yes	Yes	Yes

	1	2	3	4	5	6	7	8
(Viswa-karma) Pattar (gold-smith)	16th year	Priest here refer to a "Panda-ram" in this caste	Not in custom	Not in custom	Not in custom	Yes	Yes	Yes
(Viswa-karma) taccar (carpen-ter)	15th year	Yes	Not in custom	Not in custom	Not in custom	Yes	Yes	Yes

Note : This function is celebrated like a marriage in all the above mentioned four castes. After putting "thread", they put silver, gold etc. cord at the time of this function. For this function they take new *dhoti*, towel etc. to the boy wearing "sacred thread".

2. Puberty Rituals

This is celebrated by all the caste people when a girl attains age. These customs vary from caste to caste, even though there are basic customs. All the basic customs are given here and the change due to caste variation are indicated in the tabular column. Wherever, there is any specific custom it is mentioned under the tabular column.

1. The news of attaining age is informed to the girls mother through somebody else is compulsory.
2. Preparing the horoscope of the girl at the time of attaining age.
3. On the first day they give bath.
4. On the first day they decorate her hair with flowers ("Puccuttutal").
5. Celebrating "nalungu" on the first day.
6. While pouring water on the girl's head, it is a custom to hold a sieve above the girl's head, odd number of

married woman pour water on the head of the girl through the sieve.

7. Things that are put into the sieve.
8. First thing given to eat after pouring water.
9. Other things given to eat after pouring water.
10. Then the girl is leaving alone in separate room.
11. Pouring water on the dates 3rd, 5th, 7th, and 9th etc.
12. Preparing "Puttu" on the dates 3rd, 5th, 7th, and 9th etc. days and on puberty ritual day.
13. Relatives come prepare food, puttu etc. and serve it to the girl.
14. "Puberty rituals"—celebration.
15. Uncle is to spend money for this function.
16. They take new saree, blouse etc. to the girl for this function.
17. Girl is decorated, garlanded and seated in a chair. They give a coconut, betel leaf, nut etc. in her hand.
18. At that time they place a stone mortor and roller in the side of the girl which is cleaned, put *kumkum*, turmeric, smear sandal paste etc. on the stone and the roller.
19. After this they give decorated roller in the hands of the girl thrice.
20. Then "Puttu" is shown around the girl.
21. Relatives attend the function and give presents to the girl.
22. A grand feast is arranged.

Puberty rituals are an important custom and are celebrated in a grand manner by almost all caste people. Almost all caste people celebrate this function like a marriage. Without celebrating this function, no caste people celebrate marriage functions to the girl.

Number of Customs						
Caste	*1*	*2*	*3*	*4*	*5*	*6*
Brahmin (iyer)	not compulsory	Not in custom	Yes	Yes	Not in custom	Not in custom
Brahmin (iyangar)	not compulsory	Not in custom	Not in custom	Yes	Not in custom	Not in custom
Pillai	Yes	Yes	Yes	Not in custom	Not in custom	Yes
Isai Vellalar	Yes	Yes	Yes	Yes	Yes	Yes
Patayacci	Yes	Yes	Yes	Yes	Yes	Yes
Sengunta Mutaliyar	Yes	Not compulsory	Yes	Not in custom	Not in custom	Not in custom
Pattar (goldsmith)	yes	Yes	Yes	Yes	Not in custom	Yes
Asari (carpenter)	Yes	Yes	Yes	Yes	Not in custom	Yes
Chattiar (vysya)	Yes	Yes	Yes	Yes	Yes	Not in custom

7	8	9	10	11	12	13
Nil	milk, Plantain dhall rice	dhall rice	Yes	Not in custom	3rd day	Not in custom
Nil	milk, Plantain, sugar	dhall rice gingely oil	Yes	Not in custom	3rd day	Not in custom
Coconut, betel leaf nut, coins	Plantain sugar, milk, gingely oil	pongal	Yes	Yes	5th day	Yes
turmeric	dhall rice	egg, blackgram flour, sugar, gingaly oil plantain	Yes	Yes	Yes	Yes
gold, coin, margosa leaves	dhall rice	egg, blackgram flour	Yes	Yes	Yes	Yes
Nil	jaggery, gingely oil	dhall rice	Yes	Not in custom	2nd day	Yes
coin, turmeric paste margosa leaves	gingely oil, plantain fruit sugar	dhall rice	yes	Not in custom	on puberty ceremony day	Yes
coin, turmeric paste margosa leaves	gingely oil, plantain fruits, sugar	dhall rice	Yes	Not in custom	on puberty ceremony day	Yes
Nil	gingely oil	two type of tiffens	Yes	Not specified	Not specified	Not specified

14	*15*	*16*	*17*	*18*	*19*	*20*	*21*	*22*
Not in custom	Not in custom	Yes	Not in custom	Not in custom	Not in custom	Not in custom	Not in custom	Not in custom
Not in custom	Not in custom	Yes	Not in custom	Not in custom	Not in custom	Not in custom	Yes	Yes
5th or 7th or 9th or 11th day	Yes	Yes	Yes on the 1st day	Not in custom	Not in custom	Yes	Yes	Yes
3rd month before marri -age	Yes	Yes	Yes	Yes	Yes	Yes	Yes	Yes
15th day	Yes	Yes	Yes	Yes	Yes	Yes	Yes	Yes
11th or 16 th day	Yes	Yes	Not in custom	Not in custom	Not in custom	Yes	Yes	Yes
11th day	Yes	Yes	Not in custom	Not in custom	Not in custom	Not spe- cified	Yes	Yes
11th day	Yes	Yes	Not in	Not in	Not in	Not spe- cified	Yes	Yes
11th or 13 day	Yes	Yes	Not in custom	Not in custom	Not in custom	Not in custom	Yes	Yes

	Number of customs						
Caste	*1*	*2*	*3*	*4*	*5*	*6*	*7*
Chettiyar (sozhiya)	Yes	Yes	Yes	Not in custom	Not in custom	Yes	gold coin wooden dhall, shell
Chettiar (vaniya)	Yes	Yes	Yes	Not in custom	Not in custom	Yes	turmeric, coin, flowers
Pillai (tuluva vellalar)	Yes	Yes	Yes	Yes	Yes	Yes	turmeric
Reddiar	Yes	Yes	Yes	Yes	Yes	Yes	turmeric, margosa leaves
Naidu	Yes	Yes	Yes	Yes	Yes	Yes	turmeric
Thondai-mandala Mutaliyar	Yes	Not compul-sory	Yes custom	Not in custom	Not in	Yes leaves	margosa
Nadar	Yes	Yes	Yes	Yes	Yes	Yes	turmeric
Nayakkar (canar)	Yes	Yes	Yes	Yes	Yes	Not in custom	Not in custom
Nayakkar (tatar)	Yes	not in custom	Only on the 3rd day	Not in custom	3rd day "enney nalungu"	Not in custom	Nil
Muppanar	Yes	Yes	Yes	Yes	Yes	Not in custom	Not in custom

8	*9*	*10*	*11*	*12*	*13*	*14*	*15*
dhall rice	tiffens	Yes	Yes	Yes	Not in custom	13th day	Yes
black-gram, flour gin-gely oil	dhall rice	Yes	Yes	Yes	Not in custom	7th or 9th or 11th or 16ty day	Yes
dhall rice	gingely oil & plantain	Yes	Yes	Yes	Yes	9th day 11th day	Yes
dhall rice	egg, black-gram flour	Yes	Yes	Yes	Yes	11th day	Yes
dhall rice	pongal	Yes	Yes	Yes	Yes	13th day	Yes
dhall rice	dhall rice	Yes	Yes	Yes	Not in custom	7th day	Yes
seed of greens with stem	dhall rice	Yes	Yes	Yes	Yes	16th day	Yes
duvrai dhall rice	egg, black-gram flour sugar	Yes	Yes	Yes	Yes	16th or 22nd day	Yes
egg, gingely oil	dhall rice	Yes	Yes	Yes	Yes	16th day	Yes
egg, gingely oil	dhall rice	Yes	Yes	1st day only	Yes	16th day or 3rd month	Yes

16	17	18	19	20	21	22
Yes	Not in custom	Not in custom	Not in custom	Not in custom	Yes	Yes
Yes	Not in custom	Not in custom	Not in custom	Not in custom	Yes	Yes
Yes	Not in custom	Not in custom	Not in custom	Yes	Yes	Yes
Yes	Yes	Yes	Yes	Yes	Yes	Yes
Yes	Yes	Yes	Yes	Yes	Yes	Yes
Yes	Yes	Yes	Yes	Yes	Yes	Yes
Yes	Yes	Yes	Yes	Yes	Yes	Yes
Yes	Yes	Yes	Yes	Yes	Yes	Yes
Yes	Not in custom	Not in custom	Not in custom	Not in custom	Yes	Yes
Yes	Yes	Yes	Yes	Yes	Yes	Yes

				Number of custom			
Caste	*1*	*2*	*3*	*4*	*5*	*6*	*7*
Devar	Yes	Yes	Yes	Yes	Yes	Yes	turmeric
Udayar	No	Yes	Yes	Yes	Yes	Yes	margosa leaves
Kallar (devar)	Yes	Yes	Yes	Yes	Not in custom	Yes	turmeric
Tuluva Naickar	Yes	Yes	Yes	Yes	Yes	Yes	turmeric paddy margosa leaves, coins
Jankamar	No	Yes	Yes	Yes	Yes	Yes	turmeric, margosa leaves, holy grass
Konar (yadha-vap Pillai)	Yes	Yes	Yes	Yes	Yes	Yes	turmeric
Kuravar (Rama-joki)	Yes	Yes	Yes	Yes	No	Yes	coin, turmeric, margosa leaves
Vannan	Yes	Yes	Yes	Not speci-fied	Not in custom	Yes	betel leaf, nut, coconut, flowers coins, turmeric
Navitar	Yes	Yes	Yes	Not speci-fied	Not in custom	Yes	Coins
Cakkili	Yes	Yes	Yes	Yes	Yes	Yes	gold, coins, beads & a ring
Harijan	Yes	Not speci-fied	Yes	Yes	Yes	Yes	not mentioned

8	9	10	11	12	13	14
egg, oil	sarkkarai pongal	Yes	Yes	5th day	Yes	15th or 22nd or 3rd month before marri-iage
gingely oil	pongal	Yes	Yes	3rd day	Yes	according to the conveni-ence
egg	blackgram flour, sugar	Yes	Not in custom	1st day	Yes	16th day
dhall rice	egg, sugar, gingely oil & plantain	Yes	Yes	Yes	Yes	21st day
cooked rice	on 3rd day, egg, black-gram flour & sugar	Yes	Yes	Yes	Yes	9th day
sweet boiled rice with ghee	tiffen	Yes	Not in custom	3rd day	Yes	11th or 15th day
black-gram flour, egg & sugar	sweet boiled rice & plan-tain	Yes	Not in custom	only on the day of puber-ty cere-mony	Yes	16th day
Pepper cooked food	tiffen	Yes	Not specified	"	Yes	9th or 11th day or 3rd month
pepper cooked food	tiffen	Yes	Not specified	9th or 11th day	Yes	9th or 11th day
gingely oil black gram flour	plantain, tiffen	Yes	Not specified	16th day	Yes	16th day
black-gram flour plantain sugar, gin-gely oil	not ment-ioned	Yes	Yes	3rd day	Yes	15th day

15	*16*	*17*	*18*	*19*	*20*	*21*	*22*
Yes	Yes	Yes	Yes	Yes	Yes	Yes	Yes
Yes	Yes	Yes	Yes	Yes	Yes	Yes	Yes
Yes	Yes	Yes	Yes	Yes	Yes	Yes	Yes
Yes	Yes	Yes	Yes	Yes	Yes	Yes	Yes
Yes	Yes	Yes	Yes	Yes	Yes	Yes	Yes
Yes	Yes	Not in custom	Not in custom	Not in custom	Yes	Yes	Yes
Yes	Yes	Not in custom	Not in custom	Not in custom	Not in custom	Yes	Yes
Yes	Yes	Not speci-fied	Not spe-cified	Not spe-cified	Yes	Yes	Yes
Yes	Not spe-cified	Not spe-cified	Not spe-cified	Not spe-cified	Yes	Yes	Yes
Yes	Yes	Yes	Yes	Yes	Yes	Yes	Yes
Yes	Yes	Yes	Yes	Yes	Yes	Yes	Yes

* In Nadar caste when a girl attains age, it is informed through somebody else. Then they give the seed of greens with stem (tandukkirai) to that girl. This is done because of the belief that otherwise the embryo will not be safe.

Apart from these differences mentioned in the tabular column, the other differences regarding puberty rituals are discussed in the chapter-folk-customs sociological approach.

Marriage Customs

Marriage customs are found in every caste. Even though there are basic customs, we can find differences due to caste variation. The basic customs are given as follows and the differences are noted in the tabular column. Some customs are pertaining to a particular social group and are mentioned in the chapter folk customs-sociological approach.

1. Asking for the horoscope first from the bride's house or bridegroom's house.
2. First go and meet the other party and then compare horoscope (a) horoscope of birth time (b) horoscope of attaining age.
3. First compare the horoscope and then go and meet other party.
4. Then the girl and boy meet each other.
5. Both the party approve each other they fix the marriage.
6. Only if the marriage is fixed then only both the parties take food in each other's house.
7. Engagement is celebrated in bride's house.
8. On that day the bride's party give the dowry, ornaments etc. to the bridegroom's party.
9. Dowry, ornaments etc. are given only on the marriage day.
10. Bridegroom's party bring new saree, blouse, betel leaf, nut, plantain, flowers, turmeric, *kumkum*, sandal paste etc. to the bride.
11. Both parties exchange written documents.
12. Exchanging plates and written documents.

13. Relatives are invited.
14. Arrange a grand-feast to them.
15. On that day itself the girl and the boy are seated together.
16. Then "aalam" is shown around their head.
17. Before marriage they celebrate "nalungu" to the bride.
18. Before marriage day they celebrate "nalungu" to the bride and bridegroom in their houses respectively.
19. Marriage is celebrated in (a) bride's house, and (b) bridegroom's house.
20. Nine grains are soaked in (a) bride's house, and (b) bridegroom's houses certain days before marriage.
21. (a) Mappillai azhaippu (bridegroom's procession) before marriage day, and (b) bride's procession.
22. Inviting the bride to their house.
23. Then worship their family God in their house (in bridegroom's house).
24. On the marriage day morning they keep fasting.
25. On that day morning they tie "kankanam" (yellow string) in each other's hand.
26. On that day bridegroom go for "paradesam".
27. The bride and bridegroom are seated in a swing and five (or) seven old married woman show, "paccaip piti" (cooked rice mixed with turmeric and *kumkum*) around them.
28. Before marriage the bride and bridegroom wash and worship the feet of their parents respectively.
29. In the marriage platform only presents Siir given to the bride from her house for her marriage are placed.
30. In the marriage platform it is a custom to place (1) Saalungaravam pot (a broad mouthed big brees vessel), (2) two standing lamps, (3) Kudavilakku,

(4) paaligai, (5) "pandamuttikkaal" (row pot), (6) "otiyan" tree's bough and (7) "peepul" tree's bough.

31. There is water in the pot while placing in the marriage platform.
32. Putting stylus, milk ladle, conch, coin, lime etc. in the "Saalungaravam" pot.
33. Pandar is built three days before marriage.
34. First pillar for pandar is corrected in the (a) north eastern direction, (b) eastern direction.
35. It is compulsory to erect certain number of pillars for the pandar.
36. For all the pillars bride and bridegroom show camphor after marriage.
37. This pillar is erected by the odd number of old married women, by the bridegroom etc.
38. This is decorated by *kumkum*, sandal paste, red cloth, flower, mango leaves etc.
39. Before tying marriage badge they put "punul" to the bridegroom.
41. The brahmin priest give "atchatai" (yellow rice) to the elderly people.
42. While tying marriage badge the bride has to wear nine yards saree.
43. While tying marriage badge first knot is put by the bridegroom and the other knots are put by the bride's sister-in-law.
44. While tying marriage badge sister-in-law of the bride holds lamp in the back of the bride and bride's party have to put coins in that.
45. After this the bride, bridegroom, sister-in-law, brother-in-law go round the marriage platform thrice.
46. In the last round brother-in-law joins the hands of the couple and put fried rice in their hands and all the three put the fried rice in the fire.

47. Then the bridegroom's brother-in-law puts ring in the hands of the bridegroom.
48. In return the bridegroom puts the ring to his brother-in-law.
49. After this he puts "metti' to the bride by placing her leg in the stone mortor.
50. It is a custom to put "metti" in the toe of the bridegroom also.
51. At the time of going round the marriage platform thrice they take and put the things inside the "salungaravam" pot.
52. Tying golden plate on the forehead of the couple by their sister-in-law, mother-in-law, aunt, uncle etc.
53. After marriage they celebrate a "nalungu".
54. Giving milk and plantain to the couple immediately after tying marriage badge.
55. At the time of "nalungu", the newly married couple play with flower bunch, powdering rice cake and putting on each other's head, playing with the nosegay of the flowers etc.
56. They untie the yellow string tied before marriage.
57. Then they leave the "paaligai" in the river, erect, the peepul tree's bough in the river bank.
58. While coming back the bride takes water-pot full of water.
59. Every time when the girl enters into the bridegroom's house, it is a custom to break coconut into piece.
60. Then the couple go and come to each other's house thrice and mingle with each other's family.
61. In some castes on the marriage day itself they celebrate "First night".
62. In some castes they celebrate "First night" only after going and coming thrice to each other's house.

63. The newly married couple go round the peepul tree on the new moon day of the month "aati".

64. They give "siir" to the bride from her house (within the first year of the marriage).

(i) On 18th of the month "aati", they untie the marriage badge and tie a new one, offer the river Goddess, worship the garland etc.

(ii) For avani avittam

(iii) For "Krishna jayanthi"

(iv) For "Navaratri"

(v) For Deepawali

(vi) For Karthikai

(vii) For Pongal

(viii) For New year day.

Number of customs						
Caste	*1*	*2*	*3*	*4*	*5*	*6*
Brahmin (Iyer)	Bride's house	No	Yes	Yes	Yes	Yes
Brahmin (Iyangar)	Bride's House	No	Yes	Yes	Yes	No
Pillai	Bride-groom's House	Yes (a)	No	Yes	Yes	Yes
Isai Velalar	Either from bride's or bridegroom's house	Yes	No	Yes	Yes	Yes
Patayacci	Bridegroom's house	Yes (b)	No	Yes	Yes	Yes
Sengunta Mutaliyar	Yes	Yes (a)	No	Yes	Yes	Yes
Pattar (golds-mith)	From both sides they ask for comparison of horoscope	No (Regarding comparison either a or b)	Yes	Yes	Yes	Yes
Asari (carpenter)	From both sides they ask for horoscope	No (Reg. compa-rison either a or b)	Yes	Yes	Yes	Yes
Chettiyar (vysya)	Bride's House	No (regarding comparison either a or b)	Yes	Yes	Yes	Yes

7	8	9	10	11	12	13
Yes	Not compulsory	Yes	Yes	Yes	No	Yes
Yes	Not compulsory	Yes	Yes	Yes	No	Yes
Yes	only few ornaments are given	Yes	Yes	Yes	Yes	Yes
Yes	only dowry	ornament etc.	Yes	Yes	Yes	Yes
Yes	not compulsory	Yes	Yes	Yes	Yes	Yes
Yes	No	Yes	Yes	Yes	Yes	Yes
Yes	Yes	No	Yes	Yes	Yes	Yes
Yes	Yes	No	Yes	Yes	Yes	Yes
Yes	Yes	No	Yes	Yes	Yes	Yes

14	*15*	*16*	*17*	*18*	*19*	*20*
Yes	No	No	"Yes	No	(a)	(a) & (b)
Yes	No	No	"Yes	No	(a)	(a) & (b)
Yes	No	No	No	Yes	(b)	(a) 5 (or) 7 days before marriage (b) 3 days before marriage
Yes	No	No	Yes	No	According to the situation	(b) three days before marriage
Yes	No	No	5 or 3 days before marriage	Yes	(b)	(a) before 5 or 7 days (b) before marriage
Yes	No	No	5 days before marriage	Yes	(b)	5 days before marriage in bridegroom's house
Yes	No	No	3 days before marriage	Yes	either in (a) or in (b)	3 days before marri-iage in bri-degroom's house
Yes	No	No	5 days before marriage	Yes	either in (a) or in (b)	3 days before marri-age in bri-degroom's house
Yes	No	No	5 days before marriage	Yes	either in (a) or in (b)	3 days before marri-age in bri-degroom's house
Yes	Yes	Yes	No	Yes	(a)	3 days

21	22	23	24	25	26
(a)	Since the marriage is celebrated in bride's house only bridegroom is invited to the bride's house	No	Yes	Yes	Yes
(a) Yes	Usually the marriage is celebrated in the bride's house only bridegroom is invited to the bride's house	No	Yes	Yes	Yes
(b) Yes	Yes	Yes	Yes	Yes	No
(b) Yes	Yes	Yes	Yes	Yes	No
(b) Yes	Yes	Yes	Yes	Yes	No
(b) Yes	Yes	Yes	Yes	Yes	No
According to the situation	If the marriage is in the bridegroom's house the bridegroom's party invite the bride and put "parisam"	Yes	Yes	Yes	Yes
According to the situation	If the marriage is in the bride groom's house the bridegroom's party invite the bride and put "parisam"	Yes	Yes	Yes	Yes
(Yes) (a)	No	Even before marriage they worship the family God	No	Yes	Yes

27	28	29	30	31	32
Yes	Not in custom	Yes	Only, peepul tree's bough two standing lamps, paaligai etc.	No	No
Yes	Not in custom	Yes	Only peepul tree's bough two standing lamps, paaligai etc.	No	No
No	Yes	Yes	Yes 1, 2, 3, 4, 6, and 7	While tying marriage badge they pour water in that pot	milk ladle stylus, knife
No	Yes	No	Yes 1, 2, 3, 4, and 7.	Yes	milk ladle ring
No	Yes	No	Yes 1, 2, 3, 4, 5, & 7.	No, only while tying marriage badge they pour water in that pot	milk ladle conch, knife, stylus
No	Yes	No	Yes 1, 2, 3, 4, 5, & 7.	Yes	milk ladle knife & ring
No	Yes	No	Yes 2, 3. Kamatchi-ammam vilakku 4, 5, & 7.	It is not custom to keep that pot in the marriage platform with water	No
No	Yes	No	Yes 2, 3. Kamatchi-amman vilakku, 4, 5 & 7.	Those people do not place, this kind of pot in the marriage platform	No
No	No	Yes	No two standing lamps	No	No

33	34	35	36	37	38	39
Yes	(a)	No	No	Yes	Yes	Yes
Yes	(a)	No	No	Yes	Yes	Yes
Yes	(b)	No	No	Yes	Yes	Yes
Not specified	(b)	No	No	Bride-groom	Yes	Yes
Yes	(a)	No	No	Yes	Yes	Yes
Five days before marriage	(b)	No	No	Yes	Yes	Yes
3 days before marriage	(b)	No	No	Yes	Yes	Yes
3 days before marriage	(b)	No	No	Yes	Yes	Yes
Not mentioned	(a)	No	No	Yes	Yes	Yes

40	*41*	*42*	*43*	*44*	*45*
Yes, before marriage only three threads are there- and it is changed into six at the time of marriage	Yes	Yes	Yes	No	Yes
Yes, before marriage only three threads are there and it is changed into six at the time of marriage	Yes	Yes	Yes	No	Yes
Yes	Yes	No	No	Yes	Yes
Yes	Yes	No	all the three kinds are put by the bridegroom	Yes	Yes
Yes	Yes	No	all the three knots are put by the bridegroom	Yes	Yes
Yes	Yes	No	all the three knots are tied by the bridegroom	Yes	Yes
Yes	Yes	Yes, nine yards cotton saree	all the three knots are put by the bridegroom	No	Yes
Yes	Yes	Yes, nine yards cotton saree	all the three knots are put by the bridegroom	No	Yes
Yes	Yes	No	Yes	No	Yes

46	*47*	*48*	*49*	*50*	*51*	*52*
Yes	Yes	Yes	Yes	No	No	No
Yes	Yes	Yes	Yes	No	No	No
Yes	Yes	Yes	Yes	No	Yes	Yes
Yes	Yes	No	Yes	Bridegroom's sister-in-law puts "metti" in his toe.	Only after finishing "nalam niir catanku" (nalungu)	Immediately after marriage
Yes	Yes	Yes	Yes	No	Yes	Yes
Yes	Yes	Yes	Yes	bridegroom's brother-in-law put "metti" in his toe.	Yes	Yes
Yes	Yes	Yes	Yes	It is not in custom	It is not in custom	It is not in custom
Yes	Yes	Yes	Yes	It is not in custom	It is not in custom	it is not in custom
Yes	Yes	Yes	Yes	No	No	Yes

53	54	55	56	57	58	59	60
Yes	Yes	Yes	Yes	Yes	No	No	No
Yes	Yes	Yes	Yes	Yes	No	No	No
Yes	Yes	Yes	Yes	Yes	Yes	Yes	Yes
Yes	Yes	Yes	Yes	Yes	Yes	Yes	Yes
Yes	Yes	Yes	Yes	Yes	Yes	Yes	Yes
Not speci-fied	Yes	Yes	Yes	Yes	Yes	Yes	Yes
Yes	Yes	Yes	Yes	Yes	Yes	Yes	Yes
Yes	Yes	Yes	Yes	Yes	Yes	Yes	Yes
Yes	Yes	Yes	Yes	Yes	Yes	Yes	Yes

61	62	63	64
Yes	No	Yes (if there is any evil effect)	(1) No (2) Yes (3) No (4) Yes (5) Yes (6) Yes (7) Yes (8) Yes
Yes	No	Yes (if there is any evil effect)	(1) No (2) Yes (3) Yes (4) Yes (5) Yes (6) Yes (7) Yes (8) Yes
According to the situation	According to the situation	Yes (if there is any evil effect)	(1) Yes (2) No (3) No (4) No (5) Yes (6) No (7) Yes (8) Yes
Yes	No	No	(1) untie the old marriage badge and tie a new one on 3rd (or) 5th month after marriage (5) (6) (7) Yes
No	Yes	Yes	(1) Yes (5) (7)-Yes
Yes	No	Yes	(1) 3rd month they untie the marriage badge and tie a new one (1) (5) (7)-Yes
They select an auspicious day and celebrate the "first night"	No	Yes	(1) (2) (3) (7)-Yes
They select an auspicious day and celebrate the "first night"	No	Yes	(1) (2) (5) (7)-Yes
They select an auspicious day and celebrate the "first night"	No	Yes	(1) on the 3rd month they untie the marriage badge and tie a new one. (1) (2) (5)-Yes

Number of customs					
Caste	*1*	*2*	*3*	*4*	*5*
Chettiar (sozhiya)	Bridegroom's house	No (regarding comparison either a or b)	Yes	Yes	Yes
Chettiyar	Yes	Yes (not mentioned)	No	Yes	Yes
Pillai (Tuluva vellalar)	Both parties ask for the horoscope	Yes (a)	No	Yes	Yes
Reddiar	Either from the bride's or bridegroom's party they ask for the horoscope	Yes (both a & b)	No	Yes	Yes
Naidu	Bride's party	No (both a & b)	Yes	Yes	Yes
Thondai-mandala Mutaliyar	Bride's party	No only (b)	Yes	Yes	Yes
Nadar	Bride's party	Yes (a)	No	No	Yes
Nayakkar (canar)	Bridegroom's party	No (a)	Yes	Yes	Yes
Nayakkar (tatar)	Bridegroom's party	No (a)	Yes	Yes	Yes

6	7	8	9	10	11
Yes	Yes	on that day itself bride's parents put "metti" in the toe of the bride	Yes	Yes	Yes
Yes	Bride's house	Yes	No	Yes	Yes
Yes	Bride's house	Dowry	Other present-ations	Yes	Yes
Yes	Yes	According to the economic situation	"siir" from the bride's side	Yes	Yes
Yes	Yes	dowry only	other things needed for marriage	Yes	Yes
Yes	Yes	dowry only	other things needed for marriage	Yes	Yes
Yes	Yes	According to the situation	things needed for marriage	Yes	Yes
Yes	Yes	dowry	other things	Yes	Yes
Yes	Yes	Ornaments	other things	Yes	Yes

12	*13*	*14*	*15*	*16*	*17*	*18*
Yes (after engagement bride is sent to bridegroom's house)	Yes	Yes	No	No	Yes	Yes
Yes	Yes	Yes	No No	No	5th or 7th or 9th or 11th days before marriage	Yes
Yes	Yes	Yes	No	No	Yes	Yes
Yes	Yes	Yes	No	No	Yes, 3rd days before marriage	Not mentioned
Yes	Yes	Yes	No	No	Yes	Not mentioned
Yes	Yes	Yes	No	No	Yes, 5th days before marriage	No
Yes	Yes	Yes	No	No	Yes, 3rd or 5th days before marriage	No
Yes	Yes	Yes	No	No	3rd or 5th or 7th days before marriage	Not mentioned
Yes	Yes	Yes	No	No	Nine days before marriage	No

19	*20*	*21*	*22*	*23*	*24*	*25*
(a)	3rd days before marriage in bridegroom's house	(a) Yes	Yes	Yes	Yes	Yes (even this, these, people put punul, metti etc. to the bridegroom)
(b)	5th or 7th days before in (a) three days before in (b)	(b)	Yes	Yes	Yes	Yes
(a) & (b) according to the situation	both in (a) & (b)	(b)	Yes	Yes	Yes	Yes
(a) or (b) according to the situation	3rd days before marriage in bride's & bridegroom's house	(b)	Yes	Yes	Yes	Yes
According to the situation	This is done 3rd days before marriage where the marriage is celebrated	(b)	Yes	Yes	Yes	Yes
in (b)	7th days before marriage in bridegroom's house	(b)	Yes	Yes	Yes	Yes
in (b)	3rd days before marriage in bridegroom's house	(b)	Yes	Yes	Yes	Yes
in (b)	3rd days before marriage in bridegroom's house	(b)	Yes	Yes	Yes	Yes
in (b)	3rd days before marriage in bridegroom's house	(b)	Yes	Yes	Yes	Yes

26	27	28	29	30	31	32
Yes	No	Yes	No	Yes 2, 3, 4, stone grinder, roller, (7)	No	No
Yes	No	Yes	No	(1) (2) (3) (4) (5) & (7)	Yes	stylus, ring, milk ladle
No	No	Yes	No	(1) (2) (3) (4) (5) (7) a lamp	only at the time of tying marriage badge	conch, knife palm leaf, stylus, lemon
No	No	Yes	No	(1) (2) (3) (4) & (7)	water is there while placing the pot inthe marriage platform	knife, stylus milk lade
Yes	No	Yes	No	(1) (2) (3) (4) (5) & (7)	water is poured while tying marriage badges	milk ladle, lemon & turmeric
No	No	Yes	No	(1) (2) (3) (4) (5) & (7)	Yes	milk ladle & ring
No	No	Yes	No	(1) (2) (3) (4) & (7)	Yes	milk ladle & stylus
No	No	Yes	No	(1) (2) (3) (4) & (7)	Yes	ring, conch, knife
No	No	Yes	No	(1) (2) (3) (4) (5) & (7)	Yes, turmeric water	coral beed, sangu, mani & conch

33	34	35	36	37	38	39
Not mentioned	(a)	No	No	Yes	Yes	Yes
Yes	(a)	No	No	Yes	Yes	Yes
4 days before marriage	(b)	No	No	Yes	Yes	Yes
Yes	(b)	No	No	Yes	Yes	Yes
5 days before marriage	(a)	No	No	By brahmin priest	Yes	Yes
5 days before marriage	(a)	No	No	elderly people	Yes	Yes
3 days before marriage	(a)	No	Yes	Three married ladies	Yes	Yes
5 days before marriage	(a)	No	No	bridegroom, brahmin priest	Yes	Yes
5 days before marriage	(b)	Even numberd of pillars are to be in pandar	No	By the bride's & bridegroom's party	Yes	Yes

40	*41*	*42*	*43*	*44*	*45*	*46*
Yes	Yes	No	Yes	Yes	Yes	Yes
Yes	Yes	No	All the three knots are put by the bridegroom	Not ment-ioned	Yes	Yes
Yes	Yes	No	All the three knots are put by the bridegroom	Yes	Yes	Yes
Yes	Yes	Yes, nine yard cotton or silk saree	All the three knots are put by the bridegroom	Yes	Yes	Yes
Yes	Yes	No	All the three knots are put by the bridegroom	Yes	Yes	Yes
Yes	Yes	No	All the three knots are put by the bridegroom	Yes	Yes	Yes
Yes	Yes	Yes	All the three knots are put by the bridegroom	Yes	Yes	Yes
Yes	Yes	No	All the three knots are put by the bridegroom	Yes	Yes	Yes
Yes	Yes	No (yellow cotton saree)	All the three knots are put by the bridegroom	Yes	Yes	Yes

47	48	49	50	51	52	53
Yes	Yes	Yes	No	No	No	Yes
Yes	Yes	Yes	Yes before tying marriage badge brother-in-law puts ring in bridegroom's toe	Yes	Yes	Yes
Yes	Yes	Yes	No	Yes	Yes	Yes
Yes	Yes	Yes	bridegroom's brother-in-law puts ring in the toe of the bridegroom	Yes	Yes	Yes
Yes	Yes	Before tying marriage badge brother-in-law puts ring in the toe of the bride & bridegroom		Yes	Not in custom	No
Yes	Yes	Yes	No	Yes	Yes	No
Yes	Yes	Yes	brother-in-law's ring in the toe of the bridegroom	Yes	Yes	Yes
Yes	*dhoti* & other clothes	Sister-in-law in-law	Sister puts the ring in the toe of the bride-groom	Yes	Yes	Yes
Yes	Yes	Sister-in-law	brother-in-law	Yes	Yes	Yes

54	*55*	*56*	*57*	*58*	*59*	*60*	*61*
Yes	Yes	Yes	Yes	Yes	Yes	Yes	Yes
Yes	Yes	Yes	Yes	Yes	Yes	Yes	Yes
Yes	Yes	Yes	Yes	Yes	Yes	Yes	They select an auspicious day and celebrate "First night".
Yes	Yes	Yes	Yes	Yes	Yes	Yes	They select an auspicious day and celebrate "First night".
Yes	No	Yes	Yes	Yes	No	Yes	They select on auspicious day and celebrate "First night".
Yes	Yes	Yes	Yes	Yes	Yes	Yes	Yes
Yes	Yes	Yes	Yes	Yes	Yes	Yes	They select an auspicious day for celebrating "First night".
Yes	Yes	Yes	Yes	Yes	No	Yes	No
Yes	Yes	Yes	Yes	Yes	No	Yes	No

62	63	64
Yes	Yes	(1) (2) (5) (6) & (7) only on the day of perum-pongal these people untie the marriage badge and tie a new one.
No	Yes	(1) (2) (5) (6)–Yes
No	Yes (they go round where the margosa and peepul tree join together)	(1) (5) (6) (7)–Yes
No	If there is any evil effect, the couple go round the peepul tree	(1) (5) (7)–Yes
No	They go round the peepul tree on the new moon day of the month of "ati"	(1) (3) (5) (7)–Yes
No	Yes	(1) (5) (6) (7)–Yes
No	No	(1) (5) (7)–Yes
Yes	Yes	(1) (5) (6)–Yes
They select an auspicious day and celebrate "First night"	Yes	(1) (5) (7)–Yes

	Number of customs					
Custom	*1*	*2*	*3*	*4*	*5*	*6*
Muppanar	Both parties	No (a)	Yes	Yes	Yes	Yes
Devar	Bride-groom's party	No (b)	Yes	Yes	Yes	Yes
Udayar	Bride-groom's party	Yes (a)	No	Yes	Yes	Yes
Kallar (Devar)	bride-groom's party	No (both a & b)	Yes	Yes	Yes	Yes
Tuluva Naickar	bride-groom's house	No (both a & b)	Yes	Yes	Yes	Yes
Jankamar	Bride-groom's party	Yes (a)	No	Yes	Yes	Yes
Konar (Fadhavap Pillai)	bride-groom's party	Yes (a & b)	No	Yes	Yes	Yes

7	8	9	10	11	12
Yes	No dowry	other things	Yes	Yes	Yes
Yes	Ornament	Other things	Yes	Yes	Yes
Yes	dowry	Ornaments & other things	Yes	Yes	Yes
Yes	all the presents given to the bride for marriage	No	Yes	Yes	Yes
Yes	Other things for marriage	No	Yes	Yes	Yes
Yes	No	Yes	Yes	Yes	Yes
Yes	Yes	No	Yes	Yes	Yes

13	*14*	*15*	*16*	*17*	*18*	*19*
Yes	Yes	No	No	9 days before marriage	No	in (b)
Yes	Yes	No	No	3 or 5 or or 7 or 9-days before marriage	No	in (b)
Yes	Yes	No	No	2 days before marriage	No	in (b)
Yes	Yes	No	No	No	No	in (a)
Yes	Yes	No	No	11 days before marriage	No	in (b)
Yes	Yes	No	No	3 days before marriage	No	in (b)
Yes	Yes	No	No	3 or 5 days before marriage	No	in (b)

20	21	22	23	24	25
3 days before marriage in bridegroom's house	(b)	Yes	Yes	Yes	Yes
3 days before marriage in bridegroom's house	(b)	Yes	Yes	Yes	Yes
5 days before marriage in bridegroom's house	(b)	Yes	Yes	No	Yes
3 days before marriage in the bride's house	(a)	Inviting the bride-groom to the bride's house	No	Yes	Yes
3 days before marriage in bridegroom's house	(b)	Yes	Yes	No	Yes
3 days before marriage in bridegroom's house	(b)	Yes	Yes	No	Yes
3 days before marriage in bridegroom's house	(b)	Yes	Yes	Yes	Yes

26	27	28	29	30	31	32
No	No	Yes	No	(1) (2) (4) (5) (7)	only at the time of tying marriage badge	conch, knife & milk ladle
No	No	Yes	No	(1) (2) (3) (4) (5) (7)	Yes, water is there	knife, conch & ring
Yes	No	Yes	No	(1) (2) (3) (4) (5) (7)	While tying marriage badge water is poured in that pot	milk ladle, knife, stylus.
No	No	Yes	No	(1) (2) (3) (4) (7) & a big pot	Yes	milk ladle, knife, ring
No	No	Yes	No	(1) (2) (3) (4) (5) (7)	Yes	milk ladle, lime etc.
No	No	Yes	No	(1) (2) (3) (4) (5) (7)	Only at the time of tying marriage badge	milk ladle
No	No	Yes	No	(1) (2) (3) (4) (5) (7)	Yes	milk ladle

33	34	35	36	37	38
3 days before marriage	(a)	No	No	5 members including bridegroom	Yes
3 days before marriage	(a)	No	No	elderly people	Yes
5 days before marriage	(a)	even number of pillars are to be in pandar	No	bridegroom & married ladies	Yes
5 days before marriage	(b)	No	No	bride's party	Yes
3 days before marriage	(a)	No	No	By the person who builds the pandar	Yes
According to their desire	(b)	No	No	5 married ladies	Yes
5 days before marriage	southern west side	5 or 11	Yes	married woman	Yes

39	40	41	42	43	44	45	46
Yes	Yes	Yes	No	If there is any evil effect one knot is tied by the bride-groom and the other two knots are tied by the sister-in-law, otherwise all the 3 knots are tied by the bridegroom	Yes	Yes	Yes
Yes	Yes	Yes	No	All the three knots are tied by the bridegroom	Yes	Yes	Yes
Yes	Yes	Yes	No	Yes	Yes	Yes	Yes
Yes	Yes	Yes	No	Yes	Yes	Yes	Yes
Yes	Yes	Yes	No	All the three knots are tied by the bridegroom	Yes	Yes	Yes
Yes	Yes	Yes	No	Yes	Yes	Yes	Yes
Yes	Yes	Yes	No	Yes	Yes	Yes	Yes

47	48	49	50	51	52	53	54
Yes	No	Mother-in-law	Brother-in-law	Yes	Yes	Not ment-ioned	Yes
Yes	Yes	sister-in-law	brother-in-law	Yes	Yes	Yes	Yes
Yes	Yes	Yes	brother-in-law	Yes	Not in custom	Yes, after leaving the paaligai in the river	Yes
Yes	Yes	bridegroom	brother-in-law	No	Yes	No	Yes
Yes	Yes	bridegroom	brother-in-law	No	Yes	No	Yes
Yes	Yes	bridegroom	brother-in-law before marriage	Yes	No	Yes	Yes
Yes	Yes	mother-in-law	brother-in-law	Yes	Yes	Yes	Yes

55	56	57	58	59	60
No	Yes	Yes	Yes	Yes	Yes
Yes	Yes	Yes	Yes	Yes	Yes
Yes	Yes	Yes	Yes	Yes	Yes
No	Yes	Yes	Yes	No	Yes
No	Yes	Yes	Yes	No	Yes
Yes	Yes	Yes	Yes	Yes	Yes
Yes	Yes	Yes	Yes	Yes	Yes

61	62	63		64
If it is an auspicious day they celebrate "First night" on that day	otherwise they celebrate it on 7th or 9th day	Yes	(1)	(5) (7)
Yes	Yes	Yes	(1)	(5) (7)
According to convenience they celebrate the first night	No	Yes	(1)	(5) (7)
Yes	No	Yes	(1)	(5) (7)
Yes	No	Yes	(1)	(5) (7)
By selecting the auspicious day they celebrate "First night"	No	Yes	(1)	(5) (6) (7)
By selecting an auspicious day they celebrate "First night"	No	No	(1)	(5) (6) (7)

	Number of customs				
Caste	1	2	3	4	5
Kuravar (Ramajoki)	Bridegroom's party	No (a & b)	Yes	Yes	Yes
Vannan	Bridegroom's party	No (a) & (b)	Yes	Yes	Yes
Navitar	Bridegroom's party	No (a) & (b)	Yes	Yes	Yes
Cakkili	Bridegroom's party	No (a) & (b)	Yes	Yes	Yes
Harijan	Bridegroom's house	Yes (a)	No	Yes	Yes

6	7	8	9	10	11
Yes	Yes	Yes	No	Yes	Yes
Yes	Yes	Ornaments	Other things for marriage	Yes	Yes
Yes	Yes	Ornaments	Other things for marriage	Yes	Yes
Yes	Yes	only talk about ornaments, dowry etc.	Yes	Yes	Yes
Yes	Yes	Not compulsory	Yes	Yes	Yes

12	13	14	15	16	17	18
Yes	Yes	Yes	No	No	According to the number of relatives they celebrate "nalungu"	No
Yes	Yes	Yes	No	No	No	on the day of marriage day they celebrate "nalungu" to the bride and bridegroom
Yes	Yes	Yes	No	No	No	On the day of marriage day they celebrate "nalungu" to the bride and bridegroom
Yes	Yes	Yes	No	No	16-kind of "nalungu"	No
Yes	Yes	Yes	No	No	5 (or) 7 (or) 9 days before marriage	No

19	20	21	22	23	24	25	26
in (b)	5 or 7 days before marriage in bride's house	(b)	Yes	Yes	Yes	Yes	No
in (b)	5 days before marriage in bride's house	(b)	Yes	Yes	No	Yes	No
in (b)	5 days before marriage in bride's house	(b)	Yes	Yes	No	Yes	No
in (b)	5 or 7 or 9 days before marriage in bride's house and 3 days before marriage in bridegroom's house	(b)	Yes	Yes	Yes	Yes	No
in (b)	5 or 7 days before marriage both in bride's & bridegroom's house	(b)	Yes	Yes	Yes	Yes	No

27	*28*	*29*	*30*	*31*	*32*
No	Yes	No	(1) (2) (3) (4) (7) a pot, stone grinder, roller	Yes	turmeric with yellow string
No	Yes	No	(1) (two pots) (4) (7)	only at the time of tying marriage badge	milk ladle
No	Yes	No	(2) wooden mortor on which a hallow and lamp placed with castor oil and a wick which is lighted (4) (7)	No	No
No	Yes	No	(1) (2) (3) (4) (7) 32 pots, stone grinder	Yes	nut cutter, coin
No	Yes	No	(1) (2) (4) & (7)	Yes	nut cutter, coins

33	*34*	*35*	*36*	*37*	*38*	*49*
Not mentioned	(a)	No	No	Married	Yes	Yes
Not mentioned	Not mentioned	No	No	Not mentioned	Not mentioned	Yes
Not mentioned	Not mentioned	No	No	Not mentioned	Not mentioned	Yes
Yes	(b)	Yes 32	Yes	Yes	Yes	Yes
Yes	(a)	No	No	Yes	Yes	Yes

40	*41*	*42*	*43*	*44*	*45*	*46*	*47*
Yes	Yes	No	Yes	Yes	Yes	Yes	Yes
Yes	Yes	No	All the knots are tied by the bride-groom	Yes	Yes	Yes	Yes
Yes	Yes	No	All the three knots are tied by the bride-groom	Yes	Yes	Yes	Before putting the rice in the holy fire bridegroom's brother-in-law puts ring in his finger
Yes	Yes	No	Yes	Yes	Yes	Yes	Yes
Yes	Yes	No	All the three knots are tied by the bride-groom	Yes	Yes	Yes	Yes

48	*49*	*50*	*51*	*52*
Yes, also they give *dhoti*, towel etc. to him	Before marriage bride's uncle put "metti" to her toe	Before marriage bridegroom's brother-in-law puts "metti" to her toe	Yes	Yes
yes, Also give a set of new dress	Mother-in-law	No	Yes	Yes
Yes	Mother-in-law	No	Yes	Yes
Yes	Before marriage day bride's uncle put "metti" to her toe	Before marriage bridegroom's brother-in-law puts "metti" to his toe	Yes	Yes
Yes	Bridegroom	No	Yes	Yes

53	*54*	*55*	*56*	*57*	*58*	*59*	*60*
Yes	Yes	Yes	Yes	Yes	Yes	Yes	Yes
Yes	Yes	Yes	Yes	Yes	Yes	Yes	Yes
Yes	Yes	Yes	Yes	Yes	Yes	Yes	Yes
Yes	Yes	Yes	Yes	Yes	Yes	Yes	Yes
Yes	Yes	Yes	Yes	Yes	Yes	Yes	Yes

61	62	63	64		
Yes	No	No	(1)	(5)	(7)
Yes	No	If there is any evil effect	(1)	(5)	(7)
Yes	No	If there is any evil effect	(1)	(5)	(7)
Yes	No	Yes	(1)	(5)	(7)
No	Yes	Yes	(1)	(5)	(7)

Notes :

**1. (17) In Brahmin caste it is not in custom to celebrate puberty rituals. Instead of that they do this before marriage as follows. They decorate the girl (bride) and prepare ("puttu" etc. and place this on her shoulder hands, leg thrice. This is termed as "eerri irakkutal". Then they take "aalam" around her.

*2. (30) In cobbler caste it is a peculiar custom to place some pots apart from the things mentioned. Salt, Chilly, and bran are put bythe bride and bridegroom in three pots and they are also placed in the marriage platform.

First Pregnancy

1. If a lady becomes pregnant, then her parents take sweet, sugar etc. go and meet her in her husband's house in the 3rd month.
2. On 5th month they take five kind of tiffens, five kind of meals etc., go and meet the girl.
3. On 5th month they take black saree.
4. On 7th month they celebrate "valai kappu". They first tied margosa fiber bangle, then murukku valai, silver, golden and glass bangles.
5. In some caste they do not celebrate valaikappu, but tied vasampu (sweet-flag) on the 5th or 7th month in the chain (marriage chain) of the lady.
6. On 9th month they celebrate "siimandam".
7. They put bangles to the children and married women those who attend the function.
8. They prepare "kapparisi" at the time of "valaikappu".
9. They invite the girl to the house for delivery on 7th month.
10. They invite the girl to the house for delivery on 9th month.
11. They send back the girl to her husband's house on 3rd month after delivery by doing "siir" to her and her child.

Number of customs					
Caste	*1*	*2*	*3*	*4*	*5*
Brahmin (Iyer)	No	Yes	Yes	Yes	No
Brahmin (Iyangar)	No	only in the 5th month they decorate her with flowers	No	Yes	No
Pillai	No	Yes	No	No	Yes, 5th month both bride & bridegroom's parents tie vasambu in her chain.
Isai Vellalar	No	Yes	Yes	In 7th or 9th month	No
Patayacci	No	Yes	No	7th month	No
Sengunta Mutaliyar	No	No	No	*[1]No	No
Pattar (goldsmith)	No	Yes	No	Yes	Yes 5th month
Asari (carpenter)	No	Yes	No	Yes	Yes, 5th month
Chettiyar	No	Yes	No	*[2]No	No

6	*7*	*8*	*9*	*10*	*11*
5th month	Yes	Yes	No	Yes	Yes
6th month	Yes	Yes	No	*Yes	Yes
No	No	No	Yes	No	Yes
No	No	No	No	Yes	Yes
No	Yes	Yes	No	Yes	Yes
No	No	No	No	Yes	Yes
No	No	Yes	Yes	No	Yes
No	Yes	Yes	Yes	No	Yes
9th month they celebrate "valaikappu" as well as "siimandam"	Yes	No	No	Yes	Yes

	Number of customs					
Castes	*1*	2	3	4	5	6
Chettiyar (sozhiya)	No	Yes	No	No	Yes, in the 7th month	7th month
Chettiyar (Vaniya)	No	Yes	No	in 7th (or) 9th month	No	No
Pillai (Tuluva Vellalar)	No	No	No	Yes	Yes, in the 7th month (they tie "sukku" instead of "vasampu")	No
Reddiar	No	Yes	No	7th month	No	No
Naidu	No	Yes	No	No	No	No
Thondai-mandala Mutaliyar	No	Yes	No	7th month	No	7th month
Nadar	No	*[3]Yes	Yes	9th month	No	No
Nayakkar (canar)	No	Yes	No	7th month	No	No
Nayakkar (tatar)	No	Only sugar, plant-tain	No	7th or 9th month	No	No

7	*8*	*9*	*10*	*11*
Yes	No	No	Yes	Yes
Yes	Yes	No	Yes	Yes
Yes	No	Yes	No	Yes
Yes	Yes	No	Yes	Yes
No	No	No	Yes	Yes
Yes	No	No	Yes	Yes
Yes	No	No	Yes	Yes
Betel leaf, nut plantain, mirror etc. are given to 5 or 7 married ladles	Yes	No	Yes	Yes
Yes	Yes	No	Yes	22nd day or 3rd month

Number of customs					
Caste	*1*	*2*	*3*	*4*	*5*
Muppanar	No	Yes	No	7th (or) 9th month	No
Devar	No	Yes	No	7th month in bride's house	No
Udayar	Yes	Yes	No	7th month	No
Kallar devar	Yes	Only sugar plantain etc.	No	7th or 9th	No
Tuluva Naickar	Yes	Yes	No	9th month	No
Jankamar	No	*[4]Yes	No	9th month	No
Konar (yadhava Pillai)	No	Yes	No	7th month	No

6	*7*	*8*	*9*	*10*	*11*
No	Yes	Yes	No	Yes	Yes
No	Yes	Yes	No	Yes	Yes
7th month	Yes	No	No	Yes	Yes
No	Yes	No	No	Yes	3rd or 5th month
No	Yes	No	No	Yes	5th month
No	Yes	Yes	No	Yes	9th month
No	Yes	Yes	No	Yes	Yes

	Number of customs				
Caste	*1*	*2*	*3*	*4*	*5*
Kuravar (Ramajoki)	No	Yes	No	7th or 9th month	No
Vannan	No	Yes	No	7th or 9th month	No
Navitar	No	Yes	No	7th month	No
Cakkili	No	Yes, also golden ornaments	No	7th month	No
Harijan	Yes, cook meals and give them to the girl	Yes	No	7th or 9th month	No

6	7	8	9	10	11
No	Yes	Yes	No	Yes	Yes
No	Yes	Yes	No	Yes	Yes
No	Yes	Yes	No	Yes	Yes
No	Yes	Yes	Yes	No	Yes
No	Yes	Yes	No	Yes	Yes

Notes :

* In 9th month bride's parents prepare a sweet (appam) and parcel it in a plantain leaf and tie the plantain leaf in the belly (in that saree portion) of the pregnant lady.

*1. These people do not celebrate "valaikappu" etc. but prepare different kind of meals, go and meet the girl in the 7th month.

*2. These people celebrate the first pregnancy elaborately.

*3. These people celebrate "nalungu" on the 5th month.

*4. These people also celebrate "nalungu" on the 5th month.

Sashtiyapthapurthi and Sadhabhishegam

Sashtiyapthapurthi

This is celebrated by Brahmin (iyer), Brahmin (iyangar), Pillai, Isai Velalar, Patayacci, Sengunta Mutaliyar, Asari (Pattar-goldsmith), Taccar (carpenter), Chettiar, (Vysya, Sozhiya, Vaniya), Pillai (Tuluva vellalar), Reddiar, Naidu, Thondai-mandala Mutaliyar, Nadar, Devar, Udayar, Kallar, Tuluva Naickar, Jankamar, Konar (yadhavap pillai), Vannan, Navitar and Cakkili.

The other caste people Nayakkar (Sanar), Nayakkar (Tatar), Muppanar, Kuravar (Ramajoki) and Harijan do not celebrate this function.

Those who celebrate this function, celebrate it like a marriage. Mostly all the caste people tie a marriage badge at this marriage also. Usually this is celebrated at the age of 60, by the son, sons-in-law, daughter and daughters-in-law. Some people do this in temple. On this day they arrange a grand feast.

Brahmin (Iyer)

These people invite brahmin priest, kindles holy fire, recites holy mantras, place 60 Kalasas and anoint the couple with the water in the Kalasams.

Brahmin (Iyangar)

These people place one 'kalasa'.

Pillai

Do not place any 'kalasa'.

Isai Velalar

Place "9" kalasas. They celebrate it either in the house or in the temple according to the situation.

Patayacci

These people place "9" kalasas. Some of this caste people do this in temple.

Sengunta Mutaliyar

These people place "5" kalasas.

Asari (Pattar-Goldsmith), Asari (Taccar-carpenter)

They do not place any "kalasa".

Pillai (Tuluva Vellalar)

These people place "Kalasas", but there is no restriction in the number of kalasas.

Reddiar

Celebrate it like other caste people.

Naidu

These people place number of kalasas according to their grand son, grand daughter's number (one kalasas for each grand-son, or grand-daughter).

Thondai Mandala Mutaliyar

These people place "5" kalasas.

Nadar

They celebrate this only in the house, like other caste people.

Devar

These people celebrate this function in the temple.

Udayar

They place "2" kalasas.

Kallar (Devar)

These people do not invite brahmin priest for this fuction.

Tuluva Naickar

These people place "7" kalasas.

Jankamar

They place "one" Kalasa.

Konar (Yadhava Pillai)

They place nine Kalasas.

Vannan

They do it in a simple manner in the temple.

Navitar

They place "5" kalasas.

Cakkili

They celebrate it like other caste people.

Sadhabhishegam

This is usually celebrated by Brahmin (iyer), Brahmin (iyangar), Pillai, Isai Velalar, Sengunta Mutaliyar, Asari (Pattar-goldsmith), Asari (taccar-carpenter), Chettiyar (vysya), Reddiar, Thondai mandala Mutaliyar, Udayar and Cakkili.

Following caste people do not celebrate this function : Patayacci, Chettiar (sozhiya) Chettiar (vaniya), Pillai (tuluva vellalar), Naidu, Nadar, Nayakkar (sonar), Nayakkar (tatar), Muppanar, Devar, Kallar (devar), Tuluva Naickar, Jankamar, Konar (yadhavap pillai), Kuravar (Ramajoki), Vannan, Navitar and Harijan.

1. This is celebrated like 60th birthday marriage.
2. This is celebrated on 70th or 71st or 75th or 80th or 81st, birthday.
3. Tying marriage badge is not in custom like 60th birthday marriage.
4. This is celebrated (a) in the temple (b) in the house.
5. Relatives are invited and a grand feast is arranged.

Number of customs

Caste	1	2	3	4	5
Brahmin (Iyer)	Yes	80th year	Yes	(b)	Yes
Brahmin (Iyangar)	Yes	*80th year	Yes	(b)	Yes
Pillai	Yes	71st (or) 81st year	Yes	(b)	Yes
Isai velalar	Yes	Not mentioned	Yes	(b)	Yes
Sengunta Mutaliyar	Yes	Not mentioned	Yes	(b)	Yes
Asari (Pattar-goldsmith)	Yes	80th year	Yes	(a)	Yes
Asari taccar-carpenter)	Yes	80th year	Yes	(a)	Yes
Chettiyar (vysya)	Yes	80th Year	Yes	(b)	Yes
Reddiar	Yes	71st (or) 80th year	Yes	(b)	Yes
Thondai mandala Mudaliar	Yes	71st (or) 80th year	Yes	(b)	Yes
Udayar	Yes	71st (or) 80th year	Yes	(a)	Yes
Cakkili	Yes	80th year	Yes	(a)	Yes

*2. Sons of the couple keep a "*kumkum*" like as follows : First rice is spread on the floor, place a plantain leaf on that, place water pot on that, brahmin priest kindle holy fire and after this they anoint the couple by water in the Kumkum.

Death Customs

Death is the final end of the human life cycle and it is the most sorrowful moment of human life. At the time of death also all people celebrate the death customs in different ways even though the basic customs are same. The basic death customs are given here and the differences are mentioned in the tabular column.

1. At the moment of the death of a person relatives, son, grandson, grand-daughter, wife etc. pour (a) milk, (b) basil plant's water, (c) water dissolved in sand, and (d) coin rubbed and mixed with water are administered in the mouth of the dead person.
2. Immediately after death they give bath to the dead body and place holy ash, *kumkum* etc. on the person's forehead.
3. After this they break a coconut, place betel leaf, nut, plantain etc. show camphor and do the "vazhi kuutti vitutal" ceremony (i.e. showing the way to the dead persons).
4. After doing this they place the camphor in front of the house.
6. Only after this ceremony they send the news to the outsiders and then only they weep.
7. They place a lamp (lighted lamp) in the headside of the dead person.
8. They place a corn-measure full of paddy bathi, coconut, betel leaf, nut etc. on the headside of the dead person.
9. These people either cremate or bury the dead body.
10. Beating all kind of drums is in custom.
11. Relatives bring "vaykkarisi" to the dead person, which contains paddy, oil, cikakkay, new cloth, plantain, tander coconut etc.
12. If a lady or a male dies than that person's parents bring new cloth (kooti) to them respectively.

13. If a male dies then for his widow, her brother-in-law brings new cloth (kooti) to her.
14. They give bath to the dead body before taking to the graveyard.
15. Then they put new cloth on the dead body.
16. Ladies put rice in the house to the dead person.
17. Gents put rice in the house to the dead person.
18. Gents put rice in the graveyard to the dead person.
19. Relatives also put rice in the mouth of the dead persons.
20. Then the dead body is placed in the bier.
21. Then the eldest son and his wife go round the bier thrice by taking corn-measure full of paddy in which a lamp is burning.
22. Relatives also go round the bier thrice and all of them bow down the dead person.
23. Then they put nine grains in cow-dung, place it in the hands or legs or both in hands and legs, and place it on the well.
24. This is done on the belief that "the dead person's good-luck will stay in the house itself."
25. Dead person's grand-son, grand-daughter hold the *ghee* torch.
26. Then the relatives or friends carry the bier to the graveyard.
27. After going to the graveyard they place the bier and put "vaykkarisi" in the mouth of the dead person.
28. Then the son takes a pot 'full of water' and goes round thrice the dead body after placing it in the graveyard. A person in the back put small holes in the pot and the water from that pot is sprinkled on the dead body. After completing the third round he break the pot into peaces by standing on the leg side.
29. Then they cremate or bury the body.

30. After this they take both and return home.
31. After returning home they wash the hands, legs etc; bow down to the lamp (which is placed where the body is laid down), smear the holy ash on their forehead and then only they take food.
32. Usually it is in custom to place a lamp upto the day of funeral ceremony in the place where the dead body is placed.
33. Then they clean the house with water.
34. Till the day of funeral ceremony they do not use oil or take oil-bath or comb the hair.
35. When the dead body is in the house they never sprinkle cow-dung water or clean the house.
36. Next day they do "paal teli".
37. On that day they place milk in a pot and the ladies put coins in the pot without making noise.
38. It is in custom that the paddy used for putting "vaykkarisi" will not be kept in the house. It has to be cooked before the funeral ceremony.
39. On the day of "paal teli", they take milk, tender coconut etc. to the grave yard, pick up the bones, ash etc., put them in the pot, anoint it by means of milk, tender coconut etc. and leave it in the river.
40. Then they take back the vessels to the house.
41. After this they mourn for the dead person on 8th day or 11th day.
42. They celebrate funeral rites on 16th day.
43. On 15th day night they erect stones one or two or three in the house, anoint it and offer three times.
44. After offering thrice and the offerings at the 3rd time are given to those who attend that ceremony.
45. In the early morning of 16th day gents go to the river bank by taking the stones and do funeral rites in the

river bank (termed as "karumati turai") and leave the stone in the river.

46. After finishing funeral rites new dresses are given to the person doing funeral rites.
47. After finishing funeral rites a ring is put in the finger of the person doing funeral rites.
48. Only after this rites they take oil bath.
49. Than they do "talaikattu".
50. Then on 30th day they mourn for the dead person. (termed as "kattukku ponavarkalai vittukku azhoittal").
51. Then they Mourn for the dead person for Deepawali and Pongal.
52. Then in the first year of the death of the person they give monthly rites.
53. After that they give funeral rites for every year.
54. If a child within a year dies then these people either bury or cremate the child by boring the year.
55. They do "punniyadanam" on 9th or 11th day.
56. If an unmarried person dies then they decorate a plantain and get that dead person married with the decorated plantain tree. Then only they do the funeral rites.
57. For one year they do not celebrate any auspicious functions.

	Number of customs						
Caste	*1*	*2*	*3*	*4*	*5*	*6*	*7*
Brahmin (Iyer)	(a), (b)	Yes	No	No	No	No	Yes
Brahmin (Iyangar)	(a), (b)	No	No	No	No	No	Yes
Pillai	(b)	Yes	Yes	Yes	No	Yes	Yes
Isai velalar	(a), (b)	No	Yes	Yes	No	Yes	Yes
Patayacci	(a), (b), (c)	Yes	Yes	Yes	No	Yes	Yes
Sengunta Mutaliyar	(b) (c)	No	Yes	Yes	No	Yes	Yes
Asari (pattar-goldsmith)	(c)	Yes	Yes	Yes	No	Yes	Yes
Asari (taccar-carpenter)	(b) (c)	Yes	Yes	Yes	No	Yes	Yes
Chettiyar (Vysya)	(a), (b)	No	Yes	Yes	No	Yes	Yes

8	*9*	*10*	*11*	*12*	*13*
No	cremate	No	No	Yes	Yes
No	Cremate	No	No	Yes	Yes
Yes	Cremate	No	Yes	Yes	Yes
Yes	*Both are in custom	No	Yes	Yes	Yes
Yes	Both are in custom	Yes	Yes	If a lady dies then her parents or relatives put new cloth	Yes
No	If the body is kept in sitting position they burn it. If they carry body in the bier, they cremate it.	No	Yes	Son, Usually two clothes are put one from the parent's house and from married house.	No
They place a "Kalasa" with water in front of the dead body	These people seated the dead body in a chair and bury it.	No	No	Yes	Yes
They place a "kalasa" with water in front of the dead body	These people also seated the dead body in a chair and bury it.	No	No	Yes	Yes
Yes	Cremate	No	Yes	Yes	Yes

14	*15*	*16*	*17*	*18*	*19*	*20*
No	Yes	No	No	No	No	Yes
Yes	Yes	No	No	No	No	Yes
No	Yes	Yes	No	Yes	Yes	Yes
Yes	Yes	Yes	No	Yes	Yes	Yes
Yes	Yes	Yes	No	Yes	Yes	Yes
Yes	Yes	No	No	No	No	Yes
Yes, by the water in the "Kalasa" placed before the dead body	Yes	No	No	No	No	No, seated in a chair like bier
Yes	Yes	No	No	No	No	No, seated in a chair like bier.
Yes	Yes	Yes	No	Yes	Yes	Yes

21	22	23	24	25	26	27
No	No	No	No	Yes	Yes	No
No	No	No	No	Yes	Yes	No
Yes, the ladies with leaf, nut, measuring pot-full of paddy.	Yes	No	No	Yes	Yes	Yes
Yes	Yes	This is done only if the dead person is a lady (or) married woman (in the hand)	Yes	Yes	Yes	Yes
Yes	Yes	at the foot	Yes	Yes	Yes	Yes
All go round the bier without carrying any-thing in the hand or head	Yes	Not in custom	No	Yes	Yes	No
Yes, but they carry the "kal-asa" in the hands	Yes	in the hands of the dead body	Yes	Yes	Yes	No
Yes, but they carry the "kalasa" in the hands	Yes	in the hands of of the dead body	Yes	Yes	Yes	No
Yes, without carrying any-thing in the hand	Yes	No	No	Yes	Yes	No

28	*29*	*30*	*31*	*32*	*33*
Yes	Yes	Yes	Yes	Yes	Yes
No	Yes	Yes	Yes	Yes	Yes
Yes	Yes	[1]Yes, before coming to the house these people give lamp plate, tumbler etc. to a brahmin priest	Yes	Yes	Yes
Yes	Yes	Yes	Yes	Yes	Yes
Yes	Yes	Yes	Yes	Yes	Yes
Yes	Yes	Yes	Yes	Yes	Yes
Yes	Yes	Yes	Yes	Yes	Yes
Yes	Yes	Yes	Yes	Yes	Yes
Yes	Yes	Yes	Yes	Yes	Yes

34	*35*	*36*	*37*	*38*	*39*
Yes	Yes	Yes	No	No	milk, plantain
Yes	Yes	Yes, (on that day they cook meals without salt and put it in the river)	No	No	milk, cooked meals without salt
Yes	Yes	Yes	No	Yes	Yes
Yes	Yes	Next day (or) 3rd-day they celebrate "paal teli"	Yes	Yes	Yes
Yes	Yes	Yes	Yes	Yes, they use this paddy at the time of "paal teli" day	Yes
Yes	Yes	Yes	No	No	Yes
Yes	Yes	Yes	Yes	No	Yes
Yes	Yes	Yes	Yes	No	Yes
Yes	Yes	[2]Next day	No	Yes	Yes

40	41	42	43	44	45	46
Yes	No	15th day	No	No	No	Yes
Yes	[3]in this caste	15th day	No	No	No	[4]Yes
Yes	7th day	16th day	Yes	Yes	Yes	Yes also saree for his wife
Yes	8th day	11th (or) 16th day	two	Yes	Yes	Yes
Yes	8th day	16th day	one stone	Yes	Yes	Yes
Yes	8th day	3rd day	No	No	No	Yes
Yes	8th day	[5]16th day	one stone	Yes	Yes	Yes
Yes	6th day	16th day	two stones	Yes	Yes	Yes
Yes	No	16th day	one stone	Yes	Yes	Yes

47	*48*	*49*	*50*	*51*	*52*
Yes	Yes	No	They mourn for the dead person on 27th day 2nd, 3rd & 6th month	No	Yes
Yes	Next day	No	No	No	Yes
Yes	Yes	No	Yes	Yes	Yes
Yes	Yes	Yes	Yes, on 29th day	Yes (before 5 or 7 days before Deepawali & Pongal)	Yes
Yes	Yes	Yes	Yes	Yes	No
Yes	Yes	No	on 16th day they celebrate it for ceremonial impurity	No	No
Yes	Yes	Yes	No	No	Yes
Yes	Yes	Yes	No	No	Yes
Yes	Yes	No	No	No	Yes

53	54	55	56	57
Yes	Bury	11th day	No	Yes
Yes	Bury	Not in Custom	No	Yes
Yes	Bury	10th or 13th day	No	Yes
Yes	Bury	No	Yes	Yes
Yes	Bury	No	Yes	Yes
Yes	No	Not in custom	Not in custom	Yes
Yes	No	Not in custom	Not in custom	Yes
Yes	Yes	Not in custom	Not in custom	Yes
Yes	No	Not in custom	Not in custom	Yes

	Number of customs						
Caste	*1*	*2*	*3*	*4*	*5*	*6*	*7*
Chettiyar (Sozhiya)	(a) (b)	No	Yes	Yes	No	Yes	Yes
Chettiyar (Vaniya)	(a), (b)	No	Yes	Yes	No	Yes	Yes
Pillai (Tuluva Vellalar)	(a), (b)	No	Yes	Yes	No	Yes	Yes
Reddiar	(a), (b)	Yes	Yes	No	Yes	Yes	Yes
Naidu	(a), (b)	Yes	Yes	Yes	No	Yes	Yes
Thondai-mandala Mutaliyar	(a), (b) (c), (d)	Yes	Yes	Yes	No	Yes	Yes
Nadar	(a), (b)	No	Yes	Yes	No	Yes	Yes
Nayakkar (Canar)	(a)	Yes	Yes	No	Yes	Yes	Yes
Nayakkar (Tatar)	(a), (b)	Yes	Yes	No	Yes	Yes	Yes

8	9	10	11	12
Yes	Both are in custom	Yes	Yes	Yes, also from uncle's house
Yes	Both are in custom	Yes	Yes	Yes, also from the uncle's house
Yes	cremate	Yes	Yes	Uncle
Yes	Both are in custom	Yes	Yes, they take back the "vayk-karisi" paddy immediately	dead person's elder-brother
Place only sandal wood	Both are in custom	They blow only tatar conch	No	Parent's house
Place only sandal wood	cremate	Yes	No	Yes
Yes	Both are in custom	Yes	Yes	Yes
Yes	Bury	Yes	Yes	Parent's house
Yes, they did not place paddy full of corn-measure	the body can be either seated or laid down and buried	Yes	No	For a female her sister-in-law puts new cloth. For a male his brother-in-law puts new cloth

13	*14*	*15*	*16*	*17*	*18*	*19*	*20*
Yes	Yes	Yes	Yes	No	Yes	Yes	Yes
Yes	Yes	Yes	Yes	No	Yes	Yes	Yes
her parents	Yes	Yes	Yes	No	Yes	Yes	Yes
her relatives	Yes	Yes	Yes	No	Yes	Yes	Yes
Yes	Yes	Yes	No	No	No	No	body is seated in the bier
her parents	Yes	Yes	No	No	No	No	Yes
Yes	Yes	Yes	Yes	No	Yes	Yes	Yes
Yes	Yes	Yes	Yes	No	Yes	Yes	Yes
Yes	Yes	Yes	No	No	No	No	Yes

21	*22*	*23*	*24*	*25*	*26*	*27*
Yes	Yes	in the hands of the dead person	Yes	Yes	Yes	Yes
Yes	Yes	in the hands of the dead person	Yes	Yes	Yes	Yes
Yes	Yes	in the leg of the dead person	Yes	Yes	Yes	Yes
Yes	Yes	No	No	Yes	Yes	Yes
Yes, without carrying	Yes	Only in the well	This is done in the belief the persons who have no child at all will give birth to a child	Yes	Yes	No
Yes, without carrying anything	Yes	Both in hands and legs	Yes	Yes	Yes	No
Yes, without carrying anything	Yes	Not in custom	No	Yes	Yes	Yes
Yes, by placing a cloth around the head	Yes	in the hands of the dead body	Yes	Yes	Yes	Yes
Yes, by placing cloth above the head	Yes	in the hands of the dead body	Yes	Yes	Yes	No

38	*29*	*30*	*31*	*32*	*33*	*34*	*35*
Yes	Yes	Yes	Yes	Yes and also water in a brass pot	Yes	Yes	Yes
Yes	Yes	Yes	Yes	Yes	Yes	Yes	Yes
Yes	Yes	Yes	Yes	Yes	Yes	Yes	Yes
Yes	Yes	Yes	Yes	Yes	Yes	Yes	Yes
Yes	Yes	Yes	Yes	Yes	Yes	Yes	Yes
Yes	Yes	Yes	Yes	Yes	Yes	Yes	Yes
Yes	Yes	Yes	Yes	Yes	Yes	Yes	Yes
Yes	Yes	Yes	Yes	Yes	Yes	Yes	Yes
Yes	Yes	Yes	Yes	Yes	Yes	Yes	Yes

36	*37*	*38*	*39*	*40*
Yes	Not mentioned	Yes	Yes	Yes
3rd day	Yes	Yes	tiffens, in husked rice, dhall, milk only	Yes
Yes	if male dies his widow puts coin in the milk	Yes	Yes	Yes
Yes	Yes	Yes	Yes	Yes
5th day	Yes	No	tiffens, unhusked rice, groundnut, milk	Yes
Yes	No	No	Yes	Yes
3rd day	Yes	Yes	Yes	Yes
3rd day	Yes	Yes	Yes	Yes
3rd day	Yes	No	Yes	Yes

41	42	43	44	45	46
8th day	16th day	Not mentioned	Yes	Yes	Yes
8th day	Yes	two stones	Yes	Yes	Yes
8th day	Yes	one stone	Yes	Yes	Yes
7th day	After 13th day	three stones	Yes	Yes	Yes
7th day	11th day	Erect two stones on 10th day night	Not mentioned	11th day	Yes
8th day	3rd day	No	No	No	Yes
8th day	16th day	one stone	Yes	Yes	Yes
8th day	15th day	two stones	Yes	Yes	Yes
8th day	15th day night	one stone	Yes	Yes	Yes

47	*48*	*59*	*50*	*51*	*52*
Yes	Next day	Yes	Yes	Yes	Yes
Yes	Yes	Yes	Yes	Yes	Yes
Yes	Yes	Yes	Not mentioned	Not mentioned	No
Yes	Yes	Yes	Yes	Not mentioned	Yes
Yes	Yes	Next day	Yes	Yes	No
Yes	Yes	No	On 16th day they celebrate to remove the ceremonial impurity.	No	No
Yes	Yes	Yes	on 16th day	Not mentioned	No
Yes	Yes	Yes	30th day	Yes	No
Yes	Yes	Next day	30th day	Yes	No

53	54	55	56	57
Yes	Bury	13th day	Not in custom	Yes
Yes	Bury	7th (or) 9th day	Yes	Yes
[7]yes	Bury	11th day	Yes	Yes
[8]8 Yes	Bury	11th day	Yes	Yes
Yes	cremate	11th day	Yes	Yes
Yes	No	Not in custom	Not custom	Yes
Yes	Bury	8th day	Yes	Yes
Yes	Bury	9th or 11th day	Yes	Yes
Yes	Bury	8th day	Yes	Yes

	Number of customs					
Caste	*1*	2	3	4	5	6
Muppanar	(a), (b)	No	Yes	Yes	No	Yes
Devar	(a), (b) (c), (d)	Yes	Yes	Yes	No	Yes
Udayar	(a), (b) (c), (d)	Yes	Yes	Yes	Yes	Yes
Kallar (devar)	(a), (b)	Yes	Yes	No	Yes	Yes
Tuluva Naickar	(a), (b)	No	Yes	Yes	No	Yes
Jankamar	(a), (b)	No	Yes	Yes	No	Yes
Konor (Yadhavap Pillai)	(a), (b)	Yes	Yes	Yes	No	Yes

7	*8*	*9*	*10*	*11*
Yes	Yes	Bury	Yes	Yes
Yes	tender coconut, bathi, lamp	Cremate	Yes	Yes
Yes	broken coconut, betel leaf, nut, plantain, lamp	Bury	Yes	No
Yes	Yes	cremate	Yes	Yes
Yes	Yes	Bury	Yes	Yes
Yes	Yes	Bury	They blow conch and beat "see-mangalam"	Yes
Yes	Yes	Bury	Yes	Yes

12	13	14	15	16	17	18	19
For a female her brother-in-law puts new cloth. For a male his parents puts new cloth	Yes	Yes	Yes	Yes	No	Yes	Yes
Yes	Yes	Yes	Yes	Yes	No	Yes	Yes
If a lady dies then her parents or relatives put new cloth	Yes	Yes	Yes	No	No	No	No
Parents	Yes	Yes	Yes	Yes	Yes	Yes	Yes
Parents	Yes	Yes	Yes	Yes	Yes	Yes	Yes
Parents	Yes	Yes	Yes	Yes	No	Yes	Yes
If a female dies, then her parents put new cloth. If a male dies, then his brother-in-law puts new cloth	Yes	Yes	Yes	Yes	No	Yes	Yes

20	*21*	*22*	*23*	*24*
Yes	Yes, by carrying a cloth above his head	Yes	either in leg or in hand	Yes, family will be more fertile
Yes	Yes, by carrying a cloth above his head.	Yes	Both in hands and legs of the dead person	Yes
Yes	Yes, without carrying anything in the hand or head.	Yes	at the foot	Yes
Yes	Yes	Yes	either in the hand or leg	This is done on the belief that "the dead person's luck will not go out with him"
Yes	Yes	Yes	either in the leg or hand	"family will be fertile more and more"
Yes	Yes	Yes	Not in custom	No
Yes	Yes	Yes	at the foot	Yes

25	*26*	*27*	*28*	*29*	*30*	*31*	*32*	*33*
Yes	Yes	Yes	Yes	Yes	Yes	Yes	Yes	Yes
Yes	Yes	Yes	Yes	Yes	Yes	Yes	Yes	Yes
Yes	Yes	Yes	Yes	Yes	Yes	Yes	Yes	Yes
Yes	Yes	Yes	Yes	Yes	Yes	Yes	Yes	Yes
Yes	Yes	Yes	Yes	Yes	Yes	Yes	Yes	Yes
Yes	Yes	Yes	Yes	Yes	Yes	Yes	Yes	Yes
Yes	Yes	Yes	Yes	Yes	Yes	Yes	Yes	Yes

34	*35*	*36*	*37*	*38*	*39*	*40*
Yes	Yes	3rd day	Yes	Yes	Yes	Yes
Yes	Yes	3rd day	Yes	Yes	Yes	Yes
Yes	Yes	3rd day	Yes	No	Yes	Yes
Yes	Yes	3rd day	Yes	Yes	Yes	Yes
Yes	Yes	Yes	Yes	Yes	Yes	Yes
Yes	Yes	3rd day	Yes	Yes	Yes	Yes
Yes	Yes	Yes	Yes	Yes	Yes	Yes

41	42	43	44	45	46
8th day	[6]16th day	One stone	No	Yes	Yes
8th day	16th day	One stone	Yes	Yes	Yes
8th day	16th day	These people do not erect stones in the house	Yes	They worship the stone only in the river bank & leave the stone the river	Yes
8th day	15th day	Two stones	Yes	Yes	Yes
3rd or 8th day	16th day	One stone	Yes	Yes	Yes
7th day	11th day	Not in custom	Yes	They erect a stone in the river bank, worship it and leave it in the river	Yes
5th or 7th day	16th day	One stone	Yes	Yes	Yes

47	*48*	*49*	*50*	*51*	*52*
Yes	Yes	Next day	3rd month	Yes	Yes
Yes	Yes	Yes	3rd month	Yes	Not mentioned
Yes	Yes	Next day	Yes	Not mentioned	No
Yes	Yes	Yes	Yes	No	No
Not mentioned	Yes	Next day	Yes	Not	No
Not mentioned	Yes	Yes	Yes	No	No
Not mentioned	Yes	Yes	Yes	Yes	Yes

53	54	55	56	57
[9]Yes	Bury (or) cremate	10th day (or) 16th day	Yes	Yes
[10]Yes	Bury	9th day	Yes	Yes
Yes	Bury	10th day	Yes	Yes
Yes	Bury	7th or 9th day	Not mentioned	Yes
Yes	Bury	9th day	No	Yes
Yes	Bury	9th day	No	Yes
Yes	Bury	11th day	Yes	Yes

	Number of customs					
Caste	*1*	*2*	*3*	*4*	*5*	*6*
Kuravar (Ramajoki)	(a), (b)	No	Yes	Yes	No	Yes
Vannan	(a), (b), (b), (d)	[11]No	Yes	Yes	No	Yes
Navitar	(a), (b), (c), (d)	[12]Yes	Yes	Yes	No	Yes
Cakkili	(a), (b), (c), (d)	Yes	Yes	Yes	No	Yes
Harijan	(a)	Yes	Yes	Yes	No	Yes

7	8	9	10	11	12
Yes	Yes	Bury	Yes	Yes	If a lady dies then her parents put new-cloth. If a male dies then his brother puts new cloth.
Yes	Yes	Both are in customs	Three type of drums viz., tappattai, urumpu settu, koyil moolas	Yes	Yes
Yes	Yes	Cremate	Three type of drums viz., tappattai, urumpu settu, koyil meelam	Yes	Yes
Yes	The powder prepared by mixing turmeric, nine kinds of grains	Cremate	Yes	Yes	Yes
Yes	Yes, also knife, stick, pastel etc.	Bury	Yes	Yes	Yes

13	*14*	*15*	*16*	*17*	*18*	*19*	*20*
Yes	Yes	Yes	Yes	No	Yes	Yes	Yes
Yes	Yes	Yes	Yes	No	Yes	Yes	Yes
Yes	Yes	Yes	Yes	No	Yes	Yes	Yes
Yes	[13]Yes	Yes	Yes	Yes	Yes	Yes	Yes
Yes	Yes	Yes	Yes	No	Yes	Yes	Yes

21	22	23	24	25	26	27
Yes	Yes	in the hands	Yes	Yes	Yes	Yes
Yes	Yes	both in legs and hands	Yes	Yes	Yes	Yes
Yes	Yes	Both in legs and hands	Yes	Yes	Yes	Yes
Yes, without carrying anything	Yes	Not in custom	No	Yes	Yes	Yes
Yes, grandson holds the pot in which the flours is kept, son carries the paddy full of measuring pot	Others carry other things	Nine grains & margosa leaves.	No	Yes	Yes	Yes

28	29	30	31	32	33
Yes	Yes	Yes	Yes	Yes	Yes
Yes	Yes	Yes	Yes	Yes	Yes
Yes	Yes	Yes	Yes	Yes	Yes
Yes	Yes	Yes	Yes	Yes	Yes
Yes	Yes	Yes	Yes	Yes	Yes

34	35	36	37	38	39
Yes	Yes	Yes	Yes	Yes	Yes
Yes	Yes	Yes	Yes	Yes	Yes
Yes	Yes	Yes	Yes	Yes	Yes
Yes	Yes	3rd day	Yes	Yes	Yes
Yes	Yes	Yes	Yes	Yes	Yes

40	*41*	*42*	*43*	*44*	*45*	*46*
Yes	8th day	16th day	one stone	Yes	Yes	Yes
Yes	3rd (or) 7th day	[14]16th day	two stones	Yes	Yes	Yes
Yes	8th day	16th day	two stones	Yes	Yes	Yes
Yes	8th day	16th day	two stones	Yes	Yes	Yes
Yes	If the dead person is male on 8th-day if the dead person is female on 7th day	If the dead person is male on 16th day, if the dead person is female then on 11th day	not mentioned	Yes	Yes	Yes

47	*48*	*49*	*50*	*51*	*52*
No	Yes	Yes	Yes	Yes	Yes
No	Yes	Not immediately after "paal teli"	Yes	No	Yes
No	Yes	Yes	Yes	No	No
Yes	Yes	Yes	Yes	No	No
No	Yes	Not mentioned	Yes	Not mentioned	No

53	54	55	56	57
No	Bury	8th or 9th day	Yes	Yes
Yes	Not mentioned	11th day	Yes	Yes
Yes	Not mentioned	11th day	Yes	Yes
Yes	Not mentioned	8th day	Yes	Yes
[15]Yes	Bury	in odd numbered days	Yes	Yes

Notes :

* It is in custom to cremate and bury the dead body. These people believe if one's body is cremate they will go to heaven, if one's body is buried they will go to hell (Isai Velalar caste).

1. There is a belief in connection with this occasion; i.e., the dead person will be lighted to reach their place. So they give lamp to a brahmin priest (Pillai).
2. The death customs of Vysya Chettiyar differs from other caste people which are mentioned in the Chapter VI, Part II, Death customs.
3. On 10th day meals is given to the relatives with vata, payasam etc. On that night they give fried rice, jaggery, unhusked rice etc. to those relatives. 11th day *dhoti*, a metal pot, coins etc. are given to a brahmin, and he is fed. On 12th day they give *dhoti*, a metal pot, coins etc. to five persons (This is termed as "chavundi (or) greekhiyam"). On that day itself they give *dhoti* to another person (termed as "vastira daanam"). Also a cow is given to a person on that day itself (termed as "koo daanam"). A bamboo stick is given to another person on that day itself (termed as) "pirampu daanam" (Brahmin—Iyangar).

It is believed that the dead person holds the stick to go to heaven and so it is given as an alm. If one has land they give land to their relatives (They give small portion of the land to their relatives, which is termed as "bumi dhanam").

13th, day is termed as an auspicious day on that day sweat, tiffen, new dress are given to all in the house (Brahmin—Iyangar).

4. If the father-in-law or mother-in-law dies, one has to take *dhoti*, ring etc. to the bridegroom and a saree to the bride. (Brahmin–Iyangar).
5. On 16th day the sons of the dead person go to the graveyard, take the sand from there, make a shape of Lord Siva (*Linga* shape) and anoint it with milk, curd etc. and the priest (from this Goldsmith caste itself) come and do the "punniyadanam". This is done to remove the ceremonial impurity due to death of a person. On that day they do "punniyadanam" by sprinkling (cow's urine) "koomiyam" throughout the house, also sprinkle milk, curd etc. (Goldsmith).
6. They celebrate karumati on 16th day night. They give offerings only once (Muppanar).
7. If a lady dies with married status then yearly they give saree, blouse, turmeric, *kumkum*, betel leaf, nut, flowers etc. to a brahmin priest's wife (Pillai—Tuluva Vellalar).
8. The same custom as above caste (Reddiar).
9. They give "yearly tithi" and give rice, plantain, coins etc. to the brahmin priest (Muppanar).
10. If a lady dies with the married status these people given saree, blouse, flower, turmeric, *kumkum* etc. as alms to a brahmin priest's wife (Devar).
11. These people place a coin on the forehead of the corpse and put garland on the corpse. The dead body is kept on a bench under which sand is spread (Washerman).
12. Immediately after death they give bath to the dead body, place the holy ash on its forehead, place a twenty five paise coin on its forehead and place the dead body on bench in which sand is spread and dharbai (a kind of holy grass) is kept on the sand and on that the dead body is placed (Barber).
13. Then the new cloth is put on the body, and the turmeric powder which was offered first to the dead body, is tied in the lap by that person's sons, daughter-in-law, then they go round thrice the dead body and then they put the powder on the dead body (For this they termed as "antaratchai ceytal") (Cobbler-cakkili).
14. On 11th day evening, 15th day mid-night and on 16th day early morning they give offering to dead person (Washerman).

15. These people give yearly funeral rites for every year. On that day they give rice as alms to a priest (pandaram) or to a cow.

Apart from these customs regarding death in some castes it is compulsory to put a particular colour saree for woman dying with married status, for a-widowed lady. Also in some castes it is compulsory for the widowed ladies to wear a particular colour saree.

Pillai (Tuluva Vellalar) people put red colour new cloth if a married woman dies, to a widow white new cloth and if a lady becomes widow it is a custom that she has to wear white or red saree. Reddiar caste people also put the same colour of saree as above but it is compulsory for a widow to wear white saree.

Naidu caste people put any colour saree if the married woman died, for widows they put light yellow colour saree. It is not mentioned that a particular colour saree to be worn by the widowed lady. Nadar caste people resemble Reddiar caste people in this matter. Nayakkar (canar) put the same colour of saree as above, but widow is to wear red saree. Nayakkar (tatar) put red saree if a woman died with married status, for widows red colour saree without flower and widowed ladies do not wear flowered saree. Muppanar caste people put saree like that of Reddiar caste people but there is no restriction for widows to wear a particular colour saree. In Devar caste people if a lady died with married status they put flowered saree, if a widow dies they put white or red colour saree. They do not mention about the saree to be worn by the widowed ladies.

In Udayar caste they resemble the Reddiar caste people and there is no compulsion for widows to wear a particular colour saree.

In Kallar (Devar) caste they put flowered new cloth if the dead person is a married lady, white new cloth for widows and there is no restriction for widows to wear particular colour saree.

In Tuluva Naickar caste people, they put red colour new cloth to the married women if she dies with married status, if a widow dies they put white cloth and white cloth is to be worn by the widow compulsorily.

In Jankamar caste, they put red, yellow, green new cloth to a married lady and if a widow dies they put white cloth and there is no restriction for the widows to wear a particular colour saree.

In Konar (Yadhavappillai) caste people it is in custom that who put new cloth to the dead body has to take bath 108 times. If that person is not able to do it, the dead person's son has to do it. If a woman become widow she has to cross the pastel, new cloth and the fire by putting fire in the straw. The person after taking 108 baths has to come inside and bow down to the lamp and sit facing northern side and take the curd, tender coconut, milk etc. from others.

These are the main variations from caste to caste in each category of human life cycle.

4

Folk-Customs : Regional Variation

This chapter deals with the Regional variations in Folk-customs. This is divided into two viz., (1) Differences in custom of various castes people between Districts (South Arcot, Tanjore and Coimbatore), (2) Differences of customs of various castes people between the villages within a District. Even though the basic customs more or less resemble each other, variations are found between region to region. The differences in Folk-customs of various caste people between region to region from child-birth to Death are given in the following pages.

1. Differences in Customs of Various Caste People between Districts

Under this division three districts are compared. They are South Arcot, Tanjore and Coimbatore. Among three districts in Coimbatore district some caste people are not available. So, they are not given here. Basic customs of different caste people are given as follows and the variations are tabulated in tabular column.

Child Birth

1. Putting "kappu" to the child.
2. At the time of putting "kappu", it is in custom to put margosa fibre bangle in the hands of the child.
3. Only other types viz. silver, five metal bangle, golden bangle are put.

4. Naming ceremony.
5. Doing punniyadanam is in custom.
6. Hair removing ceremony.
7. Ear boring ceremony.

These are the basic customs regarding child birth. In the tabular column, in row the basic customs are mentioned. In the columns caste, district are mentioned. Only if the tabular column are given like this the differences can be noted easily.

Number of customs			
Caste / District	*1*	2	*3*
Brahmin (Iyer) South Arcot	Yes, on 7th or 9th day	Yes	Yes
Tanjore	Yes on 7th day	Yes	Yes
Coimbatore	—	—	—
Brahmin (Iyangar) South Arcot	11 day	Yes	Yes
Tanjore	Yes, 11th day	No	Silver mixed with white metal etc.
Coimbatore	—	—	—
Pillai South Arcot	7th day	Yes	Yes
Tanjore	7th & 15th day	Yes on 7th day	Yes, 15th day
Coimbatore	30th day	No	Five metal bangle & silver bangle only
Isai Velalar South Arcot	16th day	No	Yes
Tanjore	16th day	Yes	Yes
Coimbatore	—	—	—

4	5	6	7
11th day	11th day	1st Year	1st year
11th day	11th day	1st year	1st year
—	—	—	—
11th day	11th day	1st year	1st year
11th day	11th day	1st year	1st year
—	—	—	—
15th day	15th day	1st year	1st year
15th day	16th day	1st year	1st year
30th day	15th day	11th month	5th year
15th day	15th day	1st year	1st year
on 16th day or in 6th (or) 12th month	16th day	2nd (or) 3rd year	While removing hair they celebrate or boring ceremony
—	—	—	—

Number of customs			
Caste / District	*1*	2	3
Patayacci South Arcot	9th day	Yes	Yes
Tanjore	15th day	Yes	Yes
Coimbatore	—	—	—
Mutaliyar South Arcot	Not in custom	No	No
Tanjore	15th day	Yes	twisted bangle (murukku kappu & other bangles)
Coimbatore	Not in custom	No	No
Pattar Goldsmith South Arcot	16th day	Yes	Yes
Tanjore	15th day	Yes	Mukkappu (three metal mixed bangle)
Coimbatore	—	—	—
Chettiar Vaniya South Arcot	15th day	Yes	Yes
Tanjore	15th day	Yes	Yes
Coimbatore	—	—	—

4	5	6	7
16th day	16th day	1st year	1st year
15th day	15th day	1st year	1st year
—	—	—	—
They celebrate this function according to the situation	Not in custom	1st year	1st year
3rd or 4th month	Not in custom	1st year	1st year
3rd month	Not in custom	11th month or 3rd year	11th month or 3rd year
3rd or 5th month	13th or 15th or 16th day	1st year	1st year
15th day	16th day	1st year	1st year
—	—	—	—
15th day	15th day	1st year	1st year
15th day	15th day	1st year	1st year
—	—	—	—

Number of customs			
Caste District	*1*	*2*	*3*
Naidu South Arcot	3rd day	Yes	Yes
Tanjore	11th day	Yes	Yes
Coimbatore	on 15th day	No	First "pancavarna tandai", then only they put "ancu pancalam" kappu
Nadar South Arcot	3rd day	Yes	Yes
Tanjore	—	—	—
Coimbatore	Not in custom	No	No
Devar South Arcot	7th day	Yes	Yes
Tanjore	after 22nd day	Yes	Yes
Coimbatore	—	—	—
Udayar South Arcot	1st year	Yes	Yes
Tanjore	15th day	Not mentioned	Five metal bangle (anju panjalam kappu)
Coimbatore	—	—	—

4	5	6	7
16th day	16th day	2nd year	2nd year
11th day	11th day	1st year	1st year
within one month	9th day	11th month	within 3rd year
30th day	15th day	1st year	1st year
—	—	—	—
3rd month	Not in custom	3rd year	3rd year
16th day	16th day	1st year	1st year
After 22nd day	11th or 15th day	1st year	1st year
—	—	—	—
16th day	16th day	1st year	1st year
16th day	15th day	5th month	5th month
—	—	—	—

Number of customs			
Caste District	*1*	*2*	*3*
Vannan South Arcot	9th day	Yes	Yes
Tanjore	16th day	Yes	Yes
Coimbatore	5th day	No	Only these bangles are put
Harijan South Arcot	7th or 11th day	Yes	Yes
Tanjore	16th day	Yes	Yes
Coimbatore	3rd day	No	Only five metal bangle

4	5	6	7
9th day	9th or 11th day	3rd (or) 5th year	3rd or 5th year
16th day	16th day	1st year	1st year
3rd month	5th day	1st year	1st year
11th day	11th day	According to the economic situation	According to the economic situation
16th day	16th day	5th month	1st or 2nd or 3rd birth day
3rd month	Not in custom	3rd year	3rd year

Puberty Rituals

1. If a girl attains age she has to inform the matter (a) through somebody else to her mother, (b) directly to her mother.
2. They pour water on the first day.
3. It is in custom to hold a sieve above the head of the girl while pouring water.
4. They pour water on 3rd, 5th, 7th, 9th, and 11th etc. days.
5. They prepare "puttu" on 3rd, 5th, 7th, 9th, 11th etc. days.
6. They prepare horoscope at the time of attaining age.
7. They invite the girl inside the house on 5th day.
8. They celebrate puberty rituals on 11th day.
9. It is in custom that relatives come, cook food and give it to the girl.
10. The girl's (a) uncle (b) grand-mother is to meet the expenditure for the "puberty rituals" celebrations.

	Number of customs			
Caste / District	*1*	*2*	*3*	*4*
Brahmin (Iyer) South Arcot	(b)	Yes	No	No
Tanjore	(b)	Yes	No	Yes
Coimbatore	—	—	—	—
Brahmin (Iyangar) South Arcot	(b)	No	No	only on the fourth day
Tanjore	(b)	Yes	No	Only on 3rd day
Coimbatore	—	—	—	—
Pillai South Arcot	(a)	Yes	Yes	Yes
Tanjore	(a)	Yes	No	Yes
Coimbatore	(a)	Yes	No	Daily till the girl is invited inside the house
Isai Velalar South Arcot	(a)	Yes	Yes	Yes
Tanjore	(a)	Yes	No	Yes
Coimbatore	—	—	—	—

5	6	7	8	9	10
Only on the 3rd day	No	4th day	No	No	Uncle
Yes	No	7th day	7th day	Yes	uncle
—	—	—	—	—	—
Only on the fifth day	No	Yes	No	No	No
Not mentioned	No	4th-day	Not in custom	No	No
—	—	—	—	—	—
Only on 5th day	Yes	Yes	5th or 7th or 9th or 11th day	Yes	uncle
Only on "Puberty" ceremony day	Yes	9th day	9th day	Yes	uncle
Daily till the inside the house	Yes	16th ay	16th day	No	uncle
Yes	Yes	7th day	7th or 9th day (or) in 3rd month	Yes	uncle
Yes	Yes	11th day	16th day month	Yes	uncle
—	—	—	—	—	—

Number of customs					
Caste / District	*1*	*2*	*3*	*4*	*5*
Patayacci South Arcot	(b)	Yes	Yes	Yes	Yes
Tanjore	(a)	Yes	No	Yes	Yes
Coimbatore	—	—	—	—	—
Mutaliyar South Arcot	(b)	Yes	No	Yes	2nd day
Tanjore	(a)	Yes	No	1st, 5th, 7th days	5th, 7th days
Coimbatore	—	—	—	—	—
Pattar Goldsmith South Arcot	(b)	Yes	Yes	Yes	3rd day
Tanjore	(a)	Yes	No	Yes 7th days	11th day
Coimbatore	(b)	Yes	No	1st, 3rd & 7th days	1st, 3rd, & 7th days
Chettiar Vaniya South Arcot	(b)	Yes	Yes	Yes	Yes Yes
Tanjore	(b)	Yes	No	3rd, 7th day	3rd & 5th day
Coimbatore	—	—	—	—	—

6	*7*	*8*	*9*	*10*
Yes	7th day	15th day or 3rd month or before marriage	Yes	uncle
Yes	9th day	9th or 15th or 22nd or before marriage	Yes	uncle
—	—	—	—	—
Yes	Yes	11th or 16th day	Yes	uncle
Yes	9th day	11th or 15th or 22nd or 3rd month (or) even before marriage	Yes	uncle
—	—	—	—	—
Yes	7th day	immediately after attaining age or before marriage	Not in custom	uncle or grand mother
Yes	Yes	11th day	Yes	uncle
Yes	7th day	15th day	Yes	uncle
Yes	Yes	7th or 9th or 11th or 16th day or before marriage	Yes	uncle
Yes	9th day	15th day (or) 3rd month	Yes	uncle
—	—	—	—	—

Number of customs					
Caste *District*	*1*	2	*3*	*4*	*5*
Naidu South Arcot	(a)	Yes	Yes	Yes	Yes
Tanjore	(a)	Yes	No	Yes	5th day
Coimbatore	(b)	Yes	No	3rd & 5th day	3rd day
Nadar South Arcot	(a)	Yes	Yes	Yes	Yes
Tanjore	—	—	—	—	—
Coimbatore	(b)	Yes	No	3rd & 5th day	2nd & 4th day
Devar South Arcot	(b)	Yes	Yes	Not mentioned	Ist day
Tanjore	(a)	Yes	No	Yes	5th day
Coimbatore	—	—	—	—	—

6	7	8	9	10
Yes	13th day	13th day	Yes	uncle
Yes	10th day	11th or 15th or 22nd day or 3rd month or before marriage	Yes	uncle
No	8th day	8th day	No	uncle
Yes	16th day	16th day	Yes	uncle
—	—	—	—	—
Yes	9th day	Not in custom	Yes	uncle
Yes	Yes	9th or 11th or 13th or 16th day	Yes	uncle
Yes	15th day	15th or 22nd day or 3rd month or before marriage	Yes	uncle
—	—	—	—	—

	Number of customs				
Caste / District	*1*	*2*	*3*	*4*	*5*
Udayar South Arcot	(a)	Yes	Yes	3rd day	3rd day
Tanjore	(a)	Yes	No	Yes	5th, 7th, 9th days
Coimbatore	—	—	—	—	—
Vannan South Arcot	(a)	Yes	Yes	Yes	only on the "puberty ceremony" day
Tanjore	(a)	Yes	No	Yes	Yes
Coimbatore	(b)	Yes	No	5th & 7th days	7th day
Harijan South Arcot	(a)	Yes	Yes	Yes	3rd day
Tanjore	(a)	Yes	No	3rd, 7th 9th & 16th day	1st, 5th, 7th, 9th and 16th day
Coimbatore	(b)	Yes	No	3rd & 7th day	3rd & 5th day

6	7	8	9	10
Yes	Yes	According to the economic conditions they celebrate "puberty rituals"	Yes	uncle
Yes	15th day	15th day	Yes	uncle
—	—	—	—	—
Yes	Yes	9th or 11th or 3rd month	Yes	uncle
Yes	11th or 16th day	15th day or 3rd month or before marriage	Yes	uncle
Yes	7th day	Not in custom	Not in custom	No
Yes	Yes	15th day	Yes	uncle
Yes	16th day	16th day	Yes	uncle
Yes	5th day	First month after attaining age	No	uncle

Marriage customs

1. First the (a) bride's party or (b) bridegroom's party ask for the horoscope.
2. They compare (a) birth horoscope, (b) age attaining horoscope and (c) both of the bride, with that of the bridegroom.
3. It is in custom to exchange the (a) written document and (b) plates at the time of engagement.
4. Bride's (a) parents, (b) uncle, (c) relatives celebrate "nalungu" to her before marriage.
5. It is in custom to soak nine grains either in (a) bride's house or in (b) bridegroom's house.
6. First pillar for pandar is erected in the (a) Eastern side and (b) in the north eastern side.
7. First pillar for pandar is erected by (a) the uncle of the bride and (b) anyone.
8. Pandar is erected certain days before marriage.
9. They erect first pillar for pandar certain days before marriage.
10. They erect four pillars for pandar.
11. Marriage is celebrated (a) in the bride's house and (b) in the bridegroom's house.
12. It is in custom to put "parisam" to the bride from the bridegroom's house.
13. Before tying marriage badge yellow string is tied in the hands of the bride and bridegroom.
14. These people place "saalungaravam" pot in the marriage platform.
15. They put milk ladle, conch, lemon etc. in the "saalungaravam" pot.
16. They place (a) two standing lamps and (b) four standing lamps in the marriage platform.

17. All the three knots are tied by the bridegroom.
18. First knot is tied by the bridegroom and the other two knots are tied by the sister-in-law of the bride.
19. It is in custom that bride's sister-in-law hold the lamp in the back of the bride while tying marriage badge.
20. It is in custom to put fried rice in the hands of the bride and bridegroom, also brother-in-law of the bridegroom puts ring in the finger of the bridegroom and vice versa.
21. They put "metti" before marriage itself.
22. They tie yellow string on the forehead of the bride and bridegroom and they leave the "pali" etc. in the river.
23. They do not celebrate any "nalungu" on marriage day.
24. They celebrate "First night" only after marriage day.
25. Then within one year, the bride's party give "siir" to the bride : (a) For "aati" month, (b) avani avittam, (c) Deepawali, (d) Karthikai, (e) Pongal, (f) Krishna jayanthi and (g) Navarattri.

	Number on customs				
Caste / District	*1*	*2*	*3*	*4*	*5*
Brahmin(Iyer) South Arcot	(a)	(a)	Not in custom	Not in custom	Not in custom
Tanjore	(a)	(a)	Not in custom	Not in custom	Before marriage day in (a)
Coimbatore	—	—	—	—	—
Brahmin (Iyangar)	(a)	(a)	Not in custom	Not in custom	Not in custom
South Arcot					
Tanjore	(a)	(a)	Not in custom	Four days before marriage (b) & (c)	before marriage day
Coimbatore	—	—	—	—	—
Pillai South Arcot	(a)	either (a) or (b)	Yes	(a) & (b)	(b)
Tanjore	(b)	(s)	Not in custom	(a), (b) & (c)	Five days before marriage in (a)
Coimbatore	(b)	(b)	(b) before marriage	7 days	15 days before marriage in (a)
Isai (Velalar) South Arcot	either (a) or (b)	(a)	Yes	Yes	(b)
Tanjore	(a)	(b)	Yes	(a) & (b)	Three or five days before the marriage in (b)
Coimbatore	—	—	—	—	—

6	7	8	9	10	11
(a)	Not mentioned	Not mentioned	Not mentioned	No	(a)
(b)	Bride's father, brother	Not mentioned	Not particular	in even number	(a)
—	—	—	—	—	—
(a)	Not mentioned	Not mentioned	Not particular	No	(a)
(a)	Aged people in bride's house	7 days before marriage	Not particular	No	(a)
—	—	—	—	—	—
(b)	By five married woman	Not mentioned	5-days	No	(b)
(a)	5 married ladies & bridegroom	Not mentioned	in even number		(b) (b)
(a)	(b)	7 days before marriage	Not particular	No	(b)
(a)	By the bridegroom	Not particular	Not particular	No	(b)
(b)	Brahmin priest	Not particular	Not particular	No	(b)
—	—	—	—	—	—

12	*13*	*14*	*15*	*16*	*17*	*18*	*19*	*20*	*21*
No	Yes	No	No	(a)	No	Yes	No	Yes	No
No	Yes	No	No	(a)	No	Yes	No	Yes	No
—	—	—	—	—	—	—	—	—	—
No	Yes	No	No	(a)	No	Yes	No	Yes	No
No	Yes	No	No	(a)	No	Yes	No	Yes	No
—	—	—	—	—	—	—	—	—	—
No	Yes	Yes	milk ladle,	(a)	Yes	No	Yes	Yes	No
No	Yes	Yes	stylus, conch silver, palm leaf & silver goddess status	(a)	Yes	No	Yes	Yes	Yes
No	Yes	Yes	milk ladle	(a)	No	Yes	Yes	No	Yes
Yes	Yes	Yes	milk ladle, ring	(a)	Yes	No	Yes	Yes	No
No	Yes	Yes	conch, knife	(a)	Yes	No	Yes	Yes	No
—	—	—	—	—	—	—	—	—	—

22	23	24	25
*tying yellow string on the forehead is not in custom	celebrating "nalungu" is in custom	on the marriage day itself	(b), (c), (d), (a) (f) & (g)
[1]tying yellow string is not in custom	celebrate "nalungu"	By fixing an auspicious day	(a), (b), (c), (d), (e) & (f)
—	—	—	—
tying yellow string on the forehead is not in custom	celebrate "nalungu"	On the marriage day itself	(a), (b), (c), (d), (e), (f) & (g)
tying yellow string is not in custom	celebrate "nalungu"	On the same day	(b), (c), (d), (e), (f) & (g)
—	—	—	—
Yes	celebrate "nalungu"	According to situation	(a), (c), (c)
Yes	celebrate "nalungu"	on the marriage day itself	(a), (c), (e)
Yes	celebrate "nalungu"	on the marriage day itself	(a), (b), (c) (d), (e) & (g)
Yes	celebrate "nalungu"	on the marriage day itself	(c), (d) (e)
Yes	celebrate "nalungu"	on the marriage day itself	(a), (c), (e)
—	—	—	—

	Number of customs					
Caste *District*	*1*	*2*	*3*	*4*	*5*	*6*
Patayacci South Arcot	(b)	(a) & (b)	Yes	Yes	(b)	(b)
Tanjore	(a)	(c)	Yes	(b)	Three days before marriage in (b)	(b)
Coimbatore	—	—	—	—	—	—
Mutaliyar South Arcot	(b)	(a)	Yes	Yes	(b)	(b)
Tanjore	(b)	(b)	Yes	Yes	Three days before marriage in (b)	(a)
Coimbatore	(b)	(c)	(b)	No	No	(b)
Pattar-Gold-smith South Arcot	(b)	(a)	Yes	Yes	(b)	(a)
Tanjore	(a)	(c)	Yes	(a), & (b)	Three days before marriage in (b)	(b)
Coimbatore	—	—	—	—	—	—
Chettiar (vaniya) South Arcot	(b)	(b)	Yes	Yes	5 or 7 days before marriage in the bride's house & 3 days before marriage in bridegroom's house	(a)
Tanjore	(b)	(c)	Yes	(a) & (b)	3 days before marriage in (b)	(b)
Coimbatore	—	—	—	—	—	—

7	8	9	10	11
By married woman	Not particular	7 or 9 days before marriage	No	(b)
Married ladies, father-in-law brahmin priest	3 or 5 days before marriage	No .	No	(b)
—	—	—	—	—
By married woman	Not particular	3 days before marriage	No	(b)
(b)	3 or 5 or 7 days before marriage	Not particular	in odd number	mostly in (b) sometimes in (a)
(b)	Not particular	Not mentioned	No	(b)
(b)	Not particular	5 days before marriage	No	(b)
aged married	5 or 7 women marriage	Not particular	No	(b)
—	—	—	—	—
5 or 7 married women & bridegroom	Not particular	Not mentioned	No	(b)
married bridegroom	Not particular	3 days before marriage	No	(b)
—	—	—	—	—

12	*13*	*14*	*15*	*16*	*17*	*18*	*19*	*20*
Yes	Yes	Yes	milk ladle	(a)	Yes	No	Yes	Yes
No	Yes	Yes	conch, knife	(a)	Yes	No	Yes	Yes
—	—	—	—	—	—	—	—	—
Yes	Yes	Yes	milk ladle	(a)	No	Yes	Yes	
Yes	Yes	Yes	conch, ring key	(a)	Yes	No	Yes	Yes
Yes	No	Yes	nothing	(a)	Yes	No	No	No
No	Yes	No	No	(a)	Yes	No	Yes	Yes
No	Yes	Yes	knife, conch, stylus	(a)	Yes	no	Yes	Yes
—	—	—	—	—	—	—	—	—
No	Yes	Yes	milk ladle	(a)	Yes	No	Yes	Yes
No	Yes	Yes	conch, knife	(a)	Yes	No	Yes	Yes
—	—	—	—	—	—	—	—	—

21	*22*	*23*	*24*	*25*
Yes	Yes	Celebrate "nalungu"	According to the situation	(a), (c), (e)
No	Yes	celebrate "nalungu"	according to the auspicious time	(a), (c), (e)
—	—	—	—	—
No	Yes	No	on the same day itself	(a), (c), (e)
No	Yes	celebrate "nalungu"	on the marriage day itself	(a), (c) (e)
No	Before tying marriage badge bride's uncle tie yellow string on her forehead, leaving "pali" is not in custom	Yes	on the marriage day itself	(a) & (c)
No	Yes	Yes	Yes	(a), (b), (c) (d) & (e)
No	Yes	Yes	Yes	(a), (b), (c) & (e)
—	—	—	—	—
Yes	Yes	Yes	Yes	(a), (c), e)
Yes	Yes	Yes	Yes	(a), (b), (c) (e)
—	—	—	—	—

	Number of custom					
Caste *District*	*1*	2	*3*	4	*5*	*6*
Naidu South Arcot	(a)	(c)	Yes	Yes	Three days before marriage in (a)	(b)
Tanjore	(b)	(b)	Yes	3 (or) 5 (or) 7 (or) 9 days before marriage	Five days before marriage in (a) or (b)	(b)
Coimbatore	(b)	(a)	Yes	Yes	3 days before marriage in (a)	(a)
Nadar South Arcot	(a)	(b)	Yes	Yes	Three days before marriage in (b)	(b)
Tanjore	—	—	—	—	—	—
Coimbatore	(a)	(c)	No	(b)	No	(a)
Devar South Arcot	(b)	(c)	Yes	Yes	5 (or) 3 days before marriage (b)	(b)
Tanjore	(b)	(a)	Yes	Yes	Three days before marriage in (b)	(b)
Coimbatore	—	—	—	—	—	—
Udayar South Arcot	(b)	(a)	Yes	Yes	Five days before marriage in (b)	(b)
Tanjore	(b)	(b)	Yes	Yes	Five days before marriage in (b)	(b)
Coimbatore	—	—	—	—	—	—

7	*8*	*9*	*10*	*11*
Brahmin priest	Five days before marriage	Not mentioned	No	(b)
bridegroom and his parents	5 or 7 days before marriage	Not mentioned	No	either in (a) or in (b)
(b)	7 days before marriage	Not mentioned	3 bough pillars	(a)
Three married ladies	Three married ladies	Not mentioned	No	(b)
—	—	—	—	—
(a)	Not mentioned	Not mentioned	Yes	(a)
married	Not particular	Not mentioned	No	(b)
elderly people	Three days before marriage	Not mentioned	No	(b)
—	—	—	—	—
married ladies & bridegroom	Five days before marriage	Not mentioned	Pillar for pandar is to be in even number	(b)
married woman & bridegroom	Not particular	Not mentioned	No	(b)
—	—	—	—	—

12	*13*	*14*	*15*	*16*	*17*	*18*	*19*	*20*	*21*
No	Yes	Yes	milk ladle,	(a)	Yes	No	Yes	Yes	Yes
No	Yes	Yes	conch, knife	(a)	Yes	No	Yes	Yes	No
No	Yes	No	No	(a)	Yes	No	No	No	Yes
Yes	Yes	Yes	milk ladle, (a)	Yes	No	Yes	Yes	No	Yes
—	—	—	—	—	—	—	—	—	—
Yes	Yes	Yes	Lemon	(b)	Yes	No	Yes	Yes	Yes
Yes	Yes	Yes	ring, milk	(a)	Yes	No	Yes	Yes	No
No	Yes	Yes	knife	(a)	Yes	No	Yes	Yes	No
—	—	—	—	—	—	—	—	—	—
No	Yes	Yes	milk ladle, knife & stylus	(a)	No	Yes	Yes	Yes	Yes
Yes	Yes	Yes	knife & stylus	(a)	Yes	No	Yes	Yes	No
—	—	—	—	—	—	—	—	—	—

22	23	24	25
Not in custom only they leave the "pali"	celebrate "nalungu"	By fixing on auspicious day	(a), (c) (e) & (f)
only they leave the "pali"	celebrate "nalungu"	Yes	(a), (c), (e)
only they leave the "pali"	Yes	on the same day	(a), (b), (c), (d), (e), (f) & (g)
Yes	celebrate "nalungu"	select an auspicious day	(a), (c) & (e)
—	—	—	—
Not in custom	Yes	only after marriage day	(c) & (a)
Yes	celebrate "nalungu"	Yes	(a), (c), (d) & (e)
Yes	celebrate "nalungu"	on the marriage day itself	(a), (c) & (e)
—	—	—	—
Yes	celebrate "nalungu"	according to the situation	(a), (c) & (e)
Yes	celebrate "nalungu"	By selecting an auspicious day	(a) & (c)
—	—	—	—

	Number of customs					
Caste District	*1*	*2*	*3*	*4*	*5*	*6*
Vannan South Arcot	(a)	(a)	Yes	Yes	Three days before marriage in (b)	(b)
Tanjore	(b)	(b)	Yes	Yes	Three days before marriage in (b)	(a)
Coimbatore	(a)	(c)	(b)	(b)	Not in custom	(a)
Harijan South Arcot	(b)	(b)	Yes	Yes	three days before marriage in (b) & 5 days before marriage in (a)	(a)
Tanjore	(b)	(c)	Yes	Five days before marriage all (a) (b) & (c)	(b)	(b)
Coimbatore	(b)	(a)	(b)	No	Not in custom	(a)

7	8	9	10	11
bridegroom's party	Two days before marriage	Not mentioned	No	(b)
Three married women and bridegroom	Three days before marriage	Not mentioned	No	(b)
(b)	Not mentioned	Not mentioned	Not particular	(b)
Bridegroom	Five days before marriage	Not mentioned	Five pillars	either in (a) or in (b) or in temple
Bridegroom	Three days before marriage	Not mentioned	Not particular	(b)
elderly people	7 days before marriage	Not mentioned	No	(b)

12	*13*	*14*	*15*	*16*	*17*	*18*	*19*	*20*	*21*
No	Yes	Yes	only ring	(a)	Yes	No	Yes	Yes	No
No	Yes	Yes	Not mentioned	(a)	Yes	No	Yes	Yes	No
Yes	Yes	Yes	lemon	(a)	Yes	No	No	No	No
Yes	Yes	Yes	milk ladle, stylus, knife, palm leaf, & lemon	(a)	No	Yes	Yes	Yes	Yes
No	Yes	Yes	milk ladle,	(b)	No	Yes	Yes	[2]Yes	No
No	Yes	Yes	lemon	(a)	Yes	No	No	Yes	Yes

22	23	24	25
Yes	Yes	According to the situation	(a), (c) & (e)
Yes	celebrate	Yes	(a), (c) & (e)
No	Yes	According to the situation	(a), (c), (d) & (e)
Not mentioned	celebrate "nalungu"	on the marriage day itself	(a), (c) & (e)
Yes	Yes	on the marriage day itself	(a), (c) & (e)
No	Yes	Yes	(a), (c) (d) & (e)

Notes :

* Tying yellow string with golden plates in the forehead of the bride, bridegroom is not in custom among Brahmin (iyer) caste people. But it is in custom to leave the "pali" in the temple.

1. In the evening of marriage day (or) next day these people Brahmin (Iyangar) leave the pali in the river.
2. Before tying marriage badge bridegroom's brother-in-law puts the fried rice in the hands of the bridegroom. After tying marriage badge bridegroom's brother-in-law puts the ring in the hands of the bridegroom and in return they give only clothes to his brother-in-law.

First Pregnancy

1. In the 3rd month they prepare three kinds of tiffen, go and meet the girl.
2. In the (a) 3rd month, (b) 5th month they take black saree.
3. In the 5th month they prepare five kind of meals, go and meet the girl.
4. They celebrate "valaikappu" in (a) 5th month, (b) 7th month and (c) 9th month.
5. They do not celebrate "valaikappu" etc. but tie "vasampu" in the chain of the marriage badge.
6. They celebrate "siimandam" in (a) 8th month (b) 9th month.
7. They invite the girl to their house in (a) 7th month, (b) 9th month for delivery.
8. They send the girl to her husband's house in (a) 3rd month, (b) 5th month, (c) 7th month, (d) 9th month after delivery.

Number of customs

Caste District	1	2	3	4	5	6	7
Brahmin (iyer) South Arcot	No	(b)	Yes (b)	No	9th month	9th month	(a) (a)
Tanjore	No	(b)	Yes (b)	No	8th month	8th month	(a)
Coimbatore	—	—	—	—	—	—	—
Brahmin (Iyangar) South Arcot	No	No	Yes (a)	No	9th month	(b)	(a) or (b)
Tanjore	No	(b)	Yes (b)	No	9th month	9th month	(a)
Coimbatore	—	—	—	—	—	—	—

Caste District	*1*	*2*	*3*	*4*	*5*	*6*	*7*	*8*
Pillai South Arcot	No	No	Yes	No	Yes	No	(b)	(a)
Tanjore	No	(b)	Yes	(b)	No	No	9th	(a)
Coimbatore	Yes	(a)	Yes	(b)	No	No	(a)	(b)
Isai Velalar South Arcot	No	No	(b)	(c)	No	No	(b)	(a)
Tanjore	No	(b)	Yes	(b)	No	No	(a)	22nd or 30th day or 3rd month
Coimbatore	—	—	—	—	—	—	—	—
Naidu South Arcot	No	No	Yes	(c)	No	No	(b)	(a)
Tanjore	No	No	Yes	(b)	No	No	(b)	(a)
Coimbatore	No	No	Yes	(b)	No	No	(a)	4th month
Nadar South Arcot	No	Yes	Yes	(c)	No	No	(b)	(a)
Tanjore	—	—	—	—	—	—	—	—
Coimbatore	Yes	No	Yes	No	Yes	No	(b)	(a)
Devar South Arcot	No	No	Yes	(b)	No	No	(a)	(a)
Tanjore	No	No	Yes	(b) or (a)	No	No	(b)	(s)
Coimbatore	—	—	—	—	—	—	—	—

Caste *District*	*1*	*2*	*3*	*4*	*5*	*6*	*7*	*8*
Udayar South Arcot	Yes	No	Yes	(b)	No	No	No	(a)
Tanjore	No	No	Yes	(b) or (c)	No			(b)
Coimbatore	—	—	—	—	—	—		—
Vannan South Arcot	No	No	Yes	(c)	No			(a) or (c) or (d)
Tanjore	No	No	Yes	(b)	No	No	(b)	(d)
Coimbatore	No	No	Yes	(a)	No	No	(b)	(s)
Harijan South Arcot	Yes	No	Yes	(b)	No	No	(b)	(s)
Tanjore	No	No	Yes	(b) or (c)	No	No	(b)	16th day(or)3rd month
Coimbatore	Yes	(b)	Yes	(b)	No	No	(a)	(a)

Sashtiyapthapurthi and Sadhabhishegam

Sashtiyapthapurthi

Brahmin (Iyer)

In South Arcot these people celebrate this function place 60 kalasas and celebrate it on 60th birthday.

In Tanjore district they celebrate it on 60th birthday, place 16 kalasas.

In Coimbatore district this caste people is not available in the field where the materials are collected.

Brahmin (Iyangar)

In South Arcot these people celebrate this function on 60th, birthday, place one kalasa.

In Tanjore district they celebrate it on 60th birthday, Regarding "kalasa", they do not mention about the thing.

In Coimbatore district this caste people is not available in the field where the materials are collected.

Pillai

In South Arcot they celebrate this function on 60th birthday.

In Tanjore district they celebrate this function on 60th birthday, place 3 or 5 kalasas.

In Coimbatore district they celebrate this function on 60th birthday, place one kalasa.

Isai Velalar

In South Arcot they celebrate this function on 60th birthday. They place more kalasas than at the marriage time.

In Tanjore district they celebrate this function on 60th birthday.

In Coimbatore district this caste people are not available in the field where the materials are collected.

Patayacci

In South Arcot it is not in custom to celebrate this function.

In Tanjore district these people celebrate this function on 60th birthday and place 9 kalasas.

In Coimbatore district these people are not available in the place where the materials are collected.

Mutaliyar

These people celebrate this on 60th birthday in South Arcot.

In Tanjore District they celebrate this on 60th birthday in the temple.

In Coimbatore district these people celebrate this on 60th-birthday in the temple.

Pattar

In South Arcot these people celebrate this on 60th birthday, place a kalasam at the time of this function.

In Tanjore district they do not celebrate this function.

In Coimbatore district these people are not available in the place where the materials are collected.

Chettiar (Vaniya)

In South Arcot they celebrate this function on 60th birthday.

In Tanjore district they celebrate this function in the temple.

In Coimbatore district this caste people are not available where the materials are collected.

Naidu

In South Arcot district these people celebrate this function on 60th birthday. They place number of kalasas according to the number of grand-son, grand-daughter etc.

In Tanjore district these people celebrate this function on 60th birthday, they place 7 or odd number of kalasas.

In Coimbatore district they celebrate this function on 60th birthday. They place 9 kalasas for this marriage.

Nadar

In South Arcot they celebrate this function on 60th birthday.

In Tanjore district these people are not available where the materials are collected.

In Coimbatore district these people do not celebrate 60th birthday.

Devar

In South Arcot these people do not celebrate this function.

In Tanjore district these people celebrate these only in temple on 60th birthday.

These people are not available in Coimbatore district where the materials are collected.

Udayar

In South Arcot these people celebrate this function, place two kalasas.

In Tanjore district these people do not celebrate this function.

In Coimbatore district these people are not available where the materials are collected.

Vannan

In South Arcot these people do not celebrate this function.

In Tanjore district these people celebrate this function.

These people are not available in Coimbatore district where the materials are collected.

Harijan

In South Arcot and Tanjore districts these people do not celebrate this function.

In Coimbatore district these people celebrate this function on 60th birthday.

Sadhabhishegam

Brahmin (Iyer)

In South Arcot these people celebrate this function on 80th birthday.

In Tanjore district they celebrate this function and place 101 kalasas.

This caste people are not available in Coimbatore district where the materials are collected.

Brahmin (Iyangar)

In South Arcot and Tanjore districts these people celebrate this function on 80th birthday.

In Coimbatore district this caste people are not available where the materials are collected.

Pillai

In South Arcot on 71st or 81st birthday they celebrate this function.

In Tanjore district they celebrate this function on 80th birthday.

In Coimbatore district they celebrate this on 70th or 80th birthday.

Isai Velalar

In South Arcot and Tanjore districts they do not celebrate this function.

In Coimbatore district these people are not available where the materials are collected.

Patayacci

In South Arcot and Tanjore districts they do not celebrate this function.

In Coimbatore district these people are not available where the materials are collected.

Mutaliyar

In South Arcot they do not celebrate this function.

In Tanjore district these people celebrate this function in the temple.

In Coimbatore district they do not celebrate this function.

Pattar

In South Arcot and Tanjore districts they do not celebrate this function.

In Coimbatore district these people are not available where the materials are collected.

Chettiyar (Vaniya)

In South Arcot and Tanjore districts they do not celebrate this function.

In Coimbatore district these people are not available where the materials are collected.

Naidu

In South Arcot these people celebrate this function on 80th birthday.

In Tanjore district and Coimbatore districts these people do not celebrate this function.

Nadar

In South Arcot and Coimbatore districts these people do not celebrate this function.

In Tanjore district these people are not available where the materials are collected.

Devar

In South Arcot these people do not celebrate this function.

In Tanjore district these people celebrate this function in temple.

In Coimbatore district these people are not available where the materials are collected.

Udayar

In South Arcot they celebrate this in Temple.

In Tanjore district these people do not celebrate this function.

In Coimbatore district these people are not available where the materials are collected.

Vannan

In South Arcot, Tanjore and Coimbatore districts these people do not celebrate this function.

Harijan

In South Arcot and Tanjore districts they do not celebrate this function.

In Coimbatore district they celebrate this function on 78th or 80th birthday.

Death Customs

The basic customs regarding death are common to all the castes and are given as follows. The differences due to region are mentioned in tabular column :

1. At the time of death of a person they pour (a) milk, (b) basil plant's water, (c) water rubbed from the coin, and (d) water in which sand is dissolved, in the mouth of dying person.
2. After the death of a person these people (a) break coconut, (b) light lamp, and (c) show the camphor and do the "vazhi kuutti vitutal" ceremony.
3. Then they place the camphor (a) in the street corner, and (b) in front of the house.
4. Only after doing this ceremony they send the news outside.
5. It is in custom to (a) bury the body, and (b) cremate the body.
6. It is in customs to put "vaykkarisi" to the dead person (a) Relatives, (b) Sons, (c) daughters, and (d) others put the "vaykkarisi" in the mouth of the dead person.
7. They give bath to the dead body (a) immediately after death, (b) before taking the body to the graveyard, and (c) both time.
8. They place (a) measuring pot full of paddy, (b) broken coconut, (c) plantain, (d) betel leaf and nut, and (e) lamp on the head side of the dead person.
9. After placing the dead body they go round the bier. (a) son carrying the measuring pot full of paddy, (b) son carrying the cloth on the head, and (c) others go round the bier following him.
10. They place nine grains with cow-dung in the (a) hand

of the dead person, (b) foot of the dead person, (c) not in custom.

11. (a) Son, (b) relatives, (c) friends, and (d) anybody carry the bier.
12. They celebrate "paal teli" on (a) next day, and (b) third day.
13. They mourn for the dead person on (a) 3rd day, (b) 7th day, (c) 8th day, and (d) 11th day.
14. They celebrate "karumati" on (a) 3rd day, (b) 11th day, (c) 13th day, (d) 15th day night, and (e) 16th day.
15. They mourn for the dead person (a) 30th day, and (b) 3rd month.
16. At the time of "karumati" they give (a) cow, (b) land, (c) bamboo stick, and (d) cloth as alms to a brahmin priest in same month.
17. They give saree, blouse, flower, turmeric, *kumkum* etc. to a brahmin priest's wife if a lady dies with married status.
18. They put (a) red colour new cloth, and (b) flowered new cloth to a lady if she died with married status.
19. They put (a) white new cloth, (b) sandalwood colour new cloth, and (c) any colour new cloth on the dead body if she is a widow.
20. It is compulsory for a widow to wear white cloth.
21. If a child within a year dies they (a) bury, and (b) cremate the child.
22. They do "punniyadanam" to the child if it dies within a year.
23. They celebrate "punniyadanam" for the child (a) 3rd day, (b) 9th day, (c) 11th day, and (d) 15th day.
24. They give (a) monthly *tithi* for one year, and (b) yearly *tithi* for the dead person.
25. If an unmarried person dies then it is in custom to decorate a plantain and perform marriage with this plantain. Then only they do the death customs.

	Number of customs					
Caste-District	*1*	*2*	*3*	*4*	*5*	*6*
Brahmin (iyer) South Arcot	(a), (b)	Not in custom	No	No	(b)	Not in custom
Tanjore	(a), (b) & (d)	Not in custom	No	No	(b)	(b)
Coimbatore	—	—	—	—	—	—
Brahmin (iyangar) South Arcot	(a)	Not in custom	No	No	(b)	All put this
Tanjore	(a) & (b)	(b)	Not in custom	No	(b)	No
Coimbatore	—	—	—	—	—	—
Pillai South Arcot	(b)	Yes	(b)	Yes	(b)	Yes, All put this
Tanjore	(a), (b) & (d)	(a), (b) & (c)	(b)	No	(b)	*Yes
Coimbatore	(a) & (c)	Yes	(b)	Yes	(a) & (b)	(a)
Isai Velalar South Arcot	(a) & (b)	Yes	(a)	Yes	(b)	Yes, All put this
Tanjore	(a), (b) & (d)	Yes	(b)	Yes	(a) & (b)	(a), (b), (c) & (d)
Coimbatore	—	—	—	—	—	—

7	*8*	*9*	*10*	*11*	*12*	*13*
(a)	(a)	Not in custom	Not in custom	(a) & (b)	(a)	Not in custom
(b)	Not in custom	Not in custom	Not in custom	(b)	(a)	Not in custom
—	—	—	—	—	—	—
(a)	(a)	Not in custom	Not in custom	(a) & (b)	(a)	Not in custom
(b)	(e)	Not in custom	Not in custom	(b)	(a)	(d)
—	—	—	—	—	—	—
(c)	(a), (b) (d) & (e)	Not in custom	either in (a) or in (b)	(d)	(a)	(a)& (c)
(b)	(a)	[1]Yes	(b)	(d)	Not in custom	5th day
(b)	(b), (c), (d) & (e)	(a)	Both in (a) & (b)	(b)	(a)	(a), (c) & (d)
(b)	(b) & (c)	(a) & (c)	[2](a)	(d)	(a)	(c)
(c)	(a), (b), (c), (d), & (e)	Yes (b)	(a)	(d)	If the body is burnt then (a) other-wise 3rd (or)5th day	(a)
—	—	—	—	—	—	—

14	*15*	*16*	*17*	*18*	*19*
15th day	27th day 3rd & 6th month	(a), (b) (c) & (d)	Yes	(a)	(a)
10th day	Not in custom	(a), (c) & (d)	Yes	(a)	(a)
—	—	—	—	—	—
(b)	Not in custom	(a), (c) & (d)	Yes	(a)	(a)
(a)	12th, 13th 14th, 15th day	(a), (b), (a) & (d)	Yes	Except black they put any colour saree	No
—	—	—	—	—	—
(a)	(a)	(d)	Yes	(a)	(a)
(d)	Not in custom	Yes	Not in custom	Except black they put any colour saree	No
(a)	(a)	(a), (c) & (d)	Yes	(a)	(a)
15th-day	(a)	(a), & (c)	Yes	any colour saree	red new cloth
(a) 11th day night)	(a)	Not in custom	Yes	any colour saree	(a) or red cloth
—	—	—	—	—	—

20	21	22	23	24	25
Yes	(a)	Yes	(c)	(a) & (b)	Not in custom
Not particular	(a)	Yes	(c)	(a) & (b)	Not in custom
—	—	—	—	—	—
Yes	(a)	Yes	10th-day	(a) & (b)	Not in custom
Not particular	(b)	Yes	(c)	(a) & (b)	Not in custom
—	—	—	—	—	—
dark brown (or) red cloth	(b)	Yes	16th-day	(a) & (b)	Yes
Not particular	(a)	Not in custom	No	(a) & (b)	Not in custom
Yes	(a)	Not in custom	2nd-day	Both (a) & (b)	Yes
Only red colour saree	(a)	No	No	Both (a) & (b)	Yes
Not particular	(a)	Yes	16th day	Both (a) & (b)	Yes
—	—	—	—	—	—

	Number of customs					
Caste-District	*1*	*2*	*3*	*4*	*5*	*6*
Patayacci South Arcot	(a), (b) & (c)	Yes	(a)	Yes	Both are in custom	(a), (b), (c) & (d)
Tanjore	(a), (b) (c) & (d)	Yes	(b)	Yes	Both are in custom	(a), (b), (c) & (d)
Coimbatore	—	—	—	—	—	—
Mutaliyar South Arcot	(a) & (b)	Yes	(a)	Yes	(b)	Yes
Tanjore	(a), (b) & (d)	Yes	(b)	Yes	(b)	Yes
Coimbatore	(a), (b)	Yes	(b)	Yes	(a) & (b)	(a)
Pattar South Arcot	(a) & (b)	Yes	(b)	Yes	(a)	all put this
Tanjore	(a) & (b)	Yes	(b)	Yes	(a)	all put this
Coimbatore	—	—	—	—	—	—
Chettiar-Vaniya South Arcot	(a), (b)	Yes	(a)	Yes	either (a) or (b)	all put this
Tanjore	(a), (b)	Yes	(b)	Yes	Both are in custom	Yes
Coimbatore	—	—	—	—	—	—

7	8	9	10	11	12	13
(b)	(a),(b), (c), (d) & (e)	(a)	(a)	(d)	(a)	(a), 8th days (d)
(b)	(a), (b), (c), (d) & (e)	[3]Yes	(a)	(d)	[4](a) [5](b)	(a) or 5th day or (b)
—	—	—	—	—	—	—
(b)	Yes	(a)	(b)	(d)	(b)	(b)
(b)	Yes	Yes, (with-out carrying anything	Not mentioned	(d)	(a)	5th day (or) (c)
(b)	(a), (b), (c), (d) & (e)	No	No	(b)	3rd day	(a)
(b)	(b), (c), (d) & (e)	Yes, without carrying anything	Only on the wall	(d)	(b)	(b)
(b)	Yes	[6]Yes	Only san-dal paste	(d)	(b)	5th (or) 7th day
—	—	—	—	—	—	—
(b)	(a) & (e)	(a)	(a)	(a), (d)	(b)	(c)
(c)	(a), (e)	(b)	(a)	(d)	(b)	(c)
—	—	—	—	—	—	—

14	*15*	*16*	*17*	*18*	*19*
(e)	(a) & (b)	(a) & (d)	Yes	only colour saree	any colour saree
(d)	(a)	Not in custom	Not in custom	(a) or yellow	(a)
—	—	—	—	—	—
(c)	(a)	(a) & (d)	Yes	Yellow	(a)
(d)	(b)	Not in custom	Not in custom	(a)	(a)
(a)	(a)	Not in custom	Not in custom	(a)	(a)
11th day	(a)	Not in custom	Yes	any colour saree	any colour saree
10th day night	(a)	Not in custom	Not in custom	silk or cotton saree	(a)
—	—	—	—	—	—
16th day	30th day	(a), (c)	Not in custom	(a)	(a)
(d)	(a)	Not in custom	No	(a)	red colour *12
—	—	—	—	—	—

20	21	22	23	24	25
any colour saree	(a)	Yes	(c)	(a) & (b)	Yes
red cloth without any border	(a)	Yes	(a) or (c)	Yes	Yes
—	—	—	—	—	—
Not particular	(a)	Yes	9th day	Both (a) & (b)	Yes
any colour saree	(a)	Yes	3rd or 5th day	(a) & (b)	Yes
No	(a)	Not in custom	No	Both (a) & (b)	No
Not particular	(a)	Yes	(c)	(a) & (b)	Yes
any colour	(a)	Yes	(c)	(a) & (b)	Yes
—	—	—	—	—	—
any colour	(a)	Yes	7th or 9th or 11th day	(b)	Yes
any colour	(a)	Yes	(d)	(a) & (b)	Yes
—	—	—	—	—	—

	Number of customs					
Caste-District	*1*	*2*	*3*	*4*	*5*	*6*
Naidu South Arcot	(a), (b) & (c)	(c)	(a)	Yes	(b)	Yes, all put this
Tanjore	(a) & (b)	(a), (b) & (c)	(b)	Yes	either (a) or (b)	(a)
Coimbatore	(b)	(a) & (c)	(b)	No	Both (a) & (b)	(a), (b) & (c)
Nadar South Arcot	(a), (b)	Yes	(b)	Yes	either (a) or (b)	all put this
Tanjore	—	—	—	—	—	—
Coimbatore	(a) & (c)	(a), (b) & (c)	(b)	Yes	(a)	(b)
Devar South Arcot	(a) & (b)	Yes	(a)	Yes	either (a) or (b)	Yes, all put this
Tanjore	(a) & (b)	Yes	(b)	Yes	(b)	all put this
Coimbatore	—	—	—	—	—	—
Udayar South Arcot	(a), (b)	Yes	(a)	Yes	(b)	Not in custom
Tanjore	(a), (b) (c)	Yes	(b)	Yes	(a)	(a), (b), (c), (d)
Coimbatore	—	—	—	—	—	—

7	8	9	10	11	12	13
(b)	(a), (b), (c), (d) & (e)	Yes, both (a) & (b) also (c)	Not in custom	(b)	(d)	(a), (c) & (d)
(c)	only sandal paste	Yes, without carrying anything	Only on the wall	(b)	5th day	(b)
(b)	(a)	[7]son go round the bier	No	(b)	(a)	(a) & (d)
(b)	(a), (b), (c) (d), (e)	Yes, without carrying anything	Not in custom	(b)	(b)	(c)
—	—	—	—	—	—	—
(b)	nut (c) & (c)	Not in custom	Both (a) & (b)	(a)	Not in custom	(d)
(b)	(a), (b), (c), (d) & (e)	(a)	(a)	(d)	(a)	(a)
(c)	[8](b) & (e)	Yes, without carrying anything	(a)	(d)	(b)	(e)
—	—	—	—	—	—	—
(b)	(b), (c), (d), (e)	All go round the bier without carry ing anything	Not in custom	(d)	(a)	(c)
(b)	(a), (b), (c), (d) & (e)	(b)	If it is married women this is in custom, (a)	(d)	(a)	5th day & (b)
—	—	—	—	—	—	—

14	*15*	*16*	*17*	*18*	*19*
(a)	either (a) or (b)	(a), (b), (c) & (d)	Yes, only at the time of first "*tithi*"	cotton new cloth	(a)
(b)	(a)	(a) & vessels	Not in custom	any colour saree	(b) termed as "naar muti" saree
(c)	No	(a)	No	(a)	(a)
(a)	(a)	(a), (b),	Not in custom	(a) (c) & (d)	(a)
—	—	—	—	—	—
5th day	(b)	(a) & (d)	Yes	(a)	(a)
(e)	(a)	Not in custom	Not in custom	(a)	(a)
(d) & (e)	(a)	Not in custom	Not in custom	(b)	(a) or red cloth
—	—	—	—	—	—
10th day	(a)	Not in custom	Not in custom	(a)	(a)
10th day	only on 22nd day	Not mentioned	Not in custom	(a)	(a)
—	—	—	—	—	—

20	21	22	23	24	25
Yes	(a)	Yes	16th day	(b)	No
Not particular	(a)	Yes	(c)	(a) & (b)	No
No	(a)	Yes	2nd day	No	No
Yes	(a)	Yes	8th day	(b)	Yes
—	—	—	—	—	—
No, Only red colour	(a)	Yes	(b)	Both (a) & (b)	No
Yes	(a)	Yes	(b)	or (a)	(b) Yes
Yes	(a)	Yes	(b)	(b)	Yes
Yes	(a)	Yes	(b)	(b0	Yes
—	—	—	—	—	—
Not particular	(a)	Yes	10th day	(b)	No
Not particular	(a)	No	No	Yes	Yes
—	—	—	—	—	—

Number of customs						
Caste-District	*1*	*2*	*3*	*4*	*5*	*6*
Vannan South Arcot	(b)	Yes	(a)	Yes	(b)	all put this
Tanjore	(a) & (d)	Yes	(b)	Yes	(a) & (b)	Yes
Coimbatore	(a) & (c)	(b) & (c)	(b)	Yes	Both (a) & (b)	(a) & (c)
Harijan South Arcot	(a), (b), (c), (d)	Yes	(a)	Yes	either (a) or (b)	all put this
Tanjore	(a), (b) & (c)	Yes	(b)	Yes	either (a) (b)	all put this
Coimbatore	(a) & (b)	(b) & (c)	(b)	Yes	(a)	(a)

7	8	9	10	11	12	13
(c)	(a), (b), (c) (d) & (e)	(a)	Not in custom	(d)	(a)	(b)
(c)	(a), (b) & (c)	(b)	(a)	(d)	(b)	(c)
(c)	(a)	Not in custom	Not in custom	(b)	(b)	(d)
(c)	Yes	(a) & (c)	either in (a) or (b)	(b) & (c)	[9](a) or [10](b) according to the son	(b)
(c)	water in the copper pot, coconut & lamp	[11]Yes	Not in custom	(d)	(b)	3rd, 5th 7th, 8th & 9th day
(b)	(b)	Yes (b)	Not in custom	(b)	(a)	(a)

14	*15*	*16*	*17*	*18*	*19*
(c)	(a)	Not in custom	Not in custom	(a)	ordinary cotton saree
(d) & (e)	(a)	Not in custom	Not in custom	any colour saree	red cloth
(a)	Not in custom	Not in custom	No	(a)	(a)
(a)	(a)	(a) & (d)	Not in custom	(a)	(a)
(d)	(a)	Not in custom	[13]Yes, but to a poor people	red colour flowered saree	red colour saree
(e)	Not in custom	Not in custom	No	(a)	(a)

20	21	22	23	24	25
Not particular	(b)	Yes	(c)	(a) & (b)	Yes
any colour saree	(a) or (b)	[14]Yes	10th (or) 11th day	(b)	Yes
Yes	(a)	No	No	(b)	Yes
Not particular	(a)	Yes	(a)	(b)	Yes
any colour saree	(a)	Yes	8th or 10th day	(b)	Yes
No	(a)	No	No	(b)	No

Notes :

* Relatives bring paddy for putting "vaykkarisi", and this is spent before "karumati"—day (Tanjore district).

1. After placing the dead body they go round the bier; daughter, daughter-in-law carry the coconut in their hand while going round the bier (Tanjore district).
2. If a married woman dies with married status they take betel leaf and nut and insert it in the mouth of the dead person. Then the husband places lamp in the hands of the dead woman (his wife) (South Arcot).
3. Persons younger than the dead person go round the bier thrice, first the dead person's elder son ties some coins in a towel and he places it on his head. Then goes round the bier in front and others follow him (Tanjore district).
4. If the dead body is cremate they do "paal teli" next day (Tanjore district).
5. If the dead body is buried they do "paal teli" on 3rd day (Tanjore district).
6. All the relatives go round the bier and the dead persons eldest son puts the sand in the pit for burying the dead person after placing the dead body in the pit (Tanjore district).
7. They go round the bier by carrying cloth in the head (Coimbatore district).

8. These people place "summadu" to the head of the dead person, place tender coconut, lamp on the head side of the dead person. They also place "batti" above the headside of the dead person (Tanjore district).
9. If the female dies they do "paal teli" next day (South Arcot district).
10. If the male dies they celebrate "paal teli" on 3rd day (South Arcot district).
11. After placing the dead body in the bier, relatives go round the bier thrice; son-in-law, daughter, son, daughter-in-law, relatives go round the bier thrice. First person takes a knife, next the son-in-law carries the measuring pot full of paddy, light lamp etc. and go round the bier (Tanjore district).
12. If the widowed lady is old they put cotton saree (Tanjore district).
13. If a lady dies with the married status, they give saree, blouse, flower, turmeric, *kumkum* etc. to poor people on the day of "aati" month new moon day (Tanjore district).
14. These people do "punniyadanam" if a child dies. If the child is buried they do "punniyadanam" on 10th day, if it is cremated then they do "punniyadanam" on 16th day (Tanjore district).

II. Differences due to Regional Variation (Within a District)

In the above division regional variation between districts is discussed. This division deals with the regional variation within a district. When we look into South Arcot there are three villages from which the data are collected. Similarly, in Tanjore district there are four villages from which the data are collected. In Coimbatore district there are three villages from which the data are collected.

District		*Village*
South Arcot	1.	Valayamadevi
	2.	Thiruvandipuram
	3.	Udayarkudi
Tanjore District	1.	Thalachankadu
	2.	Kurankuputtur
	3.	Melapparumpallam
	4.	Karuvizhantanatapuram
Coimbatore District	1.	Kalapatti
	2.	Matampatti
	3.	Thondamuttur

In the following pages the differences between village to village in South Arcot, Tanjore and Coimbatore districts are discussed. Basic customs are same and they differ slightly in some aspects.

Basic customs mentioned in the above division are taken into account to this division also for the purpose of comparison.

In the Tabular column "V" notes "Valayamadevi", "Thi" denotes "Thiruvandipuram" and "U" denotes "Udayarkudi".

Customs regarding child birth, Sacred Thread ceremony, Puberty rituals, Marriage, First pregnancy, Sashtiyapthapurthi, Sadhabhishegam and Death, are given in the following pages.

South Arcot District

Number of Customs

Child Birth

Caste-Place	1	2	3	4	5 6	7	
Brahmin (Iyer) V	7th (or) 9th day	Yes	Yes	10th day	11th day	1st year	1st year
Thi	7th (or) 11th day	Yes	Yes	16th day	15th day	1st year	1st year
U	7th day	Yes	Yes	11th day	11th day	1st year	1st year
Brahmin (Iyangar) V	11th day	Yes	Yes	11th day	11th day	1st year	1st year
Thi	9th day	Yes	Yes	3rd month	11th day	3rd year	3rd year
U	—	—	—	—	—	—	—
Pillai V	7th day	Yes	Yes	15th day	15th day	1st year	1st year
Thi	—	—	—	—	—	—	—
U	3rd day	Yes	Yes	15th day	15th day	1st year	1st year
Isai Vellalar V	16th day	Not in custom	Yes	Not mentioned	Not mentioned	1st year	1st year
Thi	15th day	Yes	Yes	15th day	15th day	1st year	1st year
U	—	—	—	—	—	—	—
Patayacci V	9th day	Yes	Yes	Not mentioned	15th day	1st (or) 3rd (or) 5th year	1st 3rd (or) 5th year
Thi	9th (or) 11th day	Yes	Yes	on the day of "kappu" (or) 3rd month	9th (or) 11th day	1st year	1st year
V	3rd day	Yes	Yes	3rd month	12th day	1st year	5th year

	1	2	3	4
Viswakarma (Pattar, Asari) V	16th day	Yes	Yes	Not mentioned
Thi	7th day	Yes	Yes	3rd or 5th month
U	16th day	Yes	Five metal bangle	proper time is not mentioned
Mutaliyar (sanguntiar) V	Not in custom	Not in custom	Not in custom	They celebrate "naming ceremony (actual time is not mentioned)
Thi	7th day (or) 9th day	Not in custom	only the silver bangle	11th day
U	16th day	Yes	Only five metal bangle	1st year
Reddiar V	—	—	—	—
Thi	7th day	Yes	Yes	16th day
U	16th day	Not mentioned	Not mentioned	within a month
Chettiyar (Vysya) V	Not in custom	Not in custom	Not in custom	After 3rd or 5th or 7th month
Thi	7th day	Yes	Yes	3rd month
U	—	—	—	—

5	6	7
Not mentioned	1st or 3rd or 5th or 7th year	1st or 3rd or 5th or 7th year
13th or 15th or 16th day	1st year	1st year
16th day	1st year	1st year
Not in custom	1st year	1st year
11th day	1st year	1st year
16th day	1st year	1st year
—	—	—
17th day	1st year	1st year
16th day	1st year	1st year
9th or 11th or 13th day	1st year	1st year
16th day	3rd month	3rd month
—	—	—

Caste Place	**Number of customs**						
	1	*2*	*3*	*4*	*5*	*6*	*7*
Chettiyar (Sozhiya) V	7th day	Yes	Yes	Not mentioned	11th or 13th day	1st year	1st year
Thi	7th day	Yes	Yes	According to economic situation	9th day	3rd	3rd
U	—	—	—	—	—	—	—
Konar V	7th or 30th-day	Not in custom	Yes	16th day	16th day	1st year	1st year
Thi	—	—	—	—	—	—	—
U	17th day	Yes	Yes	16th day	16th day	1st year	1st year
Maruttuvar V	7th day	Yes	Yes	9th day	9th day	1st year	1st year
Thi	7th day or 3rd month	[1]Yes	Yes	9th day	9th day	1st year	1st year
U	7th day	Yes	Yes	one month after the child birth	16th day	after one year	after one year

	1	2	3	4	5	6	7
Vannar V	7th day	Yes	Yes	9th day	9th day	1st year	1st year
Thi	9th day	Yes	Yes	9th day	9th or 11th day	according to the vow	3rd or 5th year
U	7th day	Yes	Yes	11th day	11th day	according to the situation	1st year
Harijan Ati Dravidar V	7th day	Yes	Yes	Not in custom	Not in custom	1st year	1st year
Thi	7th or 11th day	[2]Yes	Yes	11th day	11th day	according to economic situation	according to economic situation
U	3rd day	Yes	Yes	30th day	16th day	after one year	13th month after child birth

1. First this people tie "arukampul", then only margosa fibre bangle.
2. First they tie 'arukkam naar" bangle and then only they tie margosa fibre bangle.

Puberty Rituals

Caste-Place	Number of customs				
	1	*2*	*3*	*4*	*5*
Brahmin (Iyer) V	(b)	No	Not in custom	only on the 4th day	only on the 3rd day
Thi	(b)	No	Not in custom	Only on the 5th day	only on the 5th day
U	(a)	No	Not in custom	only on the 5th day	3rd or 5th day
Brahmin (iyangar) V	(b)	No	Not in custom	only on the 4th day	only on the 3rd day
Thi	(b)	No	Not in custom	4th day	only on the 5th day
U	—	—	—	—	—
Pillai V	(a)	Yes	Yes	Yes	5th day
Thi	—	—	—	—	—
U	(a)	Yes	Yes	Alternate days	1st day
Isai Velalar V	(b)	Yes	Yes	Yes	every day
Thi	(a)	Yes	Yes	Yes	Yes
U	—	—	—	—	—

6	*7*	*8*	*9*	*10*
Not in custom	4th day	Not in custom	No	No
Not in custom	5th day	Not in custom	No	No
Not in custom	5th or 7th day	Not in custom	No	No
Not in custom	4th day	Only before marriage	No	No
Not in custom	Yes	only before marriage	No	No
—	—	—	—	—
Yes	Yes	5th or 7th or 9th or 11th day	Not in custom	(a)
—	—	—	—	—
Yes	15th day	15th day	Yes	(a)
Yes	7th day	7th or 9th day or 3rd month	Yes	(a)
Yes	7th or 11th or 15th day	3rd month or before marriage	Yes	(a)
—	—	—	—	—

Caste *Place*	Number of customs				
	1	2	3	4	5
Patayacci V	(a)	Yes	Yes	Yes	Yes
Thi	(a)	Yes	Yes	Yes	Yes
U	(a)	Yes	Yes	Yes	First day and odd numbered days
Viswakarma (Pattar, Asari) V	(a)	Yes	Yes	Not particular	Not mentioned
Thi	(a)	Yes	Yes	Yes	Yes
U	(a)	Yes	Yes	Yes	Yes
Mutaliyar (Sanguntar) V	(a)	Yes	No	Not mentioned	2nd day
Thi	(a)	No	Yes, only on the 3rd day	Yes	1st day
U	(a)	Yes	Yes	1st & 16th day	only on 1st & 16th day
Reddiar V	—	—	—	—	—
Thi	(a)	Yes	Yes	Yes	5th day
U	(a)	Yes	Yes	Yes	3rd, 7th & 9th-day

6	*7*	*8*	*9*	*10*
Yes	Not mentioned	15th day	Yes	(a)
Yes	11th day	11th day or 3rd month	Yes	(a)
Yes	9th day	16th day	Yes	(a)
Yes	Not mentioned	11th day	From fifth day onwards	(e)
Yes	9th or 11th day	11th day or 3rd month	Not mentioned	(a)
Yes	9th day	9th day	Yes	(a)
Yes	16th day	11th or 16th day	Yes	(a)
Yes	11th day	11th day	Yes	(a)
Not men-tioned	16th day	16th day	Yes	(a)
—	—	—	—	—
Yes	11th day	11th day	Yes	(a)
Yes	13th day	13th day	Not mentioned	(a)

Caste *Place*	Number of customs				
	1	*2*	*3*	*4*	*5*
Chettiar	(a)	Not mentioned	Not mentioned	Not mentioned	Not particular
Thi	(a)	Yes	Yes	Not mentioned	only on the 3rd day
U	—	—	—	—	—
Chettiar (Sozhiya) V	(a)	Yes	Yes	Not mentioned	only on the 3rd day
Thi	(a)	Yes	Yes	Yes	Yes
U	—	—	—	—	—
Konar V	(a)	Yes	Yes mentioned	Not mentioned	Only on the 3rd day
Thi	—	—	—	—	—
U	(a)	Yes	Yes	Yes	Yes
Maruttuvar V	(b)	Yes	Yes	Not mentioned	9th (or) 11th day
Thi	(b)	Yes	Yes	Yes	Yes
U	(b)	Yes	Yes	First day	30th day

6	7	8	9	10
Not mentioned	11th or 13th day	11th (or) 13th day	Not mentioned	(a)
Yes	15th day	11th (or) 15th day	Yes	(a)
—	—	—	—	—
Yes	Not mentioned	13th day	Yes	(a)
Yes	11th day	11th day	Yes	(a)
—	—	—	—	—
Yes	11th or 15th day	11th (or) 15th day	Yes	(a)
—	—	—	—	—
Yes	16th day	16th day or 3rd month	Yes	(a)
Yes	11th day	9th or 11th day	Yes	(a)
Yes	9th day	9th or 11th day or 3rd month	Yes	(a)
Yes	Yes	7th day	Yes	(a)

Caste *Place*	**Number of customs**			
	1	2	3	4
Vannan V	(a)	Yes	Yes	Not mentioned
Thi	(b)	Only on the 3rd day	Yes, only on the 3rd day	Yes
U	(b)	only on the 5th day	Yes, only on the 5th day	Yes
Harijan V	(a)	Yes	Yes	odd numbered days
Thi	(b)	Yes	Yes, uncle's wife hold the sieve	Yes
U	(a)	Yes	Yes	Yes

5	6	7	8	9	10
On the day of "puberty ceremony"	Yes	Not mentioned	9th or 11th day or 3rd month	Yes	(a)
Odd numbered days	No	11th day	11th day	Yes	(a)
5th day	Yes	15th day	15th day	Yes	(a)
3rd day	Yes	Yes	15th day	Yes	(a)
Yes	Yes	11th day	11th day	Yes	(a)
Yes	Yes	11th day	11th day	Yes	(a)

Marriage

Caste *Place*	Number of customs				
	1	2	*3*	4	5
Brahmin (iyer) V	(a)	(a)	Not in custom	Not mentioned	(a)
Thi	(a)	(a)	Not in custom	Not in custom	(a)
U	(a)	(a)	(b)	Not in custom	Only before marriage day in (a)
Brahmin (iyangar) V	(a)	(a)	Not in custom	No	(a)
Thi	(a)	(a)	(a)	Not in custom	Day before marriage day in (a)
U	—	—	—	—	—
Pillai V	(b)	(b)	Yes	First (b) and then others	(b)
Thi	—	—	—	—	—
U	(b)	(a)	Yes	(b) then (c)	3 days before marriage both in (a) & (b)
Isai Velalar V	either (a) or (b)	(c) (c)	Yes	(b) than others	5 day before marriage in (b)
Thi	(b)	(a)	(a)	(b)	3 days before marriage in (b)
U	—	—	—	—	—

6	7	8	9	10	11	12
(a)	By married ladies	Not particular	Not mentioned	Not particular	(a)	Not particular
(a)	(b)	Not mentioned	Not mentioned	Not particular	(a)	Not in custom
(a)	Brahmin priest	Three days before marriage	Not particular	even number	(a)	Not in custom
(b)	by married ladies	Not mentioned	Not particular	Not particular	(a)	No
(b)	(b)	3 days before marriage	Not particular	Not mentioned	(a)	Not in custom
—	—	—	—	—	—	—
(a)	by married ladies	5 days before marriage	Not particular	odd number of pillars	(b)	Not in custom
—	—	—	—	—	—	—
(a)	3 married women	3 days before marriage	Not particular	Not mentioned	temple	Not in custom
(b)	(b)	3 days before marriage	Not particular	Not mentioned	(b)	Yes
(a)	bridegroom	any day before marriage	Not particular	Not mentioned	either in (a) or in (b) or in temple	Yes
—	—	—	—	—	—	—

13	*14*	*15*	*16*	*17*	*18*	*19*
Yes	Not mentioned	No	(a)	No	Yes	No
Yes	No	No	(a)	No	Yes	No
Yes	Not in custom	No	(a)	No	Yes	Not in custom
Yes	No	No	(a)	No	Yes	Not in custom
Yes	No	No	(a)	First two knots are tied by the bridegroom and one knot is by the sister-in-law	No	No
—	—	—	—	—	—	—
Yes	Yes	Yes	(a)	Yes	No	Yes
—	—	—	—	—	—	—
Yes	Yes	Milk ladle stylus, knife	(a)	Yes	No	Yes
Yes	Yes	milk ladle, conch, knife	(a)	Yes	No	Yes
Yes	Yes	milk ladle ring	(a)	Yes	Not in custom	Not men-tioned
—	—	—	—	—	—	—

20	21	22	23	24	25
Yes	No, only after marriage	They do not tie the yellowstring on the forehead but only leave the "pali"	celebrate "nalungu"	on the same day	(a), (b), (c) (d), (e) & (g)
Yes	No, only after marriage	only they leave the "pali"	celebrate "nalungu"	Yes	(a), (c), (d), (e), (f) & (g) (b)
Yes	No, only after marriage	Tying golden plate is not in custom, but they leave the "pali" next day	celebrate "nalungu"	Yes	(a), (c), (d), (e) & (f)
Yes	No, only after marriage	Not in custom	They celebrate "nalungu"	on the same day	(a), (c), (e), (f) & (g)
Yes	No, only after marriage	They leave the "pali" only	celebrate "nalungu"	on the same day	(b), (c), (d), (e), (f) & (g)
—	—	—	—	—	—
Yes	No	Yes	celebrate "nalungu"	on the same day	(a), (c), (d), & (e)
—	—	—	—	—	—
Yes	only after marriage	Yes	Yes	on the marriage day itself	(a), (c)
Yes	only after marriage	Yes	celebrate "nalungu"	Yes	(a), (c) & (e)
Yes	Yes	Yes	celebrate "nalungu"	on the marriage day	(c), (d) & (e)
—	—	—	—	—	—

	Number of customs				
Caste-Place	1	2	3	4	5
Patayacci	(b)	(b)	Yes	(b) and then others	5 days before marriage in (b)
Thi	(b)	(b)	Yes	3 (or) 5 days before by (a) the (b) & (c)	3 days before marriage day in (a) & (b)
U	(b)	(c)	Yes	first (b) then (c)	Both in (a) & (b)
Mutaliyar V	(b)	(a)	Yes	(b)	Both in (a) & (b)
Thi	either from (a) or (from) (b)	(a) or (b)	(a) & (b) first	3 days before marriage first (a) then (c)	5 days before marriage in (b)
U	(b)	if (a) is not available then (b)	(a) & (b)	5 days before marriage. first then (c)	5 days before marriage in (b)
Pattar V	(b)	(b)	Yes	First (a) & then (b) & (c)	Three days before marriage (b)
Thai	either from (a) or (b)	(a)	Yes	3 days before marriage by (a) then (b) & (c)	3 days before marriage in (b)
U	(b)	(a)	(a) & (b)	3 days before marriage in (a) than (b) & (c)	7 days before marriage where the marriage is celebrated
Reddiar V	—	—	—	—	—
Thi	either From (e) or (b)	(c)	Yes	3 days before marriage first by (a) (b) & (c)	3 days before marriage both in (a) & (b)
U	(b)	(b)	Yes	3 days before marriage first in (a) & then (b) & (c)	5 days before marriage in (b)

6	7	8	9	10	11	12
(b)	(b)	Not mentioned	Not particular	odd number of pillars	(b)	Yes
(b)	5 married ladies	Day before marriage day	Not mentioned	Not particular	Either in (a) or in (b) or in the temple	Yes
(a)	Chief of that village	3 days before marriage	Not particular	16-pillars	(b)	Yes
(a)	(b)	3 days before marriage	Not mentioned	Not mentioned	(b)	Yes
(b)	odd number married ladies	3 days before marri.	Not mentioned	Not particular	(b)	Yes
(b)	elderly people	5 days before marri.	Not particular	even number of pillars	(b)	Yes
(a)	(b)	3 days before marriage	Not mentioned	odd number odd number of pillars	(b)	Yes
(b)	3 (or) married women	3 days before marriage	Not particular	Not particular	(b) (b)	Yes Yes
(b)	married woman	5 days before marriage	Not particular	Not mentioned	either in (a) or in (b)	Yes
—	—	—	—	—	—	—
(a)	married ladies	3 days before marriage	Not particular	Not mentioned	either in (a) or (b) according to the situation	No
(b)	married lady	one week before marriage	Not particular	Not mentioned	either in (a) or in (b) or in the temple	Yes

13	*14*	*15*	*16*	*17*	*18*	*19*
Yes	Yes	milk ladle conch, stylus	(a)	Yes	No	Yes
Yes	Yes	milk ladle knife & ring	(a)	Yes	No	Yes
Yes	Yes	milk ladle stylus, lime	(a)	Yes	No	Yes
Yes	Not in custom	No	(a)	Yes	No	No
Yes	Yes	milk ladle knife & ring	(a)	Yes	No	Yes
Yes	Yes	milk ladle knife etc.	(a)	Yes	No	Yes
Yes	Yes	milk ladle	(a)	No	Yes	Yes
Yes	No	No	(a)	Yes	no	Yes
Yes	Yes	milk ladle, knife, palm leaf stylus & lime	(9a)	No	Yes	Yes
—	—	—	—	—	—	—
Yes	Yes	milk ladle conch	(a)	Yes	No	Yes
Yes	Yes	milk ladle, stylus, palm leaf	(a)	Yes	No	Yes

20	21	22	23	24	25
Yes	only after marriage	Yes	Yes	Yes	(a), (c) & (e)
Yes	Not mentioned	Yes	celebrate "nalungu"	on the marriage day itself	(c) & (e)
Yes	No, only after marriage	Yes	celebrate "nalungu"	selecting an auspicious day	(a), (c) & (e)
Yes	No, only after marriage	No	Yes	on the same day	(a), (c) & (e)
Yes	No, only after marriage	Yes	celebrate "nalungu"	only after the marriage day	(a), (c) & (e)
Yes	Yes	Yes	Not mentioned	By fixing an auspicious day	(a), (c) & (e)
Yes	only after marriage	Yes	celebrate "nalungu"	on the same day	(a), (b), (c), & (e)
Yes	Not in custom	only leave the "pali"	they cele-brate "nalungu"	by selecting an auspicious day	(a), (b), (c) (e)
Yes	Not in custom	Yes	celebrate "nalungu"	selecting an auspicious day	(a), (b), (c) & (e)
—	—	—	—	—	—
Yes	only after marriage	Yes	celebrate "nalungu"	they select an auspicious day for this	(a), (c) & (e)
Yes	Yes	tying yellow string is not in custom, but they leave "pali" in the river	Not mentioned	Yes	(a), (c) & (e)

Caste-Place	Number of customs				
	1	*2*	*3*	*4*	*5*
Chettiar V (Vysya)	(a)	(a)	Yes	(c)	Not mentioned
Thi	(b)	(b)	Yes	Day before marriage day, 1st (a) than (b) & (c)	Day before marriage day in (b)
U	—	—	—	—	—
Chettiyar V (sozhiya)	(b)	(b)	Yes	(a), (b) & (c)	3 days before marriage in (b)
Thi	either from (a) or (b)	(b)	Yes	Day before marriage day first (a) than (b) (c)	Day before marriage day in (b)
U	—	—	—	—	—
Konar V	(b)	(b)	Yes	(b)	7 (or) 9 days before marriage in (a) and 3 days before marriage in (b)
Thi	—	—	—	—	—
U	(b)	(c)	Yes	3 (or) 5 days before marriage first by (b) and than by (c)	(b)
Maruttuvar V	(b)	(c)	Yes	Yes	5 days before marriage in (a)
Thi	(b)	(c)	Yes	(b) than others	(b)
U	(b)	(a)	(b)	7 days before marriage first by (b) than (c)	(a)

6	*7*	*8*	*9*	*10*	*11*	*12*
(a)	(b)	Three days before marriage	Not particular	Not mentioned	(b)	No
(b)	married ladies	3 days before marriage	Not mentioned	Not particular	(b)	No
—	—	—	—	—	—	—
(b)	by married ladies	5 days before marriage	Not mentioned	Not particular	(b)	Yes
(b)	by married ladies	3 days before marriage	Not mentioned	Not particular	(b)	No
—	—	—	—	—	—	—
(a)	(b)	3 days before marriage	Not particular	even number pillars	(b)	Yes
—	—	—	—	—	—	—
South western side	married woman	5 days before marriage	Not particular	9 or 11 pillars	(b)	Yes
(a)	married ladies	7 days before marriage	Not particular	odd number of pillars	(b)	Yes
(a)	married ladies	5 days before marriage	Not particular	Not mentioned	(b)	Not in custom
(b)	bride's party	3 days before marriage	Not particular	Not mentioned	(a)	Not in custom

13	14	15	16	17	18	19	20
Yes	No	No	(a)	No	Yes	No	Yes
Yes	Yes	milk ladle conch	(a)	Yes	No	Yes	Yes
—	—	—	—	—	—	—	—
Yes	Yes	milk ladle conch	(a)	Yes	No	Yes	Yes
Yes	Yes	milk ladle,	(a)	Yes	No	Yes	Yes
—	—	—	—	—	—	—	—
Yes	Yes	milk ladle lemon	(a)	Yes	No	Yes	Yes
—	—	—	—	—	—	—	—
Yes	Yes	milk ladle stylus & lime	(a)	Yes	No	Yes	Yes
Yes	Yes	milk ladle ring	(a)	No	Yes	Yes	Yes
Yes	Yes	milk ladle, knife, stylus palm leaf, ring & lemon	(a)	Yes	No	Yes	Yes
Yes	Yes	milk ladle,	(a)	No	Yes	Not mentioned	Yes

21	22	23	24	25
No	Only leaving "pali" is in custom	celebrate "nalungu"	on the same day	(a), (c), (d) & (e)
only after marriage	Yes	celebrate "nalungu"	by selecting an auspicious day	(a), (c) & (e)
—	—	—	—	—
Not in custom	Yes	celebrate "nalungu"	Yes	(a), (c) & (e)
only after marriage	Yes	celebrate "nalungu"	By selecting an auspicious day	(a), (c) & (e)
—	—	—	—	—
only after marriage	Yes	Yes	Yes	(a), (c), (e) & (f)
—	—	—	—	—
only after marriage	Yes	celebrate "nalungu"	By selecting an auspicious day	(a), (c) & (e)
only after marriage	Yes	Yes	Yes	(a), (c) & (e)
only after marriage	Yes	Yes	By selecting an auspicious day	(a), (c), (d) & (e)
only after marriage	Yes	Yes	on the marriage day itself	(a), (c) & (e)

	Number of customs				
Caste-Place	*1*	2	*3*	*4*	*5*
Vannar V	(b)	(b)	Yes	(a)	5 days before marriage in (a)
Thi	(b)	(a)	(a)	(b) than others	5 days before marriage in (a)
U	(b)	(c)	Yes	Yes	(b)
Harijan V	(b)	(a)	Yes	(b)	3 days before marriage in (a)
Thi	(b)	(b)	(b)	3 days before marriage first (b) than others	5-days before marriage in (a) & 3-days before marriage in (b)
U	(b)	(c)	Yes	3 days before marriage by (b) than others	(b)

6	7	8	9	10	11	12
(b)	married ladies	5 days before marriage	Not particular	Not particular	(b)	Yes
(b)	married ladies	2 days before marriage	Not mentioned	Not particular	(b)	Not in customs
(a)	(b)	7 days before marriage	Not particular	Not particular	(b)	Yes
(a)	(b)	5 days before marriage	Not mentioned	Not particular	(b)	Yes
(a)	bride-groom	5 days before marriage	Not • particular	Five pillars	either (b) or in temple	Not in customs
(b)	married ladies	3 days before marriage	Not mentioned	Not particular	(b)	Yes

13	*14*	*15*	*16*	*17*	*18*	*19*	*20*
Yes	Yes	milk ladle, ring	(a)	Yes	No	Yes	Yes
Yes	Yes	ring	(a)	No	Yes	Yes	Yes
Yes	Yes	milk ladle palm leaf, lemon	(a)	Yes	No	Yes	Yes
Yes	Yes	conch, coin margosa leaves	(a)	Yes	No	Yes	Yes
Yes	Yes	milk ladle, stylus, knife palm leaf, lemon	(a)	No	Yes	Yes	Yes
Yes	Not in custom	No	(a)	No	Yes	Yes	Yes

21	22	23	*24*	*25*
only after marriage	Yes	Yes	Yes	(a), (c) & (e)
only after marriage	Yes	Yes	according to the situation	(a), (c) & (e)
Yes	Yes	Yes	on the marriage day itself	(a), (c) & (e)
Yes	Yes	celebrate "nalungu"	on the marriage day itself	(a), (c) & (e)
Yes	Yes	celebrate "nalungu"	on the marriage day itself	(a), (c) & (e)
Not mentioned	Yes	Yes	Yes	(a), (c) & (e)

First Pregnancy

Caste / Place	Number of customs							
	1	2	3	4	5	6	7	8
Brahmin (Iyer) V	No	(b)	Yes	(b)	No	(a)	(b)	(a)
Thi	No	(a)	Yes	(b)	No	(b)	(a)	(b)
U	No	(b)	No	(b)	No	(b)	(b)	(a)
Brahmin (Iyangar) V	No	No	Yes	(b)	No	(a)	(b)	(a)
Thi	No	No	Yes	(a)	No	(b)	(b)	(a) or (b)
U	—	—	—	—	—	—	—	—
Pillai V	No	No	Yes	No	Yes, 7th month	No	(b)	(b)
Thi	—	—	—	—	—	—	—	—
U	No	No	Yes	(b) or (c)	No	No	(b)	(a)
Isai Vellalar V	No	(b)	Yes	(b) or (c)	No	No	(b)	(b)
Thi	No	No	Yes	(c)	No	No	(b)	(a)
U	—	—	—	—	—	—	—	—
Patayacci V	No	No	Yes	(b)	No	No	(b)	(a)
Thi	No	No	Yes	either (b) or (c)	No	No	(b)	(a)
U	No	(b)	Yes	(b)	No	No	(a)	(a)

Caste / Place	*1*	*2*	*3*	*4*	*5*	*6*	*7*	*8*
Mutaliyar V	No	No	7th month bride's parents go & meet the pregnant lady	No	No	No	(b)	(b)
Thi	No	(b)	Yes	(c)	No	No	(b)	either (a) or (c)
U	No	No	•Yes	(c)	No	No	(b)	(a)
Pattar V	No	No	Yes	(b)	they tie "vasa-mpu" also	No	(b)	(a)
Thi	No	(b)	Yes	either (b) or (c)	No	No	(b)	(a)or (b)
U	Yes	No	Yes	either (b) or (c)	No	No	(b)	(a)
Reddiar V	—	—	—	—	—	—	—	—
Thi	Yes	No	Yes	(b)	No	No	(a)	(b)
U	Yes	No	Yes	(c)	No	No	(b)	(a)
Chettiyar (vysya) V	No	No	5th & also in 7th month	(c)	No	(b)	(b)	(a)
Thi (a)	No	No	7th month			No	(b)	(b)
U	—	—	—	—	—	—	—	—

Caste / Place	1	2	3	4	5	6	7	8
Chettiyar (Sozhiya) V	No	No	Yes	(b) or (c)	No	No	(b)	(b)
Thi	No	No	7th mon. they celebrate 'nalungu'	(c)	No	No	(b)	(a)
U	—	—	—	—	—	—	—	—
Konar V	No	No	Yes	(b)	No	No	(a)or(b)	(b)
Thi	—	—	—	—	—	—	—	—
U	No	No	Yes	(c)	No	No	(b)	(a)
Maruttuvar V	No	No	Yes	(b) or (c)	No	No	(b)	(a)
Thi	No	No	Yes	(b)	No	(b)	(b)	(a)or (b)
U	Yes	No	Yes	(b)	No	(b)	(b)	(a)
Vannan V	No	No	Yes	(b) or(c)	No	no	(b)	(a)
Thi	No	No	Yes	(c)	No	No	(b)	(e), (c) or (d)
U	Yes	No	Yes	(b)	No	No	(b)	(c)
Harijan V	Yes	No	Yes	(b)or (c)	No	No	(b)	(d)
Thi	Yes	No	Yes	(b)	No	(b)	(b)	(a)
U	Yes	No	Yes	(c)	No	No	(b)	(b)

Sashtiyapthapurthi and Sadhabhishegam

Sashtiyapthapurthi

This is usually celebrated on 60th birthday. At that time it is usual to place certain number of "kalasa", kindle holy fire, recite holy mantras, tie a new marriage badge at that time also. This couple is anointed by the water in the "kalasas" before tying marriage badge. These are the basic customs and the slight differences are mentioned as follows :

Brahmin (Iyer)

Valayamadevi :

Place 60 kalasas.

Thiruvandipuram :

Not mentioned (i.e. they do not mentioned how many kalasas to be placed).

Udayarkudi :

Place 11 kalasas.

Brahmin (Iyangar)

Valayamadevi :

Place one kalasa.

Thiruvandipuram :

Not mentioned.

Udayarkudi :

This caste people is not available in this village.

Pillai

Valayamadevi :

Not mentioned

Thiruvandipuram :

This caste people is not available in this village.

Udayarkudi :

Celebrate this only in the temple.

Isai Velalar

Valayamadevi :

More "kalasams" are placed for 60th birthday, than at the time of marriage.

Thiruvandipuram :

Place 5 "kalasas".

Udayarkudi :

Thiscaste people is not available in this village.

Patayacci

Valayamadevi :

Do not celebrate this function.

Thiruvandipuram :

Celebrate this only in the temple.

Udayarkudi :

Place 7 kalasas.

Mutaliyar

Valayamadevi :

Not mentioned.

Thiruvandipuram :

Place one kalasam

Udayarkudi :

Place one kalasam.

Pattar

Valayamadevi :

Place one kalasam.

Thiruvandipuram :

Place 3 "kalasam"

Udayarkudi :

These people celebrate this either in the houses (or) in the temple.

Reddiar

Valayamadevi :

This caste people is not available in this village.

Thiruvandipuram :

Place one "kalasam"

Udayarkudi :

Place 3 "kalasas"

Chettiyar (Vysya)

Valayamadevi :

Celebrate like a marriage.

Thiruvandipuram :

Place 5 kalasas.

Udayarkudi :

This caste people is not available in this village.

Chettiyar (Sozhiya)

Valayamadevi :

Celebrate like a marriage.

Thiruvandipuram :

Place 5 kalasas.

Udayarkudi :

This caste people is not available in this village.

Konar :

Valayamadevi :

Do not celebrate this function.

Thiruvandipuram :

This caste people is not available in this village.

Udayarkudi :

Place 9 kalasas.

Maruttuvar

Valayamadevi :

Do not celebrate this function.

Thiruvandipuram :

Celebrate it only in the temple.

Udayarkudi :

Place 5 kalasas.

Vannan

Valayamadevi :

Do not celebrate this function.

Thiruvandipuram :

Do not celebrate this function

Udayarkudi :

Do not celebrate this function.

Harijan

Valayamadevi :

Do not celebrate this function.

Thiruvandipuram :

They celebrate this like other caste people.

Udayarkudi :

This people do not celebrate this function.

Sadhabhishegam

This function is celebrated in the 70th or 71st or 80th or

81st birthday. This is celebrated like 60th birthday, but with one difference. They do not tie marriage badge at the time of this function. Among the fourteen castes mentioned in this section only Brahmin (iyer), Brahmin (iyangar), Pillai, Chettiyar (vysya), Mutaliyar, Reddiar, Viswakarma, Barber caste people celebrate this function, other caste people do not celebrate this function. In Valayamadevi, Brahmin (iyer), Brahmin (iyangar) Chettiyar (vysya) caste people celebrate, this on 80th birthday and Pillai caste people celebrate this on 71st or 81st birthday.

In Thiruvandipuram, Brahmin (iyer), Brahmin (iyangar), Isai Velalar, Mutaliyar, Reddiar caste people celebrate this on 80th birthday. Viswakarma and Barber caste people celebrate this in temple on 80th birthday like 60th birthday.

In Udayarkudi, Viswakarma, Brahmin (iyer), Pillai and Reddiar caste people celebrate this like 60th birthday Mutaliyar caste people do "archana" in the temple on 80th birthday.

Other caste people in these three villages do not celebrate this function.

Death Customs

Caste Place	Number of customs					
	1	*2*	*3*	*4*	*5*	*6*
Brahmin (Iyer) V	(a) & (b)	Not in custom	Not in custom	No	(b)	Not in custom
Thi	(a), (b) & (c)	Not in custom	Not in custom	No	(b)	Not in custom
U	(b)	Not in custom	Not in custom	No	(b)	Yes
Brahmin (Iyangar)	(a) & (b)	Not in custom	Not in custom	No	(b)	Not in custom
Thi	(a)	Not in custom	Not in custom	No	(b)	Yes
U	—	—	—	—	—	—
Pillai V	(b)	Yes	(a)	Yes	(b)	Yes
Thi	—	—	—	—	—	—
U	(b)	Yes	(b)	Yes	(b)	Yes
Isai Velalar V	(a) & (b)	Yes	(a)	Yes	either (a) or (b)	Yes
Thi	(a) & (b)	Yes	(b)	Yes	(b)	Yes
U	—	—	—	—	—	—

7	8	9	10	11	12	13
(a)	(c)	Not in custom	Not in custom	(a) or son-in-law	(a)	27th day or 3rd or 6th month
(a)	(c)	Not in custom	Not in custom	(a) & (b)	(a)	Not mentioned
(b)	gingely seed rice, dharbai grass & lamp	Not in custom	Not in custom	(a) & (c)	(a)	(b)
(b)	(c)	Not in custom	Not in custom	(b)	(a)	Not in custom
(b)	(c)	Not in custom	Not in custom	(b)	(a)	till 11 days
—	—	—	—	—	—	—
(a)	Yes	(a) & (c)	Not mentio-ned	(b) & (c)	(a)	(c)
—	—	—	—	—	—	—
(c)	(a) & (c)	Not in custom	either in (a) or in (b)	(d)	(e)	(a) & (c)
(b)	Yes	(a) & (c)	(a)	(d)	(a) or (b)	(c)
(b)	(b) & (c)	Yes, with-out taking anything in the hand	(a)	(d)	(a)	(c)
—	—	—	—	—	—	—

14	*15*	*16*	*17*	*18*	*19*	*20*
(d)	Not in custom	(a), (c) & (d)	Yes	(a)	(a)	Not particular
(b)	Not in custom	(a), (b) (c) & (d)	Yes	(a)	(e)	Yes
10th-day	Not in custom	(a), (b) (c) & (d)	Yes	(a)	(a)	Yes
(c)	Not in custom	(a), (b) (c) & (d)	Yes	(a)	(a)	Not particular
(b)	Not in custom	(a), (b) (c) & (d)	Yes	"mull" cloth dipped in turmeric water	(a)	Yes
—	—	—	—	—	—	—
(a)	(a)	(a), (c) & (d)	Not mentioned	(a)	(a)	(a)
—	—	—	—	—	—	—
(c)	(a)	(d)	Yes	(a)	(a)	dark brown colour
(b) or (a)	(a)	(a) & (d)	Not mentioned	(a)	(c)	Not particular
(d)	(a)	(a) & (d)	Yes	only colour saree	red new cloth	only red colour
—	—	—	—	—	—	—

21	22	23	24	25
(a)	Yes	(c)	Both (a) & (b)	Not in custom
(a)	Yes	(c)	Both (a) & (b)	Not in custom
(a)	No	No	Both (a) & (b)	Not in custom
(a)	No	No	Both (a) & (b)	Not in custom
(a)	Yes	10th day	Both (a) & (b)	Not in custom
—	—	—	—	—
(a)	Yes	10th (or) 13th day	Both (a) & (b)	Not in custom
—	—	—	—	—
(b)	Yes	16th day	Both (a) & (b)	Yes
(a)	Not in	No	only (b)	Yes
(a)	Not in custom	No	Both (a) & (b)	Yes
—	—	—	—	—

Place	Number of customs					
	1	*2*	*3*	*4*	*5*	*6*
Patayacci V	(a), (b)	Yes	(a)	Yes	either (a) or (b)	Yes
Thi	(a), (b) & (c)	Yes	(b)	Yes	either (a) or (b)	Yes
U	(a) & (b)	Yes	(b)	Yes	either (a) or (b)	Yes
Mutaliyar V	(a) or water	Yes	(b)	Yes	either (a) or (b)	Not mentioned
Thi	(a) & (b)	Yes	(b)	Yes	(b)	Yes
U	(a) & (b)	Yes	(b)	Yes	either (a) or (b)	Yes
Pattar V	(a) & water	Yes	(a)	Yes	(a)	Not in custom
Thi	(a) & (b)	Yes	(b)	Yes	(a)	Not in custom
U	(a), (b), (c) & (d)	Yes	(b)	Yes	(a)	Not in custom
Reddiar V	—	—	—	—	—	—
Thi	(a) & (b)	Yes	(b)	Yes	either (a) or (b)	Yes
U	(a) & (d)	Yes	(b)	Yes	(b)	No

7	8	9	10	11	12	13
(a)	Yes	(a) & (c)	(b)	(d)	(a)	(c)
(b)	Yes	(a) & (c)	(a)	(d)	(a)	(a), (c) & (d)
(c)	Yes	(a), (b) & (c)	(b)	(b)	(a)	(c)
(b)	Yes	(a) & (c)	(c)	(b) & (c)	(a)	(c)
(b)	Yes	(a) & (c)	(b)	(d)	(b)	(b)
(b)	(b), (c) (d) & (e)	Yes, without carrying anything	(c)	(b)	(a)	(c)
(a)	(b), (c) (d) & (e)	Yes, son carries "kalasam"	(a)	Not mentioned	(a)	(c)
(b)	(b), (d) & (e)	yes, without carrying anything	only on the well	(d)	(b)	(b)
(b)	(b), (c) (d) & (e)	Yes, without carrying anything	either in (a) or (b)	(b)	(b)	(c)
—	—	—	—	—	—	—
(b)	Yes	(a)	Not in custom	(b)	(a)	(b)
(b)	(b), (c) (d) & (e)	without carrying anything	either in (a) or (b)	(d)	(a)	(a), (c) & (d)

14	15	16	17	18	19	20
(a)	(d)	(a) & (d)	Not in custom	(a)	(a)	Not particular
(a)	(a) & (b)	Not mention-ed	Yes	any colour new saree	any colour new saree	Not particular
(a)	(a)	(d)	Yes	(a)	(c)	Yes
(a)	16th day	(a) & (b)	Not menti-oned	(a)	(a)	sandal wood colour
(c)	(a)	Not in custom	Yes	Yellow new cloth	(a)	any colour saree
(a)	Not mentio-ned	Not	Not in mentio-ned	(a)	(a)	red colour saree
(a)	Not mentio-ned	(a) & (d)	Not mentio-ned	(a)	(a)	Yes
(b)	(a)	Not in custom	Yes	any colour new saree	any colour new saree	No, any colour saree
(a) or 22nd day	Both (a) & (b)	Not in custom	Not in custom	(a)	(a)	No, any colour saree
—	—	—	—	—	—	—
13 after death	(a)	(a) & (c)	Yes	(a)	(a)	Yes
(a)	(a)	(a) & (b) (c) & (d)	Yes	(a)	(a)	Yellow saree

21	22	23	24	25
(b)	Yes	16th day	both (a) & (b)	Yes
(a)	Yes	11th day	only (b)	Yes
(b)	Yes	9th day	only (b)	Yes
(a)	No	No	Both (a) & (b)	No
(b)	Yes	9th day	Both (a) & (b)	Yes
(b)	Yes	5th day	only (b)	Not mentioned
(c)	No	No	only (b)	No
(a)	Yes	(c)	Both (a) & (b)	Yes
(c)	No	No	only (b)	Not in custom
—	—	—	—	—
(a)	Yes	(b)	Yes	Not in custom
(a)	Yes	13th day	(b)	Yes

Caste/ Place	**Number on customs**					
	1	*2*	*3*	*4*	*5*	*6*
Chettiyar (vysya) V	(a) & (b)	Not mentioned	No	No	(b)	Not in custom
Thi	water & (b)	Yes	(a)	Yes	either (a) or (b)	Yes
U	—	—	—	—	—	—
Chettiyar (sozhiya) V	(a) & (b)	Yes	(a)	Yes	either (a) or (b)	Yes
Thi	water & (b)	Yes	(a)	Yes	either (a) or (b)	Yes
U	—	—	—	—	—	—
Konar V	(a) & (b)	Yes	(a)	Yes	either (a) or (b)	Yes
Thi	—	—	—	—	—	—
U	(e), (b) (c) & (d)	Yes	(b)	Yes	either (a) or (b)	Yes
Maruttuvar V	(a) & (b)	Yes	(a)	Yes	(b)	Yes
Thi	(a)	Yes	(a)	Yes	(b)	Yes
U	(a)	(b) & (c)	(a)	Yes	either (a) or (b)	Yes

7	*8*	*9*	*10*	*11*	*12*	*13*
(a)	(a)	Not mentioned	Not in custom	(d) four persons	Yes	Not in custom
(c)	Yes	Yes	(a)	(b) & (c)	(a)	(a) & (c)
—	—	—	—	—	—	—
(a)	(a), (b) (c), (d) & (e)	(a) & (c)	(a)	(b) & (c)	(a)	(c)
(c)	Yes	Yes	(a)	(b) & (c)	(a)	(e) & (c)
—	—	—	—	—	—	—
(c)	Yes	(a) & (c)	(a)	(d)	(a)	(b)
—	—	—	—	—	—	—
(b)	Yes	(a)	only the wall	(a) & (b)	(a)	(a), (c) & (d)
(b)	Yes	Yes (c)	(b)	(b) & (c)	(a)	(a) or (b)
(b)	Yes	(a)	(a)	(d)	(a)	(c)
(c)	Yes	(a)	either in (e) or in (b)	(b) & (d)	(b)	(c)

14	*15*	*16*	*17*	*18*	*19*	*20*
(c)	No	(a), (b)	Yes	(a)	(b)	Yes
(a)	(a)	(d)	Not mentioned	(a)	(a)	Not particular
—	—	—	—	—	—	—
(e)	29th-day	(a) & (d)	Yes	(a)	(a)	Yes
(a)	(a)	(d)	Not mentioned	(a)	(a)	Not particular
—	—	—	—	—	—	—
(d)	(a)	(a) & (d)	Not in custom	(a)	(a)	Not particular
—	—	—	—	—	—	—
(a)	(a)	(a) & (d)	Not in custom	(b)	(a)	Not particular
(e)	Not mentioned	(a), (c) & (d)	Yes	(a)	(b)	Not particular
(b) or (c)	(a) (a)	rice & money only	Yes, but to their daughter-in-law, not to a brahmin priest's wife	milk, saree	red colour new cloth	Not particular
(e)	either (a) or (b)	only cow	Not in custom	(a)	(a)	Yes

21	*22*	*23*	*24*	*25*
(a)	No	No	Both (a) & (b)	Not in custom
(a)	Yes	(c)	Both (a) & (b)	Not in custom
—	—	—	—	—
(a)	Yes	13th day	Both (a) & (b)	Not in custom
(a)	Yes	(a)	Both (a) & (b)	Not in custom
—	—	—	—	—
(a)	Yes	(c)	Both (a) & (b)	Yes
—	—	—	—	—
(b)	Yes	(c)	Both (a) & (b)	Yes
(a)	Yes	(c)	Both (a) & (b)	Yes
(a)	Yes	(a) or (c)	Both (a) & (b)	Yes
(a)	Not in custom	No	only (b)	No

Caste *Place*	Number of customs					
	1	2	3	4	5	6
Vannan V	(a), (b) (c) & (d)	Yes	(a)	Yes	either (a)	Yes
Thi	(b)	Yes	(a)	Yes	(b)	Yes
U	(a)	Yes	(a)	Yes	(a)	Yes
Harijan V	(a)	Yes	(a)	Yes	(a)	Yes
Thi	(a), (b) (c) & (d)	Yes	(a)	Yes	(b)	Yes
U	(d)	Yes	(a)	Yes	(a)	Yes

7	*8*	*9*	*10*	*11*	*12*	*13*
(a)	Yes	Yes, (a) & (c)	(a) & (b)	(d)	(a)	(a) or (b)
(b)	Yes	(a) & (c)	Not in custom	(d)	(a)	(b)
(b)	Yes	(a) & (c)	(a)	(b) & (c)	(b)	(c)
(c)	Yes	(a) & (c)	(a)	(b)	(a)	If it is male 8th day, if it is female 7th day
(b)	Yes	(a)	either in (a) or (b)	(b) & (c)	If a male dies they do it next day, otherwise 3rd day	(b)
(a)	Yes	(a)	(b)	(d)	(a)	(d)

14	*15*	*16*	*17*	*18*	*19*	*20*
(c)	No	(a), (b)	Yes	(a)	(b)	Yes
(a)	(a)	(a) & (d)	Yes	(a)	(a)	Yes
(a)	(a)	(a) & (d)	Yes	(a)	ordinary cotton saree	Not particular
(c)	(a)	(d)	Not in custom	(a)	(a)	Yes
(a)	(a)	(d)	Not in custom	(b)	Not mentioned	Not in custom
(e)	(a)	Not in custom	Not in custom	(a)	(a)	Not particular
(c)	(b)	only (a)	Not in custom	(a)	(a)	Not particular

21	*22*	*23*	*24*	*25*
(a)	Yes	(c)	Both (a) & (b)	Yes
(b)	Yes	11th day	Both (a) & (b)	Yes
(a)	Yes	(b)	only (b)	Yes
(b)	Yes	odd numbered days	(b)	Yes
(a)	Yes	11th day	Do not give "*tithi*" to the dead person	Yes
(a)	Yes	7th day	(b)	Yes

Tanjore District

The four villages viz. Thalachankadu, Kurankuputtur, Karuvizhantanatapuram and Melapparumpallam, of Tanjore distsrict from which the customs from child birth to death (of a human life cycle) are collected. Even though the materials are collected from eighteen castes, common caste people atleast in two villages are taken into Account for the purpose of comparison. Common caste people in the above villages are mentioned as follows :

	Thalachankadu	*Kurankuputtur*	*Karuvizhantanatat puram*	*Melapparumpallam*
1.	Brahmin (iyer)	Brahmin (iyer)	—	Brahmin (iyer)
2.	Pillai (Karkattar)	Pillai (karkattar)	Pillai (karkattar)	—
3.	Patayacci	Patayacci	Patayacci	Patayacci
4.	Naidu	—	Naidu	—
5.	Nayakkar (canar)	Nayakkar (canar)	—	Nayakkar (canar)
6.	—	Nayakkar (tatar)	Nayakkar (tatar)	—
7.	Vaniya Chettiyar	Vaniya Chettiyar	Vaniya Chettiyar	—
8.	Viswakarma	Viswakarma	Viswakarma	Viswakarma
9.	Vannan	Vannan	Vannan	—
10.	Navitar	—	Navitar	—
11.	—	—	Udayar	Udayar
12.	Harijan	Harijan	Harijan	Harijan

The basic customs mentioned in the above division is the same for this district also and the differences between the villages are noted in the tabular column. "Tha" denotes Thalachankadu, "K" denotes kurankuputtur, "KM" denotes Karuvizhantanatapuram and "M" denotes Melapparumpallam in the tabluar column.

Child Birth

Caste Place	Number of customs						
	1	2	3	4	5	6	7
Brahmin (iyer) Tha	7th day	Yes	Yes	11th day	11th day	1st year	1st year
K	9th day	Yes	Yes	9th day	9th day	1st year	1st year
KM	—	—	—	—	—	—	—
M	7th day	Yes	Yes	9th day	15th day	1st	1st (or) 3rd year
Pillai (Karkattar) Tha	7th & 15th day	Yes	Yes	15th day	15th day	1st year	1st year
K	9th & 15th day	Yes	Yes	15th day	15th day	1st year	1st year
KM	7th & 11th day	Yes	Yes	15th day	15th day	1st year	1st year
M	—	—	—	—	—	—	—
Patayacci Tha	11th day	Yes	Yes	15th day	15th day	1st year	1st year
K	13th day	Yes	Yes	13th day	13th day	1st or 3rd year	1st year or 3rd year
KM	15th day	Yes	Yes	15th day	15th day	According to the situation	According to the situation
M	15th day	Yes	Yes	1st month	15th day	1st year	1st year

Caste / Place	*1*	*2*	*3*	*4*	*5*	*6*	*7*
Naidu Tha	11th day	Yes	Yes	11th day	11th day	1st year	1st (or) 3rd year
K	—	—	—	—	—	—	—
KM	11th day	Yes	Yes	11th day	11th day	1st year	1st (or) 3rd or 5th year
M	—	—	—	—	—	—	—
Nayakkar (Canar) Tha	15th day	Yes	Yes	15th day	16th day	1st year	1st year
K	15th day	Yes	Yes	15th day	15th day	1st year	1st year
KM	—	—	—	—	—	—	—
M	16th day	Yes	Yes	16th day	16th day	1st year	1st year
Nayakkar (tatar) Tha	—	—	—	—	—	—	—
K	16th day	Yes	Yes	16th day	16th day	1st year	1st year
KM	15th day	Yes	Yes	16th day	16th day	1st year	1st year
M	—	—	—	—	—	—	—
Vaniya Chettiyar Tha	11th day	Yes	Yes	15th day	15th day	1st year	1st year
K	16th day	Yes	Yes	16th day	16th day	1st year	1st year
KM	15th day	Yes	Five metal bangle only	15th day	15th day	1st year	1st year
M	—	—	—	—	—	—	—

Caste / Place	1	2	3	4	5	6	7
Viswakarma Tha	15th day	Yes	mukk-appu silver & gol-den ban-gle	15th day	16th day	1st year	1st year
K	16th day	Yes	Yes	16th day	16th day	only in the temple	only in the temple
KM	15th day	Yes	Yes	16th day	15th day	1st year	1st year
M	15th day	Yes	Yes	16th day	15th day	1st year	1st year
Vannan Tha	16th day	Yes	Yes	16th day	15th day	1st year	1st year
K	16th day	Yes	Yes	15th day	15th day	1st or 3rd year	1st or 3rd year
KM	16th-day	Yes	Three metal bangle only	16th day	16th day	1st or 5th year	1st or 5th year
M	—	—	—	—	—	—	—
Navitar Tha	16th day	Yes	black bangle & tie "citti-rattai"	16th day	16th day the	only in the temple	only in temple
K	—	—	—	—	—	—	—
KM	16th day	Yes	Yes	16th day	16th day	only in the temple	only in the temple
M	—	—	—	—	—	—	—

Caste / Place	*1*	*2*	*3*	*4*	*5*	*6*	*7*
Udayar Tha	—	—	—	—	—	—	—
K	—	—	—	—	—	—	—
KM	15th day	Not in cus-tom	Five metal bangle only	16th day	15th day	5th month	5th month
M	15th day	Yes	Yes	16th day	16th day	1st year	1st year
Harijan Tha	16th day	Yes	Yes	16th day	16th day	5th month	1st or 2nd or 3rd year
K	15th day	Yes	black ban-gle	16th day	15th day month	5th year	1st
KM	11th day	Yes	Yes	15th day	11th day	5th month	Accord-ing to the situation
M	7th day	Yes	Yes	11th day	16th day	5th month	1st year

Puberty Rituals

Caste / Place	Name of customs				
	1	*2*	*3*	*4*	*5*
Brahmin (Iyer) Tha	(a)	Yes	Not in custom	Yes	Yes
K	(a)	Yes	Not in custom	Yes	Yes
KM	—	—	—	—	—
N	(a)	Yes	Not in custom	Yes	Yes
Pillai (Karkattar) Tha	(a)	Yes	Not in custom	Yes	9th day only
K	(a)	Yes	Not in custom	Yes	11th day only
KM	(a)	Yes	Not in custom	Yes	9th day only
M	—	—	—	—	—
Patayacci Tha	(a)	Yes	Not in custom	Yes	odd number of days
K	(a)	Yes	Not in custom	Yes	Yes
KM	(a)	Yes	Not in custom	Yes	Yes
M	(a)	Yes	Not in custom	Yes	odd number of days

6	7	8	9	10
Not in custom	7th day	Not in custom	Not in custom	No
Not in custom	7th day	Not in custom	Not in custom	No
—	—	—	—	—
Not in custom	9th day	Not in custom	Not in custom	No
Not in custom	9th day	9th day	Not mentioned	(a)
Not in custom	11th day	11th day	Not mentioned	(a)
Not in custom	9th day	11th day	Not mentioned	(a)
—	—	—	—	—
Yes	9th day	9th or 15th or 22nd day or before marriage	Yes	(a)
Yes	9th day	According to the situation	Yes	(a)
Yes	7th day	13th day	Yes	(a)
Yes	6th day	9th day	Yes	(a)

Caste Place	Number of customs				
	1	2	3	4	5
Naidu Tha	(a)	only on the 3rd day	Not in custom	Yes	Yes
K	—	—	—	—	—
KM	(a)	Yes	Not in custom	Yes	Yes
M	—	—	—	—	—
Nayakkar (canar) Tha	(a)	Yes	Not in custom	Yes	only on 11th day
K	(a)	Yes	Not in custom	Yes	only on 9th day
KM	—	—	—	—	—
M	(a)	Yes	Not in custom	Yes	only on 9th day
Nayakkar (tatar) Tha	—	—	—	—	—
K	(a)	only on the 3rd day	Not in custom	Yes	5th, 7th & 9th day
KM	(a)	Yes	Not in custom	Yes	odd numbered days
M	—	—	—	—	—

6	7	8	9	10
Yes	10th day	11th day	Yes	(a)
—	—	—	—	—
Yes	11th day	11th day	Yes	(a)
—	—	—	—	—
Yes	11th day	16th or 22nd day	Yes	(a)
Yes	11th day	16th or 22nd day	Yes	(a)
—	—	—	—	—
Yes	11th day	15th or 22nd day	Yes	(a)
—	—	—	—	—
Yes	16th day	16th day	Yes	(a)
Yes	16th day	16th day	Yes	(a)
—	—	—	—	—

Caste *Place*	Number of customs				
	1	*2*	*3*	*4*	*5*
Vaniya Chettiyar Tha	(a)	Yes	Not in custom	3rd day only	3rd day 5th day
K	(a)	Yes	Not in custom	5th day only	3rd & 5th day
KM	(a)	Yes	Not in custom	7th day only	Yes
M	—	—	—	—	—
Viswakarma Tha	(a)	Yes	Not in custom	Yes	Not mentioned
K	(a)	Yes	Not in custom	Yes	Not mentioned
KM	(a)	Yes	Not in custom	Yes	Not mentioned
M	(a)	Yes	Not in custom	Yes	Not mentioned
Vannan Tha	(a)	Yes	Yes	Yes	Yes
K	(a)	Yes	Yes	Yes	Yes
KM	(a)	Yes	Not in custom	Yes	Yes
M	—	—	—	—	—

6	7	8	9	10
Yes	9th day	15th day (or) 3rd month	Yes	(a)
Yes	11th day	15th day	Yes	(e)
Yes	15th day	16th day	Yes	(a)
—	—	—	—	—
Yes	15th day	15th day	Yes	(e)
Yes	13th day	15th day	Yes	(a)
Yes	13th day	13th day	Yes	(a)
Yes	11th day	11th day	Yes	(a)
Yes	15th day	15th day or 3rd month	Yes	(a)
Yes	15th day	According to the situation	Yes	(e)
Yes	15th day	15th day	Yes	(a)
—	—	—	—	—

Caste Place	Number of customs				
	1	*2*	*3*	*4*	*5*
Navitar Tha	(a)	Yes	Yes	Yes	Yes
K	—	—	—	—	—
KM	(a)	Yes	Not in custom	Yes	Yes
M	—	—	—	—	—
Udayar Tha	—	—	—	—	—
K	—	—	—	—	—
KM	(a)	Yes	Not in custom	Yes	Yes
M	(a)	Yes	Not in custom	Yes	Yes
Harijan Tha	(a)	Yes	Not in custom	3rd, 5th, 9th 16th day	1st, 5th 7th, 9th & 16th days
K	(a)	Yes	Not in custom	Yes	Yes
KM	(a)	Yes	Not in custom	Yes	Yes
M	(a)	Yes	Not in custom	Yes	Yes

6	*7*	*8*	*9*	*10*
Yes	9th day	11th or 13th day or before marriage	Yes	(a)
—	—	—	—	—
Yes	9th-day	11th-day	Yes	(a)
—	—	—	—	—
—	—	—	—	—
—	—	—	—	—
Yes	13th day	15th day	Yes	(a)
Yes	15th day	15th day	Yes	(a)
Yes	16th day	16th day	Yes	(a)
Yes	15th day	15th day	Yes	(a)
Yes	16th day	16th day	Yes	(a)
Yes	16th day	16th day	Yes	(a)

Marriage Customs

Caste Place	Number of customs					
	1	*2*	*3*	*4*	*5*	*6*
Brahmin (Iyer) Tha	(a)	(b)	Yes	Before marriage day, bride's sister-in-law do this	Before marriage day in (a)	(b)
K	(a)	(b)	Yes	5 days before marriage	3-days before marriage in (a)	(b)
KM	—	—	—	—	—	—
M	(a)	(b)	Yes	3 days before marriage	Day before marriage in (b)	(b)
Pillai (Karkattar) Tha	(b)	(b)	yes	before marriage day	5 days before marriage in (a)	(b)
K	(b)	(b)	Yes	before marriage day	3 days before marriage in (a)	(b)
KM before	(b) (b)	(b)	Yes	3 days before marriage	5 days	
				marriage	marriage in (a)	
M	—	—	—	—	—	—
Patayacci Tha	(b)	either (a) or (b)	Yes	only (b)	3 days before marriage in (b)	
K	(b)	(b) (a) or (b)	Yes	(b)	5 days before marriage in (b)	(b)
K	(b)	(b)	Yes	(b)	5 days before marriage in (b)	(b)
KM	(b)	(c)	Yes	(b)	(b)	(b)
M	(b)	(a)	Yes	(b)	(b)	(b)

7	8	9	10	11	12	13	14
Bride's father, brother	3 days	Not mentioned	Even number	(a)	Not in custom	Yes	No
Brahmin priest	5 days	Not mentioned	Even number	(a)	Not in custom	Yes	No
—	—	—	—	—	—	—	—
Bride's party	3 days	Not mentioned	Even number	(a)	Not in custom	Yes	No
Bridegroom & 5 married ladies	Not particular	Not mentioned	Even number	(a) (a)	Not in custom	Yes	Yes
Bridegroom & 3 married ladies	Any day before marriage	Not mentioned	Even number	(a) (a)	Not in custom	Yes	Yes
Bridegroom & 3 married ladies	Not mentioned	Not mentioned	Even number	(a)	Not in custom	Yes	Yes
—	—	—	—	—	—	—	—
Father-in-law	3 or 5 days	Not particular	Not mentioned	(b)	Yes	Yes	Yes
Brahmin priest	3 days	Not particular	Not mentioned	(b)	Yes	Yes	Yes
Married ladies	5 days	Not particular	Not mentioned	(b)	Yes	Yes	Yes
Married ladies	7 days	Not particular	Not mentioned	(b)	Yes	Yes	Yes

15	*16*	*17*	*18*	*19*	*20*
No	(a)	No	Yes	No	Yes
No	9 (a)	No	Yes	No	Yes
—	—	—	—	—	—
No	(a)	No	Yes	No	Yes
Stylus, silver palm leaf	(a)	Yes	No	Yes	Yes
Conch	(a)	Yes	No	Yes	Yes
Silver statue	(a)	Yes	No	Yes	Yes
—	—	—	—	—	—
Conch	(a)	No	Yes	Yes	Yes
Knife	(a)	No	Yes	Yes	Yes
Stylus	(a)	No	Yes	Yes	Yes
Stylus	(a)	No	Yes	Yes	Yes

21	22	23	24	25
only after marriage	No	celebrate "nalungu"	Fix a date for this	(a), (b), (c) (d) & (e)
only after marriage	No	celebrate "nalungu"	select an auspicious day	(a0, (b), (c) (d) & (e)
—	—	—	—	—
only after marriage	No	celebrate "nalungu"	on the marriage day itself	(a), (b), (c) (d) & (e)
Yes	Yes	celebrate "nalungu"	on the marriage day itself	(a), (c) & (e)
Yes	Yes	celebrate "nalungu"	on the marriage day itself	(a), (c) & (e)
Yes	Yes	"celebrate "nalungu"	on the marriage day itself	(a), (c) & (e)
—	—	—	—	—
only after marriage	Yes	celebrate "nalungu"	select an auspicious day	(a), (c) & (e)
only after marriage	Yes	celebrate "nalungu"	select an auspicious day	(a), (c) & (e)
only after marriage	Yes	celebrate "nalungu"	Yes	(a), (c) & (e)
only after marriage	Yes	celebrate "nalungu"	Yes	(a), (c) & (e)

Caste Place	Number of customs					
	1	2	3	*4*	*5*	*6*
Naidu Tha	(b)	(b)	Yes	(b) than (c)	5 days before marriage in (b)	(b)
K	—	—	—	—	—	—
KM	(b)	(b)	Yes	(b) than (a) & (c)	5 days before marriage	(b)
M	—	—	—	—	—	—
Nayakkar (canar) Tha	(b)	(a)	Yes	sister	(b)	(b)
K	(b)	(a)	Yes	sister	(b)	(b)
KM	—	—	—	—	—	—
M	(b)	(c)	Yes	sister	(b)	(b)
Nayakkar (tatar) Tha	—	—	—	—	—	—
K	(b)	(b)	Yes	(b)	(b)	(a)
KM	(b)	(a)	Yes	(b)	(b)	(a)
M	—	—	—	—	—	—

15	16	17	18	19	20
conch, knife	(a)	Yes	No	Yes	Yes
—	—	—	—	—	—
Stylus, knife	(a)	Yes	No	Yes	Yes
—	—	—	—	—	—
knife, conch	(a)	Yes	No	Yes	Yes
conch, ring	(a)	Yes	No	Yes	Yes
—	—	—	—	—	—
knife, ring	(a)	Yes	No	Yes	Yes
—	—	—	—	—	—
conch, pavazha-mani conch	(a)	Yes	No	Yes	Yes
sangu mani	(a)	Yes	No	Yes	Yes
—	—	—	—	—	—

21	22	23	24	25
only after marriage	Yes	celebrate "nalungu"	only after going & coming back thrice	(a), (c) & (e)
—	—	—	—	—
only after marriage	Yes	celebrate "nalungu"	only after going & coming back thrice	(a), (c) & (e)
—	—	—	—	—
only after marriage	Yes	Yes	only after going and coming back thrice	(a), (c) & (e)
only after marriage	Yes	Yes	Yes	(a), (c) & (a)
—	—	—	—	—
only after marriage	Yes	Yes	Yes	(a) (c) & (e)
—	—	—	—	—
only after marriage	Yes	celebrate "nalungu"	Yes	(a), (c) & (e)
only after marriage	Yes	celebrate "nalungu"	select an auspicious day	(a), (c) & (e)
—	—	—	—	—

Caste *Place*	Number of customs					
	1	2	*3*	*4*	*5*	*6*
Chettiyar Vaniya Tha	(b)	(e)	Yes	(b)	3 days before marriage in (b)	(b)
K	(b)	(b)	Yes	(b)	(b)	(b)
KM	(b)	(a) & (b)	Yes	(a) & (b)	(b)	(b)
M	—	—	—	—	—	—
Viswakarma Tha	(b)	(a)	Yes	(b) (c)	(b)	(b)
K	(b)	(b)	(a)	(b) & (c)	(b)	(a)
KM	(b)	(c)	(a)	(b)	(b)	(a)
M	(b)	either (a) or (b)	(a)	(a) & (b)	(b)	(a)
Vannan Tha	(b)	(a)	Yes	(b)	3 days before marriage in (b)	(a)
K	(b)	(b)	Yes	(b)	3 days before marriage in (b)	(a)
KM	(b)	either (a) or (b)	Yes	(b)	3 days before marriage in (b)	(a)
M	—	—	—	—	—	—

7	8	9	10	11	12	13	14
Bridegroom & married woman	3 days	Not particular	odd number	(b)	No	Yes	Yes
bridegroom	5 days	Not particular	odd number	(b)	No	Yes	Yes
married woman	3 days	Not particular	odd number	(b)	No	Yes	Yes
—	—	—	—	—	—	—	—
Aged married woman	5 or 7 days	Not in custom	Not mentioned	(b)	Yes	Yes	Yes
Aged married woman	5 days	Not in custom	Not mentioned	(b)	Yes	Yes	Yes
Aged married woman	3 days	Not in custom	Not mentioned	(b)	Yes	Yes	Yes
Aged married woman	7 days	Not in custom	Not mentioned	(b)	Yes	Yes	Yes
Bridegroom	3 days	Not in custom	even number	(b)	Yes	Yes	Yes
Married ladies	3 days	Not in custom	even number	(b)	Yes	Yes	Yes
Bridegroom & married ladies	3 days	Not in custom	even number	(b)	Yes	Yes	Yes
—	—	—	—	—	—	—	—

15	16	17	18	19	20
conch, knife	(a)	Yes	No	Yes	Yes
conch, knife	(a)	Yes	No	Yes	Yes
conch, knife	(a)	Yes	No	Yes	yes
—	—	—	—	—	—
knife, conch	(a)	Yes	No	Yes	Yes
conch, stylus	(a)	Yes	No	Yes	yes
Stylus	(a)	Yes	No	Yes	Yes
knife	(a)	Yes	No	Yes	Yes
conch	(a)	Yes	No	Yes	Yes
ring	(a)	Yes	No	Yes	Yes
knife	(a)	Yes	No	Yes	Yes
—	—	—	—	—	—

21	*22*	*23*	*24*	*25*
No	Yes	celebrate "nalungu"	only after going and coming thrice	(a), (c) & (e)
No	Yes	celebrate "nalungu"	Yes	(a) (c) & (e)
No	Yes	celebrate "nalungu"	Yes	(a), (c) & (e)
—	—	—	—	—
No	Yes	celebrate "nalungu"	only after going & coming thrice	(a), (b), (c) & (e)
No	Yes	celebrate "nalungu"	Yes	(a), (b), (c) & (e)
No	Yes	celebrate "nalungu"	Yes	(a), (b), (c), & (e)
No	Yes	celebrate "nalungu"	Yes	(e), (b), (c) & (e)
No	Yes	celebrate "nalungu"	Yes	(a), (b), (c) & (e)
No	Yes	celebrate "nalungu"	Yes	(a), (c) & (c)
No	Yes	celebrate "nalungu"	Yes	(a), (c) & (a)
—	—	—	—	—

Caste Place	Number of customs					
	1	*2*	*3*	*4*	*5*	*6*
Navitar Tha	(b)	(a)	Yes	(b)	3 days before marriage in (b)	(b)
K	—	—	—	—	—	—
KM	(b)	(c)	Yes	(b)	3 days before marriage in (b)	(b)
M	—	—	—	—	—	—
Udayar Tha	—	—	—	—	—	—
K	—	—	—	—	—	—
KM	(b)	either (a) or (b)	Yes	only (b)	5 days before marriage in (b)	(b)
M	(b)	(b)	Yes	(a) & (b)	3 days before marriage in (b)	(b)
Harijan Tha	(b)	(b)	Yes	(a)	3 days before marriage in (b)	(b)
K	(b)	(b)	Yes	(a) & (b)	(b)	(b)
KM	(b)	(c)	Yes	(a)	(b)	(b)
M	(b)	(b)	Yes	(a) (b) & (c)	(b)	(b)

7	8	9	10	11	12	13	14
Bridegroom & brahmin priest	3 or 5 days	Not in custom	Odd number	(b)	Yes	Yes	Yes
—	—	—	—	—	—	—	—
Married ladies & bridegroom	5 days	Not in custom	Odd number	(b)	Yes	Yes	Yes
—	—	—	—	—	—	—	—
—	—	—	—	—	—	—	—
—	—	—	—	—	—	—	—
Bridegroom	5 days	No	Not mentioned	(b)	Yes	Yes	Yes
Married woman	5 days	No	Not mentioned	(b)	Yes	Yes	Yes
Bridegroom	3 days	No	Even number	(b)	Yes	Yes	Yes
Bridegroom	5 days	No	Even number	(b)	Yes	Yes	Yes
Bridegroom	3 days	No	Even number	(b)	Yes	Yes	Yes
Bridegroom	3 days	No	Even number	(b)	No	Yes	Yes

15	*16*	*17*	*18*	*19*	*20*
Water	(a)	Yes	No	Yes	Yes
—	—	—	—	—	—
Water	(a)	Yes	No	Yes	Yes
—	—	—	—	—	—
—	—	—	—	—	—
—	—	—	—	—	—
conch, knife	(a)	Yes	No	Yes	Yes
milk ladle, conch	(a)	Yes	No	Yes	Yes
milk ladle, coin	(a)	No	Yes	Yes	Yes
knife, spoon	(a)	No	Yes	Yes	Yes
spoon, coin	(a)	No	Yes	Yes	Yes
milk ladle, nut cutter	(a)	No	Yes	Yes	Yes

21	22	23	24	25
No	Yes	celebrate "nalungu"	auspicious day	(a), (c) & (c)
—	—	—	—	—
No	Yes	celebrate "nalungu"	fixing an auspicious day	(a), (c) & (e)
—	—	—	—	—
—	—	—	—	—
—	—	—	—	—
No	Yes	celebrate "nalungu"	selecting an auspicious day	(a) & (c)
No	Yes	celebrate "nalungu"	Yes	(a) & (c)
No	Yes	Yes	on the marriage day	(a), (c) & (e)
No	Yes	Yes	on the marriage day	(a), (c) & (e)
No	Yes	Yes	on the marriage day	(a), (c) & (e)
No	Yes	Yes	on the marriage day	(a), (c) & (e)

First Pregnancy

Caste / Place	Number of customs							
	1	*2*	*3*	*4*	*5*	*6*	*7*	*8*
Brahmin (iyer) Tha	No	(b)	Yes	(b)	No	(a)	8th month	(a)
K	No	(b)	(b)	No	(b)	(b)	(a)	
KM	—	—	—	—	—	—	—	—
M	No	(b)	Yes	(b)	No	(b)	(b)	(a)
Pillai (karkattar) Tha	No	(b)	Yes	(b)	No	No	(b)	(a)
K	No	(b)	Yes	(c)	No	No	(a)	(b)
KM	No	(b)	Yes	(c)	No	No	(b)	(e)
M	—	—	—	—	—	—	—	—
Patayacci Tha	Yes	No	No	either (a) or (b)	No	7th month	(a)	30th day (or) (a)
K	Yes	No	No	either (a) or (b)	No	(b)	(b)	(a)
KM	Yes	No	No	(a)	No	(b)	(b)	30th day
M	Yes	No	No	(b)	No	7th month	(a)	(a)
Naidu Tha	No	No	Yes	(b)	No	No	(b)	(a)
K	—	—	—	—	—	—	—	—
KM	No	No	Yes	(c)	No	No	(a)	(c)
M	—	—	—	—	—	—	—	—

Nayakkar (canar) Tha	1st or 2nd month	No	Yes	(b)	No	No	(b)	(c)
K	Yes	No	Yes	(c)	No	No	(b)	(b)
KM	—	—	—	—	—	—	—	—
M	Yes	No	Yes	(c)	No	No	(a)	(b)
Nayakkar (tatar) Tha	—	—	—	—	—	—	—	—
K	1st or 2nd month	No	Yes	(b) or (c)	No	No	(b)	22nd day or 3rd-month
KM	Yes	No	Yes	(c)	No	No	(a)	(a)
M	—	—	—	—	—	—	—	—
Vaniya Chettiar Tha	Yes	No	Yes	(b)	No	No	(b)	(a)
K	Yes	No	Yes	(c)	No	No	(b)	(a)
KM	Yes	No	Yes	(b)	No	No	(b)	(a)
M	—	—	—	—	—	—	—	—
Viswakarma Tha	No	No	Yes	either (b) or (c)	No	No	(a)	(a)
K	No	No	Yes	(b)	No	No	(a)	(b)
KM	No	No	Yes	either (b) or (c)	No	No	(a)	(a)
M	No	No	Yes	(c)	No	No	(a)	(a)

Vannan Tha	No	No	No	either (b) or (c)	No	No	(b)	(b)
K	No	No	No	either (b) or (c)	No	No	(a)	(a)
KM	No	No	No	(b)	No	No	(b)	(b)
M	—	—	—	—	—	—	—	—
Navitar Tha	No	(a)	No	(c)	No	No	(b)	(a)
K	—	—	—	—	—	—	—	—
KM	No	(a)	No	(b)	No	No	(a)	(a)
M	—	—	—	—	—	—	—	—
Udayar Tha	—	—	—	—	—	—	—	—
K	—	—	—	—	—	—	—	—
KM	No	No	Yes	(b) or (c)	No	No	(b)	(b)
M	No	No	Yes	(c)	No	No	(a)	(c)
Harijan Tha	No	No	Yes	(c)	No	No	(b)	16th day or 3rd month
K	No	No	Yes	(c)	No	No	(b)	16th day
KM	No	No	Yes	(b)	No	No	(a)	16th day (or) 3rd month
M	No	No	Yes	(c)	No	No	(b)	(b)

Sashtiyapthapurthi and Sadhabhishegam

Sashtiyapthapurthi

This is celebrated on 60th birthday. At that time it is usual to place certain number of "kalasas", kindle holy fire, recite holy mantras, tie a new marraige badge at that time also. This couple is anointed by the water in the "kalasas" before tying marriage badge. These are the besic customs and slight variations are mentioned as follows. Among the twelve caste people taken for analysis in this division only Brahmin (Iyer), Pillai (Karkattar), Patayacci, Viswakarma, Naidu caste people celebrate this function.

Brahmin (Iyer)

Tha	—	Place 16 kalasas.
K	—	Place 11 kalasas.
KM	—	Place 60 kalasas.
M	—	Place 16 kalasas.

Pillai (Karkattar)

Tha	—	Place 3 kalasas
K	—	Place 5 kalasas
KM	—	Place odd number of kalasas
M	—	Place 3 kalasas.

Patayacci

Tha	—	Place 9 kalasas
K	—	Place 7 kalasas
KM	—	Place 11 kalasas
M	—	Place 15 kalasas

Viswakarma

Tha, K, KM, M	—	Celebrate like other caste people.
	—	Sometimes celebrate this in temple also.

Naidu

Tha	—	Place 7 kalasas
K	—	Place 9 kalasas
KM	—	Place 11 kalasas
M	—	Place odd number of kalasas

Vaniya Chettiar, Vannar and Navitar caste people celebrate this in temple. The other caste people viz., Nayakkar (canar), Nayakkar (tatar), Vaniya Chettiyar, Udayar and Harijan caste people do not celebrate this function.

Sadhabhishegam

This is celebrated on 80th birthday. This is celebrated like 60th birthday. For this marriage it is not in custom to tie marriage badge. Among the twelve caste people mentioned in this division only Brahmin (iyer), Pillai (karkattar), Viswakarma caste people celebrate this function. Other caste people viz; Patayacci, Naidu, Nayakkar (canar), Nayakkar (tatar), Vaniya Chettiyar, Vannan, Navitar, Udayar and Harijan caste people do not celebrate this function.

Brahmin (Iyer)

In all the four villages this is celebrated in the same way. They place 101 kalasas and tie a marriage badge for this ceremony also.

Pillai (Karkattar)

These people celebrate this like the above caste people.

Viswakarma

These people also celebrate this like the above caste people. In all the four villages these customs resemble more or less each other. Not only these customs, but all the other customs also more or less resemble each other since these villages are near-by to each other. So, we can find only slight variations in the customs of these village caste people.

Death Customs

Caste / Place	Number of customs						
	1	*2*	*3*	*4*	*5*	*6*	*7*
Brahmin (Iyer) Tha	(a), (b) & (c)	Not in custom	No	No	(b)	Yes	(b)
K	(a) & (b)	Not in custom	No	No	(b)	Yes	(b)
KM	—	—	—	—	—	—	—
M	(a), (b) (c) & (d)	Not in custom	No	No	(b)	Yes	(b)
Pillai (Karkattar) Tha	(a) & (b)	Yes	(b)	Yes	(b)	Yes	(b)
K	(a)	Yes	(b)	Yes	(b)	Yes	(b)
KM	(b) & (d)	Yes	(b)	Yes	(b)	Yes	(b)
M	—	—	—	—	—	—	—
Patayacci Tha	(a) & (b)	Yes	(b)	Yes	either (a) or (b)	Yes	(a)
K	(a) & (d)	Yes	(b)	Yes	either (a) or (b)	Yes	(a)
KM	(b) & (c)	Yes	(b)	Yes	either (a) or (b)	Yes	(a)
M	(a) & (b)	Yes	(b)	Yes	either (a) or (b)	Yes	(a)

8	9	10	11	12	13	14	15
(e)	Not in custom	No	(d)	(a)	Mourn for 10 days	10th day	13th day
(e)	Not in custom	No	(b)	(a)	Mourn for 10 days	10th day	13th day
—	—	—	—	—	—	—	—
(b)	Not in custom	No	(c)	(a)	Mourn for 10 days	10th day	13th day
(e)	by carrying coconut	(b)	(d)	Not in custom	5th day	(d)	in the month of "aati"
(a)	by carrying coconut	(b)	(b)	Not in custom	(b)	(a)	in the month of "aati" & ayppaci
(a)	by carriyng coconut	(b)	(b) & (a)	Not in custom	(c)	(e)	in the month of "aati"
—	—	—	—	—	—	—	—
Yes	towel with coins	(a)	(d)	*(a) or (b)	(a)	(d)	(a) & (b)
Yes	(b)	(a)	(d)	*(a) or (b)	5th day	(d)	(a)
Yes	(b)	(a)	(d)	*(a) or (b)	(b)	(d)	(a) & (b)
Yes	towel with coins	(a)	(d)	*(a) or (b)	odd number days	(d)	(a)

16	*17*	*18*	*19*	*20*	*21*	*22*	*23*	*24*	*25*
(a), (b)	Yes	(a)	(a)	any colour saree	(a)	Yes	11th-day	Yes	No
(a), (b) (c) & (d)	Yes	(a)	(a)	any colour saree	(a)	Yes	9th days	Yes	No
—	—	—	—	—	—	—	—	—	—
(a), (b) (c) & (d)	Yes	(a)	(a)	any colour saree	(a)	Yes	13th day	Yes	No
(a), (b) (c) & (d)	Yes	any colour except black	(a)	any colour saree	(a)	No	No	Yes	No
(a), (b) (c) & (d)	Yes	any colour except black	(a)	any colour saree	(a)	No	No	Yes	No
(a), (b) (c) & (d)	Yes	any colour except black	(a)	any colour saree	(a)	No	No	Yes	No
—	—	—	—	—	—	—	—	—	—
(a)	No	(a) or yellow or any colour	(a)	red colour without border	(a)	Yes	9th day	Yes	Yes
(d)	No	(a) (or) yellow (or) any colour	(a)	red colour without border	(a)	Yes	11th day	Yes	Yes
(d)	No	(a) or yellow	(a)	red colour	(a)	Yes	11th day	Yes	Yes
(a) & (d)	No	any colour	(a)	red colour without flower	(a)	Yes	9th day	Yes	Yes

Number of customs

Caste *Place*	*1*	*2*	*3*	*4*	*5*	*6*	*7*	*8*
Naidu Tha	(b)	Yes	(a)	Yes	either (a) or (b)	Not in custom	(c)	only sandal wood
K	—	—	—	—	—	—	—	—
KM	(a) & (b)	Yes	(b)	Yes	either (a) or (b)	Not in custom	(c)	sandal wood & lamp
M	—	—	—	—	—	—	—	—
Nayakkar (canar) Tha	(a)	Yes	(b)	Yes	(a)	Not in custom	(c)	(a)
K	(a)	Yes	(b)	Yes	(a)	Not in custom	(a)	(a) & (c)
KM	—	—	—	—	—	—	—	—
M	(a) & (b)	Yes	(b)	Yes	(a)	Not in custom	(c)	(a), (c) (d) & (e)
Nayakkar (tatar) Tha	—	—	—	—	—	—	—	—
K	(a)	Yes	(b)	Yes	(a)	Not in custom	(c)	(b), (c), (d) & (e)
KM	(a) & (b)	Yes	(b)	Yes	(a)	Not in custom	(c)	(b), (d) & (e)
M	—	—	—	—	—	—	—	—

9	*10*	*11*	*12*	*13*	*14*	*15*	*16*	*17*	*18*
without carrying anything	only on the wall	(b)	5th day	(b)	10th day night	(a)	(a) & vessels	No	any colour
—	—	—	—	—	—	—	—	—	—
without carrying anything	Not ment-ioned	(b) & (c)	5th-day	(a)	11th-day	(a)	(a), (d) & vessels	No	any colour
—	—	—	—	—	—	—	—	—	—
Not mentioned	(a)	(b)	(b)	(b)	9th day night	Not ment-ioned	(a)	No	(a)
Not particular	(a)	(b) & (c)	(b)	(b)	10th day	Not ment-ioned	vessels	No	(a)
—	—	—	—	—	—	—	—	—	—
Not mentioned	(a)	(d)	(b)	(b)	10th-day	Not mentio-ned	(d)	No	any colour
—	—	—	—	—	—	—	—	—	—
No	(a)	(d)	(a)	(c)	(a)	(a)	Not	No ment-ioned	(a)
No	(a)	(b), (c) or (d)	(a)	(c)	(d)	(e)	(d)	No	(a)
—	—	—	—	—	—	—	—	—	—

19	20	21	22	23	24	25
light yellow colour	Not particular	(a)	Yes	11th day	(b)	Not in custom
—	—	—	—	—	—	—
light yellow	Not particular	(a)	Yes	11th day	(b)	Not in custom
—	—	—	—	—	—	—
(a) or (b)	(a) or yellow	(a)	Yes	10th day	according to the situation (a), (b)	Yes
(a) or (b)	yellow	(a)	Yes	(c)	(b) only	Yes
—	—	—	—	—	—	—
(a)	(a) or	(a)	Yes	10th day	(a) & (b)	Yes
—	—	—	—	—	—	—
red colour without flower	Do not wear flowered saree	(b)	Yes	6th day	(b)	Yes
red without flower	Do not wear flowered saree	(b)	Yes	9th day	(b)	Yes
—	—	—	—	—	—	—

Number of customs

Caste *Place*	*1*	2	3	4	5	6	7	8
Vaniya Chettiyar Tha	(a)	Yes	Yes	Yes	either (a) or (b)	Yes	(c)	rice, lamp & batti
K	(a) & (b)	Yes	Yes	Yes	either (a) or (b)	Yes	(c)	rice, lamp & batti
KM	(b)	Yes	Yes	Yes	either (a) or (b)	Yes	(a)	rice, lamp & batti
M	—	—	—	—	—	—	—	—
Viswakarma Tha	(a) & (b)	Yes	(b)	Yes	(a)	Not in custom	(c)	two lamps
K	(b)	Yes	(b)	Yes	(a)	Not in custom	(c)	two lamps
KM	(a) & (b)	Yes	(b)	Yes	(a)	Not in custom	(a)	two lamps
M	(a)	Yes	(b)	Yes	(a)	Not in custom	(c)	two lamps
Vannan Tha	(a)	Yes	(b)	Yes	either (a) or (b)	Yes	(a)	Yes
K	(d)	Yes	(b)	Yes	either (a) or (b)	Yes	(c)	Yes
KM	(a) & (b)	Yes	(b)	Yes	either (a) or (b)	Yes	(c)	Yes
M	—	—	—	—	—	—	—	—

9	10	11	12	13	14	15
(b) & (c)	(a)	(d)	(b)	(c)	(d)	(a)
(b) & (c)	(a)	(d)	(b)	(c)	(e)	(a)
(b) & (c)	(a)	(d)	(b)	(c)	(d)	(e)
—	—	—	—	—	—	—
(c)	only sandal paste in (a)	(b)	3rd day	7th day	9th day	(a)
(c)	sandal paste in (a)	(c)	3rd day	5th day	10th day	(a)
(c)	sandal paste in (a)	(b)	3rd day	5th day	10th day	(a)
(b) & (c)	(a)	(d)	cremate then (a), bury then (b)	(c)	(e)	30th day night
(b) & (c)	(a)	(d)	(e)	(c)	(d)	(a)
(b) & (c)	(a)	(d)	(b)	(c)	(d)	30th day night
—	—	—	—	—	—	—

16	*17*	*18*	*19*	*20*
No	No	(a)	red	any colour
No	No	(a)	red	any colour
No	No	(a)	red	any colour
—	—	—	—	—
rice	Yes	any colour without black	(a)	any colour saree
vessels	Yes	any colour	(a)	Yes
(d)	Yes	red	(a)	yellow
(a)	Yes	any colour	(a)	Yes
No	Yes, to themselves	any colour	red	any colour
No	Yes, to their relatives	any colour	red	any colour
No	Yes, to their relative	any colour	red	any colour
—	—	—	—	—

21	22	23	24	25
(a)	Yes	(d)	(b)	Yes
(a)	Yes	(c)	(b)	Yes
(a)	Yes	(d)	(b)	Yes
—	—	—	—	—
(a)	Yes	10th day	(a)	Yes
(a)	Yes	10th day	both (a) & (b)	Yes
(a)	Yes	10th day	(b) only	Yes
(a)	Yes	10th day	(a) & (b)	Yes
either (a) or (b)	Yes, only if it is male	If (a) then on 10th day If (b) than on 16th day	(a) & (b)	Yes
(b)	Yes, only if	—	(a) & (b)	Yes
either (a) or (b)	Yes, only if it is male	—	(a) & (b)	Yes
—	—	—	—	—

Number of customs

Caste / Place	*1*	2	3	4	5	6	7
Navitar Tha	rub gold and give it to the dead person	Yes	(b)	Yes	(b)	Yes	(c)
K	—	—	—	—	—	—	—
KM	rub gold and give it to the dead person	Yes	(b)	Yes	(b)	Yes	(c)
M	—	—	—	—	—	—	—
Udayar Tha	—	—	—	—	—	—	—
K	—	—	—	—	—	—	—
KM	(a)	Yes	(b)	Yes	(a)	Yes	(b)
M	(b)	Yes	(b)	Yes	(a)	Yes	(b)
Harijan Tha	(a)	Yes	(b)	Yes	either (a) or (b)	Yes	(c)
K	(b)	Yes	(b)	Yes	either (a) or (b)	Yes	(c)
KM	only water	Yes	(b)	Yes	either (a) or (b)	Yes	(c)
M	(b)	Yes	(b)	Yes	either (a) or (b)	Yes	(c)

8	*9*	*10*	*11*	*12*	*13*
(a)	Yes, without carrying anything	only give lamp and take it back	(d)	(a)	(a)
—	—	—	—	—	—
(a)	Yes, without carrying anything	only give lamp and take it back	(d)	(a)	(a)
—	—	—	—	—	—
—	—	—	—	—	—
—	—	—	—	—	—
Yes	(b) & (c)	(a)	(d)	(a)	5th & (b)
Yes water in the copper pot	(b) & (c)	(a)	(d)	(a)	(b)
(b) & (a) water in the copper pot	Yes	(a)	(d)	(b)	3rd & 5th
(b) & (a) water in the copper pot	Yes	(a)	(d)	(b)	7th & 8th
copper pot, (b) & (e)	Yes	(a)	(d)	(e)	9th day
water in the copper pot, (b) & (c)	Yes	(a)	(d)	(b)	3rd, 7th & 9th day

14	*15*	*16*	*17*	*18*	*19*	*20*
(d)	(a)	No	Yes	flowered saree	white (or) red	Not particular
—	—	—	—	—	—	—
(a)	(c)	No	Yes	flowered saree	white (or) red	Not particular
—	—	—	—	—	—	—
—	—	—	—	—	—	—
—	—	—	—	—	—	—
10th day	22nd day	No	Yes	(a)	(a)	Not mentioned
10th day	22nd day	No	Yes	(a)	(a)	Not mentioned
(a)	(a)	No	Yes, to poor people	flowered red colour saree	red	any colour saree
(d)	(e)	No	Yes, to poor people	flowered red colour saree	red	any colour saree
(a)	(a)	No	Yes, to poor people	flowered red colour saree	red	any colour saree
(d)	(e)	No	Yes, to poor people	flowered red colour saree	red	any colour saree

21	22	23	24	25
(a)	Yes	9th day	only (b)	Yes
—	—	—	—	—
(a)	Yes	9th day	only (b)	Yes
—	—	—	—	—
—	—	—	—	—
—	—	—	—	—
(a)	No	No	(b)	Yes
(a)	No	No	(b)	Yes
(a)	Yes	8th day	(b)	Yes
(a)	Yes	8th day	(b)	Yes
(a)	Yes	10th day	(b)	Yes
(a)	Yes	8th (or) 10th day	(b)	Yes

** If the body is cremated then they celebrate "paal teli" next day, if the body is buried they celebrate "paal teli" on 3rd day.

Coimbatore District

The three villages viz. Madampatti, Kalapatti, Thondamuttur of Coimbatore district from which the customs from child birth to death (of a human life cycle) are collected. Even though the materials are collected from more than eleven caste people, common caste people atleast in two villages are taken into account for the purpose of comparison. Basic customs mentioned in the above divisions are the same for this district also and the changes between the villages are noted inthe tabular column. "M"—denotes "Madampatti"—village, "K"—denotes "Kalapatti" village and "Tho" denotes Thondamuttur village in the tabular column. Common caste people in the above villages are mentioned as follows :

	Madampatti	**Kalapatti**	**Thondamuttur**
1.	—	Naidu	Naidu
2.	Kongu Vellalar	Kongu Vellalar	—
3.	Harijan	Harijan	Harijan

Child Birth

Number of customs

Caste Place	*1*	*2*	*3*	*4*	*5*	*6*	*7*
Naidu M	—	—	—	—	—	—	—
K	7th day	No	only golden bangle	within one month	9th day	within one year	while removing hair
Tho	9th day	No	"panja-varna tantai", then" anju pancalam" kappu	3rd month	15th day	11th month	within three years
Kongu Vellalar	Not in custom	No	No	5th month	7th day	11th month	7th year
K	Not in custom	No	No	3rd month	Not in custom	1st year	after one year, 3rd (or) 5th year
Tho	—	—	—	—	—	—	—
Harijan M	7th day	No	Five metal bangles	3rd month	Not in custom	Not mentioned	3rd year
K	Not in custom	No	Not in custom	3rd month	12th day	11th month	5th (or) 7th year
Tho	Not in custom	No	No	3rd month	Not in custom	11th month	3rd year

Puberty Rituals

Number of customs

Caste Place	*1*	*2*	*3*	*4*	*5*	*6*	*7*	*8*	*9*	*10*
Naidu M	—	—	—	—	—	—	—	—	—	—
K	(b)	No	No	3rd & 5th day	3rd day	Not men-tioned	8th day	8th day	No	(a)
Tho	(a)	No	No	Do not pour	pre-pare it till 7th day	Not men-tioned	7th	7th day	No	(a)
Kongu vellalar M	(a)	No	No	Yes	5th day	Yes	Yes	7th day	No	(a)
K	(b)	No	No	3rd, 5th	3rd day	Yes	Yes	immediately after attaining age (or) within a week	No	(a)
Tho	—	—	—	—	—	—	—	—	—	—
Harijan M	(b)	No	No	3rd & 5th day	3rd, 5th day	Yes	Yes	1st month after attaining age	No	(b)
K	(b)	No	No	5th day	5th day	Yes	6th day	6th-day	No	(a)
Tho	(b)	No	No	Yes	daily	Not mentio-ned	7th 9th day	on the same day of invi-ting the girl inside the house	No	(a)

Marriage Customs

Number on customs

Caste Place	*1*	*2*	*3*	*4*	*5*	*6*	*7*	*8*
Naidu M	—	—	—	—	—	—	—	—
K	(b)	(a)	(a)	(b)	three days before marriage in (a)	(b)	(b)	7 days
Tho	(b)	(a)	(a)	(a)	Not in custom	(b)	(a)	7 days
Kongu Vellalar M	(b)	(a)	No	(b)	No	(a)	(a)	4 days
K	(b)	(a)	No	No	No	(a)	(b)	4 days
Tho	—	—	—	—	—	—	—	—
Harijan M	(b)	(a)	(a)	7 days before marriage in (a)	Not in custom	(a)	elderly people	7 days
K	(b)	(b)	(b)	(b)	8 days before marriage in (a)	(b)	(b)	8 days
Tho	(b)	(a)	(b)	Not mention-ed	7 days before marriage in (a)	(a)	elderly people	3 days

9	*10*	*11*	*12*	*13*	*14*	*15*	*16*	*17*	*18*	*19*
—	—	—	—	—	—	—	—	—	—	—
Not particular	Not particular	(b)	No	Yes	No	No	(a)	Yes	No	No
Not particular	Not particular	(b)	No	Yes	No	No	(a)	Yes	No	No
Not particular	No	(a)	No	Yes	No	No	(b)	Yes	No	No
Not particular	No	(b)	No	No	No	No	(a)	Yes	No	No
—	—	—	—	—	—	—	—	—	—	—
Not particular	Not mentioned	(b)	No	No	No	No	(a)	Yes	No	No
Not particular	No	(a)	No	No	No	No	(a)	Yes	No	No
Not particular	Not mentioned	(a)	No	Yes	No	No	(a)	No	Yes	No

20	21	22	23	24	25
—	—	—	—	—	—
No	Yes	They leave "pali" only	Yes	on the same day	(a), (c) & (d)
No	Yes	Yes	Yes	Yes	(a), (b), (c), (d) or (e), (g) & (f)
No	Yes	they leave the "pali" only	Yes	Yes	(a), (b), (c),
No	No	Yes	No	on the marriage day	(a), (c) & (e)
—	—	—	—	—	—
No	Yes	No	Yes	Yes	(c)
No	Yes	only they leave the "pali"	Yes	on the marriage day	(c) & (c)
No	Yes	Yes	Yes	Yes	(a), (c), (d), & (e)

* (f)—According to the economic situation.

First Pregnancy

Caste Place	Number of customs 1	2	3	4	5	6	7	8
Naidu M	—	—	—	—	—	—	—	—
K	No	No	No	(b)	No	No	(a)	4th month
Tho	No	No	Yes	(b)	No	No	(b)	(b) or (c)
Kongu Vellalar M	Yes	No	Yes	(b)	No	No	(a)	(a)
K	No	No	Yes	(b)	No	No	(a)	(a) or (d)
Tho	—	—	—	—	—	—	—	—
Harijan M	Yes	(b)	Yes	(b)	No	No	(a)	(a)
K	Yes	No	Yes	(b)	No	No	(a)	4th month
Tho	Yes	No	Yes	(b)	No	No	(a)	(a) or (b)

Sashtiyapthapurthi and Sadhabhishegam

Sashtiyapthapurthi

Naidu

Kalapatti—They celebrate this on 60th year, place 9 kalasas.

Madampatti—This caste people are not available in this village.

Thondamuttur—Not in custom.

Kongu Vellalar

Madampatti—It is not in custom to celebrate this function.

Kalapatti—This is celebrated on 60th year, place 9 kalasas, and these people do not tie a marriage badge at the time of this celebration.

Thondamuttur—This caste people is not available in this village.

Harijan

Madampatti, Kalapatti, Thondamuttur—It is not in custom to celebrate this function.

Sadhabhishegam

Naidu

In Madampatti this caste people is not available and it is not in custom to celebrate this in other two villages.

Kongu Vellalar

In Thondamuttur village this caste people is not available and in other two villages it is not in custom to celebrate this function.

Harijan

It is not in custom to celebrate this function among this caste people.

Death Customs

Number of custom

Caste Place	*1*	*2*	*3*	*4*	*5*	*6*	*7*	*8*
Naidu M	—	—	—	—	—	—	—	—
K	(b)	No	No	No	(a)	Yes	(b)	(a)
Tho	(d)	No	No	No	(a)	Yes	(b)	(a), (b), (c) (d) & (e)
Kongu Vellalar M	(a)	No	No	No	(a)	No	(b)	(a), (c), (d) & (e)
K	(a), (b), (c) & (d)	No	No	No	(a)	No	(b)	(a)
Tho	—	—	—	—	—	—	—	—
Harijan M	(a) & (c)	No	No	No	either (a) or (b)	Yes	(c)	(a) & (c)
K	(a) & (b)	No	No	No	(a)	No	(b)	(a)
Tho	(a), (b), (c) & (d)	No	No	No	(a)	Not mention-ed	(b)	(a)

9	*10*	*11*	*12*	*13*	*14*	*15*	*16*	*17*	*18*
—	—	—	—	—	—	—	—	—	—
without carrying anything	No	(b)	(a)	Not in custom	(a)	(b)	No	Yes	(a)
(b)	(b)	(a)	(b)	Not in custom	(a)	(b)	No	Yes	(a)
(b)	No	(b)	(b)	(a) & (b)	11th-day	No	No	No	(a)
No	No	(b)	(e) or (b)	(c) or (b)	Next day (or) (a)	(b)	No	No	(a)
—	—	—	—	—	—	—	—	—	—
No	No	(b) & (a)	(a)	No	(a)	No	No	No	flowe-red saree
(b)	No	(b)	(a)	(a)	(a)	No	No	No	red
Not in custom	No	(b)	(b)	(a) & (d)	(a)	No	No	No	(a)

19	20	21	22	23	24	25
—	—	—	—	—	—	—
(a)	No	(a)	Yes	2nd day	(b)	Yes
(a)	Yes	(b)	Yes	11th day	(b)	Yes
(a)	No	(a)	No	No	(b)	Yes
(a)	Yes	(a)	No	No	(b)	Yes
—	—	—	—	—	—	—
sandal colour saree	Not particular	(a)	Yes	Next-day	(b)	No
white	No	(a)	No	No	(b)	No
(a)	Yes	(a)	No	No	(b)	No

In this analysis of variations in the customs of various caste people due to region we can find out the variations in the customs between Districts and between the villages in the same district. In some aspects we do not find any variation. In some aspects we find such difference. In some aspects all the customs resemble each other—this may be due to migration of the people in other region from place to place. In some aspects much difference is find since each and every caste people keeping their own way of traditional methods without leaving their culture.

5

Folk-Customs : Rural and Urban Area Differences

Rural area people have a sense of unity. The relation between the rural area people are intimate. They know each other personally and their customs, conventions and culture are common. Rural people take part in religious celebrations. Structurally and functionally the rural area (village) is a unit. In rural areas, people assist each other and thus they have close neighbourhood relations. Rural area people have deep faith in religion and deities. Their main occupation is agriculture which largely depends upon the vagaries of nature. The farmer acquires an attitude of fear and awe towards natural forces and start worshipping them. The village people lead a simple life. Their behaviour is natural, live a peaceful life, free from mental conflicts. They are sincere, hospitable and hard-working. The level of morality is high. The inhabitants of the village are strongly attached to old customs and traditions.

Taking up the social aspects of urban community, the city is a way of life. The word 'urbans' suggests this way of life; it indicates fashionable living, wide acquaintance with things and people and political manner of speech. Generally speaking, the urban communities are identified as large, dense and heterogeneous and the rural communities as small, less dense and homogeneous, yet no hard and fast line can be drawn.

Namalasanasa is one of the feature of urban community. A citizen may live for several years in a city and may not know the names of one third of the people who live in the same city area. "The urban world puts a premium on varied recognition". In short, urban contacts are segmental, class extremes characterize urban community. Social heterogeneity is also one of the characteristic feature of urban area. The personal traits, the occupations, the cultural life and the ideas of the members of the urban community vary widely than those of the rural inhabitants. Urbanities become night dwellers, not neighbours.

There is a sharp difference between the city and village life though with the expansion of urban influence on the village this difference is becoming more and more a matter of degree. However, in spite of the recent trends of urbanisation, the village still retain many of their traditional features and present a sharp contrast with the urban life.

Thus rural area mostly consists of villages and urban area is a town area. In rural area, we can find mostly uneducated people whereas in urban area educated people are more in number. In rural area, the relations between the primary groups and families are intimate. The family fulfills the needs of its members in all aspects of their life and exercises control over them. It is through the family that the new members are initially introduced to the customs, conventions and culture of the society. In rural areas the relationship among the people are direct and intimate so that often the entire village is organised like a family. Moreover, the life of the people in rural area is simple and economical and have very limited needs. The spirit of ambition and competition is generally absent. Less comparing to urban life.

This is not so in urban area. In urban area, mostly joint family system is not found, (there may be few exceptions). So, the new members in a family do not generally know the proper customs conventions, and culture of their ancestors. So, it is not possible for them to maintain the customs etc. of their ancestors in their life.

The major social factors which influence the life of the Indian rural community are caste system, joint family, various laws of marriage as well as social and religious customs and traditions etc. Any change in any one of these factors results in changes in the rural community. The change may take place due to the influence of urban community people. When the people in the rural area come into contact with the people in urban area, they adopt and imitate the way of life of the urban community people atleast in some aspects. So, changes occur among the rural community people.

In urban areas, all the members of a family are to be seen pursuing their individual paths. Regarding folk-customs, the differences in customs of rural and urban area is discussed in this chapter. The main customs of human life cycle viz. (1) Child birth, (2) Sacred thread ceremony, (3) Puberty rituals, (4) Marriage customs, (5) First pregnancy, (6) Sashtiyapthapurthi and Sadhabhishegam and (7) Death customs differ in rural and urban communities.

In rural area the child birth is celebrated grandly. They celebrate "kappu" (putting are—rings to the child), cradling ceremony, naming ceremony, punniyadanam, hair removing ceremony and ear boring ceremony without fail at proper time. The people in rural area are afraid of Gods and Goddess, have faith in ghosts and evil effects and so they celebrate every custom without fail. The urban community people also celebrate these customs, but they do not celebrate them at proper time. Sometimes they never remove the hair of the child and bore the ear of the child. Now-a-days we can notice some children without the ear bored, in urban areas. They think that it is not must, but in contrast to this, the rural area people think that it is must to observe these customs at proper time.

In Brahmin (iyer), Brahmin (iyangar), Viswakarma (Carpenter, Goldsmith) caste people celebrate "sacred thread ceremony". This, is celebrated with pomp and show like a marriage in rural areas. Urban community people also celebrate this but in a simple manner. Mainly the economic factor is the reason for this. In urban areas, each and everything is costly and it is very difficult to celebrate any function in a grand manner. Particularly middle class family is very much affected by the economic status.

Regarding "Puberty Rituals", rural area people celebrate this for seven (or) eleven days. After inviting the girl inside the house they celebrate the rituals in grand manner. They invite relatives, friends, beat auspicious drums, celebrate this celebration. Moreover, after the girl attaining age they never allow the girl to go outside alone till marriage. This is strictly followed in olden days and also now-a-days in most of the rural areas. The reason for the slight change in rural areas, is the spread of education. This is not so in urban areas. In urban areas they celebrate "puberty rituals" very simply.

Moreover, they do not take much care for this occasion. Also they allow the girl to go outside before marriage itself. This is due to modernization and educational system among the urban community people. In urban society, they do not celebrate this that much care like that in rural areas.

While looking into Marriage ceremonies, rural area people celebrate this with much fear and care. They celebrate each and every custom without fail. "Marriages are made in Heaven"— This proverb reveals that marriage is an auspicious function which is the turning point in the life a human being only if the married life is proper, then the whole life of the married couple will be peaceful. Rural area people have much faith in religion etc. they celebrate everything in the proper way. Marriage customs are many in number and mostly resemblance can be found between caste to caste and region to region. Even though the basic customs are same, they vary slightly from caste to caste and region to region. It may be due to their traditional way of celebrating certain functions to keep up their culture, they celebrate these function in their own way.

In urban areas also they celebrate marriage customs, but in a simple manner. Rich people celebrate the function in grand manner to show their wealthy position, but they do not do it in proper manner as in rural areas. Other people in urban area celebrate marriage functions simply. This may be due to economic condition. In those days marriage is celebrated for four or five days. Now-a-days everything is finished on the marriage day itself. We can point out that economic condition, educational progress, modernization and the time limit for the working people as reasons for the above. Moreover, marriage functions are reduced very much in urban areas. Simply they arrange the marriage in a temple and after finishing marriage they arrange for a grand-feast for those who attend the function.

Pregnancy is considered to be a most admirable one among the people in rural areas. In rural areas after marriage, next year itself they expect a child from the couple. If it is not so, then they feel very much and the bridegroom's parents ask her son to marry another girl, thinking that his first wife is not fit for giving birth to a child. Also they scold her as barren woman. They treat the girl very cruelly. In urban areas it is not so. Since mostly both the married couple are educated, they planned their way of life and their parents also understand the situation. So, child is not a problem for them. Also if both the husband and the wife are working people, then it is very difficult for them to take care of the child, if they have a child. In rural areas, they believe that only if the pregnant lady's desire is fulfilled then only her child will be healthy. Otherwise they believe that child to be born will be an unhealthy one. So, they take much care of the pregnant lady. In urban areas even though they take care of the pregnant lady, they allow her to go outside if she is a working woman. So, regarding pregnancy, rural and urban people mainly differs in one respect viz., rural area people do not allow the girl to go out after celebrating "kappu", but urban area people allow the girl to go for her work even after celebrating "kappu". After delivery, in rural areas they send back the girl and the child only on 3rd or 5th or 7th month. According to the situation, they send the girl and her child, within one or two months after delivery to her husband's house in urban areas.

60th birthday, 80th birthday are celebrated both in rural and urban areas. It is usual that the sons, son-in-law, daughters and daughters-in-law together spend money for this function.

They believe that doing "Sashtiyapthapurtti" (60th birthday) to their parents will give them good fortune. Also they got the heartful blessing of their aged parents. Urban area people celebrate this to show their economic status. Moreover, some people do not care in celebrating this function to their parents in urban areas. The same condition for 80th birthday also.

Death is the last moment in a human life. To satisfy the dead person, people do so many ceremonies after the death of the person. In rural areas, they do each and every ceremony for the dead person with much care, faith and fear. They want to fulfill the desire, wishes of the dead person, even though they do not know what is the desire, wish etc. of the dead person. They promptly do every custom to a dead person. They do the funeral ceremonies properly. If a person dies on Saturday, Wednesday etc. then they tie a chicken with the bier and bury or cremate it with the body. They thought that the chicken is a companion for the dead body. This is done on the belief that if a person dies on Saturdays, etc. than there occur three more deaths, i.e. the dead person is in need of companion. So, to avoid more deaths they do it like this. Likewise if a person dies on "ashtami", "navami" tithi-days then some caste people scatter fried rice, flower etc. all the way to the graveyard. This is also done to satisfy the dead person. These area people mourn on 3rd, 8th, or 11th-day, on that day they prepare edibles liked by the dead person and offer them to him/her. They celebrate "funeral rites" (karumati) on 3rd or 10th or 11th or 15th or 16th day, on that day dead person's relatives prepare various kind of edibles and bring them to the dead person's house. In the dead person's house also they prepare edibles etc. liked by the dead person and all the things are divided into three parts and offered thrice to him/her. In the same way, they mourn for the dead person on 30th day or 3rd month. These people termed this ceremony as "kattukku poonavarkala vittukku azhaittal" i.e. they believe that the dead person will again come, mingle with their family and bless the family members.

Also they give "monthly" and "yearly" tithi for the dead

person. At that time they give alms to a brahmin priest. These are all done on the belief that the dead person will be satisfied that his / her family member never forget him/her and bless the family members to have a prosperous life. If a married lady dies with married status then they take new saree, blouse, flower, betel leaf, nut, plantain etc., offer it to her and give it to a brahmin priest's wife. Likewise if we take into account of all the death customs, we can point out the beliefs of the people in rural area.

Urban area people also do the death customs, but not with so much care for details. They also mourn for the dead person, do funeral rites etc. but with shortest period. They also give yearly tithi to the dead person according to their economic situation. Even though they do all the ceremonies of death, they do not do it properly, like the people in rural area. In urban areas, mostly people are living in congested area, and also they live in rented house. Only some are living in their own house. It is not possible for the urban area people, living in rented house to do all the death ceremonies. Even though they celebrate death custom, they do not give much importance to all the death ceremonies. Urban area people have no faith in ghosts, rebirth etc.

In rural area, they have faith in ghosts, in rebirth etc. and so they specially do each and every custom with much care and faith. On the "funeral rites" day they give cow, cloth etc. as alms to brahmin priest. This kind of action is said to help that dead person's soul in crossing a river viz., "Vaitharani" Similarly oil, mirror etc. also given as "alms" to a brahmin priest. This kind of action is considered to be favourable for the many passage of the soul over barren deserts and difficulties due to illusions. Giving cloth, bamboo stick, fans etc., at the time of funeral rites or on the day of "paal teli" are considered as capable of producing on departing souls, comforts skin to those derived while using them when alive. The souls of men who have reached a particular super-physical world after death to rise to higher worlds and the rites for the dead performed by the relatives lifts them up to those levels.

Urban area people also give certain kind of alms at the time of doing "funeral rites". But they are not very particular about this. Thus in every Folkloristic material we can find rural and urban area difference. Moreover, the influence of urban community people is found among certain rural area people. But regarding Folk-customs, urban influence is not found among rural area people. Rural area people following their own way of tradition, culture etc. without break, which are handed down from generation to generation, but urban people do not so.

Critical Analysis of Folk Customs : A Sociological Point of View

Every society is having its own way of celebrating functions, rituals and ceremonies, by following their tradition. They follow their tradition from their ancestor period itself. Folk-customs are also followed by every society by following their tradition. Present system of society is not able to follow their tradition fully but they follow the basic concepts of their tradition on their celebrations, functions, rituals and ceremonies. Is it possible for us to say that the folk customs are completely changed or completely vanished; No, certainly not. Still they are surviving in one or other form. It is celebrated by keeping basic traditional events in simple manner according to the time, place and economy.

All social group people celebrate the customs regarding birth, puberty, Sacred thread ceremony (pertaining to particular social groups), marriage customs, Sashtiyapthapurthi, Sadhabhishegam and death. Regarding birth at present period 95% of the child are born in hospitals. Natural birth is almost rare. In this aspect all social group people follow the same type of activities. There is no change. Just 5% of the child are born in natural context. The reason may be courage, good health and belief. Regarding the ceremonies of child birth, the ceremonies like cradling, naming, ear boring and hair removing are performed simply by following basic traditional concepts. Still all society people are having broad mind in giving feast on occasions to relatives and friends. Likewise, the guests are able to present presentations on the basis of their status. In this aspect of giving feast, no change is found. At present feast is arranged through hotels.

Regarding puberty ceremony lot of changes are seen. Present days science and education grow tremendously. So, the puberty ceremony celebrations are shrinked to one to two hours. Moreover, it is not celebrated in grand manner. Only few, still follow the grand manner celebration, they arranged the celebration in *Mandapa* like a marriage, invite close relatives and friends. Some rich people do this ceremony elaborately to show their status. Likewise, in interior villages they celebrate this ceremony in grand manner.

Likewise, sacred thread ceremony is celebrated by following the basic concepts of the traditional methods by those social group people who celebrated sacred thread ceremony. In present days, they invite close relatives for this functions. Time and economy are the basic factors for slight change in the celebrations.

Regarding marriage ceremony, all social group people give importance to the agreement of the horoscopes of the bride and bridegroom; still they are having strong belief in the agreement of the horoscopes. Tradition is followed almost by all the social groups in main events and concepts of marriage celebrations. Tying marriage badge in marriage celebrations is an important event. In present days, Register Marriage, Dynamic marriage systems are followed by few but 90% of the social group people, belief in God and Goddesses followed the traditional marriage celebrations. There may be slight changes but the basic concept of the marriage is still celebrated by all social group people.

Likewise importance is given to the first pregnancy by all social group people. Still they follow the traditional celebrations regarding first pregnancy of a women. Since it is important to keep the lady in happy mood this celebration is celebrated. This celebration consists of the basic Psychological concepts. People believe that the celebrations for the first pregnant lady gives happiness and the child will be born in fine manner.

Some social group people celebrated Sashtiyapthapurthi (60th or 61st birthday) and Sadhabhishegam (80th or 81st birthday) in the house following traditional concepts. Some celebrate it in the temple. Present trend is that all social group people celebrate this celebrations in Thirukkatayur Temple of Tamilnadu. According to the economic conditions it is celebrated in this temple in grand or simple manner.

Death customs are followed as per tradition by all social group people. Some people make it simple but many people follow the tradition. Still some people celebrate death customs in grand manner following their tradition. Some celebrate it for showing their status.

So, the customs of life cycle of a human depends upon the tradition and the society. They perform every custom depending upon their society pattern. We can conclude that 'society' is an important factor for the variations in celebrations and ceremonies of human life cycle.

Critical Analysis of Folk Customs : An Anthropological Point of View

Customs are the only, main source for understanding the unlettered, uncivilized peoples. Since they do not leave any biographies and written historical documents about them. So for knowing the culture of the unlettered people, customs acts as a bridge. No man is without habits, which leads to customs. Customs reflects the culture.

This book follows the functional method among various methods for studying the culture through marriage customs. This method is based on the assumption that every cultural element has a definite functional role. On the basis of this functional role the culture can be easily understood. According to the definition of Malinowski the different elements of culture are inter-related with each other. Each element satisfies human needs in a particular way. So to understand culture, it is better to study the function, which it performs.

Marriage customs are discussed through Anthropological point of view. Marriage is the centre point of every human life cycle. Mostly regular marriage pattern is 'Monogamy' type. According to the Hindu law 'one man is equal to one women' and so this is followed by all social group. This itself shows our culture. Likewise in a normal family husband and wife are having equal importance and equal rights. This pattern of marriage creates stability in the family. The laws regarding inheritance of the property is properly laid done though this kind of marriage pattern and the distribution of property is equal.

Culture is not a time bound aspect. It is always intertwined with the life of people. So, it is impossible to separate culture and people which is reflected through their customs. Customs may change due to different time, economic and social factor's but do not change from the basic concepts of tradition. So, we can define culture as a constant concept eventhough it depends on the customs, habits, beliefs etc. of the people which may be variables. Constant factor depends upon variables i.e., culture depends upon customs, habits and beliefs with the basic concepts of traditions.

Critical Analysis of Folk Customs Caste Variation

Tamilnadu is the treasure house of castes and its sub-groups. So, it is quite natural for differences among the customs between castes. Even among the same castes differences are found because of the sub-castes. Some customs resemble each other but the basic concepts of tradition is followed by each caste people. Since the basic concepts of tradition resembles in almost all criteria among the people resemblance is found in some customs. Likewise due to place, time and migration variation is found. Moreover, each caste people is having their own tradition from their ancestor's period and so the variation is unavoidable.

In each and every life cycle ceremony this variation is found. Regarding this concept time is not a factor for variation but the social change is the constant factor for the same.

Critical Analysis of Folk Customs-Regional Variation

Lands are classified according to its nature in Sankam poetry. People living in plains are having some tradition according to its nature. Likewise people of hilly region, people of ocean region, people of forest region, people of field region etc. were having their tradition on the basis of their native land. Nativity is a common concept which cannot be separated from each human being. Likewise the tradition of nativity is also followed by every human and so the regional variation is unavoidable. This variation is common to all life cycle ceremony. Eventhough the variations are common, they depend upon the basic concepts of tradition. So, tradition is a constant concept upon which the variations are taken place according to the caste, region etc.

Critical Analysis of Folk Customs : Rural Vs Urban Area Differences

Rural people still perform their customs following their tradition. They celebrate each and every event without fail. They are having strong belief in performing each and every event of their customs and habits. Also people believe that if an event is left then god will punish them. So, rural area people perform every custom perfectly. Urban area people also having belief in performing customs, but their environment is different from rural area. Present days urban area is congested; living places are small. It is difficult to celebrate each and every custom and events perfectly. So, customs are celebrated with important events only. But the customs are performed following the basic concepts of tradition. Eventhough these people are having faith and belief on God, there is no other way for them. That is why, they are celebrating only important events of a custom.

Moreover, the growth of education, scientific innovation and Globalization create some changes in the celebrations and so the difference is found between rural and urban areas. Time is also a factor for the change. At present, rural areas are also having some developments. But these developments never affect their customs and celebrations in any way. This is the established truth to be mentioned.

Conclusion

The origin of custom is obscure. Many customs arose to satisfy the fundamental needs of man especially those connected with his self-preservation, tendencies, procreation and the like. They are obeyed more spontaneously because they grow slowly. As long as customs spontaneously prevail, they are the strongest ties in building up a social order. All customs are not irrational.

When we look into the social role of customs, customs regulate social life. It is an important means of controlling social behaviour and its importance in society cannot be minimized. Customs preserves our culture and transmit it to the succeeding generations, bring people together and develop social relationships among them. Enemies are turned into friends by custom. It is needless to say that Hinduism is alive today because of customs. It would have died long ago if not the Hindus been forced to abide by customs.

Customs provide stability and a feeling of security in human society. The language which the child learns, the occupations with which he became familiarized, the forms of worship that he follows, the games which he plays all are offered to him through customs. Customs play an important part in personality building. From birth to death man is under the influence of customs. He is born out of marriage, a custom, he is brought up according to the customs and when he dies he is given last rites as laid down by customs. Customs mould his attitudes and ideas.

Customs are universal. There is no country or community wherein customs are not found. In India with the spread of western education the observance of customs has loosened, still the old woman folk of the country continue to observe them. It is thus evident that customs play a major part in regulating our social behaviour. They determine our culture, preserve it and transmit it from generation to generation. Customs exercise much a powerful hold over man that they can be called the "king of man". They are observed not simply because people's sentiments and feelings of personal obligation support them.

Custom is both treated as democratic and totalitarian at the some time. It is democratic because it is made by the group, everybody contributes to its growth. It is totalitarian because it effects every sphere of self-expression, private and public, it influences our thoughts, beliefs and manners. The authority of customs diminishes in complex society where impersonal relations largely replace personal contact and where individuals are removed from the direct control of the group as a whole.

Customs is enduring; custom is transmitted from generation to generation, and custom only is followed from time immemorial. Custom is spontaneous, grows in society by itself and followed as a matter of habit. Custom is followed by all the members of a community and this universal following creates social bonds between them. Custom is concerned with the initiate life and temperament of the group.

Thus, custom never vanishes as long as the human civilization continues. Each and every moment of a human life cycle is based on a custom. Without custom, nothing will happen in a human life cycle. So, custom and folks of a country are never separable from each other. From every point of view i.e., from sociological point of view, from Anthropological point of view etc., custom plays an important role in human life cycle. Thus custom will exist till the human civilization continue without any break.

Part-II
FOLK-CUSTOMS

6

Folk-Customs : Introduction

Date collection

For this project data have been collected from three districts viz., (1) South Arcot, (2) Tanjore, and (3) Coimbatore.

South Arcot

In South Arcot from three villages viz., (1) Valayamadevi, (2) Thiruvandipuram and (3) Udayarkudi data have been collected.

Valayamadevi

Valayamadevi is a village consisting of Total population 3492. Among 3492, male members are 1617 and female members are 1675. This village is divided into two parts viz. kiizh valayamadevi (the eastern part of the village) and meel valayamadevi (the western part of the village). It is not considered here and the collection has been made in both divisions. Total number of castes in this village is eighteen. This village is 25 km from Chidambaram, but it is considered under chidambaram taluk itself.

Mostly 70% of the people in this village are uneducated and only 20% of the people are educated upto High school level and 10% of the people are educated above high school level.

About the Informants

I have selected one informant in each caste. All the informants are above forty years except the one in Barber caste who is 27 years and Isai Velalar who is 30 years old. The materials are collected from both sex. Among the eighteen caste people there is only one family in Nadar caste. They are not available at the time of data collection. The particulars about the informants are given in the tabular column as follows.

Particulars about the informants

No.	Caste	Name	Sex	Age	Educa-tion	Native place	Present residence	Address	Other par. if any
1	2	3	4	5	6	7	8	9	10
1.	Brahmin (Iyer)	Mrs. K. Jayalakshmi	Female	45	Unedu-cated	Kanchipuram	Valayama-devi	Mrs. K. Jayalakshmi Kizh Valayamadevi Chidambaram taluk	
2.	Brahmin (Iyangar)	Mrs. kr. Lakshmi	Female	50	Unedu-dated	Arsonmangalam	Valayama-devi	Mrs. R. Lakshmi, Mel valayamadevi Chidambaram taluk	
3.	Pillai (Karkattar)	Mrs. Saraswati Mrs. Tiripuram	Female	42 60	unedu-cated	Paradur	Valayama-devi	Mrs. Saraswathi Kizh Valayamadevi Chidambaram taluk	
4.	Isai Velalar	Mrs. Sundaram bal	Female	30	educated up to high school level	Melakalattur near kumhahonam	Valayama-devi	Mrs. Sundarambal Kizh Valayamadevi Chidambaram taluk.	
5.	Patayacci (Vanniyarkula kshattriyas)	Mrs. P. Vairam	Female	43	educated upto High school	Iravankudi Jayankondam taluk	Valayama-devi	Mrs. P. Vairam Kizh Valayamadevi Chidambaram taluk	working as a secondary school teacher in vala-yamadevi

1	2	3	4	5	6	7	8	9	10
6.	Senkunta Mutaliyar	Mr. Cirrambala Mutaliyar Mrs. Ankmyiyammal	Male Female	64 50	uneducated	Vennanthur, Salam dist.	Valayamadevi	Mr. Cirrambala Mutaliyar Main Road, Valayamadevi Chidambaram taluk	—
7.	Viswakarma (Pattar-goldsmith)	Mrs. Asothai	Female	45	uneducated	Palayankottai (near chidam-(baram)	Valayamadevi	Mrs. Asothai Kizh Valayamadevi Chidambaram taluk.	— —
8.	Vysya Chettiyar	Mr. R. Vankatesan Chettiar	Male	42	educated upto High school level	Chidambaram	Valayamadevi	Mr. R. Venkatesan Chettiar Kizh Valayamadevi Chidamabaram taluk	speaks Telugu as well as Tamil. working as a school teacher in Valayamadevi
9.	Sozhiya Chettiar	Mrs. Cinnapponnu	Female	50	uneducated	Kurinjippadi	Valayamadevi	Mrs. Cinnappannu Kizh Valayamadevi Chidamabaram taluk	—
10.	Vaniya Chettiar	Mrs. Apurvam	Female	50	uneducated	Turinjimedu (CDM taluk)	Valayamadevi	Mrs. Apurvam Kizh Valayamadevi Chidambaram taluk	— —

1	2	3	4	5	6	7	8	9	10
11.	Devar	Mr. Chidambaram	Male	45	unedu-cated	Valayamadevi	Valayama-devi	Mr. Chidambaram Kizh Valayamadevi Chidambaram taluk	
12.	Vannan (Washerman)	Mr. R. Ramalin-gam	Male	40	unedu-cated	Valayamadevi	Valayama-devi	Mr. R. Ramalingam Kizh Valayamadevi Chidambaram taluk	—
13.	Navitar (Naruttuvar Barber)	Mr. N. Palani sami	Male	27	unedu-cated	Valayamadevi	Valayama-devi	Mr. N. Palanaisami Kizh Valayamadevi Chidamabaram tk.	—
14.	Konar (Yadh-avappillai)	Mrs. Kaliyanamma	Female	40	unedu-cated	Idayankudi-kadu, Mincurutti	Valayama-devi	Mrs. Kaliyamma Kizh Valayamadevi Chidamabaram tk.	— —
15.	Cakkili	Mr. Ramu	Male	55	educated upto high school	Valayamadevi	Valayama-devi	Mr. Ramu Kizh Valayamadevi Chidamabaram tk.	He is an Ex-ser-vice-man
16.	Kuravar (ramajoki)	Mrs. Kenna-mma	Female	57	educa-tion upto high school level	Kavaslkkudi (sethiya-tappu)	Valayama-devi	Mrs. Kannamma Kizh Valayamadevi Chidambaram tk.	These people are not "kura-vas" like "nari kurvas", but these

1	2	3	4	5	6	7	8	9	10
									people are named as 'kuravas' they mentioned their caste "Ramajoki"
17.	Adi Dravidar (Harijan)	Mr. Carkkarai Mrs. Cinnamma	Male Female	55 60	educated upto high school level	Valayamadevi	Valayamadevi	Mr. Carkkarai Kizh Valayamadevi Chidambaram tk.	—
18.	Nadar—Informants are not available in this village.								

Thiruvandipuram

This village is ten kilometres from Cuddalore. Totally this village is 50 km away from Chidambaram. This village consists of Total number of population 2715. Among 2715, male are 1369 and female are 1346. Nearly there are sixteen caste people in this village. In the census report of this village they divide the total population into three division viz., (1) Forward community, (2) Backward community and (3) Harijan. In the forward community there are 350 males and 320 females, in the backward community there are 1019 males and 1026 females and in the Harijan community there are 35 males and 36 females. About the informants all the details are given as follows in the tabular column.

About the Informants

S.No.	Caste	Name	Sex	Age	Education
1.	Brahmin (Iyer)	Mrs. N. Saroja	Female	40	S.S.L.C
2.	Brahmin (Iyangar)	P.T. Srinivasan	Male	48	VIth Std.
3.	Pillai (Tuluva Vellalar)	R. Ampuja valli & Her mother	Female	20 45	S.S.L.C.
4.	Pillai (Isai Velalar)	Mrs. Kannamma	Female	50	Nil
5.	Viswakarma Kammalar (Goldsmith)	Mrs. Lokanayaki	Female	66	VIth Std.
6.	Viswakarma (Asari-working by using stone)	Mr. M. Velayuta-Asari	Male	70	Nil
7.	Viswakarma (Asari-carpenter)	Mr. Sivalinga Asari	Male	62	Nil
8.	Chettiyar	Mr. Sambath	Male	45	VIII Std.

Native Place	*Present Residence*	*Address*	*Other Particulars if any*
Thiruvandipuram	Thiruvandipuram	Mrs. N. Saroja, 2/14 East car at, Thiruvan-dipuram, Cuddalore-2 Pincode-607401	—
Thiruvandipuram	Thiruvandipuram	Mr. P.T. Srinivasan, car street, Thirvandipuram, Cuddalore tk.	—
Thiruvandipuram	Thiruvandipuram	R. Apujavalli, 1.3. A, Thiruvandi-puram Cuddalore tk.	—
Therazhundur	Thiruvandipuram	Mrs. kannamma, Car street, Thiruvandipuram, Cuddalore tk.	—
Thiruvandipuram	Thiruvandipuram	Mrs. Lokanayaki, 102, Car. Street, Thiruvandipuram Cuddalore tk.	—
Thiruvandipuram	Thiruvandipuram	Mr. M. Velayuta Asari Car, Street, Thrivandipuram, Cuddalore tk.	—
Thiruvandipuram	Thiruvandipuram	Mr. Silvalinga Asari Car, St., Thrivandipuram Cuddalore tk.	—
Cuddalore	Thiruvandipuram	Mr. Sambath Chettiar Car, Street, Thiruvandipuram, Cuddalore tk.	—

S.No.	*Caste*	*Name*	*Sex*	*Age*	*Education*
9.	Chettiyar (Sozhiya)	Mr. P. Vairakkannu Chettiar	Male	64	VI Std.
10.	Mutaliyar	Mr. M. Jayaraman	Male	50	S.S.L.C.
11.	Reddiar	Mrs. V. Jayalakshmi	Female	70	Nil
12.	Jankamar (Devar)	Mrs. Krishnavani	Female	39	Nil
13.	Maruttuvar (Barber)	Mr. Marimuttu	Male	51	S.S.L.C.
14.	Eekali (Washerman)	Mr. Govindam Meastri	Male	70	Nil
15.	Patayacci	Mrs. Kamala	Female	60	S.S.L.C.
16.	Harijan	Mr. G. Dhanabal	Male	47	Nil

Native Place	*Present Residence*	*Address*	*Other Particulars if any*
East Marudur	Thiruvandipuram	Mr. P. Vairakkannu Chettiar Car Street, Thiruvandipuram Cuddalore tk.	—
Thiruvandipuram	Thiruvandipuram	M. Jayaraman, 4521, Middle Street, Thiruvandipuram 607401	—
Sinkili Koil	Thiruvandipuram	Mrs. V. Jayalakshmi, 2/6 Car Street, Thiruvandipuram	—
Kavarappattu (near Cuddalore)	Thiruvandipuram	Mrs. Krishnaveni, Middle Street, Thiruvandipuram	—
Cuddalore, O.T.	Thiruvandipuram	Mr. Marimuttu, 4/40 4th Street, Thiruvandipuram	—
Thiruvandipuram	Thiruvandipuram	Mr. C. Govindan Meastri, Veedam Garden St., Thiruvandipuram	—
Thiruvandipuram	Thiruvandipuram	Mrs. Kamala, Car Street, Thiruvandipuram	—
Oeeri (Thiruvandipuram)	Thiruvandipuram	Mr. G. Dhenabal, Dtteri, Thiruvandipuram, Cuddalore tk.	—

Udayarkudi

Udayarkudi is a village 25 kms from Chidambaram. Total population of Udayarkudi is 1273. Among 1273, male members are 676 and female members are 597. Total number of castes in this village is 17. This is a rural area consisting of 78% of uneducated people. 15% of the people are educated upto school level and 5% of the people are educated above school level. In this village also the total population is divided into three viz., (1) Forward community, (2) Backward community and (3) Harijan. In the forward community there are 4 males and 5 females, in the backward community there are 664 males and 589 females and in the Harijan community there are 6 males and 4 females. About the informants all the details are given in the tabular column as follows :

About the Informants

S.No.	*Caste*	*Name*	*Sex*	*Age*	*Education*
1.	Brahmin (Iyer)	T. Mangalam	Female	50	S.S.L.C.
2.	Pillai	G.K. Kalcitrasi	Female	29	VI Std.
3.	Patayacci	T. Sivagnanam	Male	60	Nil
4.	Viswakarma	T. Subramaniyam	Male	36	S.S.L.C.
5.	Viswakarma (Kammalar)	B. Kasturi	Female	33	3rd class
6.	Mutaliyar (Senguttar)	V. Muthukumaran	Male	46	P.U.C.
7.	Thondalman-dale Mutaliyar	A. Rajappan	Male	55	S.S.L.C.
8.	Tuluva Naickar	G. Duraisamy	Male	57	B. Lit.
9.	Reddiar	S. Baskaran	Male	33	P.U.C.

Native Place	*Present Residence*	*Address*	*Other Particulars if any*
Udayarkudi	Udayarkudi	T. Mangalam, 23, Thyagaraja Pillai St. Udayarkudi, K. Koil.	—
Thiruchinnopuram	Udayarkudi	C.K. Kalai Arasi, w/o G. Kalaiyamoorthy Pillai, thiruchinna-puram, Lalpet post.	—
Venkatesapuram	Udayarkudi	T. Sivagnanam, Puthu Street, Udayarkudi.	—
Kattumannarkoil	Udayarkudi	T. Subramaniam, 57, mele viti, Udayarkudi	—
Cuddalore	Udayarkudi	B. Kasturi, w/o Bangarusamy, Udayarkudi, Kattumanmar Koil	—
Udayarkudi	Udayarkudi	V. Muthukumaran, 32, North at, Udayarkudi Kattumannarkoil	—
Puthanari, (Tirunalvali dt.)	Udayarkudi	A. Rajappan, 42, North Street, Udayar-kudi, K. Koil (tk)	—
Kizhacharuval	Udayarkudi	D. Durasisamy, 23, West, Street, Udayar-kudi, K. Koil.	—
Kattumannarkoil	Udayarkudi	S. Baskaran, 14, Bajanai madattaru, Udayarkudi, K. Koil.	—

S.No.	*Caste*	*Name*	*Sex*	*Age*	*Education*
10.	Naidu	S. Savithri	Female	25	S.S.L.C.
11.	Nadar	S. Solamuttu Nadar	Male	74	3rd Std.
12.	Kellar (Devar)	P. Ramachandran	Male	39	M.R.M.Ed.
13.	Udoyar (Kulala)	D. Lakshmi	Female	35	S.S.L.C.
14.	Konar (Yadhavap pillai)	Kuppammal	Female	40	Nil
15.	Vannar	T. Masilamani	Male	50	8th Std.
16.	Maruttuvar (Barber)	M. Kuppusamy	Male	40	S.S.C., B.T.S. L.C. certificate in Phy. Edu-cation (Hr.)
17.	Harijan	H. Jayakumar	Male	30	M.A. B.Ed.

Native Place	*Present Residence*	*Address*	*Other Particulars if any*
Edamanal	Udayarkudi	S. Savithri, w/o M. Sugumarramanujam, Periyar Nagar, Udayarkudi, K.Koil.	—
Udayarkudi	Udayarkudi	S. Solamuthunadar, 4, new North Street, Udayarkudi, K.Koil.	—
Madurai	Udayarkudi	P. Ramachandran, 11, danakkara Stret, Udayarkudi, K. Koil.	—
Udayarkudi	Udayarkudi	D. Lakshmi, No. 6, Kulala Street, Udyarkudi, K. Koil	—
Udayarkudi	Udayarkudi	Kuppammal, Periyarnagar Udayarkudi.	—
Kandamangalam	Udayarkudi	T. Masilsmani, Venkateswara Dry Cleaners Udayarkudi.	—
Kalavellore, Tiruppuvanam Ramnad dist.	Udayarkudi	M. Kuppusamy, PRG Higher Secondary School Udayarkudi, K. Koil.	—
Tharapuram	Udayarkudi	N. Jayakumar, Tanakkars Street, Udayak-kudi, K. Koil.	—

Tanjore District

In Tanjore district from four villages viz. (1) Thalachankadu, (2) Kurankuputtur, (3) Malapperumpallam (Karaimadu) and (4) Karuvizhantanatapuram data for the analysis have been collected.

Thalachankadu

This village consists of Total population 1960. Among 1960, male members are 1010 and female members are 950. Total number of castes in this village is thirteen. This village is 45 km from Chidambaram and is in Trabanquer Taluk. All the informants are uneducated in this village. Mostly 90% of the people in the village are uneducated. Only 10% of the people are educated upto High school or above level. The other informations regarding the informants are given in the tabular column as follows :

All the informants are above 30 years and below 80 years. Materials are collected from both sex.

Details about the informants

S. No.	*Caste*	*Name*	*Sex*	*Age*	*Edu-cation*	*Native Place*
1.	Brahmin (Iyer)	Mrs. Nilambal	Female	60	Nil	Thalachankadu
2.	Brahmin (Iyangar)	G. Ranganatha Iyangar	Male	50	Nil	Thalachankadu
3.	Pillai (Karkarttar)	Mrs. Saraswathi	Female	40	Nil	Raadambur
4.	Patayacci	Mrs. Gouriyamma	Female	45	Nil	Kavaripum-pattinam
5.	Naidu	Mrs. Govindammal	Female	45	Nil	Rajamannarkudi
6.	Nayakkar (Canar)	Mrs. Joti	Female	22	Nil	Peruntottam
7.	Vaniya Chettiyar	Mrs. Pattammal	Female	40	Nil	Thirucirram-balam
8.	Viswakarma (Asari-Carpenter)	Mrs. Mankalam	Female	70	Nil	Thalachankadu
9.	Viswakarma (Pattar-Goldsmith)	Mrs. Soundram	Female	45	Nil	Tiripuvanam
10.	Muppanar	Mrs. Chellamma	Female	45	Nil	Mayiladuturai
11.	Vannar	Mrs. Cinnamma	Female	50	Nil	Katiramangalam
12.	Navitar	Mrs. Navaniitham	Female	45	Nil	Ayappadi (near Poraiyar)
13.	Harijan	Mrs. Ratnampa	Female	56	Nil	Velanagar

Present Residence	*Address*	*Other Particulars if any*
Thalachankadu	Mrs. Nilambal, Thalachankadu, Thanjore Dt.	—
Thalachankadu	G. Ranganata Iyangar, Pandaravaadai St. Thalachankadu P.D. Tanjore dt.	—
Thalachankadu	Mrs. Saraswathi, Vellalar St. Thalachangadu P.D. Tanjore dit.	—
Thalachankadu	Mrs. Gouriyamma, West St., Thalachankadu P.O. Tanjore Dt.	—
Thalachandkadu	Mrs. Govindammal, West St., Thalachankadu P.O., Tanjore Dt.	—
Thalachankadu	Mrs. N. Joti, Mill St., Thalachankadu P.O. Tanjore Dt.	—
Thalachankadu	Mrs. Pattammal, Kile viti, Thalachankadu P.O., Tanjore Dt.	—
Thalachankadu	Mrs. Mankalam, Pandaravadai St. Thalachankadu P.O., Tanjore Dt.	—
Thalachankadu	Mrs. Soundaram, Thalachankadu P.O., Tanjore Dt.	—
Thalachankadu	Hrs. Cellamme, Thirumanjana viti, Thalachankadu P.O., Tanjore Dt.	—
Thalachandadu	Mrs. Cinnamma, Thalachankadu P.O., Tanjore Dist.	—
Thalachankadu	Mrs. Navaniitham, Kilattaru, Thalachankadu P.O., Tanjore Dist.	—
Thalachankadu	Mrs. Ratnampa Thalachankadu P.O. Tanjore Dist.	—

Kurankuputtur

This village consisting of Total population 873. Among 873, Male members are 460 and female members are 413. Total number of castes in this village is nine. This village is 46 km away from Chidambaram and is also considered to be in Trabanquar Taluk. All the informants in this village are also uneducated. 95% of this village are also uneducated and only 5% of the people are educated. Details about the informants are given in a tabular column as follows :

Details about the informants

S. No.	*Caste*	*Name*	*Sex*	*Age*	*Edu-cation*	*Native Place*
1.	Brahmin (Iyer)	Mr. Ramachandran	Male	50	Nil	Kurankuputtur
2.	Pillai (Karkattar)	M. Radhakrishnan	Male	42	Nil	Thalachankadu
3.	Patayacci	Mr. Kaliyaperumal	Male	55	Nil	Kurankuputtur
4.	Nayakkar (Canar)	Mr. S. Samikannu	Male	52	Nil	Narimedu
5.	Nayakkar	Mrs. Bhavani	Female	35	Nil	Sattenur
6.	Vaniya Chettiyar	Mr. P. Arikrishnan	Male	45	Nil	Kurankuputtur
7.	Devar	Mrs. Amudam	Female	45	Nil	Kurankuputtur
8.	Vannar	Mr. Rajendran	Male	48	Nil	Kurankuputtur
9.	Harijan	Mr. Uttirapati	Male	35	Nil	Kurankuputtur

Present Residence	*Address*	*Other Particulars if any*
Kurankuputtur	Mr. Ramachandran, Kurunkuputtur, Thalachankadu, P.O. Tanjore Dt.	—
Kurankuputtur	M. Radhakrishnan, Vellala Street, Kurankuputtur, Thalachankadu, P.O. Tanjore Dt.	—
Kurankuputtur	Mr. Kaliyaperumal, Main Road, Kurankuputtur, Thalachankadu, Tanjore Dt.	—
Kurankuputtur	Mr. S. Samikannu, Main Road, Kurankuputtur, Thalachankadu, P.O. Tanjore Dt.	—
Kurankuputtur	Mrs. Bhavani, Kurankuputtur, Thalachankadu, P.O. Tanjore Dt.	—
Kurankuputtur	Mr. P. Arikrishna, Main Road, Kurankuputtur, Thalachankadu, P.O. Tanjore Dt.	—
Kurankuputtur	Mrs. Amudham, Kurankuputtur Thalachankadu, P.O. Tanjore Dt.	—
Kurankuputtur	Mr. Rajendran, Milattaru, Kurankuputtur, Thalachankadu, P.O. Tanjore dt.	—
Kurankuputtur	Mr. Uttirapati Kurankuputtur, Thalachankadu P.O. Tanjore Dt.	Mr. Uttirapati sings folksongs (all type of songs) very well and his songs were recorded during my visit

Melapperumpallam (Karaimadu)

Melapperumpallam (Karaimadu) is a village of total population 1328, Male members are 648 and female members are 660. This village is situated in between Thalachankadu and Kurankuputtur. Total number of castes in this village is 5. Mostly 95% of this village people are uneducated. Either from Thalachankadu or from Kurankuputtur we can reach this place which is two to three kilometers away from these village. Details about the informants are given in tabular column as follows :

S. No.	*Caste*	*Name*	*Sex*	*Age*	*Educ-ation*	*Native Place*	*Present Residence*	*Address*
1.	Patayacci	Mrs. Kiliya-mma	Female	42	Nil	Karaie-du	Kari amadu	Mrs. Kili-yamma karaimedu Mela Str. melapperu-mnpallam, Tranqubar tk.
2.	Nayakkar	P. Mamickam	Male	40	Nil	"	"	P. Manickam Nayakkar st. Karatimadu Melapperu-mpallam
3.	Viswa-karma (Pattar)	S. Algarsmy	Male	58	Nil	"	"	S. Algarsamy Karaimedu Mele st. Mele Perum-pallam
4.	Udayar	Mr. Govind-araj	Male	47	Nil	"	"	Mr.Govindaraj Nayakkar st. Melap-parum-pallam Tranquba tk.
5.	Harijan	M. Kaliya-moorthy	male	45	Nil	"	"	R. Kaliya-moorthy Colony, Melap-perum-pallam P.O. Tranqulbar tk.

Karuvizhantanatapuram (Cavadi)

Total population of this village is 1757, Male members are 906 and female members are 851. Total number of castes in this village is 12. This is 42 km from Chidambaram and is also in Trabanquar Taluk. We have to cross this village to reach Thalachankadu or Kurankuputtur. This village is also a rural area. 60% of the people are uneducated, 10% of the people upto school level and 5% of the people above school level are educated. Details about the informants are given in the tabular column as follows :

Details about the informants

No.	Caste	Name	Sex	Age	Education	Native Place
1.	Brahmin (Iyer)	Mr. Parthasarati	Male	65	School level	Karuvizhantanta-puram
2.	Isai Velalar	Mrs. Taiyalnayaki	Female	45	unedu-cated	Parambur
3.	Patayacci	Mr. S. Ganesan	Male	46	Nil	Karuvizhantanta puram
4.	Naidu	Mr. Rangarajulu Naidu	Male	56	Nil	Nataraja Pillai savadi
5.	Nayakkar (Tatar)	Mr. Akara Nayakkar	Male	65	Nil	Nataraja Pillai savadi
6.	Vaniya Chettiyar	Mr. Rajakannu Chettiyar	Male	58	Nil	Kurankuputtur
7.	Viswakarma (Acari-carpenter)	Mr. Kuppusamy Asari	Male	60	Nil	Karuvizhantanata puram
8.	Mutaliyar (Senguntar)	Mrs. Kosalai	Female	50	Nil	Karuvizhantanata-puram
9.	Vannar	Mr. Kunju	Male	56	Nil	Karuvizhantanata-puram
10.	Navitar	Mr. Ranganatan	Male	50	Nil	Cankiruppu
11.	Udayar	Mr. Koluntamma	Female	60	Nil	Panankattankudi
12.	Harijan	Mr. Nagappan	Male	60	Nil	Karuvizhantanata-puram

Present Residence	*Address*	*Other Particulars if any*
Karuvizhantanatapuram	Mr. Parthasarati, North st., Thalachankadu P.O. Tanjore St.	Nil
Karuvizhantanatapuram	Mrs. Taiyalnayaki, 183, West St. Karuvizhantanatapuram Thalachankadu P.O. Tanjore Dt.	Nil
Karuvizhantanatapuram	Mr. S. Ganesan, North Street, Karuvizhantanatapuram, Thalachankadu P.O. Tanjore Dt.	Nil
Karuvizhantanatapuram	Mr. Rangarajulu Naidu, Main Road, Cavadi, Karuvizhantana-tapuram, Tanjore Dt.	Nil
Karuvizhantanatapuram	Mr. Akora Nayakkar, Main Road, Cavadi, Karuvizhantanatapuram Tanjore Dt.	Nil
Karuvizhantanatapuram	Mr. Rajakannu Chettiyar, Main Road, Cavadi, Karuvizhantana-puram, Tanjore Dt.	Nil
Karuvizhantanatapuram	Mr. Kuppusamy Asari, Mutaliyar St., Karuvizhantanatapuram, Thalachankadu P.O. Tanjore Dt.	Nil
Karuvizhantanatapuram	Mrs. Kosalai, Karuvizhantanat-puram, Thalachankadu P.O. Tanjore Dt.	Nil
Karuvizhantanatapuram	Mr. Kunju, Main Road, Karuvizhantanatapuram, Cavadi, Tanjore Dt.	Nil
Karuvizhantanatapuram	Mr. Ranganatan, Cankiruppu St. Cavadi P.O., Thalachankadu Tanjore Dist.	Nil
Karuvizhantanatapuram	Mrs. Koluntamma, 4/37, Karuvizhantapatapuram, Thalachankadu, Tanjore Dt.	Nil
Karuvizhantanatapuram	Mr. Nagappan, Karuvizhantana-tapuram, Thalachankadu, P.O. Tanjore Dt.	Nil

Coimbatore District

In Coimbatore District from three villages viz., (1) Madampatti, (2) Kalapatti and (3) Thondamuttur Data are collected.

Madampatti

This village is 10 km away from Coimbatore. Total population of this village is 6697. Among 6697, males are 3270 and females are 3427. Total number of caste people is 7. Among 10 castes only 5 castes people respond for the questions and so data are collected from 6 caste people. In some caste two informants are selected for material collection. The village is a rural area, and consists of mostly uneducated people. The details about the informants are mentioned in the tabular column.

Details about the informants

S. No.	Caste	Name	Sex	Age	Education	Native place	Present	Address	Other Particulars if any
1.	Kongu Vellalar	Puvattal	Female	39	Nil	Andipalayam	Madampatti	Puvattal, c/o Murugosami Kavundar, pudev road tottam, Madampatti, P.O Coimbatore-10.	Nil
2.	Nadar	Kaliyammal	Female	45	Nil	Sundappalayam	Madampatti	Kaliyammal, c/o the above address	Nil
		Pappal	Female	60	Nil	Kunnattur	Madampatti	Pappal, c/o Karuppanna Nadar, Putur road Madampatti P.O., Coimbatore-10.	
3.	Kavundar	Velattal	Female	50	Nil	Chettiappalayam	Madampatti	Velattal, c/o Murugasamy Kavundar, Pudu road tottam, Madampatti (P.O.) Coimbatore-10	Nil
4.	Vannan	Naccal	Female	70	Nil	Challappa	Madampatti	Naccal, Palani c/o Murugasami Kavundar, Pudur road tottam, Madampatti, P.O. Coimbatore-10.	
		Palani	Male	30	Nil	Challappa	Madampatti		
5.	Harijan	Marudal	Female	50	Nil	Pudur	Madampatti	Marudal, Palanal, Mayandi, Kasa c/o Murugasamiktottam, Madampatti P.O. Coimbatore-10	Nil
		Palanal	Female	50	Nil	Madampatti	Madampatti		
		Mayandi	Male	49	Nil	Madurai	Madampatti		
		Kasa	Female	45	Nil	Nilakkottai	Madampatti		

Kalapatti

Total population of this village is 4761. Among 4761, male are 2296 and female are 2465. This is 12 km away from Coimbatore. Totally 14-caste people are there is this village. Among the fourteen caste people only 7 caste people respond for the questions. This area contains 95% of uneducated people and 15% of the people educated upto a certain level. In some castes more than one informant is selected for material collection. The details about the informants are given in the tabular column.

Details about the informants

S. No.	Caste	Name	Sex	Age	Education	Native Place	Present Residence	Address	Other Particulars if any
1.	Pillai	Mrs. Hamsabai	Female	47	Higher grade teacher	Madurai	Kalapatti	Mrs. Hamsa Bai, Thilakar St. Kalapatti Coimbatore-641061	Nil
2.	Sozhiya Vellalar	Dulasiyammal	Female	43	Nil	Kalapatti	Kalapatti	Dulasiyammal, 8/9, Thuluvar Street, Coimbatore-61	Nil
3.	Kongu Vellalar	Palaniyammal	Female	45	Nil	Kalapatti	Kalapatti	Palaniyammal, 3/9, Thilaher Street, Kalapatti P.O., Coimbatoare-61,	Nil
		Mrs. Lakshmi	Female	48	Nil	Kalapatti	Kalapatti	Mrs. Lakshmi, 9/9 Thilakar St. Kalapatti P.O. Coimbatore-61	
4.	Naidu	D. Uma	Female	23	P.U.C.	Coimbatore	Kalapatti	D. Uma, 15/11, Pilliyarkovil St. Kalapatti, Coimbatore	Nil
		Mrs. Sulochana	Female	30	S.S.L.C.	Kalapatti	Kalapatti	Mrs. Sulochana, 13/118, Pillaiyar Koil street, Kalapatti, Coimbatore.	

S. No.	Caste	Name	Sex	Age	Education	Native Place	Present Residence	Address	Other Particulars if any
5.	Mutaliyar	Mrs. Ponnammal	Female	45	Nil	Kalapatti	Kalapatti	Mrs. Ponnammal, w/o Maruthasala Mutaliyar, Karthikeya minning factory, Kalapatti Coimbatore-61.	Nil
		Mrs. Palaniyammal	Female	40	Nil	Kalapatti	Kalapatti	Mrs. Palaniyammal, w/o Palanlyappan, kattur, Kalapatti P.O., Coimabtore.	
6.	Harijan	Kuppamma	Female	40	Nil	Kalapatti	Kalapatti	Kuppamma, Kalapatti, Coimbatore.	Nil
		Mrs. Thulasi	Female	30	Nil	Kalapatti	Kalapatti	Mrs. Thulasi, w/o Rangan, Kalapatti, Coimbatore-61	

Thondamuttur Village

Total population of this village is 8570. Among 8570, males are 4500 and females are 4070. This is 16km away from Coimbatore. Totally 10 castes are there in this village. Among the 10 caste people only 5 caste people respond for the questions. This area contains 95% of uneducated people and 5% of the people educated upto certain level. In some castes more than one informant is selected for material collection. The details about the informants are given in the tabular column.

Details about the informants

S. No.	Caste	Name	Sex	Age	Education	Native Place	Present Residence	Address	Other Particulars if any
1.	Naidu	Rajalakshmi	Female	40	6th Std.	Muthupalayam	Thondamuttur	Rajalakshmi, Muttirapalayam, Thondamuttur Coimbatore.	Nil
		Meenakshi	Female	44	Nil	Thondamuttur	Thondamuttur	Meenakshi, Thondamuttur, Coimbatore.	Nil
2.	Kavundar	Ponnammal	Female	35	Nil	Thondamuttur	Thondamuttur	Ponnammal, Thondamuttur, Coimbatore.	Nil
		Rajammal	Female	54	Nil	Madampatti	Thondamuttur	Rajammal, Thondamuttur Coimbatore.	Nil
3.	Kavutar	Ponnattal	Female	45	Nil	Kombanur	Thondamuttur	Not mentioned	Nil
		Arukkani	Female	20	Nil	Kombanur	Thondamuttur	Arukkani, Thondamuttur Coimbatore.	Nil
4.	Kurumba Kavutar	Mayilattal	Female	35	know to read & write	Thondamuttur	Thondamuttur	Mayilattal, Thondamuttur, Coimbatore.	Nil
		Karuppattal	Female	40	Nil	Thondamuttur	Thondamuttur	Karuppattal, Thondamuttur, Coimbatore.	Nil
5.	Harijan	Marattal	Female	60	Nil	Thondamuttur	Thondamuttur	Marattal, Thondamuttur, Coimbatore.	Nil
		Palaniyammal	Female	65	Nil	Thondamuttur	Thondamuttur	Palaniyammal, muttur, Coimbatore.	Nil

In this part some of the collected songs (not all the songs, to reduce the page limit) during my data collection are given in phonemic transcription. Also a sample of questionnaire is given (which is translated into English, but is used in Tamil for the purpose of data collection). While collecting materials from more or less 30 castes the materials are collected. But I have delimited the number of castes into 30. I have not mentioned the customs of Sozhiya Vellalar, Kongu Vellalar, Kavundar, Kavundar, Kurumba Kavutar and Parvata Rajakulam (Meenavar-Fisherman) caste people.

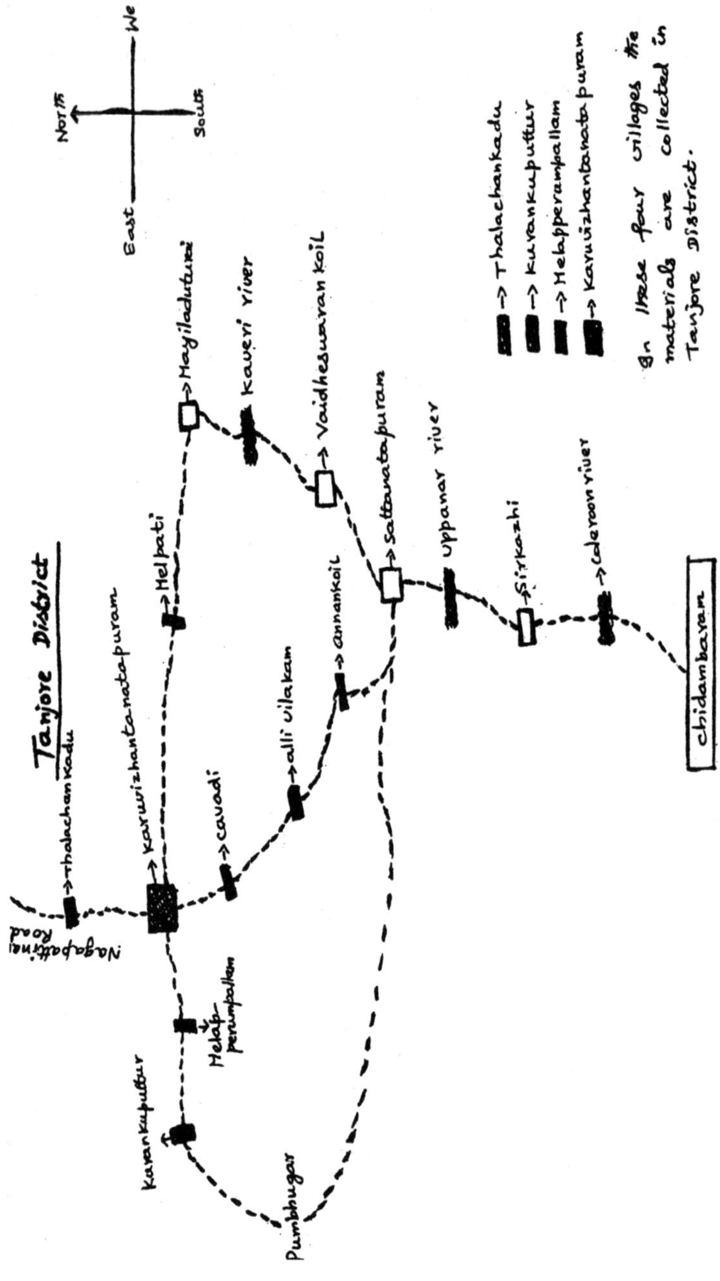

North
South
East
We
Tanjore District
Nagapattinai Road
Thalachankadu
Karuvizhantanatapuram
Helpati
Mayiladuturai
Kaveri river
Vaidhesuaran koil
Sattanatapuram
Uppanar river
Sirkazhi
Coleroon river
Chidambaram
annankoil
alli vilakam
cavadi
Mehap perumpallam
Karankuputtur
Pumbhugar
Thalachankadu
Kuvankuputtur
Mehapperampallam
Karuvizhantanatapuram
In these four villages the materials are collected in Tanjore District.

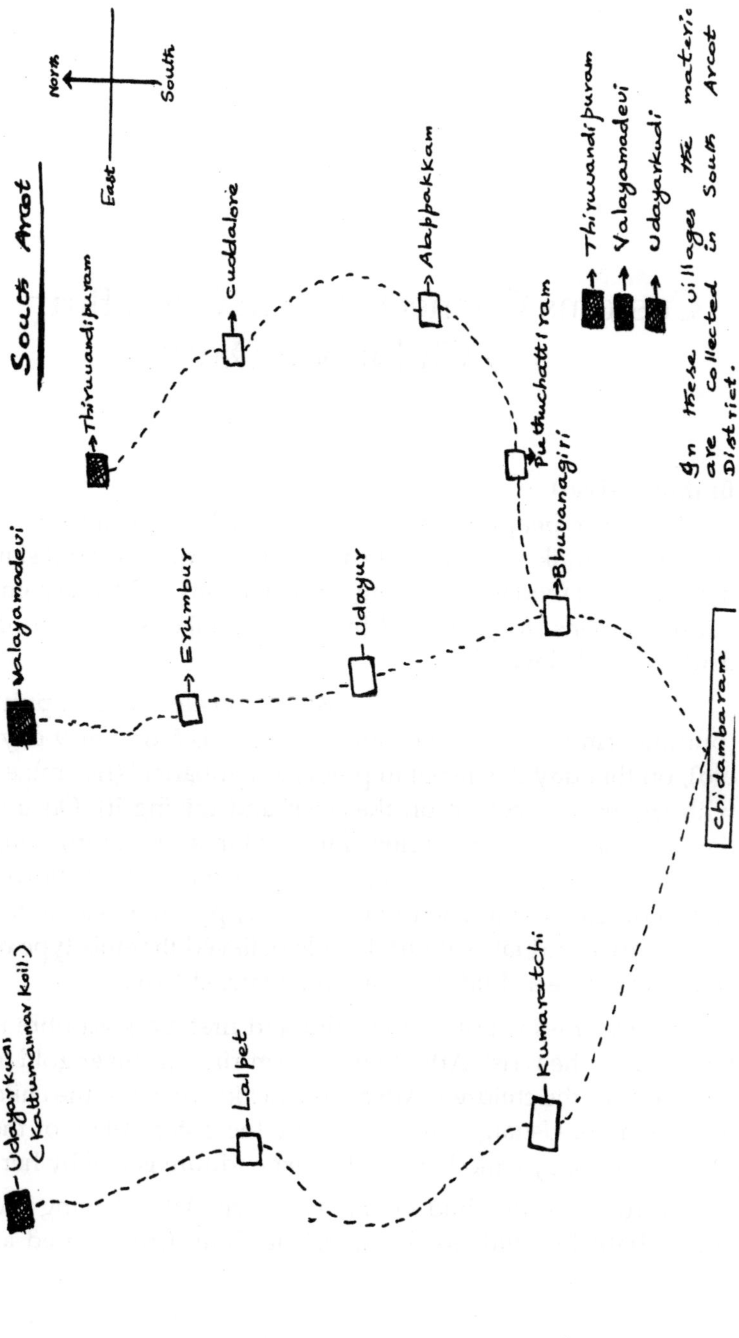
South Arcot
North
South
East
Thiruvandipuram
Cuddalore
Abppakkam
Puthuchattiram
Bhuvanagiri
Valayamadevi
Erumbur
Udayur
Chidambaram
Udayarkudi
(Kattumannar koil)
Lalpet
Kumaratchi
Thiruvandipuram
Valayamadevi
Udayarkudi
In these villages the materi
are collected in South Arcot
District.

7

Customs Connected with Child Birth and Childhood Days

Brahmin (Iyer)

This caste people give bath to the newly born child. They administer donkey's milk to the newly born child to avoid skin diseases. Diet food is given from 5th to 30th days and it contains various greens, food cooked in steem, brinjal, snake gourd, drumsticks, beans etc.

On 7th or 9th day it is a custom to celebrate "kappu" (putting arm-rings to the children when it is 5 or 7 or 9 days old), on that day it is usual to prepare "kapparici" (rice mixed with jaggery, placing it on the oven and mixing it). On this day, First they clean the roller (kuzhavi) in a pair of grinding stones and put sandal paste, turmeric powder, *kumkum*, flower and a new cloth on it. Then a married lady puts the roller in the cradle thrice and takes it out. People believed that this type of action will give a child to a childless married lady.

A new dress is put on the child and first margosa fibre is tied around the wrist. After that put arm-rings in silver gold in the hands of the children. After this function they put the child in the cradle. Usually, this is done by the sister-in-law of the newly born baby's mother and the expenditure is met by her.

On 10th day, the child's father is invited. After shaving and taking bath he kindless the sacrificial holy fire (termed as

"Diitchai valarttal") and take food with "vata" and *paayasam* (a sweet dish). On 11th day they celebrate a ceremony to remove the ceremonial impurities due to the birth of a child (termed as "*punniyadanam*") etc. ("*punniyadanam*" sacred gifts made to brahmans or others on special occasions, i.e. meritorious alms being bestowed on special occasions as at birth of a child. On this day Brahmin priest (sasstrikal) comes and recites, a section of the *Vedas* including prayers and hymns and kindless the sacred fire). This function is done for the purpose of "saanṭhi kazhittal-tittu kazhittal" (to remove ceremonial impurities from ceremonic, child birth etc.). They buy new clothes to the child and its parents for this occasion.

On the 3rd month after the child's birth it is a custom to buy new clothes, big type of brass pot (tavalai), another type of small size brass or silver pot (kutam) and all the other type of presents (siirvarisai-presentations) to the child's mother. Then her parents arrange a grand party to her, her husband and his family members and send her to her husband's house.

On the first date (star) of birth of the child, it is a custom to perform "Aayishoman". This is done to prolong the life of the child. On the day, they bore the ear of the child and shave it's hair. This has to be done compulsorily on the first birthday of the child. Only after this, they take the child out of the house, first to the temple. Only after this, they send the child to other places.

When a child finishes it's fifth year, they admit the child to the school. At that time child's parents give presents to the teacher according to their economic status. When the child is admitted in a school it is a custom to prepare rice mixed with jaggery and take it to the school, along with betel leaf, nut, plantain, camphor etc. There they offer worship to God in the school. They also bring paddy-full of corn-measure (marakkaal) to the school and give a turmeric root (manjal kompu) in the hands of the child. Then they hold the hands of the child and make it write first in the paddy by means of turmeric root.

Brahmin (Iyangar)

This people give bath to the newly born baby immediately after it's birth and they administer donkey's milk to the child to avoid skin diseases. They give diet food from 2nd to 41 days and it contains brinjal, ladies finger etc.

On 11th day after child's birth these people celebrate three functions on the same day viz., (1) punniyadanam, (2) naming ceremony (3) kaappitudal. "Punniyadanam" is done like the above caste people. On that day evening they celebrate "naming ceremony" on that occasion they write few names on the paddy and put black (or) red thread across the paddy, place the child on the thread in the direction east to west, and tie the thread in it's waist. After that, the child's mother whispers the child's father's name (i.e. her husband's name) in the years of the child and take the child from the paddy. At that time they place *kumkum* (or) collyrium on the forehead of the child.

On the same day child's aunt puts the arm-rings to the child. First she puts margosa fibre round the wrist of the child, then silver arm rings and *maravattai kappu* (made of a mixture of iron, copper and silver metels) and also the anklet around the leg (near the leg palm). On this day it is a "must" to buy *dhoti,* some golden ornaments to the child's father.

On this day itself they celebrate *"virai daanam"* (giving various kind of seeds etc. to some brahmins)—a ceremony celebrated, in the child's father's house people who are to meet the expenditure for this function. On this day they give paddy, betel leaf, nut, plantain, fruits, twenty five or fifty paise coin to some brahmins as alms. At the time of presenting these things, the brahmins who get the alms have to spread the *dhoti* tied around their waist and the child's father has to put these alms in the *dhoti*. These alms are compulsorily first put in a corner after the brahmins went to their houses. When the mother of the child is sent to her house on 5th or 7th or 9th month with the child, it is usual to prepare a sweet, another tiffen which is saltish. They have to buy a silver shell and a milk ladle, silver tumbler, a vessel for keeping the milk, saree for the child's mother etc. Then they give these things to the child's mother etc. Then they give these things to the child's mother and then only they send her to her husband's house with her child. The customs like "Aayishoman", "Ear boring" ceremony etc. resemble the above caste people. Removing hair of the child is not compulsory, but they do it if there is any supplication to the God like giving the hair of the child to the God. As in brahmin (iyer) caste people the child has to sit in it's uncle's lap and goldsmith bores the ear and puts a golden wire immediately in the ear. They invite relatives for this occasion and arrange a grand feast to them. Child's mother's parents have to spend money and buy *dhoti* etc. to the child's father, saree etc. for the mother, a bowl for giving food to the child, betel leaf, nut, a big plate, another big plate full of sugar, the golden wire for the ear of the child etc. On that day in bridegroom's house they has to give a grand dinner.

At the age of 5, the child is admitted in the school. At that time they take new dresses, slate, book etc. for the child and they give money to the teacher according to their economic status.

Pillai

This caste people give bath to the newly born baby. After giving bath they put the child in a leaf viz. "murukam leaf" to avoid skin diseases. For the same reason they administer donkey's milk to the child. Diet food is given to the mother from 3rd to 7th day once a day and from 7th to 15 days twice a day. This diet food includes dried food stuff (vattal), garlic (puundu), chilly etc. which are ground and a number is prepared and this is given to the mother of the newly born baby. They also give betel leaf's water with korajan to the child.

As in Brahmin caste, this caste people also celebrate "kappu" to the child on 7th day after the child's birth. On that day first margosa fibre is tied around the child's wrist. These people insert margosa leaves in front of the pial and fix a margosa stick in front of the pial, where the child is born.

(belief—*This custom is in vogue because it is a belief that ghost won't enter and take out the child from that place when there is margosa leaves, stick* etc.) On that day, Meals are cooked with seven green leaves and given it to the child's mother. An old married lady mixes 9 varieties of grain in the cowdung and places it on the wall.

On the 15th day after the child's birth "punniyadanam" is done. If the first baby is a male then it is in custom to give "virai daanam" as in the iyangar caste. On that day new dresses are put on the child and the child is placed in a big plate and pen, notebook etc. are kept by the side of the child. Then they invite a brahmin and give him sugar, plantain, fruits, paddy, grains, coins etc. and similar gifts are given to four other persons. On that day they invite relatives and a grand feast is arranged for them. On that day itself these people put arm-rings and at that time they tie the fibre of the white coarse plant (vallerukku naar) around the waist. They put the golden arm rings for the hand, silver rings for the leg, tie the gold or silver rope chain around the waist (*Belief : The white coarse plant is tied around the waist since it is a belief that the blemishes will not affect the body of the child).*

When celebrating the ceremony "putting arm rings" there is an important function celebrated by this caste people. It is in custom to give offerings to Goddess Mariyamman on that day. They place "kalasas" before Goddess Mariyamman, pour water inside it and place Margosa leaves in the kalasam. They offer a mixture of rice and jaggery at that time. When offerings are given to Goddess Mariyamman, they tie a yellow string with a piece of turmeric root to the mother and the child. Also on that day, they prepare an edible viz. "kaayappiti"—which is made by mixing and powdering the gingely seeds and jaggery and this powder is given a round shape by pressing it in the hands.

It is a custom to bore the ear and remove the hair of the child on the date of the birth star in the first year. They make a golden ear-ring. When boring the ear the child is to sit in it's uncle's lap and the goldsmith bores the ear. For this ceremony, a new dress is to be bought for the uncle. On that day rice with jaggery is mixed and a brahmin priest comes and kindles the holy fire. A new dress is worn to the children on that day. Relatives attend the function and a grand feast is arranged for them. That day itself they celebrate "naming ceremony" (If someone has a supplication to their family God they will do the "naming ceremony" accordingly). In the fifth year, the child is admitted to the school and according to their economic status, presentations are given to the teacher in the school.

Isai Velalar (Pillai)

When a child is born, immediately they give both to the child. As soon as the child is born they give European saffron, garlic and a medicine prepared in the house to the mother. They give diet food from 3rd to 7th day and this diet food contains garlic, brinjal and fish. "Korajanai' with betel leaf water is given to the child. They give oil bath to the child on 3rd, 5th and 7th day. On 16th day they celebrate "kappu". On that day they tie (1) silver anklet, maravattai kappu (five metal mixed ring) etc. for the leg; (2) odd number of small black beadstring bangles, vasampu (a corus calamus) tied in a thread golden arm-ring for the hands; (3) small white beads stringed chain for the neck; and (4) white coarse fibre for the waist. They take new dresses to the child on that day. Child's uncle gives presentations according to their economic situation (presentations like money, vessel, ornaments etc.). Only on that day the child's mother has to be given full bath and she is decorated and she wears marriage saree (or) new saree and the others place *tilak* on her forehead for the first time after the child's birth. On the date of birth star of the child the ear boring, and removing hair is to be done compulsorily. During the ear boring ceremony, the child is to sit in it's uncle's lap. On this day the presentation are brought from uncle's and aunt's house. They, in return, give presentations, from the child's house.

When the child completes five years, it is admitted to the school and according to their economic situation, they give presentations to the teacher. These people also follow the customs of the Patayacci caste people viz., they take betel leaf, nut, plantain, camphor, turmeric root and the rice and jaggery mixture and offer it to God.

Patayacci

These people give bath one hour after the child birth. If the child is affected by a skin disease viz. "karappaan", then they put the child on the 'came' (caladium nymphs sifolium) leaf. Otherwise they put the child in the floor itself. These people give donkey's milk to the child to avoid skin diseases. Immediately after birth these people give first cold water to the mother, then European Saffron (kumkumappu) and betel leaf and then they grind and give garlic. These people give diet food to the mother only from 3rd day to 15th day on odd numbered days. It consists of "poriccakkuzhampu" and "cooked rice". In this they put dried food stuff, garlic, the unripe fruit of horse-radish tree. They give betel leaf and some kind of oil and European Saffron to the child.

On 9th day they put "kappu" to the child. On that day they tie (1) baalamani—a stringed white or small black beads to the neck; (2) fibre of the white coarse plant and a black thread to the waist; (3) Vasambu (a corus columns) and puundu (garlic) to the hand; and (4) silver ankle to the leg. They also put golden arm rings to the child's hand. On 16th day "punniyadanam" is celebrated. On that day new ornaments and new dresses are put to the child. On that day brahmin priests come and kindle the sacrificial holy fire and recite holy mantras. This is done on the belief that this ceremony will remove the ceremonial impurities due to child birth. Only after finishing this ceremony they allowed the girl to join inside the house. On that day they invite relatives and arrange a grand feast for them.

"Ear boring ceremony" and "removing hair" are celebrating on the first date of birth star. This can be done both in the house as well as in the temple. While boring the ear the child is to be seated on its uncle's lap, goldsmith bores the ear and put the golden wire immediately. It is not compulsory to celebrate the function in the first date of birth. If there is some obstruction then they celebrate this in 3rd or 5th year etc. They invite guests and the guests give presents like money, gold, new cloth etc. to the child. They take the child outside first on 30th day or 3rd month, to the temple and give offerings to God. Then they send the child outside without hesitation.

In the 5th year they admit the child in the school by taking betel leaf, nut, plantain, camphor, turmeric root and the rice mixed with jaggery. They offer these things to God.

Sengunta Mutaliyar

This caste people give both to the child and mother immediately after birth and if the child is affected by the disease "karappaan", then they put the child on the leaf of the "karappaan plant" (Lapidaga this cristata). They give donkey's milk (or) "rasam" from the shop to the child to avoid skin diseases.

According to the body situation of the mother they give diet food to her from 3rd to 5th day. After this they give these medicene twice daily upto 15th day. They give "Korojanai" with betel leaf water to the child.

On 15th day they celebrate "kappu" to the child. First margosa fibre bangle is put, than they put twisted bangle (murukkam kappu), silver bangle, golden bangle etc. They put the child in the cradle on 16th day, buy new cloth, prepare rice mixed with jaggery and kozhukkattai. According to the star, the "name" of the star, sex of the child they name the child. "naming ceremony" is celebrated on 3rd or 4th month in the temple. They invite relatives and give them a grand feast. It is not in custom to celebrate "punniyadanam". They worship their family God on 16th day and take the child to the temple on 22nd day or 3rd month.

On the first date of birth star they bore the ear of the child and remove the hair. Usually, they celebrate this in the temple. They buy new cloth to the child and the child is to be seated on it's mother's lap while boring the ear and they put golden ear ring immediately.

Child is admitted to the school in the 5th year. They follow give only sweets to the children in the school. They do not celebrate any other custom apart from the above mentioned one.

Asari (Pattar-Viswakarma)

These people give bath to the child immediately after it's birth and give donkey's milk to avoid skin diseases. They give diet food from 5th to 13th day to the mother which contains garlic, brinjal, avarai (a kind of beans) etc. on 16th day they celebrate "kappu" to the child. First they tie the fibre of the margosa tree to the hand, then golden arm ring to the hands silver anklet to the leg, stringed small white or black beads to the neck. Relatives are invited for this function and they present gifts to the child. That day a grand-feast is arranged to all the relatives who attend the function. On 13th or 15th or 16th day these people celebrate "punniyadanam" to remove the ceremonial impurities due to child birth, on 30th day or 3rd month they take the child out first to the temple.

On the first date of birth star they celebrate "ear boring ceremony" and remove the hair. They celebrate these functions either in the temple or in the house. For this function these people take new dresses to the child and its mother. At the time of ear boring the child is to sit in its uncle's lap, anyone can bore the ear and put the golden earring. Child's grand father spends the money for this celebration. If it is not possible to celebrate these functions on the first birthday, they celebrate these in 3rd, or 5th or 7th year.

In the 5th year, they admit the child to the school, at that time they give some money to the teacher, give sweets to the children in the school and take new dresses to the school going children.

Asari (Viswakarma-Carpenter)

Customs of these people resemble those of the above caste (goldsmith) people except in one or two aspects. They give diet food from 3rd to 15th day to the mother which contains pepper, garlic, brinjal, dried food stuff (Vadakam), coriander seed etc. fried on oil and by grinding all together and prepared as "sambar", the greens cooked and mashed.

They celebrate "kappu", "Naming ceremony" on 15th day. On 16th day they do "punniyadanam". After 16th day they take the child to the temple, "Ear boring ceremony" and removing hair is done on the first birthday. For this ceremony they buy new clothes for the father, mother and the child and celebrate this ceremony like a marriage. At the time of boring the ear the child is seated in it's uncle's lap, goldsmith pierces the ear and puts the golden earring. The expenditure for this ceremony belongs to the child's uncle and they celebrate this ceremony either in the house or in the temple.

Chettiyar (Vysya)

Immediately after birth these people give bath to the child and administer donkey's milk to the child. From third day onwards they give "diet food" to the mother of the child. On 9th or 11th or 13th day they give full bath to the mother of the child and the day on which the full bath is given to the mother, that day "punniyadanam" is celebrated. An important custom prevails among this caste people, viz., on the 19th day of the child's birth, it is a practice that, the child's mother has to (it is must) wash clothes by taking them to the tank.

They celebrate "Naming ceremony" in 3rd or 5th or 7th month. On that day all the expenditure is met by the child's mother's house. They invite all the relatives to attend the function, child's uncle has to buy and give golden bangles for the hand, golden chain for the neck, silver anklet for the leg, silver milk-ladle, the plank in plastic or ever silver for the child's swinging hammock made of cloth (eenai), new clothes for the child and it's parents, new cloth for the swinging hammock (this cloth has to be a nice cloth with embroidery on it), flowers, plantains, betel leaf, nut, sandal paste, sweets, sugar, two fine towels etc. on that day. That day a grand feast has to be arranged for the guests (all these are child's mother's house's expenditure). Those who are willing to give presentations used to give parentations to the child there itself.

On that day night they put the child in the swinging hammock (eenayil poodutal). First a grinding stone is cleaned, washed and *kumkum*, sandal paste, turmeric powder, flower, a new cloth are put on it and that grinding stone is put into the swinging hammock by the child's aunt, relatives etc. thrice. (This is done on the belief that those who have no child and if that person do this, she may give birth to a child). Only after this ceremony, child's grandmother or aunt or married woman put the child in the swinging hammock. That day they give cooked food, sweets, etc. to the persons who attend the function.

When the persons return after finishing the function, it is a practice to give betel leaf, nut, plantain, turmeric, *kumkum*, flowers, blouse piece or eversilver vessel etc. to the ladies (This caste people are very particular about the "blouse piece" given to the unmarried and married ladies along with the *kumkum* etc.).

These people perform "Aayishoman" ceremony (This is done in the belief that this ceremony gives a long life to the child). That day, they give alms to a brahmin priest. Relatives and guests attend the function and a grand feast is given to all the members. Mainly uncle and aunt must attend the function on that day. On the first date of the birth star they bore the ear of the child. The child sits on it's mother's or father's or uncle's lap and the goldsmith bores the ear of the child and puts golden ear-rings on the same day. On that day, they prepare the mixture of rice and jaggery. "Aayishoman" and "Ear boring" ceremony are performed on one and the same day.

When the child completes five years they admit the child to the school and arrange a grand feast in the house.

Chettiyar (Sozhiya)

This people give bath to the child as soon as it is born. Then they administer donkey's milk to the child. They give diet food from 3rd to 9th day and it contains brinjal, food without any hot things like chilly etc. On 7th day they celebrate "kappu" and tie first the margosa fibre arm-ring, golden arm-ring etc. Acorus calamus (vasambu), garlic (puundu) etc. string in a thread and tied to the arm of the child. They put small white or black beads stringed in a thread around the neck, tie white coarse fibre to the waist and put a silver anklet to the leg, on that day itself they put the baby in the swinging hammock. on 11th or 13th day they celebrate "punniyadanam". In this caste they celebrate "punniyadanam" for the first child only. That day brahmin priest comes and kindles holy fire and it is usual to give alms to that brahmin.

On the first birthday, they celebrate "Ear boring ceremony" and remove the hair. At the time of boring the ear the child has to sit in it's uncle's lap and goldsmith bore the ears. They take new dresses for the child, child's parents, invite friends and relatives to the function. A grand feast is given to all who participate in the function.

When the child completes five years, they admit the child to school by giving sweets to the school children.

Chettiyar (Vaniya)

These people give bath to the newly born baby and they give donkey's milk to the child is affected by the skin disease viz. "karappaan", otherwise they give mixture from the shop. They give donkey's milk to prevent the skin diseases affecting the child. They give "diet food" from 3rd to 7th day, and it contains drumstick, brinjal etc. They give "kooroojanai" with betel leaf water to the child. They put "kappu" on 15th day.

They tie white coarse fibre to the waist, margosa tree's fibre, gold, silver arm-rings for the hand. On that day, all the presentations will be given from child's mother's house. They prepare rice mixed with jaggery and they put the child in the swinging hammock. After that golden ornaments are put into the measuring pot it is shaken and a name is given to the child. On that day new clothes are taken to the child and its parents.

Only on that day they close the "venniir kuzhi", the hole made for observing the water when the child is given bath immediately after its birth. It is a belief that the water which is used to give bath to the child was not stepped on, by any others and also it is a belief that if the water is on the earth without being in the hole, ghost will seize the child.

They bore the ear of the child on the first birth date, they seat the child on it's uncle's lap and the goldsmith bores the ear of the child. For this ceremony the presentations are to be brought from the child's uncle's house. For this presentation, from the child's house, they have to give presentation as a return.

When the child completes five years, it's uncle comes and after fixing an auspicious date he admits the child to school with proper presentations.

Pillai (Tuluva Vellalar)

As soon as a child is born, these people give bath to the child. Immediately after birth these people administer donkey's milk to the child to avoid skin diseases. They give diet food to the mother from 3rd day to 7th day. This contains brinjal, garlic etc. They put "kappu" in the parents' house on 11th day; they put silver and golden bangles only. On that day they take new dresses, prepare rice with jaggery, invite relatives etc. They put the child in the cloth cradle on 11th day and they use new cloth for this cradle. "Naming ceremony" is celebrated on 11th day and for this function they invite relatives. On the same day they celebrate "punniyadanam", to remove ceremonial impurities due to child birth. When the mother goes out she takes marogsa leaves, iron etc. in her hand to avoid seizure by ghosts. After "punniyadanam", they take the child outside first to the temple. These people remove the hair of the child on the first birthday and celebrate "Ear boring ceremony" on the same day. For this they take new dresses to the child only. While boring the ear, the child is to be seated in its uncle's lap, the goldsmith bores the ear and immediately they put golden ear rings. The child's mother's parents spend for this ceremony. These people admit the child to school in the 5th year, they give some money to the teacher and give sweets to the children in the school.

Reddiar

This caste people give bath to the child immediately after its birth and give donkey's milk to the child. They give diet food to the mother from 3rd to 9th day and it contains brinjal, garlic, etc. They put "kappu" on 7th day in the child's house. First they put margosa fibres bangle, then five metal bangle, silver bangle and golden bangle. The take new dresses to the child, prepare rice mixed with jaggery and relatives attend the function. They put the child in the cradle on 11th day by using the mother's marriage saree. On 16th day they celebrate "Naming ceremony", relatives attend the function. On 11th day itself they do "punniyadanam" to remove the ceremonial impurities due to child birth. When the mother goes out she takes margosa leaves, iron things etc. to avoid seizing by ghosts. They take the child in the 3rd month to the temple. The other customs resemble (regarding ear boring, removing hair etc.) the other caste people. These people also admit the child when it completes 5th year, in the school like other castes.

Naidu

This caste people give bath to the child immediately after birth. They give donkey's milk or rasam from the shop and also the "oil of karappaan plant" to the child, to avoid skin diseases. They give diet food from 3rd day onwards which contains "poriccakkuzhampu" without tamarind. They celebrate "kappu", "cradling ceremony", "Naming ceremony", "punniyadanam" on 11th day. "Kappu" is celebrated in the girl's house, first they put margosa fibre bangle, "mukkappu" (three metal mixture bangle), silver bangle etc. They buy new clothes to the child and new dresses for the mother. "Naming ceremony", "punniyadanam" etc. resemble the above caste people. They take the child to the temple in the 3rd month.

They celebrate "Ear boring ceremony" and removing the hair of the child in the first or 3rd birthday. Regarding the customs for this ceremony, these people resemble the other caste people. The expenditure for this ceremony is to be met by the uncle, they do this ceremony either in the house or in the temple. For all the above functions they invite relatives and arrange a grand feast for them. Admitting the child in the school etc. resemble the other caste people.

Thondaimandala Mutaliyar

The child is given bath as soon as it is born. These people do not put the child in the leaves and give donkey's milk. Diet food consists of brinjal, garlic, pepper etc. mixed and prepared like a sambar. At the time of "kappu", they put margosa fibre's kappu, silver and golden bangle to the child. On 16th day they celebrate "Naming ceremony", "Ear boring ceremony" and remove the hair of the child. For this function they take new dresses to the child only. While boring the ear the child is to sit in its aunt's lap, goldsmith bores the ear and puts the golden earring immediately. This is celebrated in the child's mother's parent's house or in the temple.

The child is admitted to school in the fifth year, they give money to the teacher, distribute sweets to the children in the school. They do not poke rice with jaggery and take new cloth to the child for this occasion. The other customs resemble the Sengunta Mutaliyar caste people regarding child birth and childhood days.

Nadar

Diet food is given to the new mother from 3rd to 16th day and it contains drumstick, fish, dried fish etc. on the 3rd day they put "kappu" in the child's mother's house. They first put "margosa fibre" bangle, then five metal bangle, silver bangle and golden bangle. On that day they take new dress to the child, poke rice with jaggery and invite relatives, on 30th day they put the child in the child's father's grand-mother's marriage saree. On the same day they celebrate "Naming ceremony". First they go to the temple, offer to their family God and then only they celebrate "Naming ceremony".

They celebrate "punniyadanam" on 16th day, to remove the ceremonial impurities due to child birth. "Hair removing ceremony" and "Ear boring ceremony" is celebrated on the first birthday of the child.

They take new dresses to the child and its parents for this ceremony. Child's uncle spends money for this function. The other customs regarding child birth is the same as in other castes.

Nayakkar (Canar)

This caste people give bath to the child immediately after birth and if it is affected by the skin disease like "karappaan" etc. they put the child on the leaf. They do not give donkey's milk to the child. Immediately after giving birth to a child the mother has to take only milk and bread. They give "diet food" from 3rd to 11th day. They give tiffen in the morning, food with sambar in the afternoon, and no food in the night. They give "kooroojanai" with betel leaf water. They put "kappu" on 15th day, in the mother's house. First they put margosa fibre's bangle, then silver, golden bangle, anklet for the leg etc. On the same day they put the child in the cradle, celebrate "Naming ceremony" etc. on that day they poke rice with jaggery, buy new clothes. Relatives attend the function and a grand feast is arranged for them. On that day itself they celebrate "punniyadanam" (termed as "patinaaru kumpitutal"), brahmin priest comes, kindles holy fire to remove the ceremonial impurities due to child birth.

They take the child on the 3rd month to the temple and after that they allow the child to go out. They remove the hair, celebrate the "Ear boring ceremony" on the first birthday. They take new dresses to the child, it's parents, while boring the ear the child is seated on it's uncle's lap, the goldsmith bores the ear and puts the golden wire in it's ear. The child's uncle has to bear the expenditure for this ceremony, this is usually celebrated in the house and if there is any vow they do it in the temple. They admit the child to the school in the 5th year, take plantain, sugar, sweets etc. and distribute it to the school children.

Nayakkar (Tatar)

Almost all customs resemble the other caste people except the following.

These people give donkey's milk to the child only if the skin disease "karappaan" is on the child. They give "diet food" from 3rd to 5th day and this mainly contains brinjal, drumstick, sambar (i.e. varral kuzhampu—the sambar which is dried to a semi-solid state). On the 16th-day these people celebrate "kappu", "cradling ceremony" and "naming ceremony" etc. they use new cloth for the cradle. For the "naming ceremony" relatives come, they arrange a grand feast to the relatives. Uncle has to bear the expenditure for this ceremony. After 16th day the ceremonial impurities are removed. "Ear boring ceremony" is celebrated on the first birthday or 3rd or 5th birthday. They bore the ear only at the time of supplication at the temple. For this also the child's uncle has to bear the expenditure. At the time of boring the ear, they buy new clothes, seat the child in it's uncle's lap and the goldsmith bores the ear.

Muppanar

This caste people give bath to the child as soon as it is born. They give "diet food" from 5th day to 16th day. It contains garlic, pepper, fish, salt and dried fish etc. They give "kooroojanai" with betel leaf water to the child.

On the 16th day they put "kappu" to the child in mother's house, they put margosa fibre bangle first, then silver and golden bangles, they prepare the rice mixed with jaggery on that day and put new clothes to the child. "Naming ceremony", "cradling", "punniyadanam" are also celebrated on the same day. They invite relatives and arrange a grand feast for them. At the time of "punniyadanam", brahmin priest comes, kindles the holy fire, doing so removes the ceremonial impurity due to child birth. These people take the child first to the temple on the 30th day or 3rd month. They remove the hair and celebrate "Ear boring ceremony," on the first birthday of the child. For this occasion from the child's uncle's house they take clothes, ornaments etc. At the time of boring the ear the child is seated on it's uncle's lap and the goldsmith bores the ear of the child and puts the golden earring to the ear immediately. All the expenditure except meals is to be born by the child's uncle and from mother's house they bear the expenditure for the meals. This function may be celebrated in the house as well as in the temple. They give new cloth for cradling child.

They admit the child to the school in the 5th year. At that time they give some money to the teacher and distribute sweets to the children. They buy new clothes for the child while admitting the child in school.

Devar

The customs regarding child birth resemble the customs in other castes. These people give "diet food" from 3rd to 15th day (if it is a first child) twice a day to the mother. They use dried food stuff material, garlic, tamarind, brinjal, dry fish (Karuvaatu), drumstick for "diet food". These people also give donkey's milk to avoid the attack of skin diseases. If the child is the first child they pour water (give full bath) on the 15th day to the mother. For other children they give full bath on the 11th day. They celebrate "punniyadanam" on 11th or 15th day to remove the ceremonial impurities due to child birth. After twenty two days they put "kappu", celebrate "cradling ceremony" and "Naming ceremony".

They celebrate "Ear boring ceremony" and remove the hair on the first birthday of the child, which is celebrated either in temple (or) house. The expenditure is beared by the child's uncle. Other customs resemble the other caste people. Also they celebrate birthday to the child once a year.

Udayar (pot-makers)

Customs of this people resemble the other caste people with slight variation. The variations are mentioned here. They give diet food for the mother on 3rd, 5th and 7th day. They add "samakkuzhampu" with the diet food. On 15th day in the child's mother's parents house they put "kappu" to the child. They put only "anju panjalam kappu" to the child and put the child on the same day in the cradle. On that day they prepare the mixture of rice and jaggery, buy new clothes for the child etc. They celebrate "Naming ceremony" on 15th day do "punniyadanam", invite the brahmin priest who kindles holy fire to remove the ceremonial impurites due to child birth. They take the child to the temple in the third month.

In 5th month, they remove the hair of the child, bore the ear of the child and while boring the ear they seat the child on it's uncle's lap and the goldsmith bores the ear and puts the golden earring immediately to the child. They celebrate this function either in the temple or in the house.

Kallar (Devar)

The child is given bath immediately after its birth and they administer donkey's milk to the child. Diet food is given to the mother from 3rd to 30th day which contains fish sambar, rasam, garlic sambar, grains, tuvaiyal (a kind of side dish) etc. on 16th day, in the child's mother's house they put "kappu", first they put margosa fibre "kappu", then five metal bangle, silver and golden bangle. On that particular day they poke rice with jaggery, take new dresses and invite guests to the house. On the same day they celebrate "Naming ceremony" and on the 21st day they do "punniyadanam" to remove the ceremonial impurities due to child birth in the temple. After one year they remove the hair of the child and celebrate "Ear boring ceremony" on the same day in the temple. While boring the ear the child is to be seated in it's uncle's lap, goldsmith bores the ear, puts the golden earring immediately and the child's uncle is to spend for this. In the 6th year beginning, the child is admitted to the school, they give money to the teacher, give sweets to the children and they take new dresses to the school going children.

Tuluva Naickar

The child is not given both immediately after birth. Diet food is given to the mother for 11 days, which contains cooked food, dried ginger and "kataiccalavu", cambar, on 9th day in the child's mother's house "kappu" is celebrated. First they put margosa fibre bangle, five metal bangle and then golden bangle to the child. On this day they take new dresses to the child, poke rice with jaggery and the relatives attend the function. On 30th day the child is put into the cloth cradle by using new cloth. "Naming ceremony" is not celebrated separately. On 11th day they do "punniyadanam" to remove the ceremonial impurities due to child birth.

On 30th day the child is taken outside, to the temple. On the first birthday they remove the hair of the child and in the 5th year they celebrate "Ear boring ceremony". For this they take new dresses only to the child, the child is seated in it's uncle's lap, goldsmith bores the ear and he puts the golden ear ring immediately. This is celebrated in the house of the child's mother's parents who meet the expenses for this ceremony. In the 5th year the child is admitted to the school, sweets are distributed to the children in the school and they take new dresses to the school going children.

Jankamar

Most of the customs regarding "child birth" resemble the "Reddiar" caste people except in the following customs, these people include brinjal rasam etc. in the "diet food" given to the mother. On 7th day they put "kappu" which is mixed variety of iron, silver, copper metals and also put golden bangle. On 9th day they put the child in the cloth cradle. On the same day they do "punniyadanam" to remove the ceremonial impurities due to child birth. In the 3rd month they celebrate "Naming ceremony" and relatives attend the function. In the same month they take the child outside, first to the temple. In the first year these people remove the hair of the child and celebrate "Ear boring ceremony" on the same day. For this occasion these people take new dresses to the child, the child is seated in it's uncle's lap, goldsmith bore the ear and puts the golden ear-ring immediately. This is usually done in the temple and the child's mother's parents spend for this.

Konar (Yadhavappillai)

Diet food is given from 3rd to 16th day to the mother which contains beans, drumstick, fish, dried fish etc. They celebrate "kappu" in the husband's house (they come to the bride's house). On 7th or 30th day they put "kappu" on that day they tie the five types of metal mixed bangle to the child's hand, poke rice with jaggery and give it to all the guests. On 11th day they allow the child's mother inside the house. They celebrate "punniyadanam" on 16th day. They close the "venniir kuzhi" on this day. On the same day itself it is in practice to put the child in the swinging hammock. Guests are invited to the function and a grand dinner is given to them. On that day new dress is bought for the child and put in a big plate which contains the rice, plantain etc. and is taken back. On this day it is in practice to give food, rice etc. to washerman and barber. When the child and its mother return back to their house both the bride's and bridegroom's parents have to give presentations (siirvaricai). On the date of the birth star, it is usual to put new dress to the child and a feast is given. "Ear boring", "Hair removing" etc. are not compulsory, in the first year itself. They remove the hair in the temple and celebrate "Ear boring ceremony" either in the temple or in the house according to their situation. While boring the ear the child has to sit in it's uncle's lap and goldsmith bores the ear of the child and puts golden ear ring immediately. They admit the child to school in the 5th year without doing any special custom.

Kuravar (Ramajoogi)

These people give bath to the child immediately after it's birth. They give diet food to the mother from 3rd to 16th day which contains brinjal, dried fish etc. On 7th day they put arm rings to the child. The "siir" for this has to be given from her mother's house if it is not possible, "siir" can be given from the child's father's house. It is in practice to tie first the margosa fibre and only after that all the other rings. On 16th day they celebrate "punniyadanam" (They do not invite the brahmin priest, kindle holy fire etc.). For this occasion they take new dresses to the mother, child etc. They give bath to both and new dress is to be worn. Guests and relatives attend the function. A grand feast is arranged for the guests.

On 30th day after child's birth, from the child's father's house they come and take the child and it's mother to their house. Within this thirty days in child's mother's house they have to give the ornaments needed to the child and it's mother. They bore the ear of the child and remove the hair in the first year. Even though this is in custom, there is no compulsion to do this at the completion of the first year, but this is to be done before the marriage. They admit the child in the school when it completes the fifth year.

Vannan (Eekaali-washerman)

Some customs regarding child birth resemble the other caste people except in the following aspects. They give donkey's milk immediately after child birth to avoid skin diseases. Diet food for the mother is given from 7th day to 3rd month and it contains dried fish, brinjal, garlic, Cennakonni (kind of fish) etc. on 9th day in the parent's house they put "kappu" to the child. First they put margosa fibre "kappu", then five metal kappu, silver kappu and golden kappu. On the same day they put the child in the cloth cradle, celebrate "Naming ceremony" and relatives attend the function. On 11th day they celebrate "punniyadanam" and allow the mother to join inside the house.

On 16th day after giving birth to a child, coarse fibre, Acorus calamus (vacambu) covered with gold tub are tied in the arm of the child. In 3rd month new dresses are purchased for the mother, child, it's father; silver, golden arm rings are tied to the arm of the child, silver or golden string is tied around the waist. Then the child and the mother are send to her husband's house. They invite relatives and they give presentations to the child and arrange a grand feast for all the guests. Regarding "Ear boring ceremony" and remove the hair they resemble the patayacci caste people. They admit the child in the school in the 5th year (without any special custom).

Navitar (Maruttuvar : Barber)

Some customs of child birth resembles the above caste people in some aspects but there are differences. They give "diet food" from 3rd to 7th day which contains the greens, "Cennakonni" (a kind of fish), brinjal, garlic etc. They put "kappu" in the house where the child is born. On 7th day they tie margosa fibre around the arm, on 9th day they do "punniyadanam" and 16th day they tie coarse fibre around the waist. On the same day they celebrate "Naming ceremony". They take the child outside in the 3rd month to the temple (Goddess Mari's temple). They remove the hair and the "Ear boring ceremony" on the first birthday and they take new dresses to the parents and the child for this ceremony. The other ceremonies regarding the child birth resemble the washerman people. They admit the child in 5th year to the school.

Cakkili (Cobbler)

They give bath to the child immediately after its birth. They mix thirty two medicinal items and after powdering it, it is usual to give that medicine to the mother of the child. This is given for 16 days. On 7th day they tie margosa fibre arm-ring to the child. This is done by the grand-father (Child's mother's parents) and grand mother. They have to prepare the rice with jaggery and invite relatives and friends. First, margosa fibre arm ring is tied and only after that according to the economy the other arm rings are put in gold and silver.

On 16th day they do "punniyadanam" and is usually done by the ladies and the parents of the bride and bridegroom, on that day (Pandaaram-priest for this caste people) comes, kindles holy fire. After that they give rice, alms to the Brahmin. This people celebrate a function as "sooru uuttum dinam" (food giving ceremony) between first and fifth year of the child. That day child's uncle comes bringing rice mixed with jaggery, sweets, meals, plantain bunch, coconut bunch and other presentation things and he has to do this ceremony to the child.

When the child completes five years they admit the child in the school. It is a custom that, the child's uncle has to admit the child to school. That day it is a custom to prepare rice with jaggery and give it to the children in the school. Also they give some money (as "guru datchanai") to the teacher and the child is admitted to the school.

Harijan (Aadi Dravidiar)

They give bath to the child immdiately after birth. They give "diet food" from 3rd to 11th day which includes rice seed (perum siirakam), brinjal, garlic, cumin etc. They give betel leaf, koorajanai and sugar to the child. They celebrate "kappu" on 7th day, first they tie margosa fibre and only after that they tie other kind of bangles to the child. On the same day they tie white coarse fibre to the waist. They prepare rice with jaggery, sugar, betel leaf, nut, plantain and offer them to the deity. On 16th day itself they celebrate the "Naming ceremony", "punniyadanam" etc. In the 3rd month they take the child outside first to it's father's house. According to the economic situation they celebrate "Ear boring ceremony", they take new dresses to the child and its parents. At the time of this cermeony the child is to be seated in it's uncle's lap, priest ("Pandaaram" for this caste people) bores the ear and puts the golden earring. Usually this is done in the temple and the child's mother's parents spend for this. When the child completes five years it is admitted to the school. At that time they give sugar to the school children.

8

Customs Regarding "Sacred Thread Ceremony" and "Puberty Rituals"

I. Sacred Thread Ceremony

This custom is in vogue only among some caste people viz. (1) Brahmin (iyer), (2) Brahmin (iyangar), (3) Asari (Carpenter), and (4) Asari (Kammalar pattar-goldsmith).

Brahmin (Iyer)

These people celebrate this ceremony at the age of fifteen of a boy. This is celebrated as a marriage and so it is called "punul kalyaanam". For this function they invite relatives and close friends. Brahmin priests come, place kalasas, kindle holy fire and recite holy *mantras*. Then they anoint the boy with the water in the "kalasas" and put the sacred thread on the chest of that boy. After this they put silver and gold cord to the boy. At the time of tying the sacred thread, that boy has to wear the five fold *dhoti* (panjakaccam) and a towel around his waist. The various items to be bought on this day are silver sacred cord, gold sacred cord, vessel made of five metals or silver used by advanced religionists to holy water purification and a small silver spoon or ladle used by Brahmins to take water from a cup on ceremonial purifications (panjapaattrauttrani), silk *dhoti*, ever silver (or) silver big plate etc. Relatives and friends attend the ceremony. They give presentations according to their economic status. That day a grand feast is held.

Brahmin (Iyangar)

At the age of fifteen it is in practice to do "punul kalyaanam". Brahmin priests come, kindle holy fire and recite holy *mantras*. In a pot a thread is tied and water is kept in the pot. Paddy is spread on the floor, a plantain leaf is put on it and on the plantain leaf rice is spread. Then on that rice, the above said pot is kept, then on that mango leaf bunch is kept and on that a coconut is kept (It looks like a "kumpam"—a water pot adorned with mango leaves and coconut). Then after reciting the holy *mantras* and kindling holy fire, brahmin priest anoints the boy who is going to have the sacred thread. After that he puts sacred thread to the boy and then put silver, gold cord. Before the day of this function these people celebrate "taatiyaadaanam". For the sacred thread ceremony they invite relatives and close friends. They give presents to the boy according to their economic status. For all the persons who attend the function, these people arrange a grand feast.

The boy who wears the sacred thread has to recite *mantras* when he happens to meet aged persons. Also he has to do "sandayavandanam", "madya vandanam" etc. (worship at any of the three stated periods), (reciting *mantras* three times daily) and has to pray to God.

Asari (Kammalar, Pattar Goldsmith, Taccar)

Sacred thread ceremony in both the goldsmith and carpenter caste are more or less resemble each other. At the age of 15 (or) 16 of the boy, they invite priest (called 'iyer') in their caste itself. He comes, kindles the holy fire and then the sacred cord is tied to the boy. The boy who is having this ceremony has to wear new *dhoti*, new towel and first sacred thread is tied, then silver and gold cord is tied. These people also celebrate this like "big marriage". They invite relatives, friends and a grand feast is given to the relatives and guests who attend the function. They give presents to the boy. It is usual to buy new silk *dhoti*, new towel for the boy who undergoes this ceremony.

II. Puberty Rituals

Brahmin (Iyer)

When a girl attains her age, on the first day, she does not take bath. She is made to sit on a stool, they decorate the girl with garlands and flowers and give her milk and plantain. After that they give dhall rice on that day.

Second day they cook rice and give it to her and as on the first day, second day also they garland her with flowers. On the 3rd day they cook a meal cake cooked in steam (puttu). On 4th day they give full bath to the girl and she is allowed to stay with other members of the house. On 5th day they give oil bath to the girl and make her wear new clothes. Then they give her meals with "vadai" (a cake made of blackgram and rice flour fried in ghee) and Paayasam (rice boiled in milk). There is a belief that at the time of menstruation if the girl has to come out of the house she has to keep margosa leaf, things made of iron, with her, otherwise they believe that ghosts will seize her.

Brahmin (Iyangar)

When a girl attains her age, on the first day, they plait her hair beautifully and decorate her hair with flowers and garlands. They drew flour drawings on the floor made her sit on it and they give her milk, plantain and sugar to her. First these are given to the girl, only after that they give dhall rice and gingely oil and after that they give "pongal" (cooked rice). Second day, they give her some tiffen. Only on the 3rd day they prepare "puttu", appam (sweet rice cake) etc. They place mydha flour, rice flour and jaggery in a tender plantain leaf ("nuni vaazhai ilai") and they tie these things to the waist of the girl. At that time relatives sing "nalungu" songs. On that occasion they give betel leaf, nut etc. to married woman. There is a peculiar custom among this caste people. Before the day of marriage, when the menses comes to the girl, they keep paddy in a measuring pot in which they place lighted lamp on the right side. On the left side they place stone mortor, small silver pot on the left side and without spilling anything, the whole thing is taken around the head of the girl thrice.

Pillai

In this caste, these people note the date of puberty, star of that date etc. Then they seat thegirl in a wooden seat, a married woman holds a sieve above the head of the girl, put coconut, betel leaf, nut, coins etc. into the sieve and five married woman pour water on the girl through that sieve. After that the girl wears a new dress and a lamp is lit before her.

Then they give first (1) plantain, sugar, milk, gingely oil to eat. This caste people give the dress worn by the girl when she attains her maturity to the washer woman. The above edibles are given to the girl in the belief that it gives strength to the waist. Moreover, ten or twelve children are made to sit with the girl and they give pongal (cooked rice), appalam (a kind of thin cake made of blackgram flour), karuvadaam (a kind of cake made of rice and chilly mix), vadai (a kind of cake) and paayasam (rice boiled with milk) etc. to eat.

On 2nd, 3rd and 4th day they prepare some special tiffen like a sweet and a kaaram etc. and offer them to God. Fifth day they prepare "puttu" (cake cooked in steam). If the 5th day is an auspicious day, then on that day itself they celebrate "puberty rituals". Otherwise they celebrate it on 7th, 9th or 11th day. For this ceremony they invite relatives and friends. Relatives would bring new saree, blouse etc. and decorate the girl. On this day relatives and friends give presentations to the girl and that day there will be a grand feast in the girl's house for all those who attend the function.

Isai Velalar

When a girl attains her age the news is announced to the others through the washer woman. First the girl's uncle has to give her bath and then she is seated, a sieve is hold above the girl's head in which gold, coin, margosa leaves etc. are put and five or seven or nine married woman pour water on the girl's head through the sieve. After pouring water the girl is invited inside the house and these people do "nalungu" to the girl. At this time, they garland the girl, then they smear sandal paste, put *kumkum* on the forehead. First, they give dhall rice to the girl and then egg and the same amount (egg amount) of gingely oil is given to the girl.

They give bath to the girl on 3rd, 5th, 7th and 9th days. Relatives come and cook food and give it to the girl on odd numbered days like 3rd, 5th and 7th. Whenever the relatives come, cook and give food, they prepare "puttu" also every day. If the relatives do not want to cook and give food to the girl they give vessels, ornaments etc. as presentations to the girl. In this caste, in the girl's house it is must to cook "puttu" everyday till the girl is allowed to come inside the house.

They celebrate "puberty rituals" on 7th or 9th, day (if not possible in the 3rd month). They announce this date to the girl's uncle's house, then to aunt's house and only later to the other relative house. For this "rituals" first uncle's, then aunt's presentations have to come. Then these presentations are taken to a temple and they are taken back to the house in a procession accompanied by beating drums. These people celebrate this function like "patayacci" caste people. The food expenditure of the puberty ceremony day belongs to the girl's house.

After this "nalungu" is done to the girl. First the girl has to sit in her own dress and then her uncle has to give her a new dress which is brought by him. Then she has to wear that uncle's saree and sit. Then the uncle has to garland the girl. They smear sandal paste and *kumkum* to the girl and to the "nalungu". After "nalungu" celebration, the garland in the girl's neck is removed by her uncle only.

When a girl attains her age, her uncle has to pour (give her full bath) water on her head. It is must that he has to pour water first on her head. He has to bring new dress, betel leaf, nut, plantain, sandal paste, powder, soap, comb, ribbon, bangles, *kumkum*, turmeric powder etc. It is a customs that 3, 5 or 7 married women pour water on that girl's head (i.e., odd number of married woman). At the time of pouring water it is poured through a sieve. Married woman hold a sieve above the girl's head in which the members in the house put some gold, coin, margosa leaves etc. After giving her full bath, it is a custom to perform a ceremony anointing the girl. The ceremony is named as "nalungu". At the time of this ceremony they garland the girl, smear sandal paste, place *kumkum* on her forehead. After that they give dhall rice first to eat, then egg, blackgram flour. These people believe that these things give strength to the waist and so they give these things to the matured girl. After that, the girl wears new dress.

Relatives come in odd numbered days and cook food, prepare "puttu" (food cake cooked in steam), and serve them to the girl on 3rd, 5th, 7th day etc. They celebrate "puberty rituals" on 15th day which is termed as "manja tanni surrutal". This is celebrated by her uncle and it is a must for him. They celebrate this function like a big festival. According to economic status some people celebrate this ceremony in 3rd month or even before the marriage day itself.

At the time of this ceremony, they put new dresses, garland, ornaments etc. in the girl and a coconut is given to the girl and she has to hold the coconut in her hand. On one side of the girl they place a grinding stone and a roller. They clean it decorate it with *kumkum,* sandal paste, turmeric powder, flowers etc. They prepare "puttu" on this day, they show it around the girl. Then they give this to the girl. They made the girl to sit and "aalam" (the water in which turmeric and chunam was mixed) in which the margosa leaf is put is also shown around the girl.

After that, the decorated roller is given thrice to the girl and got back. Relatives and friends come on this day and they give presents like vessel, ornaments, money etc. They arrange a grand feast for all the members (on that day) who attend the function. This ceremony is done only on an odd numbered day. Only after this ceremony the matured girl is allowed to come outside (The belief for doing this ceremony is "ghosts will not seize the girl" if this ceremony is celebrated). Also if the girl has a necessity to go outside the house at the time of menses and also before doing this ceremony, it is a practice to give margosa leaves, iron etc. in her hands and allow her to go out.

When the "puberty rituals" is not celebrated immediately, it is a practice atleast to show the "puttu" around the girl before allowing her to go out. This is done within the house without inviting friends and relatives. Only after this ceremony they allow the girl to go out. Otherwise even if there is a necessity this caste people never send the girl outside. These people also give the dress of the girl worn while attaining the age, to the washer woman.

Sengunta Mutaliyar

When a girl attains her age, this news is to be sent to her uncle. He comes and builds a hut and send the girl inside the hut (This hut is made up of two millet mate and it looks like a small hall). After that the girl is given full bath (without sieve etc.). They mix gingely oil, jaggery etc. and they give it to the girl to eat as a first edible after attaining the age. After that dhall rice is given to her to eat. The dress which is worn by the girl when she attains her age is given away to the washer woman. There is no other custom in practice on the first day. Second day "puttu" (food cake cooked in steam) is cooked. Among this caste people also it is in practice that relatives come and cook food, give it to the girl. On 11th or 16th day they celebrate a ceremony "tirattu currutal" (puberty ceremony). On that day the girl is decorated and is made to sit in a seat. Then the "puttu" and the "food" cooked with all kind of side dishes are shown around the girl and they give these cooked food and "puttu" etc. to the washerwoman. For all these sixteen days washerwoman gives the change of dress to the girl.

Asari (Pattar-Kammalar-goldsmith, taccar-carpenter)

The girl who attains age is seated and five (or) seven married women pour water through the sieve which is held above the girl's head in which coin, turmeric paste, margosa leaves etc.

are put. Then they give new dresses to the girl and decorate her hair with flowers and seat the girl in seat. Then they show "aalam" (lime mortor mixed with turmeric powder dissolved in the water) around the girl and they give gingely oil, plantain, sugar etc. to eat as a first edible after attaining her age. Non-vegetarian people give egg also along with the above mentioned things. Only after this, dhall rice is given to the girl.

Second day blackgram flour and jaggery is mixed and cooked, in that, ghee and sugar are mixed and it is given to the girl. Third day they give three tiffens (like idli, cream cake, puttu, bajji etc.) to the girl. From the fifth day onwards it is in practice for relatives to come and cook food and give it to the girl. On 11th day a brahmin priest comes and does "punniyadanam". At that time he kindles the sacred fire and after finishing this ceremony "puberty rituals" are celebrated. At the time of puberty ceremony the girl's uncle brings her new saree, ornaments etc. On that day relatives and friends come and they give presents like vessels, money, ornaments etc. to the girl. A grand-feast is given to all the participants in the ceremony.

Chettiyar (Vysya)

If a girl attains age they informs the matter to her mother through somebody else. Then the girl is given full bath and decorated and she is seated facing east. Then gingely oil is given in the morning daily to take inside. On 7th day, 5 or 7 or 11 married women give full bath to the girl and decorate her, on that spot itself. Then these married women also have to take oil bath and then give a feast to the girl. After that the girl's parents give plantain, flower, turmeric and *kumkum* to these married women. Daily two varieties of tiffen are given to the girl. Relatives come and cook tiffen and give it to the girl. On 11th or 13th day Brahmin priest comes, kindles holy fire and do "punniyadanam".

On that evening the girl is decorated and her hair is plaited and all in the house sing and make merry. If the girl's parents are rich they invite friends also for this occasion. Relatives give presents to the girl. On that day afternoon or in the evening they celebrate "*tatipam*" to remove the ceremonial impurity. For that, five standing lamps are kept in the position of a square and five thread for a wick are put in five faces of the lamp and the wick is lit. These five lamps are connected by five or seven threads, and inside this the girl and the other seven members sit. Then sandal paste, *kumkum* etc. are smeared on the girl and the other seven members give *kumkum* and turmeric (both made like a ball) to the girl. The girl decorates her leg with these balls and she does this for the other seven members with her and throws away the balls so as to hit the wall on her back. After that she gives turmeric, *kumkum,* blouse piece to other seven members with her. Then one among the seven cut the thread connecting the five lamps by sharp knife and after this, the seven members take oil bath and a grand feast is given.

Chettiyar (Sozhiya)

When a girl attains her age, first relative are invited and they will give her bath. A sieve is held above the girl's head in which gold, coin, wooden doll (marappaacci), shell for a milk-ladle etc. are put and five married women pour water through the sieve on the girl's head. After giving bath to the girl, they give dhall rice to the girl to eat first. On that day the presentations come from the uncle's house. Relatives attend the function and a grand feast is arranged for those who attend the function.

Chettiyar (Vaniya)

When a girl attains her age, first a sieve is hold above the head of the girl in which turmeric, coin, flowers etc. are put and odd numbered married women pour water on the girl's head through the sieve. After pouring water first blackgram flour and gingely oil are given to her to take inside and after that dhall rice is given to her to eat. These people give the dress of the girl, when the girl first attains her age, to the washerwomen. On 3rd, 5th and 7th day they cook "puttu".

According to their economic condition, on 7th or 9th or 11th or 16th day or before the marriage "puberty ceremony" is celebrated. For puberty rituals the presentations have to come from the girl's uncle's house. On the "puberty ceremony" day it is a custom to put "nalungu" in the uncle's saree. (Presented for this ceremony by the uncle to the girl).

Pillai (Tuluva Vellalar)

If a girl attains her age, she informs the matter through others to her mother. On the first day they pour water over the girl by keeping sieve above her head, two married ladies hold the sieve and turmeric is put into the sieve. After that anybody can pour water into the sieve. After this they leave the girl in a separate room, decorate her hair with flowers. Then they give dhall rice first to eat and then gingely oil and plantain. On the first day itself they prepare "puttu". After this they pour water on 3rd, 5th, 7th, 9th day and prepare "puttu" on these days. They prepare the horoscope at this time of puberty.

Then they invite the girl on 7th or 9th day inside the house. The girl's uncle, aunt etc. are to do "siir" for this "puberty rituals" which is celebrated on 9th or 11th day. For this, they take new saree. On the first day itself after pouring water they put "nalungu" to the girl by smearing sandal paste, *kumkum* etc. and put "garland" on her. Relatives come and cook food on odd numbered days. If it is not possible to do the "puberty rituals", they cook "puttu" and show it around the girl's head and only after that they send the girl outside. If it is necessary to go out the girl takes margosa leaves, iron etc. to avoid seizure by ghosts. These people give the dress of the girl at the time of attaining age to a washerwoman.

Reddiar

On the first day these people give shall rice after giving bath to the girl. They pour water on the first day by placing sieve above the head of the girl, washerwoman holds the sieve, turmeric, margosa leaves etc. are put into it and nine aged ladies pour water in the sieve. These people invite the girl inside the house on 11th day and celebrate "puberty rituals" and the girl's uncle does the "siir" for this function. The other customs regarding puberty rituals are the same as those of "Patayacci" caste people.

Naidu

If a girl attains her age she is to inform the matter to her mother, through somebody else. Then they pour water on the head of the girl. They do not prepare "puttu" on the first day. They leave the girl in a separate room, decorate her hair with flowers, do "nalungu" to the girl by smearing sandal paste and *kumkum*. They prepare the horoscope of the girl at the time of attaining age. They give dhall rice first after pouring water. They pour water on 3rd, 5th, 7th and 9th day and prepare "puttu" on 3rd, 5th, 7th and 9th day. They invite the girl inside the house on 13th day and celebrate "puberty rituals" on the same day. Her uncle does 'siir" for this function. The other customs regarding puberty rituals resemble the other caste people.

Thondaimandala Mutaliyar

Most of the customs regarding the puberty rituals, resemble the other caste people. Following are some exceptions. When a girl attains age, married women hold a sieve, put margosa leaves in that, the girl's uncle's wife pours water on her head through the sieve. After pouring water on the first day they do not celebrate "nalungu" but smear turmeric, sandal paste etc. to the girl. Then they leave her in a separate room, give her only dhall rice. Then they pour water on 3rd, 5th, 7th days, prepare "puttu" mixed with jaggery and another "puttu" mixed with curd on these days. The girl is invited into the house on 7th day and on the same day they celebrate 'puberty rituals", take new saree and her uncle is to spend for this occasion. Relatives do not come and cook food etc. and serve them to the girl. If it is not possible to celebrate "puberty rituals", then this caste people prepare "puttu" and show it around the girl and only after this they send the girl outside.

Nadar

When a girl attains puberty, the mother is informed through somebody else. Then they give the seed of greens with stem (tandukkiirai) to that girl. This is done because of the belief that the embryo will be safe. They pour water on 1st, 3rd, 5th, 7th, 9th and 10th days and prepare "puttu" on all the ten days. While pouring water, married ladies pour water and the other customs regarding puberty resemble the other caste people. They invite the girl inside the house on 16th day and the girl's uncle is to spend money for "puberty rituals" and he has to take new saree for the girl. All the other customs regarding "puberty rituals" resemble the other caste people.

Nayakkar (Canar)

These people pour water on the head of the matured girl and this is usually done by married women. These people leave the girl in a separate room and she is to be in that room for 11th days. On this day they decorate her with flowers and they note the time of maturity. They give "dhuvarai dhall rice" immediately after giving bath and on the 3rd day they give egg, blackgram flour and sugar to eat. They give full bath to the girl on odd numbered days 3rd, 5th, 7th, 9th etc. They prepare "puttu" only on the eleventh day. On the third day they prepare "blackgram flour kali" and give it to the girl. On the 11th day, they give her full bath and allow her to come inside.

The celebrate "puberty rituals" on 16th or 22nd day, all the expenditure is to be borne by the girl's uncle. On this occasion the girl wears new saree. She is decorated with flowers, garlands, they keep plantain, coconut, betel leaf, nut etc. in her hand. After pouring water on the first day they celebrate "nalungu" and smear sandal paste, place *kumkum* etc. Giving "blackgram" flour is to give relief from the hip-pain. The relatives come and cook food, "puttu" etc. on odd numbered days and give it to the girl.

On the day of "puberty rituals", these people place stone

mortor and roller and decorate it with sandal paste and *kumkum,* then they give the decorated roller into the hands of the girl thrice. The relatives give presents to the girl and a grand feast is arranged for them. They never send the girl out, without doing this celebration. However, if it is necessary to go out she is to take margosa leaves, iron etc. otherwise they believe that ghosts will seize her. They give the cloth to the washerwoman and she gives cloth to the girl till she is allowed to come inside the house.

Nayakkar (Tatar)

This caste people pour water only on the 3rd day and this has to be done by the uncle. Upto 16th day the girl is to be in a separate room. They prepare "puttu" on 5th, 7th and 9th day. After giving bath on the first day they first give egg, gingely oil to eat and then "dhall rice". They pour water on 3rd, 5th, 7th, 9th, 11th, 13th and 16th day and allow the girl inside the house. On 16th day itself they celebrate "puberty rituals" and the uncle spends money for this celebration. This people also invite relatives and they cook food, prepare "puttu" and give it to the girl on odd numbered days. There is no restriction for pouring water i.e. anybody can pour water on the girl's head.

They do "ennay nalungu" on the 3rd day. For all these, uncle has to bear the expenditure. They give iron, sickle, margosa leaves, broomstick etc. in the hands of the girl and they believe that ghosts will not seize the girl.

Muppanar

Most of the customs resemble the other caste people. Those different from others are listed here. The girl is to be in a separate hall for 10 days, these people prepare "puttu" on the first day itself and for other days the relatives who prepare meals also prepare "puttu". They invite the girl inside the house on 16th day after giving full bath. These people celebrate "puberty rituals" on 16th day or in the 3rd month and on that day they do "nalungu". At the time of "nalungu" they put garland on the girl. There is no restriction for putting the garland to the girl, but when it is taken out from her neck, only her uncle should do it.

Devar

If a girl attains age she is to intimate it through other persons to her mother (if she says it directly to her mother they believe that the girl will be affected by diseases). On the first day they give her full bath and give her new cloths to wear. They give full bath on 3rd, 5th, 7th, and 9th etc. days and on the 15th day they give her full bath and allow the girl inside the house. On 5th day these people cook "puttu". On the first day after giving her full bath these people first give egg, oil to take inside, then they give her "sweet rice" (Sarkkarai pongal). On these days they never take mutton etc.

These people celebrate "puberty rituals" on 15th or 22nd day or in the 3rd month or before marriage according to the economic status. They note the time of attaining puberty and prepare horoscope according to this time. The expenditures are met by the girl's uncle. In this caste also relatives come, cook food and give it to the girl on odd numbered days. On all these days the relatives prepare "puttu" and give it to the girl. All the other customs resemble the other caste people.

Udayar

If a girl attain age it can be informed directly to her mother by the girl herself. Then they seat the girl in a separate room, on the first day they pour water, relatives hold a sieve above the head of the girl, put margosa leaves in the sieve, an old married woman pours water through the sieves on the head of the girl. On that day they do "nalungu" by smearing sandal paste, *kumkum* etc., prepare "puttu", leave her in a separate room, decorate her hair with flowers. After this, first they give "gingely oil" to the girl. After this they pour water on the 3rd day, prepare rice, Kezhvaraku (millet) "puttu" on this day. They prepare horoscope of the girl at the time of attaining age. On 5th day they invite the girl inside the house. According to their convenience they celebrate "puberty rituals" and the girl's uncle is to spend money for this. They take new saree on this day. The other customs resemble the other caste people regarding "puberty rituals".

Kallar (Devar)

When a girl attains puberty, in this caste it is in custom to inform the news to her mother through somebody else. Then they buy sugar, plantain, flower etc. washerwoman and relatives are invited, she pour water on the girl's head. On the 1st day while pouring water they prepare "puttu", leave the girl in a separate room, decorate her hair with flowers. While pouring water to the girl on the first day girl's uncle's wife holds sieve, puts turmeric in the sieve and uncle's wife pours water through sieve. They prepare the horoscope of the girl attaining age. After this these people give egg, blackgram flour, sugar etc. to the girl to eat. They invite the girl inside the house on 16th day and after the 16th day the girl's uncle, aunt do "siir" and celebrate "puberty rituals". At that time they take new saree to the girl. Relatives come on odd numbered days, and prepare "puttu", cook food and serve them to the girl.

On the day of "puberty rituals", the girl wears new saree, they garland her, give coconut etc. in her hand and seat her in a chair. At that time stone mortor and roller are placed on the side of the girl which are decorated by *kumkum*, sandal paste etc. and this roller is given thrice into the girl's hand and got back and relatives give presentations to the girl. The girl is sent outside only if the "puberty ritual" is finished or if the girl is to go outside necessarily they prepare "puttu" and send her outside. Otherwise they never allow the girl to go outside. At the time of attaining age, when the girl goes outside she is to take margosa leaves or iron things to avoid seizure by ghosts. They give the dress at the time of attaining age to the washerwoman and she is to give the change of dress to the girl till she comes inside the house.

Tuluva Naickar

If a girl attains age it is to be mentioned by somebody else to her mother. On 1st day they pour water by holding a sieve above the girl's head, three married ladies hold the sieve, put turmeric, paddy, margosa leaves and coins in it. Any body can pour water through the sieve, put "nalungu", smear sandal paste and *kumkum* etc. leave the girl inside a separate room. Then they decorate the girl's hair with flowers on the first day.

Then they give dhall rice, then egg, sugar, gingely oil and plantain to take inside. They pour water on the girl on 1st, 3rd, 5th, 7th, 9th, and 11th days and prepare food on 3rd, 5th, 6th, 9th... and on the day of inviting the girl inside the house. They prepare the horoscope of the girl at attaining age. On the 21st day they invite the girl inside the house. On the same day they celebrate "puberty rituals" and the girl's uncle is to do "siir" for this celebration. On odd numbered days, relatives come, prepare food and serve them to the girl. No presentation will be given to the girl and other custom regarding "puberty rituals" resemble the above caste people. They never send the girl outside before celebrating "puberty rituals". At the time of attaining puberty they give margosa leaves or iron things to avoid seizure by ghosts. The dress worn by the girl on the day of attaining age is given to the washerwoman.

Jankamar

In this caste, the girl attaining age can inform the matter to her mother directly. They pour water on the first day itself. On this day they smear sandal paste, *kumkum* etc. and do "nalungu" to the girl. The girl is garlanded and her hair is decorated with flowers. After pouring water on the first day these people give "cooked rice" first to eat and only on the 3rd day, they give egg, blackgram flour and sugar.

They pour water on 3rd, 5th, 7th and 9th days and prepare "puttu" on these days. They also prepare horoscope of the girl at this time. While pouring water on the first day they hold a sieve above the girl's head. Usually, married ladies hold the sieve, put turmeric, margosa leaves and holy grass (arukam pul) inside the sieve and the married ladies pour water in the sieve.

They invite the girl inside the house on 9th day. On this day itself these people celebrate "puberty rituals" and the uncle takes new saree for this occasion and the other expenditures are met by the parents. On odd numbered days relatives come and cook food and prepare "puttu" and serve it to the girl. The other customs regarding puberty rituals resemble the other caste people.

Konar (Yadhavappillai)

When the girl attains puberty on the first day she is given full bath. The cloth worn on that day is given to the washer woman. For the girl, presentations come from her uncle's house. After giving full bath, a new cloth is given to her to wear. Then a kind of sweet boiled rice (Sarkkarai pongal) in which little amount of ghee is added is given to her to eat as a first edible. On the 2nd day some tiffen is given to her. Only on the 3rd day "puttu" is cooked. On the 5th day relatives come, cook and give food to the girl. On the 11th or 15h day "puberty rituals" is celebrated and all kinds of presentation have to come from the girl's uncle's house for that day. That day three "puttu" is cooked and all the three "puttu" are taken around the girl and one of the three "puttu" is given to the washerwoman. The other two are given to the those who attend the function (All the three "puttu" are done by the rice mixed with jaggery). After showing the "puttu" around the girl, she is allowed to come inside the house. "Puberty rituals" are celebrated like a marriage by these caste people. This ceremony can be celebrated before marriage also. Without celebrating the "puberty ceremony" the girl must not go out ("turai mitikkaamal vassalil sellakkuutaatu") is a strict custom among these people. So, these people strictly never allow the girl to go out of the house before puberty ceremony is celebrated.

Kuravar

When the news of maturity of a girl is known, a separate

hall is built and she is sent inside the hall. Then they send this news to her uncle. Her uncle comes with presentations for the girl. A sieve is held above the head of the girl in which coin, turmeric water, margosa leaves etc. are put and odd numbered married woman pour water through the sieve on the girl's head. They give blackgram flour, egg and sugar first to eat to the girl and then decorating her, she is sent to the separate room. Then a kind of sweet boiled rice (sarkkarai pongal) and plantain are given to the girl to eat. This people cook "puttu" only on the day of "puberty ceremony". On other days they give only some varieties of tiffen. According to the economic condition the "puberty rituals" are celebrated on 16th day. Otherwise whenever possible they do it accordingly. The matured girl is allowed to go out after her bath whether the "puberty rituals" is celebrated or not. On the day of "puberty ceremony", the girl is taken to the river or tank bank and the puberty rituals are done there itself. On that day friends and relatives come with presentations and a grand feast is arranged for those who attend the function. All the expenditures belong to the girl's house. They do not give the cloth worn when the girl attains her age to the washerwoman.

Vannan (Eekaali-Washerman)

The girl who comes to age is seated and sieve is held above the girl's head in which betel leaf, nut, coconut, flowers, coins, turmeric etc. are put and five (or) seven married woman pour water through the sieve on the girl's head. Then they give "pepper cooked food" first to eat to that girl. After that in odd numbered days relatives cook and give food to the girl. After this 9th or 11th day or on the third month according to their convenience they celebrate the puberty rituals. On the day of "puberty rituals", the presentations have to come from the girl's uncle's house. On that day "puttu" is cooked and it is shown around the girl. Relatives and friends attend the function and a grand feast is arranged to them. The participants of this function give presents to the girl.

Navitar (Maruttuvar–Barber)

The girl who comes to age is seated and a sieve is held above the girl's head and coins are put into the sieve and her uncle pours water through the sieve on the girl's head. After that "pepper cooked rice" is given to the girl to eat first. On odd numbered days relatives would cook and give food to the matured girl. After that 9th or 11th day "puberty rituals" is celebrated. Then "puttu" is cooked and it is shown around the girl. Relatives and friends who come to attend the function give presents to that girl.

Cakkili (Cobbler)

When a girl attains her age, that girl's uncle has to pour water on the girl's head. A sieve in which gold, coins, beads, a finger ring (this was put by the uncle's wife in the sieve) etc. are put and held above the girl's head and water is poured through the sieve. After pouring water, the ring in the sieve is put into the finger of the girl. Then a green hut (a separate hut) is built and the girl is sent into the hut. From 1st to 32 days the girl has to be in the separate hut. After pouring water, gingely oil, blackgram flour, plantain etc. are given to the girl to eat as first edible after attaining age. This caste people never give cooked food for three days, only some tiffen are given to the girl, to eat. Only after pouring water on the third day, they give food. These people pour water once in three days interval on the girl's head. For this thirty two days, this girl will not eat meat etc.

They celebrate "punniyadanam" on 16th day and for this (pandaaram-priest), priest comes and kindles holy fire on that day, friends and relatives attend the function. After finishing "punniyadanam" they give alms to the priest. Only after "punniyadanam" is finished the girl is allowed to come inside the house. Even though the girl is allowed to come inside the house, on the 16th day she is again sent to the separate hut and she has to be there for thirty two days compulsorily. After this thirty two days the date and time of maturity of the girl is noted by the uncle's house people and those who are to do the "puberty rituals" will celebrate the puberty ceremony. The ritual customs are same as those of other caste people.

Harijan (Adi Dravidar)

The news of attaining age of a girl is sent to the uncle and he has to pour water on the girl first. After pouring water a new dress ("kayiru paavadai and daavan"—they turn this "kayiru paavaddi" as "koovandi paavadai") has to be given for her to wear. Then plantain, sugar, and some varieties of food are given to close neighbourers. After this, they ask the girl to sit and sieve is held above the girl's head and five pots (kudam) of water is poured on the girl's head through the sieve. Then oil and "sikakkay" is smeared on the head of the girl and a new saree has to be given to the girl. Then they give feast to all the members. These people also give the dress of the girl when she attain her age to washerwoman. After pouring water, these people give a mixture of blackgram flour, plantain, sugar, gingely oil to the girl to eat as a first edible. Only on the 3rd day the "puttu" is prepared 2nd day they give "vadai", "paayasam" etc. to the girl. Only on odd numbered days they give her full bath. On these days relatives come, cook food and give it to her. On 15th day "puberty rituals" are celebrated on that day plantain, sugar, flowers, betel leaf, nut, new dress etc. has to be bought. The expenditures for this celebration is not spent by the uncle. On that day they decorate the girl and "puttu" is taken around the girl. On that day relatives and friends will come and give presentations to the girl. A grand feast is arranged to the guests.

9

Marriage Customs

Brahmin (Iyer)

These people send the horoscope of the bride to the bridegroom's house and they ask for the bridegroom's horoscope for the purpose of comparison. If both the horoscopes agree, then the bridegroom and his party come and see the bride in her house. If they agree then they fix the marriage. These people take food in the bride's party even before fixing the marriage.

The engagement is celebrated in bride's house. At the time of engagement bridegroom does not attend the function. On that day the dowry, ornaments etc. are to be given to the bridegroom's party. On that day close relatives will come and in front of all the relatives, they write the "Lakhna Pattirikai" (the paper in which the auspicious day, time etc. for marriage are noted). On that day from the bridegroom's house they bring and give new saree, blouse, betel leaf, nut, plantain, flowers, turmeric, *kumkum*, sandal paste etc. to the bride.

These people celebrate "puberty rituals" only at the time of marriage. Before the day of marriage the girl is decorated and seated, seven or nine things are shown around her by 7 or 9 married women. The seven or nine things are shown around the girl and these things are placed in the parts of the body like head, shoulder, hand, leg and taken back. The expenditure for this function belonged to the girl's parent. These people believe that "the ghost will not seize the girl and inauspicious things will not affect her", by doing this function.

Marriage is celebrated in the girl's house. Before marriage day "bridegroom's procession" (maapplillai azhaippu) is arranged. Before the procession milk, sugar etc. are given to the bridegroom and he is seated and new dresses, mirror, powder, comb chappel etc. are also given to the bridegroom. This procession is accompanied by fire works (vaana vetikkai) etc. in a grand manner. After this function, tiffen is given to the bridegroom and then the bride and bridegroom sit together. Brahmin priest recites *mantras*, the aged people bless the couple and then coconut, betel leaf, nut, plantain, flowers, *kumkum*, turmeric, sandal paste, saree, blouse piece, *dhoti*, towel etc. are given to the couple. This function is termed as "sabhataambhuulam".

After on the marriage day, there is a function known as "paradeesikkoolom". At that time, the bridegroom has to wear nine yards *dhoti* and a towel and hold a bundle of cloth. A friend or brother-in-law of the bridegroom hold the umbrella for the bridegroom at this time and then the bridegroom undertakes "yaathraadaanam" (This function means that the bridegroom is angry with the father-in-law). Father-in-law stops the bridegroom and tells him that he will give in marriage his daughter to the bridegroom and takes back the bridegroom to the house. Then the bride and bridegroom are seated in a swing and the aged woman show the "paccaip piti" (the cooked rice mixed with turmeric powder and *kumkum* and made like a ball) around the bridegroom and bride thrice in clockwise and thrice in anti-clockwise direction. On the marriage platform except the presentation (siir) given to the bride from her parent's house, nothing is placed like in other castes.

After this function, the girl has to change her dress, to wear nine yard saree. Then the girl and the boy are seated in front of the brahmin priests who recite holy *mantras* and kindle the holy fire. Then the girl sits on her father's lap, a small ploughing instrument is placed on the head of the girl (the belief in this is that "the girl will lead her life in a fertile manner") and taken back. Then the bridegroom ties the marriage badge on the bride's neck and the bridegroom tied one knot and the other two knotes are completed by the sister-in-law. The time of marriage (i.e., at the time when the bridegroom ties the marriage badge) the bride wears the saree in a deep red or purple colour. This saree has to be worn on all the festival and ceremonial days (but now this system is changing). These people wear two marriage badges, one from bride's house, another from bridegroom's house.

After this ceremony, the marriage dress is changed by the bride and bridegroom. Then the couple are seated in front of the brahmin priests who kindles the holy fire, then doing "paaligai puja" (the mixture of nine kind of grains are soaked in water and they will grow up like a small plant, this is called as "paaligai"), and then the relatives bless the couple. The relatives and friends give presents and immediately the feast is given. This feast is called as "samabandi boojanam" because at the same time both the bride's and bridegroom's party took food.

On the evening of the marriage day the couple are seated and "nalungu" is done. At the time of "nalungu" the bride has to give betel leaf, nut etc. to the bridegroom by singing songs. Rolling of coconut, plucking of the coconut from the bride or bridegroom's hand by the other and flowers from each other's hand are part of "nalungu". These games are termed as "tiruvilaiyaadalkal", then the rice cakes fried in oil are powdered and put on one another's head (bride and bridegroom). In this game if the bride pluck the coconut from the bridegroom then it is a belief that the bride lead her husband. If the bridegroom won in the play he will lead the wife. After the "nalungu" is finished, camphor is lighted and around 6'o clock they take the "paaligai" and with trumphat they go to the tank (or) river and then they leave the "pali" in the tank or river. Then on that night the couple go to the bridegroom's house along with the presentations for marriage (siir varissi) and with variety rice (kattu saadam). The presentations like cot, vessels, ornaments etc. have to be sent. Then a reception is held in the bridegroom's house. For this all the "siir" are prepared again in the bride's house. The half of the expenditure for the reception is from the bride's house. They celebrate "First night", usually on the same day. After marriage within one year it is a custom to celebrate some ceremonies and do "siir" to the bride and bridegroom from bride's house. These people give "siir" and celebrate the functions like

(1) *Kaaradaiyaan noompu*—For this pot, a little earthen pot, the face of Goddess Lakshmi in silver etc. with other kinds of "siir saaman" (presentations) has to be given to the bride.

(2) *Aati maappillai azhaippu*—In the bride's house they has to give *dhoti*, ring, silver goblet to the bride and bridegroom and has to give a grand-feast to them.

(3) *Aavani avittam*—Bride's party has to put the sacred thread to the bridegroom by giving *dhoti*, towel, etc. to him. A grand feast has to be arranged.

(4) *Navarattiri*—Dolls made up of clay, clothes etc. has to be given to the bridegroom's house.

(5) *Talai Deepawali*—Before the 'Deepawali day night, the couple has to be invited to the bride's house, tiffen and dinner has to be given. On the next day early morning white milk *dhoti*, saree, etc. have to be given and the bridegroom has to be seated in a wooden plank and the oil has to be smeared like "Oil nalungu". Then 51 types of tiffen has to be prepared on that day.

(6) *Karthikai Deepam*—Fried rice seed, unhusked rice (aval), Lamp etc., has to be bought and given to the bride along with the other presentations.

(7) *Pongal*—The pot made up of white metal, big size spoon etc. with other kind of presentation has to be given to the bride.

Brahmin (Iyangar)

This caste people resemble the above caste people in many

aspects, except the following : Only if the marriage is fixed, the bridegroom's party will take food in the bride's house. On the day of engagement it is a custom to exchange written documents mentioning the news of the alliance between the bride and bridegroom. On that day they give ornaments for the marriage to the bridegroom's party, if not possible then they give it before marriage.

Before the day of marriage in the early morning the bride and bridegroom have to take oil bath. Then on that day evening "bridegroom's procession" (termed as "janavaasam") is arranged. The marriage is celebrated in the bride's house itself. The mixture of nine grains has to be cooked in water, two days before the marriage day in the bride's house.

After tying marriage badge (customs resemble the above caste people) the couple are seated facing each other and a coconut smeared with turmeric powder is given to them. They roll coconut and play. After this the couple go round the marriage platform thrice and the bridegrooms brother-in-law place the hand of the couple on each other's and puts fried rice-seed on their hand thrice. Then the bridegroom puts the ring in his brother-in-law's hand and then uncle and aunt put the "metti" in bride's toe and then only the couple exchange their garlands.

After marriage, "nalungu" is arranged. In this the newly married couple play with nose-gay of the flower, powdering the rice cake (appalaam) putting on each other's head, play pallaankuzhi (a tablet with fourteen holes for play etc.), etc. while other stand around the couple. After this the "paaligai" is taken to a tank and the peepul tree's bough is fixed in the bank of the tank or the river. After the "paaligai" is left in the tank a ceremony viz., "gragappraveesam" is celebrated. At this ceremony the bride is sent to the bridegroom's house along with saree, *dhoti*, betel leaf, nut, plantain, flowers, variety rice, rice cake, vadakam etc.

Then within one year these people give "siir" to the bride from her parents. (1) *Aati*—In the milk from coconut, sugar has to be put, the bridegroom has to be invited to the house (bride's) and this milk (termed as "aatippaal") has to be given to the bridegroom. Then "parupputtenkaay" (a sweet made of ground, pulse and jaggery) has to be prepared and given. (2) *Avanai avittam* :—This is done as per above caste people. (3) *Navarattiri*—This is also done as per above caste people. (4) *Talai Deepawali,* (5) *Karthikai,* (6) *Pongal*—For these functions also these people do the "siir" as per above caste people. (7) *Sri Jayanthi*—Shape of Lord Krishna in silver has to be bought and has to give them to the bride. For "Nalunku song" refer following page.

Pillai

They first examine the agreement of horoscopes. In olden days only from the bridegroom's house come to see the bride (In this connection a proverb is told *"oru ponnu paakke venti sila seruppu teeynju pookum").* But now-a-days only from the bride's house they send the horoscope and if the horoscopes as well as both parties agree marriage is fixed. Engagement is celebrated in bride's house. This caste people termed the engagement as *"muhuurtta oolai ezhututal";* at that time saree, blouse piece, engagement ring etc. are brought from the bridegroom's house to the bride and relatives come and in their presence the marriage is fixed. On that day the date, time etc. of marriage is fixed and a grand feast is given to all the members who attend the function.

Marriage is celebrated in the bridegroom's house. The first pillar for the "Pandar" is erected in front of the marriage hall and is decorated with mango leaves, turmeric, *kumkum,* a new cloth (termed as "kusumpu tuni") and is erected by five married woman and bridegroom. The nine grain is soaked only in the bridegroom's house five days before marriage. It is a belief that the growth of this nine grains soaked in water shows the future life of the newly married couple. According to the growth of the grains, the life of the newly married couple is believed to be decided by destiny.

Before the day of marriage it is usual, to do "nalungu". For the bride-her uncle and for the bridegroom—his uncle do the "nalungu" celebration. At the time of "nalungu" for the bride and bridegroom their uncle dip the sacrificial grass in the oil and places it on their head, then "Sikakaay" and then both the bride and bridegroom are given bath. Then they make "pillayaar" (shape of Lord Ganesh) and then do *puja* for it (This type of "nalungu" is changing now-a-days). Then from the bridegroom's house they come and take the girl to their house. When the bride enters into the house of the bridegroom, her mother-in-law gives her a measuring pot full of paddy in which a lamp is lit and then invites her into the house.

They place "alunkaravam (a broad mouthed big brass vessel in which the milk ladle, a stylus (ezhuttani), leaf etc. are put), 'granite grinding stone and roller', 'kuda vilakku' (a kind of lamp), 'peepul tree's bough', 'row of pots placed one on each other (termed as "panta muttikkaal paanai") in which odins woodier's bough is tied etc. in the marriage platform. Then in the marriage platform the bridegroom tie the marriage badge to the bride. At this time water is filled up in the pots on the marriage platform. These people tie only one marriage badge to the bride and also the marriage badge is brought from the bridegroom's house.

Then the bride and bridegroom hold each other's hand and go round the marriage platform thrice and at the third time they have to take the things thrice in the broad mouthed brass vessel and put them back. Then the hands of the couple are joined and the brother-in-law of the bridegroom put the fired rice seed into their hand. Then they put a ring to the bridegroom and the bridegroom gives a ring for his brother-in-law. After this the bride places her leg on the grinding stone and the bridegroom puts the "metti" in her leg. Then rice is spread on the floor and a plantain leaf is placed on it and the bride has to stand on it. Then the mother-in-law, sister-in-law tie the plate of gold on the forehead of the bride and the mother-in-law, sister-in-law of the bridegroom tie gold coins on his forehead. Then a grand feast is given to all the members who attend the function.

After this they celebrate—"naalaam niir satangu"—i.e. "nalungu" (on these days only next day after marriage, this ceremony is celebrated, now-a-days they celebrate it on the same day). Then the "paaligai", peepul tree's bough etc. are taken to the tank or river and submerged in the water and the peepul tree's bough is erected in the bank of the tank. There is a belief that the growth of this peepul tree's bough shows the future life of the newly married couple. Then the bridegroom is taken to the bride's house. Then the couple go and come to each other's house thrice and after that they celebrate the ceremony "first night".

Then within one year of the marriage they give "aaticciir". On the 18th of the month of "aati" (July-August) they celebrate "aati perukku". On that day the garland of the marriage is left in the river. Among these caste people, they do not have the custom to untie the marriage badge at the time of "sati perukku". In the month of "Ayppasi", they invite the couple to the bride's house and presentations are given for Deepawali. For "Pongal" they go to the bridegroom's house and give presentations to the bride. They do not invite the couple to the bride's house for "pongal".

Isai Velalar (Pillai)

This caste people ask for the other's horoscope either from bride's or from bridegroom's party. They compare horoscopes and if they do agree they put the flower before God or Goddess in the temple. If they get the permission then they fix up the marriage. Engagement is done in the bride's house. On that day all the presentations has to be brought from the bridegroom's house. Only the expenditure for fest belong to the bride's house (After this all the customs resemble the customs of washerman caste people).

These people celebrate the marriage in the bridegroom's house. They celebrate three types of "nalungu" before marriage. First is on the morning of the day before the marriage, second while the bride is taken to the bridegroom's house and third on the marriage day before the girl enters the marriage platform.

They put "parisam" to the girl and she is taken to the bridegroom's house. The nine grains are soaked in bridegroom's house five days before the marriage ceremony.

At the time of marriage the bride and bridegroom take oil bath. Before tying the marriage badge both the bride and the bridegroom tie yellow string (kankanam) to each other's hand, and the bridegroom puts the "metti" on bride's toe. On the marriage platform the broad mouthed big brass vestsel is placed. Also "kuda vilakku", seven pots (to keep the "pali"), the pepul tree's bough tied with the pot, adorned with *tilak* and a red cloth, kuda vilakku—in the center peeppul tree's bough etc; are placed. After this the seven pots are placed.

The pot where the peepul tree's bough is tied is filled with water. These people wear silk saree at the time of marriage (On those days they wear only cotton saree termed as "saamip putavai"). Then the bride and bridegroom worship the feet of their parents. Then brahmin priest comes, recites holy *mantras* and kindles holy fire. The sister-in-law holds the lamp, and the bridegroom tie the marriage badge to the bride's neck. Then the bride and the bridegroom exchange garlands. Then his brother-in-law joins the hands of the bridegroom and bride and puts fried rice-seed on his hand. Then he puts the ring on this finger. After this bride's younger sister or elder sister puts the "metti" on bridegroom's toe. The newly married couple's relatives tie the golden plate on the forehead of the couple. After this they celebrate "naalaam niir satangu" "nalungu" (as in other castes) and only after this they take and leave the "paaligai" in the river or tank. This people celebrate "nalungu" like other caste people. Then the couple untie the yellow string from each other's hand. At the time of leaving "paali", the bride has to take the "saalungaravam" pot and leave the "paali" in the tank and carry water in that pot from the tank. The bridegroom again carries the peepul tree's bough and erect it in the garden, of their house and has to pour water. There is a belief that if the bough grow well then the life of the newly married couple also will be like that of peepul tree's bough.

According to the growth of the peepul tree's bough, the life of the couple will be settled. In this caste also the couple go and come to each other's house and mingle with each other's family.

In the month of "aati" the bride's parents give "siir" (presentations) and they worship the marriage garland and leave it in the river on 18th, of this month. For Deepawali and Pongal also the bride's party has to give presentations. It is in custom among this caste people that they untie the marriage badge only in odd numbered months like 3rd or 5th and tie a new one.

Patayacci

In this caste first from the bridegroom's house they have to see the bride's horoscope and if the horoscopes agree then both parties will seat in one another's house and if all the things click they fix the marriage and only if the marriage is fixed both parties will take food in one another's house.

Bridegroom's party has to come to the bride's house and then the engagement is fixed. At the time of engagement betel leaf, nut, plantain, fruit, ornaments, flowers, new dresses etc. are brought from the bridegroom's house to bride's house. On that day, brahmin priest comes and fix the auspicious date, time etc. for marriage. The bride, wearing new saree has to pay respect to all the close relatives and aged persons. On that day a grand feast is given to all those who attend the function.

In this caste five (or) seven (or) nine days before marriage "nalungu" is celebrated for bride by her relatives and each relative brings new dress to the bride and gives her a grand feast. Only after the "nalungu" is finished, the bride take bath and wear new dresses. For this "nalungu" also all kind of presentations will be brought by the relatives. "Nalunku" is usually of two types. One is named as "ennay nalungu" and other named as "sandana nalungu". First one is done with oil and the second one is done with sandal paste. Nine grains are soaked in water nine or seven days before the marriage in bridegroom's house and in this caste this is done in both bride and bridegroom's house. When the bride is taken to the bridegroom's house this "paaligai" is also taken to the bridegroom's house, with the bride. Then it is a custom to offer *puja* for God or Goddess of the bridegroom's house after the bride has been invited to his house. At that time they offer meals, sweet cooked rice, the saree that has to be worn at the time of tying marriage badge (the saree is only cotton saree not the silk saree), *dhoti*, the marriage badge etc.

Next day the marriage is celebrated. In the marriage platform broad mouthed big brass vessel, new pots rowed pots on one another, paaligai, peepul tree's bough, stone grinder and roller etc. are placed. First the bride and bridegroom tie a yellow thread tied with a turmeric piece (term as "kankanam") to each other. At the time of marriage brahmin priest puts "punul", then the silver, gold punul is put by the relatives. At the time of marriage they invite brahmin priest who kindles holy fire and recites *mantras*. Before tying marriage badge, the bride and bridegroom worship their parent's feet (termed as "paada puujai") by pouring water and cleaning it and worship by placing flowers etc. If the marriage is celebrated in the bridegroom's house, mother of the bride does not attend the function (if it is celebrated in chultry, temple etc. both the mother and the father of the bride will attend the marriage), then the bride worships her father's feet only. At the time of tying marriage badge the bride's sister-in-law keeps a lamp at the back of the bride. This is termed as "naatti vilakku pitittal". For this money has to be given to the sister-in-law from the bride's house.

After tying the marriage badge bride's brother places the bride's and bridegroom's hand one on the other and puts fried rice seed on their hand and then they put it in the holy fire. Then the bride's brother goes in front, the couple follow and they go round the marriage platform thrice. Then the bridegroom places the bride's leg on the stone mortor and puts the 'metti' on her toe. After this the couple take the milk ladle, a stylus, palm leaf from the broad mouthed vessel thrice and puts them back again in the vessel. Then his brother-in-law puts the ring to the bridegroom and vice versa. Then uncle, aunt, sister-in-law tie the golden plate on the forehead of the bride. Then only the yellow string tied before marriage has to be untied by someone else. Then they took "paaligai" and the "peepul tree's" bough and went to the river or tank. They leave the "paaligai" in the river, errect the peepul tree's bough on the river bank or on the bank of the tank. Then the bridegroom has to go to the bride's house.

Then it is in custom for the bride and bridegroom to go, to each other's house and mingle with each other's family thrice. The third time bride's parents arrange a feast, sweets, tiffens etc. and do a ceremony "sampantam kalattal" (mingle with each other's family). After this the bridegroom's party do the same. Then within a year in the month of aati, they do "aati siir" and give presentations. On 18th of this month, they leave the marriage garland in the river after worshipping it, untie the marriage badge and tie a new one. On the day before Deepawâli, new dresses, presentations etc. are given to the couple and are invited to the bride's house and presentations are given to them and after celebrating the function they go back to their house. In the month of "tai", "Pongal" presentations are given to the bride and taken to the bridegroom's house. On the day of new moon day of the month of "aati" the couple go round the peepul tree.

Sengunta Mutaliyar

First from the bridegroom's house they go to see the bride's house. Before the horoscopes are examined these people see the girl and then only they check the agreement of the horoscopes and if they agree they will fix the marriage in the girl's house. If the horoscopes agree, they select on auspicious day and fix up the marriage. It is not in custom like "engagement" etc. On the day in which the marriage is fixed, relatives attend the function and a grand feast is arranged.

The day before the marriage day a ceremony viz. "pariyam pootutal" is celebrated. On that day from the bridegroom's house they come with a silk saree and with other presents, accompanied by trumphets etc. to the bride's house and put the "pariyam" and take food and then return back to their house. Only after putting "pariyam" (donation, fee, presents etc. by the bridegroom to the bride before proceeding to the house for marriage, as jewels, apparel, money, rice, fruits etc., in some parts stipulated for) they will send the girl to the bridegroom's house. On that day itself it is usual to worship their family God by offering saree, blouse, *dhoti*, towel etc. and three kind of tiffen etc.

The marriage is celebrated in the bridegroom's house. The nine grains soaked in water is prepared in the bridegroom's house before five, seven or nine days of the marriage day. When putting the "Pandar" it is usual to erect a "Muhuurthakkaal" (First pillar for pandar) and it is erected three days before the marriage day. This is usually erected in the north-east direction (termed as "iicaaniya muulai" (or) "sani muulai"). This first pillar is termed as "pandakkaal" by this caste people. A bamboo stick to which a yellow cloth containing the nine kind of grains, coin etc. are kept is tied and also mango leaves are tied. Then five members hold the bamboo stick and erect it.

On the platform where marriage ceremony takes place broad mouthed big brass vessels, two covers for it, row pots on one another, nine kalasams for keeping the "paaligai" (these kalasams are brought from potter's house), peepul tree's bough, stone mortor, roller, a mortor ("ural" termed as "kundaani") are kept. With all the above things these people tie a turmeric. First "atai" (a kind of cake made of the mixture of rice, kinds of dhall etc.) is made and given to the bridegroom. Then they put oil "nalungu" to him. This is done to the bridegroom by his sister and nine elderly people in the bridegroom's house. A similar "nalungu" is done to the bride in her house on the same manner. Then they take bath. The saree to be worn at the time of marriage is bought by the bridegroom's people and this is a cotton saree and not a silk saree. The "marriage badge" also has to be brought from bridegroom's house. Then the bride and bridegroom are seated together, brahmin priest will come and recite *mantras*, kindle holy fire.

Then in a big plate two broken coconuts, a coconut, plantain, flowers, betel leaf, nut, *kumkum* etc. are placed and camphor is lit and the brahmin priest shows it to all the relatives and gives it to the bridegroom. Then he gives 'atchadai' (rice mixed with turmeric powder) to all the people and when the brideg-room ties the marriage badge to the bride, they put the yellow rice on the couple by blessing them to live a long and prosperous life. Then the bride and bridegroom change garlands and they go round the marriage platform thrice. Then the bride's sister-in-law tie the golden plate on bride's forehead. Then the couple are invited from the marriage platform and are given milk and plantain. After this they go to the bride's house (it is in custom to wear "pottuttaali" [small round size marriage badge] and they can marry again when she became a widow).

After marriage the couple go and come thrice to each other's house and mingle with each other's family as in other castes. After this the relatives cook food and feed the newly married couple. Then within one year these people give "siir" for the month of "aati" 21 coconuts, a new plate etc. are bought and the couple are invited to the bride's house. On the day of Deepawali, in Ayppasi month, new dresses, golden presentations etc. are given to the couple inviting them to the bride's house. On the day of "Pongal" they buy new pot (big vessel in the type of pot) etc. and they take it to the bridegroom's house.

Asari (Pattar-Kammalar-Goldsmith, Taccar-Carpenter)

First from the bridegroom's house they have to see the horoscope of the bride and if the horoscopes agree, then they select on auspicious day and fix up the marriage. These people take food in each other's house only if the marriage is fixed or they take food if they are relatives. Bridegroom's party come to the bride's house and fix up the marriage. On that day bridegroom's party bring all the *"varisai saamaangal"*, like betel leaf, nut, flowers, *kumkum,* turmeric, sandal paste, plantain, sarees, blouse piece etc. to the bride's house. After the date has been fixed the bride wears new saree and the garland from the bridegroom's house and bow down to the aged people. On that day relatives come and a grand feast has been arranged.

Before the marriage "nalungu" is done to the bride in the bride's house. First her parents do the "nalungu". Five days before marriage they soak nine grains in water in the bridegroom's house. These people celebrate a ceremony viz. "*kaappu kattutal*" before marriage. On that day a new pot is bought, it is decorated by turmeric powder, *kumkum* etc. and a yellow string is tied round it. Then five married women put paddy in that pot and pour water on the paddy and light and show the camphor. Then with that fire of the camphor they kindle fire in the hearth and the paddy is boiled and it is ground to become rice. Then before the bride is taken to the bridegroom's house they worship and offer to their family God by cooking the above said rice.

On the day before the marriage day the bridegroom's party invite the bride's party and at that time bride's party take white metal vessel, other vessels with them. While coming, bridegroom's party come with all kind of presentations ("siir varisai") like saree, blouse piece, *dhoti,* towel etc. to invite the bride's party. In the marriage hall five new pots (sompu), five coconuts, flowers, coins, betel leaf, nut, stone grinder and roller are kept. Before beginning the marriage both the bride and bridegroom tie the yellow string in each other's hand and then do obeisance at the feet their parents. These people, at the time of marriage, compulsorily wear nine yards saree or the upper portion of the saree in the right side and then only they tie the marriage badge. First the bridegroom's house marriage badge is tied to the bride, at that time bride's sister-in-law hold the lighted lamp. Then the couple go round the marriage platform thrice.

Then the bridegroom puts the "metti" in the toe of the girl and they take the "paaligai" to the river or tank. They leave the "paaligai" in the river or tank and erect the peepul tree's bough in the bank of the river or the bank of the tank. After this the bride takes water in the water pot from the river or the tank and they return back to the house.

After the marriage, this caste people celebrate a ceremony (viz., "Naakavalli muhuurttam"). For this the expenditure has to be borne by the bride's house. The bride and bridegroom have to be seated with new dresses etc. and the bridegroom tie the second marriage badge to the bride. Then the couple play the "pallaankuzhi", nose-gye of the flower etc. They also crush the fried rice cake and put it on one another's head, and they roll the coconut etc. After this bridegrom's brother-in-law puts the ring in his finger. After this ceremony bride's uncle, aunt, sister-in-law tie the golden plate on the forehead of the bride. Then the couple go and come to each other's house and mingle with each other's family. Second time bride's party take tiffens and they mingle with each other's family. Third time from the bridegroom's house they do the same.

Within one year of the marriage, bride's party do "siir" to the bridegroom in the month of "aati". On the day of "aati perukku", they untie the marriage badge, again tie a new one with badge and gundu (gundu-golden round shaped thing tied on both sides of the badge) and then they leave the garland in the river. For "aavani avittam", they buy a new "panja paattra uttrani", new dresses and prepare a feast with "vata" and "paayasam". On the day of Deepawali the couple are invited to the bride's house, they do tiffens, buy new clothes and give a grand feast. For karthikai they give rice for "mao villakku", i.e. rice flour mixed with jaggery etc. For Pongal they give sugar, plantain etc. and take these to the couple in the bridegrom's house.

Chettiyar (Vysya)

These people compare horoscopes. First only from the girl's house they have to ask for the horoscope in the bridegroom's house. First from the girl's house they go and see the bridegroom's house and when they go there they take flowers, betel leaf and nut, plantain etc. with them. If the horoscopes agree they fix up the marriage. After this from the bridegroom's house they go to the bride's house and when they go over there they take flowers, plantain, betel leaf, nut, two blouse pieces etc. with them. If they agree, then they, i.e. from the bridegroom's house, will meet and discuss about the dowry etc. In this discussion itself they talk about the things for "sacred thread ceremony" (termed as "vadugu"), the things like silver plate, silver panjapaatram used by advanced religionist, to hold water for purification and a silver spoon (panjapaatra uttrani), silver pot, silver goglat, chappal, umbrella, chair (or) wooden seat, apart from this, they talk about the five tiffens, silver vessels, the rate for "aavani avittam", for the first night, for Deepawali, for the ceremony in which changing the marriage badge etc. Then, only if the rates and other things are agreed they select an auspicious day for the engagement. On that day they fix up the marriage and bridegroom's party bring betel leaf, nut, plantain, saree, blouse, flowers, *kumkum*, sandal paste, turmeric etc. Bride's party buy new dresses for the bridegroom and buy ring or chain. On the engagement day itself bride and bridegroom are seated side by side. Then bride's and bridegroom's father exchange the plates with each others before the brahmin priest. On that day relatives and friends attend the function. For both the parties there will be a common broker and both the parties have to give a deposit amount to him. This is for not changing their words. All the details are written in a document and given to both party. On the same day they put ornaments to the girl. Then the dresses from bride's to bridegroom's party and bridegroom's party to bride's party are given to the bridegroom and bride respectively. Then they wear new dresses and they sit together in a seat. Then they show "aalam" around them and arrange a grand feast for these who attend the function.

Before the marriage "nalungu" is done to the bride and bridegroom by their parents respectively. At the time of "nalungu" they put oil and Tilak on their forehead, they give food to them and give presentations. They select an auspicious day and worship their family God. Only after worshiping their family God, they will prepare all materials for the marriage. Marriage is celebrated in the bride's house. Bride's party go and invite the bridegroom with his relatives and they allot a separate room for the bridegroom and at the time of entering that room bride's party has to give bridegroom's pant, shirt, towel, soap, comb, *dhoti* etc. to his father and the expenses are done by the bride's party. Then, the "bridegroom's procession" (termed as "etirkola azhaippu") is celebrated and a feast is arranged.

The bride's and bridegroom's dresses, the presents given for the marriage etc. are placed separately in five plates and the "varisai saamaangal" (betel leaf, nut, plantain, flowers, *kumkum*, sandal paste, turmeric etc.) are kept in the bride's house. Then the bride and bridegroom are taken to a temple with trumphets and they exchange garlands in the temple, and they are taken back in a procession to the marriage place. Both stand and "aalam" is shown around them and a coconut is broken and they are brought to the marriage platform. Then the bride's house presents are given to the bridegroom's party and the deposit amount is got back from the broker. The golden ornaments are taken by the brahmin priest and he recites *mantras* and gives them back. The expenditure for Pandar belong to both party. Then the exchanging of plates is done, i.e. like the bride and the bridegroom has to be married to each other. Then "aalam" is shown to the bride and the bridegroom and then they are fed. At this time the pillar for pandar has been erected with odins tree's bough, decorating it with sandal paste, *kumkum*, a new cloth and showing camphor. This has been erected in the "iisasana muulai", i.e. in the north-eastern direction.

On the marriage day "nalungu" is done. The bride, bridegroom and their parents are seated in the same platform and the oil, sikakkay are placed thrice on them and they take bath. At this time the "nalungu" songs are sung. At this time dresses are given to other bridegroom from the bride's house. At the time of 'bridegroom's procession" itself they have to keep the "vadugu" (punul) things like an exhibition. After this for both the bride and the bridegroom they tie the gold plate on their forehead (This is termed as "passiyam kattutal"). Then the "punul ceremony" is performed. The thread, gold, silver punul are put by the bride's side or bridegroom's side five married women, after the brahmin priest recites the *mantras*. Mother-in-law places the colluriyum to the bridegroom by using a silver wire to avert evil eye. Then the bridegroom takes the stick, books, bag, banian tree's leaves, peepul tree's leaves, his brother-in-law holds the umbrella to him and the bridegroom went for the "kasi yaathirai". After this he comes back and the bridegroom has to place his feet on which mother-in-law pours water, father-in-law cleans his feet and puts sandal paste, *kumkum* etc. like worshiping the feet of the elderly people. Then the bridegroom's party invites the bride's party and the bridegroom's party give saree, blouse etc. to the bride's parents by placing them on a big towel. Then the bride and bridegroom join hands; 'aalam' is shown around them and a coconut is broken piece by piece and both of them are taken to the marriage hall.

In the marriage hall, marriage hall stick (manavarai kazhi) is erected, two plantain leaves with rice on them are placed and on that pots lime mortor is smeared are placed and in front of each pot seven or nine lamps are lit. Then the two marriage badges are tied in two yellow strings (these people wear "pottuttaali"—round shaped marriage badge) and placed on these pots. The nine grains are soaked only in the bride's house three days before the marriage day. A stone grinder and roller are placed on the marriage platform.

Then the bride and the bridegroom kindle the fire and worship the marriage badge on the pot. Then they do the feet worship to their parents. After this on one side the bride, bride's parents and on the other side the bridegroom, the bridegroom's parents are seated. The bride, bridegroom, their parents recite *mantras* and exchange betel leaf and nut. Then the marriage badge is placed in a coconut (in the same plate flowers, plantain etc. are there) is to be blessed. Then a stool is put and the bride sits on its facing east and place her right leg toe on it and the bridegroom is seated opposite to her i.e. facing her and he has to trample on her toe. The brahmin priest recites *mantras* and the bridegroom among the two marriage badges takes one and ties it on the bride's neck and places *kumkum* and lime on it. Then he ties the other marriage badge in the same way. Then those who attend the marriage give presents to the couple. Then to all the members betel leaf, nut, sweets are distributed.

Then the bridegroom's younger (or) elder sister ties the bride's saree's border and the towels of the bridegroom.

Then the bride's younger (or) elder brother takes the hand of the couple and go round the fire place and joins the hand of the couple and puts the fried rice-seed and close their hands. Then the fried rice has to be put in the fire (termed as "jajalu pacceti"). Like this three times they have to repeat the ceremony. Then they have to go again to the marriage platform and then the bridegroom gives sandal paste and places *kumkum* to his brother-in-law. *Dhoti*, towel, shirt, ring etc. are given to him from the bridegroom's house and the brahmin priest recites *mantras* and gives it to the bridegroom's brother-in-law. Then the brother-in-law wears the dresses and 'aalam' is taken by the bridegroom's relatives. In this 'aalam' money has to be put. Then bridegroom's sister (younger or elder) is asked to untie the knot and she would do it only if she is given ornament (or) money. Then they place a stone grinder and a stool, bride is to be seated on this stool, bridegroom ties the yellow string (on which a round coin and black beads on both sides are string) on the forehead of the bride. Then she place her right leg on the stone grinder and the bridegroom puts "metti" on her toe. Like this for the left leg also.

Then the bride gives the "vayanam". In this two winnows are smeared with turmeric powder and in the corners *kumkum* is smeared in a line and in that blouse place, coconut, plantain, flower, turmeric, yellow string with marriage badge, *kumkum*, colluriyum, mirror and coin like marriage badge etc. are placed in one winnow and with other winnow it is covered and give one set to the brahmin priest's wife, another set to her mother and the third set to her sister-in-law (totally, three set of winnows are given).

After this they worship their family Goddess "Kannikaa Parameswari". In this *puja* a bachelor has to take bath in the river or tank and draw water in a pot and place mango leaves, coconut, flowers, saffron on it and bring it to the marriage place. The bridegroom and bride go near him, invite him by singing songs and then that pot is placed in the marriage platform and it is decorated like a Goddess and worshipped and offerings are made.

After marriage they celebrate a function viz. "Baanuvu". For this function bridegroom's party bring saree, blouse etc. Those things are placed on a seat, the bridegroom and bride stand facing each other. Then the brahmin priest makes an elephant (shape) in salt and another in "dhuvarai" dhall. Then the bridegroom asks the bride "shall we take the elephant to the river in order to give it bath". Then the bride makes fun of him. After this the couple sit facing each other and "nalungu" is celebrated. In this function, the bride puts salt, dhuvarai dhall etc. around the head of the bridegroom thrice and she sings at that time. Then she powders the fried rice cake and throws thrice on their relatives head. Then comb, soap, mirror, bread, plantain, milk, sweets etc. are given to the bridegroom. The bridegroom also does the same and give the same things to the bride. At that time bridegroom's relatives sing songs. Then the bride and bridegroom play with nose-gay of flower. They termed this as "urutti taandutal". Then the bride takes "aalam" to the bridegroom and he puts a ring in that plate. Then the couple untie the string to each other's hand.

The pillars tied in the marriage hall are connected at the bottom and the bride's and bridegroom's saree, *dhoti,* blouse, towel, shirt, couple's parent's clothes are placed in a big plate under the pillars, milk is poured, coconut, plantain etc. are offered to it. After this grand feast is given to all those who attend the marriage. In that feast, bridegroom and the bride sit opposite to each other and take food. Then bridegroom's party and the bride's party make fun of each other. The bridegroom puts the sweet served to him on the bride's leaf and she has to eat it compulsorily.

When the feast is going on, the bride's party give turmeric, *kumkum*, blouse piece or eversilver vessel etc. to the female section of their party and the bridegroom's party also do the same thing. They termed this as "manjal kumkumam vazhankutal" (presentations given to the bride from her house) to the bridegroom's party. Then with the couple they go to the bridegroom's house. At that time bride's party has to cook variety rice like tamarind rice, sweet rice, curd rice etc. and give it to the bridegroom's party. Within one week of the marriage, first the bride's party invite the couple to their house. At that time, they have to take betel leaf, nut, plantain, orange, five coconut, five turmeric, two blouse piece, sandal paste, *kumkum*, a silver vessel etc. with them and bring them to their house. Before this, the bridegroom's party give a grand feast to the bride's party. Then they go to the bride's house with coconut, plantain etc. and invite them. At that time the bride's party has to prepare a sweet and a tiffen and give it to them and send them back. Like this they repeat this three times.

Then within one year of the marriage these people celebrate some function. In the 3rd month after marriage they untie the marriage badge and tie a new one (taali piriccu koorttal). An auspicious day is selected, as said before (at the time of engagement) bride's party come with presentations, two sovereigns gold, small pipe like things in gold (this pipe has to be in twenty five, thirty, forty, sixty or seventy in number) etc. On that day five married woman untie the thick marriage badge string from the bride's neck, and then tie the marriage badge and these pipes etc. in two thin strings and tie this on the bride's neck. This ceremony has to be done between 3 to 6 P.M. on that day and the five married women and relatives, have to be given a feast.

Apart from this, after marriage in the first "aati" month,

bride's party has to give presentations, eversilver vessels, sweets, tiffens, two blouse pieces etc. to the bridegroom's party. At the end of the month "aati" (around July 15th) the bride has to be invited to her house and given presentations in a plate. At the month "Aavani" begins (around August 15th) the bridegroom comes and take back the bride to his house.

Then for the first night the bride's party has to give cot, bed, new dresses for the couple, bearau, one (or) two sovereigns gold chain, sweet, other tiffens etc. plantain, flowers, betel leaf, nut etc. With these things this ceremony has to be done in bridegroom's or bride's house. This is termed as "saanthi muhuurtham".

Then for "aavani evittam", they invite the bridegroom with presentations, new dresses, ring or wrist watch etc. has to be given through the brahmin priest by reciting *mantras*. Few days before Deepawali, bride's parents come with a big vessel, a small pot, two silver bowls, soap, sikakkaay, gingely oil, flowers, plantain, coconut, two blouse piece etc. and request them to send the couple to their house, then before Deepawali bride's party has to go to the bridegroom's house and invite the couple to their house. Then from the bride's house they have to buy new dresses for both according to the economic status, they have to put one sovereign, gold ring or other golden ornaments. For all these occasion in bride's house the couple have to be invited to the bride's house and presentations have to be given.

Chettiyar (Sozhiya)

In this caste first from bridegroom's house they ask for the bride's horoscope and they compare the horoscopes. If the horoscopes agree then they fix up the marriage. Only if the marriage has been fixed they will eat in one another's house otherwise they won't. They celebrate engagement only in the bride's house. On this day itself the ornaments from bride's and bridegroom's house are worn by the bride. Relatives and friends attend this function and a grand feast is given to them.

On the engagement day itself bride's parents put ring ("minji") in the toe of the bride. After the engagement, the girl is sent to the bridegroom's house and she will be there till the marriage is celebrated. This custom is changing now-a-days. In these days after sending the bride to the bridegroom's house after the engagement, she is taken back again to her parent's house.

Marriage is celebrated in the bride's house. The nine grains are soaked in water three days before marriage in the bridegroom's house. Now-a-days this is done where the marriage takes place. On the marriage day morning "nalungu" is celebrated to the bride and bridegroom in their houses. Then these people cook "manappongal" and place it on three plantain leaf and offer it to God. Before the marriage badge is tied both the bride and bridegroom tie the yellow string to each other's hand. Before tying the "kankanam", punul and the metti are put to the bridegroom.

In the marriage hall they place paaligai, peepul tree's bough, stone grinder, roller, kuttu vilakku (termed as "aayirankaal pandi") are placed. This caste people do not place "salun-karavam" the broad mouthed big vessel in the marriage platform). Before the marriage the bridegroom undertakes "paradeesikkoolam" and then the bride and bridegroom worship their parent's feet. Brahmin priest comes, kindles the holy fire, recites *mantras* and gets the blessings of the elderly people and gives the marriage badge to the bridegroom and he ties it on the bride's neck. Then his brother-in-law puts the fried rice seed on the couple's hands by placing one on the other and then they go round the marriage platform. After this they celebrate a ceremony viz. "Naakavalli muhuurttam". At the time of this ceremony a cloth cradle is constructed and the couple swing it, they play "pallaankuzhi", they look at themselves in the mirror. They exchange betel leaf and nut, powder the rice cake and put them on one's head. Only after this they untie the string tied in their hands before marriage and bride's relative ties golden plate on her forehead.

After all these functions, they take the "paaligai" to the river or tank, leave it in the river or tank, erect the peepul tree's bough on the bank of the river or tank, the bride takes water from the river or tank. When the bride enters into the house with water a coconut has to be broken. Then they give milk and plantain to the couple. On the new moon day immediately after marriage the couple go round the "peepul tree".

Within one year of the marriage these people (bride's party) do "siir" in the month of aati for "aati perukku" (18th of the month aati", for aavani avittam, in the month of ayppasi (i.e. for Deepawali), Karthikai, Pongal. Only on the day of "Pongal" (perumpongal) this people untie the marriage badge and tie a new one.

Chettiyar (Vaniya)

This caste people resemble the Soozhiya Chettiyar people in some aspects except the following. These people celebrate "engagement" in the bride's house and fix the date for marriage on that day itself (It is not in custom to send the girl to bridegroom's house immediately after engagement like the above caste people).

These people celebrate the marriage in the bridegroom's house. They soak the nine grains in water five or seven days before marriage in the bride's house and three days before in the bridegroom's house. This is termed in the bridegroom's house (i.e. the nine grains soaked in water in the bridegroom's house) as "*mutakkuppali*". According to the number of relatives "nalungu" is celebrated to the bride 5 or 7 or 9 or 11 days before marriage. The first pillar for "pandar" is erected by five or seven married woman along with the bridegroom in the direction "sani muulai" (i.e. north-eastern side). Before marriage, bridegroom sister puts "punul" to him. This caste people also do the custom "Paradesik koolam poodal". At that time they visit a Lord Ganesh temple, and the bridegroom's brother-in-law cleans the feet and places *Tilak* on his feet and puts the "minji" in his toe.

On the marriage day they spread paddy, a bed-sheet is

spread on it and the bride and bridegroom are seated on this. In the marriage hall these people place standing lamp, peepul tree's bough, bread mouthed big vessel (salunkaravam), kuda vilakku, the row pot on one another (pandamuttikkaal paanai), paaligai etc. Before tying the marriage badge they celebrate a "nalungu" to the bride and bridegroom. Brahmin priest comes kindles holy fire, recites *mantras* and then the bridegroom ties the marriage badge on the bride's neck. After the marriage, aunt, sister-in-law, uncle etc. tie golden plate tied in a string on the forehead of the bride. Then like other caste people, these people also celebrate "naalaam nirr satangu" (Amboogam punnutal) which resembles the "naakavalli satangu" of other castes. After this they take and leave the "paaligai" in the river, erect the peepul tree's bough on the river bank and the bride brings water in the pot. After this a grand feast is arranged. Then the couple are invited to the bride's house.

Then within one year of the marriage these people give presentations (1) in the month of "aati"—untie the marriage badge, tie a new one and leave the garlands in the river, (2) in the month of "aavani" for "aavani avittam", (3) in the month of "Ayppasi" for "Deepawali", and (4) for Pongal. At the time of untying the marriage badge they tie "gundu" (round shaped ball like thing, in which there is a hole which is also made up of gold) with the new marriage badge.

Pillai (Tuluva Vellalar)

These people compare the horoscope prepared at the time of birth and from both sides they ask for horoscope. First they go and meet the concerned party and then only they compare horoscopes. If the horoscopes agree the bride and bridegroom meet each other and if they agree they write 'muhuurtha oolai". On this day they give, from the bride's side, only the dowry amount. Usually, these people take food in each other's house, only if the "engagement" is finished. At the time of engagement they exchange plates and get the written document of the engagement. For this function they invite relatives and friends and arrange a grand feast.

Before the marriage day, bride's uncle, aunt etc. put "nalungu" and also the relatives put "nalungu" to the bride. Nine grains are soaked in bride's and bridegroom's house. Marriage can be celebrated according to the situation, i.e. either in bride's or in bridegroom's house. They put "pandar" four days before marriage. The first pillar for pandar is erected in the eastern side by the married ladies and is decorated with turmeric, mango leaves, sandal paste and *kumkum*. Before the marriage day the bridegroom's party come to the bride's house, bring presentations to the bride and after going to the bridegroom's house they make offerings to God. The day before marriage, these people put "nalungu" to the bride and bridegroom in their houses respectively. On the marriage day bride and bridegroom keep fasting, they tie yellow string to each other's wrist. They decorate the marriage platform separately, place "saalungaravam", a big pot, a lamp, two standing lamps, "pandamuttikkaal paanai" with which peepul tree's bough is tied. They bring this pot newly from the potter's house. They fill the "saalungaravam" pot with water at the time of tying marriage badge, put conch, knife, palm leaf, stylus and lemon into it.

Before tying the marriage badge the brahmin priest kindles holy fire recites holy *mantras*, place the marriage badge in a plate which contains coconut, plantain, flower, betel leaf, nut etc. gets the blessings of the elderly people gives yellow rice and flower. At the time of tying marriage badge the elderly people scatter the rice and flower over the couple and bless them usually the three knots are put by the bridegroom, at that time sister-in-law of the bride hold the lamp and others put coins in the lamp.

After tying marriage badge the couple, sister-in-law, brother-in-law go round the marriage platform and after this brother-in-law joins the hands of the couple, puts fried rice seed and all put it in the holy fire. Then he puts ring in the finger of the bridegroom and in return the bridegroom again puts the ring to his brother-in-law. After this, the bridegroom puts ring in the toe of the bride. While going round the marriage platform thrice, third time the bride and bridegroom take the things inside the "saalungaravam pot" and put them again back into it. After this they invite the couple in a separate room and give plantain and milk to them. After this they celebrate a function viz. "naalaam niir satangu". At that time bride's and bridegroom's mother-in-law, sister-in-law, uncle, relatives tie coins on the forehead of the couple. At this time they play pallankuzhi, crushing fried rice cake, playing with nose-gay of the flowers, rolling coconut, changing betel leaf, nut etc. After this they take and leave the "paaligai" in the river, the bride take water in the pot, erect the peepul tree's bough in the house. They break coconut each time before the bride entering into the house.

They fix an auspicious date, take new dresses etc. for the "first night". Then the couple go and come to each other's house thrice and they mingle with each other's family. At the time of "aati" new moon day, they go round the margosa and peepul tree (joined together). Within one year of the marriage they take new dresses, ornaments, worship the garland on 10th of the month "aati". Then they do "siir" for Deepawali, Karthikai and Pongal.

Reddiar

These people compare the horoscopes of both the boy and the girl. First they visit each other's house and either from the boy's or from the girl's house they exchange horoscopes. They use both the birth horoscope and age attaining horoscope for the purpose of comparison. If the horoscopes do not agree they put flower before God in the temple and get the permission of the *deity*. These people do "nalungu" to the girl 3 days before marriage and first "parents" do it and then the bride's uncle, relatives do it.

These people soak the nine grains three days before marriage in the bride's and bridegroom's house. They build "pandar", 3 days before marriage and the first pillar for the pandar is erected by the married ladies in the eastern side which is decorated with turmeric, mango leaves, red cloth, sandal paste and *kumkum*. Usually, the washerman ties white cloth in the pandar. Marriage is celebrated as per the desire of the bride or bridegroom's party. The bride wears cotton or silk saree at the time of tying marriage badge. Before tying the marriage badge these people put "punul" to the bridegroom, relatives put silver and golden thread. First the brahmin priest puts the thread "punul" to the bridegroom. At the time of tying marriage badge bride wears nine yards saree. While tying marriage badge all the three knots are tied by the bridegroom. Then bridegroom puts "metti" to the bride and bridegroom respectively. After going round the marriage platform thrice, the bride and bridegroom are seated in a separate room and given milk and plantain to eat.

After finishing "Naakavalli muhuurttam", they leave the "paaligai" in the river, erect peepul tree's bough in the house and each time when the bride enters the house they break a coconut. They play all the games at the time of "Naakavalli Muhuurttam", done by other caste people. They select on auspicious day for "first night", take new dresses and celebrate it. If there is any evil effect, the couple go round the peepul tree. In the third month after marriage these people untie the marriage badge and tie a new one. Then within one year of the marriage from the bride's house they do "siir" to the bride for (1) in the month of "aati", (2) Deepawali and (3) Pongal. The other customs resemble those of other caste people regarding marriage.

Naidu

In this caste, first bride's party compare the horoscope with that of bridegroom's party and then only they go and meet the bridegroom's party. Both the horoscopes of the bride are compare with that of bridegroom. If the horoscopes never agree they put flowers in the temple and get the permission of God or Goddess. If they agree, then the bride and bridegroom meet each other. Then they fix the "engagement" which resemble the other caste people. They put "nalungu" the day before marriage and the bride's uncle also puts "nalungu". Nine grains are soaked in water three days before marriage in the bride's house where the marriage is celebrated. Five days before marriage they build "pandar", erect first pillar for "pandar" in the north-eastern side; brahmin priest erects the pillar which is decorated with turmeric, mango leaves, red cloth and sandal paste.

Washerman ties white cloth in the pandar. Yellow string is tied by the brahmin priest to the bridegroom and bridegroom ties yellow string to the bride. They put milk ladle, turmeric and lime fruit in the "saalungaravam" pot, place 6 pandamuttukaal rows, each contains five pots and these are brought newly from potter's house. They erect peepul tree's bough in the marriage platform and place two standing lamps. The other things placed in the marriage platform are the same as in other castes.

Before tying marriage badge the bridegroom does the "paradeesam pootal" (going to the temple) etc. The bride wear silk saree while tying marriage badge. All the three knots are put by the bridegroom. Bridegroom's brother-in-law puts fried rice seed each time while going round the marriage platform thrice. Before tying marriage badge brother-in-law puts ring in the toe of the bride and bridegroom. It is not in custom to tie yellow string with golden plate on the forehead of the couple. Immediately after marriage they seat the bride and bridegroom in a separate place and give plantain and milk to the couple. The other customs resemble the other caste people regarding marriage. After this they take the nine grains, leave it in the river, bridegroom takes the peepul tree's bough, erects the bough in the house, bride takes a pot full of water. There is no custom of breaking coconut, or celebrate "nalungu" etc. They celebrate "First night" only after fixing an auspicious day and take new dresses to the couple. Only for the "new moon day" of the month of "aati" month, the couple go round the peepul tree. Within one year they (bride's parents) give "siir" to the bride in the month of (1) aati, (2) for Deepawali, (3) for Pongal and (4) for Krishna Jayanthi. The other customs regarding marriage resemble the other caste people.

Thondaimandala Mutaliyar

The horoscope prepared during attaining age is used for comparison purpose for marriage. If the horoscopes do not agree then they do not proceed further and if the horoscopes agree then the bride and bridegroom meet each other. This caste people eat food only if the engagement is fixed, otherwise they never take food in each other's house even if they are relatives. At the time of engagement they get the written document and exchange the plates. Five days before marriage "nalungu" is done to the bride. Nine grains are soaked in water seven days before marriage in bridegroom's house where the marriage is celebrated. Pandar is built three days before marriage, first pillar for pandar is erected in the eastern side, the elderly people in the house erect this pillar which is decorated with turmeric, mango leaves, red cloth, sandal paste and *kumkum*. There is no restriction for the number of pandar pillars, but for all the pillars the couple light and show camphor and washerman ties white cloth to the pandar. The other customs regarding marriage resemble the above caste people.

On the marriage day the bride and bridegroom keep fasting, then the brahmin priest ties yellow string in the wrist of the bridegroom and the bridegroom ties yellow string in the wrist of the bride. In the "saalungaravam" pot water is placed before tying marriage badge, they put the milk ladle and ring into it. In the marriage platform they place "pandamuttikkaal" pot which are bought newly from the potter's house, two standing lamps erect the peepul tree's bough separately (sometime they tie this with the "pandamuttikkaal" pot). It is not in custom to put "punul" to the bridegroom in this caste.

While tying marriage badge all the three knots are tied by the bridegroom to the bride and they do not put "metti" to the bridegroom. Immediately after tying marriage badge the couple's uncle, aunt, sister-in-law, relatives tie the golden plate tied in yellow string on the forehead of the couple. After going round the marriage platform the couple are seated in a separate room and given milk and plantain.

Before going to leave the "paaligai", a "nalungu" is celebrated. At that time the couple play pallankuzhi, crushing fried rice cake etc. like other caste people. Then on that day evening they take the "paaligai" to the river, leave it in the river, the bride takes pot full of water and the peepul tree's bough is erected in the house. While the bride enters each time into the house, they break a coconut. "First night" is celebrated on the same day and they take new dresses for this function. Then within one year of the marriage, "siir" is done to the bride from her house (1) in the month of "aati", (2) for Deepawali, (3) for karthikai and (4) for Pongal. The other customs regarding marriage resemble the Sengunta Mutaliyar caste people.

Nadar

In this caste, first bride's party go and meet the bridegroom's party and then compare the "puberty horoscope" of the bride with that of bridegroom. If the horoscopes never agree they do not allow the bride and bridegroom to meet each other. If the horoscope agree then they fix the engagement which resembles the customs of the other caste people. They do "nalungu" to the bride three or five days before marriage and first bride's uncle is to do "nalungu" and then others do it. Two days before marriage bridegroom's party soak the nine grains in water where the marriage is celebrated. They build "pandar" three days before marriage, three married ladies erect the first "pillar" for pandar in the north eastern side, which is decorated with mango leaves, red cloth, sandal paste, *kumkum* etc. and the washerman ties white cloth in the pandar. Bride and bridegroom show camphor to all the pillars in the pandar.

In this caste, the yellow string is tied by the brahmin priest to the bridegroom and by the bridegroom to the bride. They place Saalungaravam, Kudavilakku, peepul tree's bough, in the marriage platform. Water is poured in the "saalungaravam" pot even before placing the pot and they put milk ladle, stylus for writing etc. and two standing lamps are placed in the marriage platform. The bride is to wear nine yards silk saree while tying marriage badge. "Sacred thread" (in thread) is put by the brahmin priest to the bridegroom before tying marriage badge. While tying marriage badge all the three knots are tied by the bridegroom. After marriage, bridegroom puts "metti" to the bride and brother-in-law's daughter puts "metti" to the bridegroom. They tie yellow string tied with golden plate on the forehead of the couple immediately after tying marriage badge. After going round the marriage platform thrice, newly married couple are seated separately and they give milk and plantain to the couple.

On that evening they take the "paaligai" to the river, bridegroom carries the peepul tree's bough, leaves the "paaligai" in the river and while returning from the river the bride takes water in the pot. Everytime the bride enters into the house they break a coconut. Peepul tree's bough is erected in the house.

After this function they celebrate a "nalungu". At that time they play the things like other caste people. They select an auspicious day and fix "First night" on that and they take new clothes for this function. Then within a year after marriage bride's party give "siir", to the bride for (1) "aati" month, (2) Deepawali and (3) Pongal.

Nayakkar (Canar)

These people compare the horoscope at the time of birth of the bride and bridegroom. They give dowry, ornaments etc. to the bride only at the time of marriage. Other customs resemble the patayacci caste people. These people celebrate "nalungu" 3 or 5 or 7 days before marriage to the bride and her sisters do this. Relatives also do this to the bride. They soak nine grains three days before marriage in bridegroom's house. Pandar for marriage is built five days before marriage. The first pillar for

"Pandar" is erected in north-eastern side, bridegroom, brahmin priest, married woman all together erect this pillar which is decorated with mango leaves, flower, dharbai grass (holy grass), cikapput tuni (red cloth), turmeric and *kumkum*. In the pandar the washerman ties white cloth. The day before marriage the bridegroom's party come to the bride's house to invite the bride to their house and at that time they bring "siir' to the bride and after returning to their house they worship their family deity. On this day they put "parisam" to the bride by bringing saree, blouse, other kind of presentations etc. on the morning of the marriage day the bride and bridegroom tie the yellow string to each others hand.

They place on the marriage platform "saalungaravam pot", Kudavilakku, peepul tree's bough, two standing lamps. These people keep water in the pot and put ring, conch, knife etc. in it. Peepul tree's bough is placed separately in the marriage platform. At the time of tying marriage badge these people wear silk saree. After tying the marriage badge these people put silver, gold "punul" to the bridegroom and it is put by the uncle, sister-in-law, sister. First the silver thread is put. Brahmin priest comes, kindles holy fire, places the marriage badge in a plate along with coconut, plantain, flower, gets the blessings of the aged people and gives flower, atchadai (turmeric powder and rice mixed) to put them on the couple when the marriage badge is tied.

At the time of tying marriage badge all the three knots are tied by the bridegroom, his sister holds lamp in the back of the bride in which bride's relatives put coins. After tying marriage badge first these people put the "punul" to the bridegroom, then the couple, bride's sister-in-law, bridegroom's brother-in-law go round the marriage platform thrice; after this, bridegroom's brother-in-law puts the ring in the finger of the bridegroom and in return, they give *dhoti*, other clothes to the brother-in-law.

Sister-in-law of the bride puts the "metti" by placing the leg of the bride on the stone mortor. Bridegroom's sister put the "metti" to him. After going round thrice, these people take and put back the things in the "saalungaravam" pot and they seat the couple in a seat give milk and fruit to them. Before this, the golden plate is tied in a string is tied by the uncle, aunt and sister-in-law on the forehead of the bride.

After finishing all the ceremonies, they take and leave the "paaligai" in the tank, the bride takes water in a pot, erect the peepul tree's bough in the garden of the bridegroom's house. After marriage the couple go round the peepul tree thrice. Then the couple go and come to each other's house and mingle with each other's family. After this they go to a temple and only after this they celebrate "First night" and they use marriage saree for this function. Within one year of the marriage these people do "siir" (1) in the month of "aati", (2) in the month of Ayppasi (for Deepawali which is celebrated in the bride's house) and (3) in the month of tai, i.e. for Pongal. They take all kind of presentations to the bridegroom's house and celebrate the function there and come back.

Nayakkar (Tatar)

More or less all the customs regarding marriage resemble the above caste people.

"Nalunku" is celebrated to the bride nine days before marriage. The nine grains are soaked in water three days before marriage where the marriage is celebrated, i.e. usually in the bridegroom's house. Pandar is built five days before marriage. The first "pillar" for the pandar is erected by the bridegroom's and bride's party, which is decorated by the dharbai (holy) grass, mango leaves, turmeric, *kumkum*, flower etc. and is erected in the eastern side. Usually the pillars in the pandar is to be in even number. The bridegroom's party invite the bride, the day before marriage. They bring a silk saree, blouse, ornaments etc. and put the "parisam" for the bride. At that time a marriage badge in the round shape is tied in a black bead chain to the bride by her parents. They worship their family deity. Before marriage the relatives of the bridegroom and bride cook food and give them respectively.

Then the bride and bridegroom tie the yellow string to each other. In the marriage platform they place "pandamuttikkaal" pot, Saalungaravam pot, the peepul tree's bough (erected separately). In the Saalungaravam pot turmeric water (yellow water) is placed and in that coral bead (pavazha mani), cangu mani (a kind of bead), conch etc. are put. At the time of tying marriage badge the bride is to wear yellow saree, her sister-in-law holds a lamp in bride's back and bride's relations put coins in that lamp. When tying the marriage badge all the three knots are tied by the bridegroom. Then the bride, bridegroom, his brother-in-law, bride's friend go around the marriage platform thrice. Then his brother-in-law puts the fried rice in their hands and all the three put it in the fire. Only after this, his brother-in-law put the ring in bridegroom's finger and in return bridegroom puts the ring in his brother-in-law's finger. Before all these things, immediately after tying the marriage badge, golden plate tied to a string is tied by the bride's aunt, sister-in-law etc. Then they seat the couple and give milk and fruit to them. After this, bride's sister-in-law puts the "metti" in her toe and bridegroom's brother-in-law puts the "metti" in his toe.

Before leaving the "paaligai" these people celebrate "naalaam niir satangu." At this time the bridegroom goes to the river bank—bride takes old cloth, meals etc. to the river bank and invite his back to the house. Before he enters into the house bride places the ploughing instrument, sow the nine kind of grains in that place. Then they take "aalam", and erect the peepul tree's bough in the garden of the bridegroom's house. Only after this, these people leave the "paaligai" in the tank.

Then the couple go and come thrice to each other's house and mingle with each other's family. After this, they select a proper auspicious day and celebrate the "First night", usually this is done in the first or third month and they never take new saree for this purpose. The newly married couple go round the peepul tree if there is any evil effect to them. Within one year of the marriage these people do "siir" (1) in the month of "aati" (2) for Deepawali and (3) for Pongal.

A different custom among this people is that while tying marriage badge they hang a curtain between the bride and bridegroom and only in this situation bridegroom tie the marriage badge to the bride.

Muppanar

These people compare the horoscope of the bride and bridegroom and in other aspects they resemble the other caste people.

In the bridegroom's house they soak the nine grains in water three days before marriage. They put "Pandar", three days before marriage, the first pillar for Pandar is erected in the north-eastern side by five members including the bridegroom. This pillar is decorated by red cloth, yellow string, Dharbai (holy grass), mango leaves, *kumkum* and sandal paste. Washerman ties white cloth in the pandar. From the bridegroom's house they come to invite the bride the day before marriage day. They bring saree, clothes, ornaments, plantain, sugar, mirror etc. Then after returning back to their house they worship their family deity. On the day of marriage they tie yellow string in each other's hand. They place pandamuttikkaal, paaligai, saalungaravam pot, two standing lamps etc. on the platform. They decorate the marriage platform separately. They put conch, knife, milk ladle etc. in the "Saalungaravam" pot. The "Pandamuttikkaal" is in one row and they keep eleven pots in the row. These pots are bought newly from the potter's house. They erect the peepul tree's bough separately and fill up the Saalungaravam pot with water at the time of marriage.

They put "punul" to the bridegroom before tying marriage badge. His uncle puts silver, golden threads to the bridegroom. First he puts silver thread. Then the brahmin priest kindles holy fire, place the marriage badge in the plate along with coconut, betel leaf, plantain, flower etc. give atchadai (rice mixed with turmeric powder) to them to put it on the head of the couple when the marriage badge is tied. At this time, sister-in-law of the bride holds the lamp and the bride's party put coins in that.

If there is any evil effect, bridegroom puts only one knot and the other two are put by her sister-in-law. Otherwise all the three knots are put by the bridegroom. After tying marriage badge they exchange garlands. After this, the couple, bride's sister-in-law go round the marriage platform thrice, bridegroom's brother-in-law puts the fried-rice in the hands of the couple, they put the fried rice in the fire. Then he puts the ring in the finger of the bridegroom. Then bride's mother-in-law puts the ring in her toe by placing her legs on the stone mortor. Bridegroom's brother-in-law puts the ring in his toes. While going round the marriage platform thrice the couple take and put the things in the "saalungaravam" pot. Then bride's sister-in-law, mother-in-law etc. tie the golden plate on her forehead. After this they give fruit and milk to the couple.

Then they take the "paaligai" to the river or tank and leave it in the river or tank, the bride takes water in the water pot. Each time when the bride enters into the house, her mother-in-law breaks a coconut into pieces. Then the couple erect the peepul tree's bough in their house and pour water brought from the river or tank. After this only they arrange a grand feast. If the day is an auspicious day they celebrate "first night" and take new clothes for this. Otherwise they celebrate the function on 7th or 9th day. It is in custom among this caste people, that the couple go round the peepul tree after marriage. Then the couple go and come to each other's house and mingle with each other's family. Within one year after marriage they give "siir" to the bride and bridegroom (i.e. bride's party give) in the month of "aati", for Deepawali, and for Pongal.

Devar

This caste people also compare the horoscope of the boy and the girl. First from bridegroom's party they get the girl's horoscope and if they agree with each other they go and meet the bride's party. These people compare the horoscope prepared at the time of attaining age of the bride with that of bridegroom. If there is no agreement, they put flower in front of the deity and if it is agreeable they proceed further in the matter. Then if everything is alright they celebrate "engagement" in the bride's house. The other customs regarding this ceremony resemble the other caste people.

They celebrate the "nalungu" to the bride 3 or 5 or 9 days before marriage. The nine grains are soaked in water three days before marriage in bridegroom's house where the marriage is celebrated. Pandar is built three days before marriage and the elderly people in the house erect the first pillar for "Pandar" in the north-eastern side. This pillar is decorated with red cloth, margosa leaves, dharbai (holy) grass, mango leaves. Moreover, the washerman ties the white cloth in the pandar. After this on the marriage day these people celebrate "Sikakkaay Kazhittal" like Patayacci caste people. The other customs more or less resemble the other caste people.

These people spread paddy in a place and then put a mat on it, on this mat the bride and bridegroom are seated and than only the marriage badge is tied. These people put knife, conch and ring in the "Saalungaravam" pot. Then "arasaanikkaal" is also erected separately in the marriage platform.

The other customs after this resemble the Nayakkar (tatar) caste people.

These people celebrate the "First night" on the marriage day itself. These people go and come thrice and mingle with each other's family. The newly married couple go round the peepul tree. Other customs resemble the Nayakkar (tatar) caste people.

Udayar

In this caste bridegroom's party go and meet the bride's party and then compare the horoscope of the bride and bridegroom. They use the horoscope of the bride at the time of birth. If the horoscopes never agree then they put flower in the temple and get the permission of the God or Goddess. Then the bride and bridegroom meet each other. They fix the engagement and they get the written document of the engagement. The other customs regarding "engagement" resemble the other caste people.

Two days before marriage they celebrate "nalungu", to the bride. First bride's uncle does it and then others do it. Five days before marriage they cook nine grains in the bridegroom's house where the marriage is celebrated. Five days before marriage they build "Pandar" for marriage, first pillar for pandar is erected by the bridegroom and married ladies, erect the pillar in the north-eastern side, which is decorated by turmeric, mango leaves, red cloth, sandal paste and *kumkum*. The pillar for "Pandar" is to be in even number and the washerman ties white cloth in the pandar.

On the marriage day morning bride and bridegroom do not fast, the bridegroom ties yellow string in the wrist of the bride and the bride to the bridegroom. The other customs resemble the other caste people. They decorate marriage platform separately, place "Saalungaravam", Kudavilakku etc. pour water at the time of tying marriage badge, put milk ladle, knife, stylus etc. into it. Then they also place "Pandamuttikkaal" in three rows and each row contains five pots. Peepul tree's bough is tied with this "Pandamuttikkaal" pot. They also place two standing lamps in the marriage platform.

Before tying marriage badge they worship the feet of their parents (bride and bridegroom), place the legs on the stone mortor and show the arundadi (a star) etc. At the time of tying marriage badge relatives put thread and silver sacred thread to the bridegroom. While tying marriage badge first knot is put by the bridegroom and the other two are put by the sister-in-law. Bridegroom puts "metti" to the bride and brother-in-law puts "metti" to the bridegroom, both before tying marriage badge. The other customs regarding marriage resemble the other caste.

Immediately after marriage they take "paaligai", bride-groom carries the peepul tree's bough, erect it in the house. Bride takes pot full of water and everytime when she enters the house they break coconut. After this they celebrate "nalungu" and in that the newly married couple play pallaankuzhi, crushing fried rice, playing with the nose-gay of flowers, rolling coconut, giving betel leaf, nut to each other etc. According to the convenience they celebrate "First night" and take new dresses for this function. The other customs regarding marriage resemble the Naidu caste people. Then within one year of the marriage bride's parents do "siir" for (1) the month of "aati", (2) Deepawali and (3) Pongal.

Kallar (Devar)

For marriage, from the bridegroom's house they ask for the horoscope of the bride and if it agrees then they go and meet the bride's party. Two horoscopes, i.e. the birth as well as the horoscope prepared at the time of puberty are used for comparison purpose. If the horoscopes agree then the bride and bridegroom meet each other. If they agree each other then the "engagement" is fixed, they give the "siir" etc. at that time itself, and only if the marriage is fixed the take food in each other's house and if they are relatives they take food even if the marriage is not fixed. At the time of engagement they get the written document and exchange plates. For this celebration they invite relatives and friends and arrange a grand feast. These people do not do "nalungu" to the bride before marriage.

Nine grains are soaked in water three days before marriage in the bride's house where the marriage is celebrated. Five days before marriage the pandar for the marriage is built, the first "pillar" for the pandar is erected in the eastern side by the bride's party which is decorated by turmeric, mango leaves, red cloth, sandal paste and *kumkum*. Washerman ties white cloth in the pandar. The day before marriage day the bridegroom's party come to the bride's place. On the marriage day morning the bride and bridegroom tie yellow string to each other's wrist.

Separate marriage platform is decorated, "saalungaravam," big pot, kudavilakku, two standing lamps, peepul tree's bough etc. are placed. While placing "Saalungaravam" there is water inside it and they put milk ladle, knife and ring into it. Before tying marriage badge in this caste they celebrate few function viz. "Sikakkaay kazhittal" (the brahmin priest does this), the bride and bridegroom exchange garlands and do *"puja"* at the foot of their parents respectively. Usually, the bride wears silk saree while tying marriage badge. Before tying marriage badge the brahmin priest places the marriage badge in a plate where coconut, plantain, flower etc. are placed, gets the blessings of elderly people, give yellow rice, flower etc. in the hands of the elderly people and recite holy *mantras,* kindles holy fire and get the blessings of elderly people while tying marriage badge. While tying marriage badge first knot is put by the bridegroom and the other two by the sister-in-law, the sister-in-law holds the lamp in the back of the bride and bride's party puts coin in the lamp. Going round thrice the marriage platform, putting fried rice into the holy fire, putting ring in the hands of the bridegroom and in return he puts the ring in the hands of the bride etc. are in custom in this caste also. 'Metti' is put to the bride by the bridegroom and to the bridegroom by his brother-in-law. It is not in custom to take and put the things in the "saalungaravam" pot by the couple.

Immediately after tying marriage badge bride's and bridegroom's aunt, sister-in-law, uncle, relatives tie yellow string on the forehead of the couple and after this the couple are seated in a separate room and they give plantain and milk etc. to the couple. It is not in custom to celebrate "nalungu" before or after leaving the "paaligai" on that day evening they take the "paaligai", leave it in the river and erect the peepul tree's bough in the house. On the same day they celebrate "First night" and they do not take new dresses for this celebration.

After marriage the couple go and come thrice to each other's house and mingle with each other's family. On the 18th of the month "aati", the couple go round the peepul tree and the bride's parents do "siir" to the couple on this day. Then within one year of the marriage the bride's party do "siir" (1) in the month of "aati", (2) for Deepawali and (3) for Pongal.

Tuluva Naickar

Most of the marriage customs resemble the other caste

people except in the following aspects. They celebrate "nalungu" to the bride eleven days before marriage and first the bride's uncle is to do this. Nine grains are soaked in water three days before marriage in the bridegroom's house where the marriage is celebrated.

"Pandar" is built three days before marriage and the first "pillar" for pandar is erected by the person who builds the pandar in the north-eastern side. This pillar is decorated with turmeric, mango leaves, sandal paste, *kumkum* etc. and the washerman ties white cloth to the pandar. On the marriage day the bride and bridegroom do not fast, the bridegroom ties yellow string to his wrist by himself and he ties the yellow string to the bride. These people build a separate marriage platform place "Saalungaravam", big pot, Kudavilakku etc., place water in the Saalungaravam, put milk ladle, lime etc. into it, place two pandamuttikkaal pots each contains five pots which are brought newly from the potter's house. Peepul tree's bough is erected separately and they place two standing lamps in the marriage platform.

The bride wears silk saree while tying marriage badge. All the three knots are put by the bridegroom while tying marriage badge. After tying the golden plate tied with a string on the forehead of the couple, they are invited into a separate room and given milk and plantain. Regarding other marriage customs they resemble the other caste people. There is no "nalungu" at all after marriage in this caste. On the marriage day evening they take the "paaligai", bridegroom carries the peepul tree's bough, leaves the "paaligai" in the river. Bride takes water in the water pot and they erect the peepul tree's bough in the house. Everytime when the bride enters their house they break coconut. On the same day they celebrate "First night" and take new dresses for the celebration. After marriage the couple go and come thrice to each other's house and mingle with each other's family. Then within one year of the marriage they give "siir" to the bride (1) in the month of "aati", (2) for Deepawali, and (3) for Pongal.

Jankamar (Devar)

These people compare the horoscope of the boy and the girl. Usually, the bridegroom's party go and meet the bride's party and only if the bridegroom's party like the bride's party they exchange horoscopes. They use birth horoscope of the girl for the purpose of comparison. If the horoscope do not agree, these people do not proceed further. If the horoscopes agree, the bride and bridegroom meet each other. If they agree then they celebrate "engagement". They give "siir" etc. only at the time of marriage. The other customs regarding this resemble the other caste people.

They put "nalungu" to the bride, 3 days before marriage and first bride's parents do this celebration. Relatives and uncle also do this. This caste people build "Pandar" for marriage according to their desire and they erect the first pillar for "Pandar" in the eastern side five days before marriage. This is decorated with turmeric, mango leaves, sandal paste and *kumkum* and erected by five married ladies. Washerman ties cloth in the pandar. Marriage is celebrated in the bridegroom's house. On the marriage day morning the bride and bridegroom do not fast. In the "saalungaravam" pot these people pour water only at the time of tying marriage badge. They put milk ladle in the "Saalungaravam" pot. They erect the peepul tree's bough separately and two standing lamps are also placed in the marriage platform. The bride wears cotton saree at the time of tying marriage badge.

These people put "punul" to the bridegroom before marriage. Brahmin priest put the "thread punul" and "silver punul" to the bridegroom. Bridegroom's brother-in-law puts ring to the bridegroom at the time of putting ring in the toe which is put by the bride. In return the bridegroom puts ring to his brother-in-law. After tying marriage badge the bridegroom puts "metti" to the bride. There is no custom of tying golden plate tied in a yellow string on the forehead of the bride and bridegroom. After going round the marriage platform the couple are seated in a separate room and the parents give milk and plantain.

Immediately after marriage these people take the "paaligai", peepul tree's bough etc. to a river and leave the "paaligai" in the river and erect the peepul tree's bough on the bank of the river. Everytime the bride enters the house, these people break a coconut. There is no "nalungu" at all before (or) after, leaving the "paaligai" in this caste. First night is celebrated in the bride's house by selecting an auspicious day and they buy new dresses for this function. After marriage the couple do not go round the peepul tree. Within one year of the marriage the bride's parents give (1) "aati siir", (2) "Deepawali siir", (3) siir for Karthikai and (4) Pongal siir, to the bride. The other customs of this caste people regarding marriage resemble the other caste people.

Konar (Yadhavappillai)

Regarding comparison of horoscopes first from the bridegroom's house compares the horoscopes with that of the bride, if it agrees then only they go and meet the bride's party. Both (the puberty as well as the birth horoscope) the horoscopes are compared with the horoscope of the bridegroom. If the horoscopes never agree then they put flowers in the temple and get the permission of the God or Goddess. Moreover, these people have a new customs as follows to check the agreement of the horoscope. They cook "rice", divide them into three parts put gold, silver, copper powder in the three parts respectively. Then they place it to the crow and if the crow takes the food mixed with silver powder then they proceed further in this matter. If everything is alright, the bride and bridegroom meet each other. Then they fix the "engagement" and regarding engagement etc. they resemble the other caste people.

They do "nalungu" to the bride 3 or 5 days before marriage and her uncle does it first and then others do it. They soak nine grains in water in the place where the marriage is to be celebrated (marriage is usually celebrated in bridegroom's house, now-a-days, they celebrate it in the bride's house also). Three days before marriage. Five days before marriage they build pandar, first pillar for pandar is erected in the south-western side, married woman erect the pillar decorate with turmeric, mango leaves, *kumkum*, sandal paste etc. They erect 9 or 11 pillars in the "pandar" and for each pillar the newly married couple are to show camphor. In the "pandar", washerman ties white cloth.

They do not place "pandamuttikkaal", but place one more pot in the marriage platform. Regarding other customs they resemble the other caste people. Bride wears silk saree while tying marriage badge. Before tying marriage badge, bridegroom's sister put golden "punul" to him. After marriage bride's mother-in-law puts ring in her toe and bridegroom's brother-in-law puts ring in his toe. The other customs regarding marriage resemble the other caste people. Regarding leaving the "paaligai" in river etc. doing "siir" within one year to the bride etc. resemble the Patayacci caste people.

Kuravar (Rama Jooki)

Among these people also, the bridegroom's party is to ask for the bride's horoscope and compare them. If the horoscopes agree then they fix up the marriage. Only if the marriage is fixed they take food in one another's house. They celebrate the engagement in the bride's house. They invite relatives and friends and arrange a grand feast for this function. Bride's parents spend money for this occasion. Apart from this all the other customs about the engagement resemble the other caste people.

The marriage is celebrated in the bridegroom's house. The nine grains are soaked in water in the bride's house seven or five days before marriage. When the girl is taken by he bridegroom's party, the "paaligai" is also taken with them. The bride's relatives put "nalungu" according to the number of relatives. All type of "nalungu" are celebrated to the bride. They erect the first pillar for pandar in "iisaaniya muulai" (in the north-eastern side). On the marriage platform the broad mouthed big vessel (this vessel is decorated with a yellow string tied with turmeric), pot, kudavilakku, paaligai, peepul tree's bough, stone grinder, roller etc. are placed.

When the bride is invited to the house, her uncle puts the "metti" to her toes and this is put from the parents house. Before the marriage, both the bride and bridegroom tie the "kankanom" on each other's hand. Then they worship the feet of their parents. Then "punul" is put to the bridegroom and the marriage badge is tied to the bride and the brother-in-law puts the "metti" to the bridegroom. At the time of tying the marriage badge sister-in-law puts the "metti" to the bridegroom. At the time of tying the marriage badge sister-in-law of the bride holds the lamp near bride's back. After the marriage is finished brother-in-law places the hands of the bride and bridegroom one on the other and puts the fried-rice seed and puts the ring for the bridegroom and in return he put the ring on the finger of the brother-in-law. Also they give *dhoti*, towel to the brother-in-law. Then for the bride, aunt, sister-in-law, uncle tie the golden plate on her forehead. Then the "paaligai" is sub-merged in the tank and the peepul tree's bough is erected on the bank of the tank. After the feast is finished, the bride and bridegroom are taken to the house of the bride on that day itself.

These people also go and come to each other's house three times and they mingle with each other's family. In the month of first aati after marriage, they worship the garland, untie the marriage badge and tie a new one. For this ceremony the yellow string has to come from the bride's house. For Deepawali, Pongal etc. bride's parents give "siir" to the couple and invite them to their house.

Vannan (Washerman)

The custom regarding comparing horoscope, engagement etc. resemble the above caste people. They celebrate the engagement only in the bride's house. On that day betel leaf, nut, plantain, flowers, new saree, ornaments, blouse, turmeric, *kumkum*, sandal paste etc. are brought by the bridegroom's party. They select an auspicious day and the marriage is fixed. If the bride's and bridegroom's party plan to provide ornaments etc. to the bride and bridegroom, these have to be provided on the engagement day itself. On that day relatives attended the function and a grand feast is given to those who attend the function, from the bride's house. On the day of engagement the bride and bridegroom sit near each other and they wear a garland on their neck. Brahmin priest comes and he selects an auspicious day, time etc. and note them in two papers and place it in the plate and give the plate in the hand's of the bride's and bridegroom's father. In that plate they also place betel leaf, nut, plantain, coconut, *kumkum*, turmeric, sandal paste, flowers etc. The priest writes in that paper along with the auspicious day, time etc., that this girl is to be given in marriage to that boy and vice versa. Then both bride's and bridegroom's father exchange the plates. On that day the girl is decorated beautifully and after the plates are exchanged by each party, the bridegroom's party give the presentations to the girl. She wears the new saree, ornaments, garland etc. given by the bridegroom's party and bow down to the aged persons. After that they give betel leaf, nut, plantain, flower, sugar etc. to the friends who attend the function.

The marriage is celebrated in the bridegroom's house. Relatives and the bride's uncle cook food and give it to her till she leaves her house. The nine grains are soaked in water only in the bride's house five days before marriage. Bridegroom's party come to invite the bride and take food in the bride's house. They put "parisam" to the girl and at that time the bride wears silk saree and the bride is taken to the bridegroom's house.

When the bride comes to the house of the bridegroom these people do a ceremony viz. "mariyammanukku pataittal" (worshiping Goddess Mariyamman). On that day these people tie the "kappu", i.e. new pot tied with yellow string new stone hearth is built and the paddy is boiled in that pot by using the new stone hearth. They termed this as "kappu katti nel veeka vaittal" (By tying kappu and boil the rice). Then this paddy is grounded as rice and using this rice, mutton, vegetables etc. are cooked. This cooked food, the wedding saree, blouse (wedding saree cotton saree), *dhoti*, towel, shirt etc. are placed before Goddess Mariyamman and offerings are given. Only after this is done these clothes are used at the time of marriage.

Then on the morning of the marriage day for the bride and bridegroom "nalungu" is celebrated. This is termed as "mananalungu". In the marriage platform paddy is spread, on that a bedsheet is spread and first the bride is seated on this and the "nalungu" is celebrated. After this, for the bridegroom also "nalungu" is done in the same way.

In the marriage hall paaligai, odins bough, peepul tree's bough decorated and tied with red cloth, mango leaves, kappu, turmeric powder, *kumkum* etc. and erected by placing the sand on the side of the Saalungaravam (i.e. the broad mouthed big brass vessel), kudavilakku, wooden mortor in which a hollow and lamp which is filled with castor oil (the oil has to be the "castor oil" it is very important) and a wick is put in that lamp, stone grinder and roller etc. are placed. Then the bride and the bridegroom worship their parent's feet with flowers etc. respectively. After this these people celebrate a ceremony "manappongal pataittal".

For this ceremony coconut is scraped, then plantain, jaggery etc. are mixed with this and it is prepared like "Panjaamirtam" and is put in five or seven plantain leaf, betel leaf, nut, plantain etc. also are placed in the leaf. Bride's and bridegroom's parents are present at the time, then the bride breaks a coconut and light a camphor and show it to the deity and kneel down. The bridegroom also does the same thing. Only after this ceremony, the marriage badge is tied to the bride. At the time of tying the marriage badge, married women fill up water in the two broad mouthed big vessel placed in the marriage hall, when the bridegroom ties the marriage badge the bride's sister-in-law holds the lamp in the back of the bride and the relatives of the bride put coins in that lamp. Then the bride and the bridegroom exchange garlands. Then the couple go round the marriage platform thrice and then the bride's brother joined the hands of the bride and the bridegroom, put fried rice-seed and the ring in the bridegroom's finger. In return the bridegroom puts a ring and give a set of new dress to his brother-in-law. Then the bride and bridegroom take the things in the broad mouthed big vessel thrice and put them back in the same vessel. Then for the bride the mother-in-law puts the "metti' in her toe. Then the bride and bridegroom are seated and they give milk and plantain to them. The bride's aunt ties the golden plate tied in a string on her forehead, then the sister-in-law and then her uncle tie this golden plate tied in a string on her forehead. Then a feast is given. After the feast only they take the "paaligai" to the tank.

After the marriage they celebrate a ceremony viz. "kappu kalaital". The couple play Pallaankuzhi, powdering the fried rice cake and putting on one another's head, sister-in-law blow the bride on her cheek and the couple blow one another on one another's cheek. Then they untie the yellow string on their hand, at this time they keep betel leaf, nut, coconut, rice etc. only after this they go to the tank for submerging the "paaligai", the bridegroom carries the peepul tree's bough and the erect it on the tank of the bank. The bride carries the water in the pot while returning from the tank. Then before going to the house, they go to the temple and break coconuts and light camphor. Then only they have to return to the house. When the girl enters the house before the marriage badge is tied to her and also when she brings water from the tank after marriage, they have to break a coconut. Then the couple starts to the bride's house. Then the couple go and come thrice to each other's house and mingle with each other's family. The other customs regarding marriage resemble the patayacci caste people.

Navitar (Barber)

Most of the customs regarding comparison of horoscope, engagement, marriage etc. resemble the above caste people. These people place the paaligai, wooden mortor on which a hallow and lamp placed with castor oil and a wick and it is lighted, two standing-lamps for the two sides, rowed pots on one another, peepul tree's bough, stone mortor etc. In this caste before the fried rice-seed is put on the hands of the couple by the bridegroom's brother-in-law, the ring is put in the finger of the bridegroom by his brother-in-law. The bridegroom also does the same to his brother-in-law. All the other customs resemble the washerman caste people. In this caste it is a must to give new vessels for pongal to the couple.

Cakkili (Cobbler)

Regarding comparison of horoscope these people resemble the washerman caste people. The "engagement" is done in the bride's house. On that day they talk about the ornaments, money to be given in the marriage etc. For this function they invite friends and relatives and arrange a grand feast.

The marriage is celebrated in the bridegroom's house. When the pandar is built, it has to contain 32 pillars and for all the 32 pillars the bride and bridegroom has to show camphor and worship them. Before marriage these people do 16 "nalungu" to bride and it is done by the bride's uncle, aunt, elder sister, younger sister etc. The nine grains are soaked in water 5 or 7 or 9 days before marriage day in the bride's house and three days before in bridegroom's house.

In the marriage platform 32 pots (separated in three rows, in each row the pots are placed on one another), broad mouthed big vessel, stone grinder, peepul tree's bough, kuda vilakku, etc. are placed. Salt, chilly and bran are put by the bride and bridegroom in the three pots (they place the pots on one another), which are also placed in the marriage platform. Before tying the marriage badge the bride and bridegroom have to tie the "kankanam" on each other's hand and worship their parent's feet. When the bride is taken to the bridegroom's house before the marriage day, her uncle puts the "metti" to her toe. For the bridegroom "punul" is put by the uncle and his brother-in-law puts the "metti" to his toe. Only after these customs are completed, bridegroom ties marriage badge to the bride and at this time they pour water in the broad mouthed big vessel. Immediately after the marriage badge is tied, they celebrate a ceremony viz. "puttu kumpitutal" (worshiping ant hill). At that time the newly married couple, friends, relatives all go to the forest and worship their family God "Maduari Viran" (also called as "maatasaami"). Bark of the cassis auriculate (aavaaram seti), is cut and erected on an ant-hill. Then goat, cock, etc. are killed and offered to it (This plant's bark is used to tan leather. So, this plant is worshiped as a deity by these people since this plant's bark helps them in their work viz., repairing the chappels etc. So, they worship this first immediately after the marriage). At this time they will sing and dance. After finishing this ceremony, these people return to their house and worship the God in the house.

Then bride's aunt, sister-in-law, uncle tie the golden plate tied in a string on her forehead. Relatives and friends give presents to the newly married couple. Then the pots kept on one another are separated by the couple and they take the things like nut cutter, coin etc. in the broad mouthed big brass vessel thrice and put them back in the vessel. Then they take the "paaligai" and leave it in the tank or river. Before leaving "paaligai" the couple untie the "kankanam" in their wrist and put it in the tank. Then they erect the peepul tree's bough on the bank of the tank or river (some people erect this bough in their house garden itself). Then the couple give feast to their uncle and after the feast, the bridegroom is taken to the bride's house.`

After marriage the couple go and come to each other's house and mingle with each other's family. For the newly married couple bride's parents give "siir" (1) in the month of "aati", the couple worship the marriage garlands, untie the marriage badge and tie a new one and leave the garlands in the river. (2) For Deepawali. For this they have to give thirty two kind of "siir" like ghee, coconut, plantain, sickle, knife etc. (3) Next for Pongal. For both Pongal and Deepawali they invite the bride and bridegroom to the bride's house.

Harijan (Aadi Dravidar)

These people termed the comparison of horoscope as "guru

paarttal". They observe the same customs for comparison, engagement etc. as patayacci caste people. They celebrate the "engagement" in the bride's house. On that day itself bride wears all the ornaments given by the bridegroom's party. For not changing their words they get the signature of each other's party. Relatives attend the function and a grand feast is arranged for them.

Usually the marriage is celebrated in the bridegroom's house. They celebrate "nalungu" to the bride five or 7 or 9 days before marriage in her mother's house. First uncle is to do "nalungu" to the bride. At that time oil Sikakkaay, sandal paste etc. are given and then they do the "nalungu". At that time soap, comb, mirror etc. are provided. When the girl is invited to the bridegroom's house they bring saree, the presentation things for putting "parisam", and after putting "parisam" and with that saree they invite her to their house.

They soak nine grains in water both in bride's and bridegroom's house five or seven days before marriage. They place broad mouthed big brass vessel (in that nut cutter, coins etc. are put), peepul tree's bough tied with the rowed pot on one another (the pots are five or seven in number), stone grinder, kudavilakku, two lamp etc. in the marriage platform.

Before marriage the bride and bridegroom tie the yellow string, i.e. "Kankanam" to each other's hand. Then they celebrate "kinni nalungu". After that the bride and bridegroom worship their parent's feet. Brahmin priest ("Pandaaram"—priest for this caste), recite *mantras,* kindle holy fire and the marriage badge is tied. Then the brother-in-law place the bride's and bridegroom's hand on each other and puts the fried rice-seed on it. Then the couple bow down the elderly people and get their blessings. After that the washerman is called and he untied the "kankanam" from the hands of the couple. After that the bridegroom puts "metti" (minji) on the bride's leg (The other customs resemble the Patayacci caste people). Then they take the "paaligai" to the tank or river and leave it in the river or in the tank, erect the people tree's bough on the tank or river bank. Then with all kinds of auspicious drums the bride carries water from the river or tank. After this the couple go and come to each other's house thrice and mingle with each other's family.

Then within one year of the marriage bride's party give siir (1) in the month of "aati", they worship the marriage garland and untie the marriage badge and tie a new one. On that occasion it is a practice to buy new clothes, (2) For Deepawali and (3) for Pongal. Both for Deepawali and for Pongal they go and meet the couple with all kind of presentations and invite them to their house.

10

Customs During First Pregnancy

Brahmin (Iyer)

In the 5th month the pregnant lady has to be invited, a black saree is bought and a feast is given to her. Flowers, garlands are put on her on this day. In 7th month they celebrate "valaikappu" (putting all type of bangles to the hand of the pregnant lady). Gold, glass bangles are put on that day and also they put flower garlands. Five type of meals ("masakkai saadam") has to be prepared and a feast has to be given to her. These are all done by the bride's house.

In the 8th month, in the bridegroom's house they do "Siimandam" (a ceremony performed among the brahmins for a woman in her first pregnancy). On that day new saree, *dhoti*, dhall mixed with jaggery and made like a pyramid, murukku (a tiffen), lattu (a sweet) and other kind of tiffens etc. have to be prepared by the bride's house and taken to the bridegroom's house. On that day the couple are seated, a pot of water is poured on them. Then the brahmin priest kindles the holy fire, with the rice-corn and puts a *tilak* on the lady's forehead and they put it on her shoulder etc. For this celebration the saree, *dhoti* etc. have to come from the bridegroom's house to the bride's house. In the 9th month from the bride's house they have to go and bring the girl to their house. After delivery they send the girl to her husband's house in the 3rd month by doing "siir" to the child and its mother.

Brahmin (Iyangar)

In the 5th month, in the bridegroom's house they give oil bath to the pregnant lady, comb the hair and decorate her hair with flowers. Then they give betel leaf, nut etc. to ten married women. In the seventh month in the bride's house they buy a new saree and garland her hair with flowers. In this month in the bride's house they celebrate "valaikappu". On that day they prepare "kaapparisi" (rice mixed with jaggery) and put silver, five metal bangle ("anju panjala kappu"), golden bangle, glass bangles etc. They put bangles to those who attend the function.

In the 8th month they celebrate "siimandam" in the bridegroom's house. They buy new saree, kindle holy fire, invite relatives and give a feast to them, 9th month in the bride's house they make a "sweet" (appam) and parcel it in a plantain leaf and tie the plantain leaf to the pregnant lady's belly (in that saree portion). Then they bring the girl to their house. Three months after delivery they send the girl to her husband's house by doing "siir" to the child and its mother.

Pillai

In the 5th month these people prepare and take some kind of tiffens in the bride's house, go and see the pregnant girl. In the 7th month in both bride's and bridegroom's house they tie vasampu (sweet flag) in gold and tie it in the marriage badge chain. For this ceremony they take a new saree for the girl. There is no other customs like valaikappu, siimandam etc. In the 7th month they bring the girl to their house. Three months after delivery they send the girl to her husband's house by doing "siir" to the child and its mother.

Isai Velalar

If a lady becomes pregnant these people take a new black saree in the 5th month from the bride's house (black saree is termed as "masakkai karuppu"). If the black colour is not acceptable (for some families there is a belief that black will not be acceptable to their family God or Goddess), they take other colours. In 5th month they prepare 5 or 7 variety of meals and tiffens, go and meet the pregnant lady to her house. On 7th or 9th month they celebrate "valaikappu". For this also, the bride's party has to give 'siir' to the girl and celebrate the function. While putting "kappu" (bangles) first margosa fibre bangle is put and only after that golden bangles are put. The expenditure for feast belong to the bridegroom's party. After this function, they bring her to their house. If the "kappu" is celebrated on the 7th month, they again send her to her husband's house and in the 9th month they select an auspicious day after new moon day and bring her back to their house. If the "kappu" is celebrated on the 9th month this is not in practice. After delivery they send the girl back to her husband's house in the 3rd month and do "siir" etc. to the child and it's mother.

Patayacci

If a lady becomes pregnant bride's party prepare five kind of meals (meals, tiffens etc.) and take them to the bridegroom's house and see the lady. In the 7th month they celebrate "valaikappu" in the bride's house. First they tie margosa fibre bangle to the lady, then five metal bangle (copper, gold, white metal, silver, lead), gold or silver bangle, glass bangles. Then they prepare jaggery mixed with rice, jaggery mixed with groundnut, gingely mixed with jaggery all made in the shape of pyramids. These are given as presentation with other kind of presentations to the lady. At the time of "kappu" the pregnant lady is seated and they put all kinds of bangles. Immediately after this celebration they bring the girl to their house and send her back to the bridegroom's house. Then they bring the girl in the 9th month to their house. After delivery they send the child and it's mother to her house in the 3rd month by doing "siir".

Sengunta Mutaliyar

If a lady becomes pregnant these people go and see the pregnant lady in the 7th month with different kind of meals and bring her to their house. They again send her back to the bridegroom's house. In the 9th month they bring her to their house for delivery and after delivery in the 3rd month they send her back to her house by doing "siir" to her and her child. There is no custom of doing "valaikappu" etc. in this caste like other caste people.

Asari (Pattar-Kammalar-Goldsmith, taccar-Carpenter)

In the fifth month, they prepare five kind of tiffen, five kinds of meal etc. inform about the pregnancy of their girl to their relatives, take plantain, sugar etc. go and meet the pregnant lady in the bridegroom's house. Then they tie the vasampu (sweet flag) in the gold and tie it to the pregnant lady's chain and invite her to their house and send her back to the bridegroom's house again. In the 7th month they celebrate "kappu". First they put margosa fibre. Then silver bangles, golden bangles etc. At that time, they take ground nut mixed with jaggery in pyramid shape (termed as "katalai pillayaar"), sweets mixed with jaggery in pyramid shape (termed as "mittaay pillayaar"), gingely mixed with jaggery (termed as "ellu pillayaar") and they prepare rice mixed with jaggery (kaapparici). Also they take new saree to the girl, take all other kind of presentations and they go and celebrate the "kappu". After this they bring the girl to their house and send her back in the 3rd month after delivery to her husband's house by doing "siir".

Chettiyar (Vysya)

If a lady become pregnant, then this caste people go to the bridegroom's house in the 5th month by selecting an auspicious day. On that day they prepare three kind of tiffens, keep it in an eversilver vessel with coconut, flower, plantain, betel leaf, nut, 2 blouse pieces, sandal paste and with all the other kinds of "siir" they bring the girl to their house. At the end of that month the bridegroom takes her back to his house. In 7th or 9th month for 3 days or 5 days, they decorate the girl and seat her in a chair and sing songs. At the end of this ceremony they give plantain, betel leaf, nut, sundal (a kind of dish) in a vessel to all those who attend the function and give turmeric, *kumkum* etc. to the married ladies.

In the 7th month bride's party prepare five kind of tiffens, sweet etc. keep them in an eversilver vessel and with all the other presentations (as specified at the time of engagement) they go and bring the lady to their house. Again the bridegroom at the end of that month takes her back with him. In the 9th month they celebrate "valaikappu", "siimandam" etc. For this, the bride's party has to give all kind of presentations with 7 type of tiffens (sweet and kaarm), saree, blouse, shirt, pants for husband, two bangles for the lady and go to the bridegroom's house. Then in the bridegroom's house they kindle holy fire, and recite *mantras* with a brahmin priest and do some ceremonies and take back the lady to the bride's house. After delivery they send the girl and her child in the 3rd month by doing "siir" to them.

Chettiyar (Sozhiya)

If a lady becomes pregnant then bride's parents prepare tiffens, go and meet the lady and return back in the 5th month. In the 7th month relatives come and tie vasampu (sweet flag) and celebrate "siimandam". The couple are seated and this is done like a marriage itself. There is no custom like "valaikappu" (putting bangles in the bride's hand). On that day itself they bring the lady to their house and after delivery they send her to her husband's house by doing "siir" to her and the child, in the 3rd month.

Chettiyar (Vaniya)

Bride's parents prepare five kind of meals, go and meet the pregnant lady in the 5th month. In the 7th (or) 9th month they celebrate "kappu". First margosa fibre bangle, then gold and silver bangles are put to the lady. They poke the rice with jaggery. Relatives attend the function and a grand feast is given. If they celebrate "kappu" in 7th month, they bring the girl to their house and send her back to her husband's house. Again they bring her to their house in the 9th month and after delivery they send her back to her husband's house in the 3rd month by doing "siir" to her and her child.

Pillai (Tuluva Vellalar)

If a lady becomes pregnant they tie dried ginger with the marriage badge in 7th month, prepare tiffens etc. Then they celebrate "valaikappu" in the same month, put golden bangles. At the time of this function bridegroom is also invited with the bride and is celebrated in the bride's house. They put bangles to the married ladies who attend the function. Immediately after this function they invite the bride to her house and after delivery they sent her back to her husband's house in the 3rd month. While returning they do "siir' to the child and send them back to her husband's house.

Reddiar

If these people come to know that a lady is pregnant they prepare five kind of meals and go to her house and see the girl. The other customs of doing "valaikappu" etc. resemble the Patayacci caste people.

Naidu

When this caste people come to know that a lady is pregnant they prepare five kind of tiffens, go and meet the girl in her house. These people do not celebrate "valaikappu" or "siimandam". They invite the bride in the 9th month for delivery and three months after delivery they do "siir" and send back the child and the mother to their house.

Thondaimandala Mutaliyar

On the 7th month they celebrate "valaikappu" in the bride's house, they put margosa fibre bangle and five metal bangle, bridegroom is with the bride at this time, they put bangles to the other married women attending the function. In the bridegroom's house they celebrate "siimandam" in the same month and they bring the girl to their house in 7th month for delivery and send her back in the 3rd month after delivery and do "siir" to the child and the mother. The other customs regarding first pregnancy resemble the "Patayacci" caste people.

Nadar

If a lady is pregnant, then in the 5th month they take black saree, prepare five kind of meals, five kind of tiffens and do "nalungu". In the 9th month they celebrate "valaikappu" First they put "margosa fibre" bangle, then silver and golden bangle. This is celebrated in the bridegroom's house, but the bridegroom will not be with the bride. They put bangles to the married ladies who attend the function. They take the girl to their house in 9th month for delivery and three months after delivery they send the girl to her husband's house by doing "siir" to the child and the mother.

Nayakkar (Canar)

These people's custom regarding first pregnancy resemble the other caste people except in one or two aspects. They give betel leaf, nut, plantain, mirror, comb etc. to five (or) seven married women. They put bangles in their hands also.

Nayakkar (tatar)

In this caste, bridegroom's parents send word through somebody about this to the bride's house in the first or second month. In the 5th month they take sugar, plantain etc. and go to the bridegroom's house. They celebrate "valaikappu" in the 7th or 9th month. The other customs resemble those of other caste people. They send her back on 22nd day or 3rd month to her house.

Muppanar

These people celebrate "valaikappu" in 7th or 9th month in the bride's house. After delivery they take new clothes, ornaments to the child and it's mother etc. when she goes back to her house. The other customs resemble the other caste people regarding first pregnancy.

Devar

These people celebrate "valaikappu" in the bride's house. All the other customs resemble the washerman caste people regarding first pregnancy.

Udayar

If a lady become pregnant then her parents go and meet her in her husband's house in the 3rd month. In the 5th month they take five kind of meals, five kind of tiffens etc. and meet her. In 7th month they celebrate "valaikappu" and "siimandam" in the bridegroom's house. On that day bridegroom is with the bride and these people put bangles to the married ladies attending the function. On this day they put margosa fibre bangle, then five metal bangle, silver bangle and golden bangle. Then they take the girl to their house and again send her back to her husband's house. Only in the 9th month they invite her to her parent's house for delivery and in the 3rd month after delivery they send back the child and it's mother by doing "siir" to them.

Kallar (Devar)

If a lady is pregnant then her parents go and see her, in the 3rd month. In the 5th month they take sugar, plantain etc. and meet her. In the 7th or 9th month they celebrate "valaikappu", put margosa fibre bangle first and then silver, golden bangles are put. At the time of celebrating this ceremony the bridegroom is also with her, they put bangles to the married woman who attend the function. After "valaikappu", they take back the girl to their house for delivery and after delivery in 3rd or 5th month they send the girl back to her husband's house by doing "siir" to the girl and the child.

Tuluva Naickar

If a lady is pregnant, in the 3rd month three kind of tiffens are prepared and they go and meet her in her husband's house. In the 5th month they prepare five kind of meals and five kind of tiffens and again go and meet her in her husband's house.

They celebrate "valaikappu" in the 9th month in the bridegroom's house, they put margosa fibre bangle first to the bride. At the time of "valaikappu" her husband is also with her and they put bangles to the married ladies attending the function. After this they invite the girl to their house in the 9th month for delivery and send back the girl after delivery in the 5th month and do "siir" to the child and it's mother.

Jankamar (Devar)

If the people come to know that a lady is pregnant then they prepare five kind of meals, five kind of tiffens and put "nalungu" to the bride. In 9th month these people celebrate "valaikappu". First they put margosa fibre bangle, glass bangles and golden bangles. On that day the bridegroom is also with the bride. On that day these people put bangles to the ladies who attend the function. This is celebrated in the bridegroom's house. In the 9th month they bring the girl to their house for delivery and after delivery they send the girl back to her husband's house in the 9th month and do "siir" to the mother and the child.

Konar (Yadhavapillai)

If one knows that a lady becomes pregnant, then the bride's parents prepare five kind of meals, tiffen etc. go and meet the pregnant lady and come back. In 7th month they put margosa tree's fibre bangle, suul kappu (silver bangle) and golden bangle. All the other customs resemble the patayacci caste people. They bring the lady in the 7th month and send her back and again bring her in the 9th month or they bring the lady in the 7th month and send her back after delivery in the 3rd month. There is no restriction for this in this caste. While sending the girl to her house, her parents do "siir" to the girl and her child.

Kuravar

Bride's parents prepare meals, take all kind of presentations, go and meet the pregnant lady in the 5th month. In 7th or 9th month they celebrate "valaikappu", first they put margosa tree's fibre bangle and then silver bangle to the lady. On that day relatives come and a grand feast is given to all. If the "kappu" is celebrated in the 7th month, they bring her to their house and send back. Again they bring her to their house in the 9th month. After delivery they send the girl and the child in 3rd month by doing "siir" to them.

Vannan (Washerman)

If a lady becomes pregnant, in the 5th month bride's parents prepare meals, tiffens, three kinds of pickle etc. take them, go and meet her in the bridegroom's house. They bring the girl to their house. Again they send her back to the bridegroom's house. In 7th or 9th, month they go and put "kappu" with ground nut, gingely (both) mixed with jaggery ("katalai", "ellu" pillayaar), rice or groundnut mixed with jaggery and take bangles, plantain, sugar, betel leaf, nut, flowers and all other kind of presentations when they go to celebrate "kappu". First they put margosa tree's fibre bangle, glass bangles, five metal mixed bangles, golden bangles etc. and bring her to their house. After delivery they send the girl and the child to her husband's house in the 3rd month by doing "siir".

Navitar (Barber)

The customs are same as above caste people (i.e., Washerman people).

Cakkili

When a lady becomes pregnant, bride's parents prepare five kind of meals, make a golden ornament go and meet her in the bridegroom's house in the fifth month. In the 7th month, they celebrate "valaikappu", in the bride's house. First they put margosa fibre bangle, then other kind of bangles and bring her to their house. Only after the delivery they send her back to her husband's house in the 3rd month by doing "siir" to the child and it's mother (Some people in this caste send back the girl to the bridegroom's house and again bring her back in the 9th month now-a-days).

Harijan (Adi Dravidar)

These people, in the bride's house cook meals, mutton etc. They take and give them to the pregnant lady in the 3rd month. In the 5th month they prepare five kind of meals go and give presentations to the lady and come back. They put "kappu" in the 7th or 9th month. First they put margosa tree's fibre bangle, silver bangle, golden bangle, golden ornaments, nose ring, ear ring, finger ring etc. on that day they poke rice with jaggery. They buy plantain, sugar and prepare gingely mixed with jaggery (all pillayaar), rice mixed with jaggery (arici pillaiyaar), ground nut mixed with jaggery (katalai pillayaar) etc. Relatives attend the function and a grand feast is arranged for those who attend the function. If they celebrate the "kappu" in the 7th month the girl has to return to her husband's house and she will come back again in the 9th month. If the "kappu" is done in the 9th month she will go to her house in the same month and only 3 months after delivery she goes to her husband's house. At that time bride's parents do "siir" to the mother and her child.

11

Sashtiyapthapurthi and Sadhabhishegam

Brahmin (Iyer)

This caste people celebrate this ceremony like a marriage itself. These people place—kalasams, brahmin priest kindles holy fire, recites holy mantras and anoint the couple with the water in the kalasams. Then they tie a marriage badge for this marriage also. They take new dresses to the couple. This is usually celebrated by the sons and daughters of the couple. Relatives attend the function and a grand feast is given to them.

Brahmin (Iyangar)

In this caste brahmin priest kindles the holy fire and recite holy mantras by placing "kumpam", i.e. (kalasam). They seat the couple together and the water in the "kumpam" is poured on the couple. This is done by the sons and daughters of the couple. For this function marriage badge, saree, *dhoti*, etc. are taken and this is celebrated like a marriage itself. Relatives are invited and a grand feast is arranged.

Pillai

These people also celebrate the 60th birthday. This is done in the wife's house. The couple's daughters and sons celebrate this marriage. For this marriage also they take saree, marriage badge etc. These people invite relatives and friends and arrange a grand feast and do this like a marriage itself.

Isai Velalar

These people celebrate 60th birthday. On that day the brahmin priest comes, kindles holy fire, recites holy mantras, places "5" kalasas anoint the couple with water in these "5" kalasas. At this time also they tie marriage badge again, this is done by the son, son-in-law, daughter-in-law and daughter. These people celebrate this in the house or in the temple according to the economic condition.

Patayacci

These people place "9" kalasams in the marriage platform and all the other customs resemble the other caste people. Some people of this caste celebrate this simply only in the temple.

Sengunta Mutaliyar

This caste people celebrate the 60th birthday and celebrate it like a marriage itself. They place "9" kalasas, tie marriage badge once again. All the other customs resemble the above caste people.

Asari (Pattar-Goldsmith, Taccar-carpenter)

This caste people also celebrate this function. The couple's parents, brother-in-law have to take new saree and *dhoti*. New marriage badge has to be made and the "saradu" (yellow string) is tied as in the marriage. All the other customs regarding this function resemble the brahmin caste people.

Chettiyar (Vysya, Sozhiya, Vaniya)

These people also celebrate 60th birthday and they celebrate it like a marriage and it resembles the ceremonies of 60th birthday of other caste people.

Pillai (Tuluva Vellalar)

These people celebrate this in the temple and the customs resemble the customs of other people. There is no restriction of number of "kalasams" placed in the marriage hall.

Reddiar

These people also celebrate this function like other caste people.

Naidu

The people place number of kalasas according to their grand-son, grand-daughter's number (one kalasa for each grand-son or grand-daughter) and celebrate this function like other caste people.

Thondaimandala Mutaliyar

These people place 5 kalasas in the marriage hall and the other customs resemble the other caste people.

Nadar

These people celebrate this function in the house like other caste people.

Nayakkar (Canar), Nayakkar (tatar), Muppanar

These three caste people do not celebrate this function.

Devar

These people celebrate this function in the temple and they tie a marriage badge at the time of this marriage.

Udayar

It is in custom to celebrate this function. They place "two" kalasas and other customs resemble the other caste people. This is usually celebrated in the house.

Kallar (Devar)

This caste people celebrate 60th birthday in the temple. For this function they take new saree and tie marriage badge at that time also. This is celebrated by the sons, daughters, son-in-law, daughters-in-law etc. They do not invite brahmin priest for this function.

Tuluva Naickar

It is in custom to celebrate 60th birthday (Sashtiyaptha-purtti) in this caste. On that day the brahmin priest recites holy mantras, kindles holy fire, places seven kalasas, anoint the couple with the water in the kalasas, they take new dresses to the couple, tie a marriage badge at that time also. They celebrate this in the temple and the sons, daughters, sons-in-law and daughters-in-law do it.

Jankamar

These people celebrate this function. On that day the brahmin priest comes, kindles holy fire, places one "kalasa", recites mantras and anoint the couple with the water in the "kalasa". For this occasion new dresses are taken for the couple and at this time also they tie marriage badge. This is usually celebrated by the sons, daughters, sons-in-law and daughters-in-law. Usually, these people celebrate it in a temple.

Konar (Yadhavappillai)

These people celebrate this marriage like Patayacci caste people except with one difference; i.e. they place nine kalasas at the time of marriage and the celebrate it usually in the temple.

Kuravar (Ramajoki)

This caste people do not celebrate this function.

Vannan

These people celebrate this only in the temple in a simple manner. They do "arccana" to the deity in the temple.

Navitar

This caste people celebrate this as in other caste, i.e. they place five kalasas in the marriage hall and other customs resemble the other caste people.

Cakkili

This people celebrate this like marriage itself and it resemble the other caste people.

Harijan

It is not in custom to celebrate this function by this caste people.

Sadhabhishegam

This is usually celebrated in the 71st or 80th year of a couple. Only some caste people do this marriage.

Brahmin (Iyer)

In the 80th year, these people celebrate this function. This is celebrated like a marriage, the couple are anointed and a feast is given (People believe that the seeing of this marriage will give good luck and bright future. So, people bow down the aged couple's feet and get their blessings).

Brahmin (Iyangar)

In the 80th year, sons of the couple keep a "kumpam" as follows : First rice is spread on the floor, on that a plantain leaf is placed, a pot with water is kept on that, they kindle holy fire and only after this they anoint the couple by the water in the kumpam. After that they get their blessings.

Pillai

These people celebrate this function in the 71st or 81st year or instead, they do it for God and Goddess, anoint God and Goddess. This is celebrated like "Sashtiyapthapurthi" in the house itself by some people of this caste.

Isai Velalar

They celebrate this function like "Sashtiyapthapurthi" with one difference. They do not tie marriage badge at the time of this function.

Patayacci

It is not in custom to celebrate this function.

Sengunta Mutaliyar

These people celebrate this like "Sashtiyapthapurthi" with one difference, i.e. they do not tie marriage badge for this function.

Asari (Pattar, Kammalar-Goldsmith, taccar-carpenter)

In the 80th year they celebrate this in temple and anointing is done to God and Goddess. Some celebrate this like "Sashtiyapthapurthi" but in this function tying marriage badge is not done.

Chettiyar (Vysya)

In the 80th year they celebrate this function.

Chettiyar (Sozhiya), (Vaniya)

It is not in custom to celebrate this function by these caste people.

Pillai (Tuluva Vellalar)

These people do not celebrate this function.

Reddiar

These people, celebrate this function like "sashtiyapthapurthi' in the 71st or 80th year, with a light difference they do not tie marriage badge at the time of this function.

Naidu

They do not celebrate this function.

Thondaimandala Mutaliyar

In the 71st or 80th year, these people celebrate this function like "Sashtiyapthapurtti".

Nadar

It is not in custom to celebrate this function among this caste people.

Nayakkar (Canar), Nayakkar (tatar), Muppanar, Devar

It is not in custom to celebrate this function among this caste people.

Udayar

At the age of 71 or 80—these people worship and anoint, God or Goddess in the temple.

Kallar (Devar)

It is not in custom to celebrate this function among this caste people.

Tuluva Naickar

These people do not celebrate this function.

Jankamar

These people do not celebrate this function.

Kenar (Yadhavappillai) : These people do not celebrate this function.

Kuravar (Ramajoki) : These people do not celebrate this function.

Vannan (Washerman), Navitar (Maruttuvar-Barber) : These caste people do not celebrate this fucntion.

Cakkili

This people celebrate this function in 80th year.

Harijan

There is no custom of celebrating this function among this caste people.

12

Death Customs

Brahmin (Iyer)

At the moment of the death of a person dying person's wife, husband, son, daughter, grandfather, grandmother, relatives pour the basil plant's water, milk etc. drop by drop in the mouth of the dying person. These people cremate the dead body. Immediately after death, a brahmin priest comes, new pot is bought, he recites holy mantras, then they give bath to the dead body, place the holy ash or *kumkum* on the dead person's forehead, new dress is worn and the uncles, son-in-law or son take the body to the graveyard. First son has to light the funeral pile and it is a custom to put ring on his finger (It is saying as "kolli vaitte kaikku mootiram poota veentum"). The new cloth (kooti) to the dead person has to come from the person's house connected by the marriage affinity (sambandi). After placing the body in the graveyard, sons and sons-in-law go round the body and anoint the body (This is termed as giving "mootcha patavi"). Then they kindle the fire. These people never keep the dead body for long time for any reason and they cremate the body on the same day of death. After cremating the body, they do "paal teli" ceremony next day. On that day they take milk, plantain etc. to the graveyard, take the ash of that dead person, pick up the bones and leave it in Cavery (or) in a river. On 15th day they give "maasiyam" (a ceremony for a dead person). Like this they do this ceremony on 27th day, 3rd and 6th month.

After the completion of the first year of the death of a person it is in practice to do funeral rites every year in the same *"tithi"* of the death of a person. On that day new *dhoti*, saree, vessels etc. are bought and feast is given. After this every year they do the funeral rites in the same *"tithi"* of the death of a person.

If a child within a year dies then these people bury the child and do "punniyadanam" on 11th day.

Brahmin (Iyangar)

At the moment when a person is dying, that person's relatives or the person who is very much close to the dying person pour basil plant's water, milk etc. drop by drop in the dying person's mouth. These people also cremate the dead body. Usually, the first son puts the funeral pile to the dead body and the grand-son holds the ghee torch (ney pandam). They give bath to the dead body before taking it to the grave yard, place namam or *kumkum* in that person's forehead, garland it, putting new cloth on it ánd take it to the graveyard.

Next day they celebrate a ceremony "paal teli". On that day the meal is cooked without salt and put into the river. Then within 10 days of the death of the person they have to give a *dhoti*, pot made up of white metal, spoon, lamp, coins etc. as alms to a person. On 10th day meals is given to the relatives with vata, paayasam etc. On that night they give fried rice, jaggery, unhusked rice etc. are poked, a sweet (mysuurpaaku) is also prepared, some tiffens are made and given to those "relatives". On 11th day *dhoti*, a metal pot, coins etc. are given to a brahmin and he is fed. On 12th day they give *dhoti*, a metal pot, coins etc. to five persons (For this ceremony they termed as Chavundi (or) Greekkiyam). On that day itself they give *dhoti* to another person. (termed as "vastira daanam"). Also a cow is given to a person on that day itself (termed as "koodaanam"). A bamboo stick is given to another person on that day itself (termed as "pirampu daanam") (It is believed that the dead person holds the stick to go to heaven and so it is given as an alm). If one has land they give land to their relatives (They give small portion of the land to their relatives "buumi daanam").

The 13th day is termed as an auspicious day. On that day sweet, tiffen, new dresses are given to all in the house. Next day they take oil bath. If the father-in-law or mother-in-law dies, one has to take *dhoti,* ring etc. to the bridegroom and saree to the bride. Then they give monthly alms ("maata tevasam or maasiya soota kumbam"). They do funeral rites every year. These people do not perform any ceremonies if a child died within a year.

Pillai

At the moment of the death of a person, basil plant's water is poured by the relatives drop by drop. Immediately after death, they place a measuring pot full of paddy, two standing lamps, coconut, betel leaf, nut, plantain etc. and light three torches (pandam) and then they show the way to the dead person ("vazhi kuutti vitutal"). Only after this ceremony they send the death news to others and also only after this they weep. These people also cremate the dead body. The eldest son has to light the funeral pile.

After making the way clear to the dead person they give bath to the body, ladies put five paise coin and rice in the mouth (vaykkarisi—a ceremony of putting rice into the mouth of a corpse before burning). After that they place the body in bier, then with the betel leaf, nut, measuring pot full of paddy etc. the ladies go round the bier and bow down to the dead body. Gents put the rice in the mouth only in the graveyard. After doing funeral to the dead body in the graveyard and while returning to the house after taking bath, they give lamp, plate, tumbler etc. to a brahmin priest as alms (daanam) (There is a belief in connection with this occasion, i.e., the dead person will be lighted to reach their place. That is why they give lamp to a brahmin priest). After this they return to the house, wash their leg, hands etc. bow down to the lamp which is lit in the place where the dead body was put before and place holy ash on their forehead and only after this they take food.

Next day they celebrate "paal teli". On that day these people take tender coconut, milk, a big pot etc. to the graveyard, pick up the bones and anoint it with tender coconut, milk, put it in the big pot and leave it in the river. On 8th day they mourn (termed as 8-m dukkam) for the dead person. This is done on the 7th day itself. They cook the dhall, make a tiffen (bajji), a kind of grain (pottukkatalai) mixed with jaggery, prepare "paniyaaram" (sweet-rice flour mixed in the jaggery), and the other edibles liked by the dead person and offer it to the dead person and give it to a washerman. The unoffered tiffens are taken by the others. On 16th day (kal caayttal), they celebrate "karumati". On that day they prepare the shape of a man using blackgram dhall's flour, recite mantras and offer it, leave it in the water. After this ceremony, they give clothes from the parent's house. They have to give *dhoti*, ring for the person who do the funeral ceremonies and also saree for his wife. On 30th day they cook food and offer it to Lord Ganesh, then go to a temple and only after this they come back and take food. These people do monthly "maaciyam" to the dead person. The first son (who puts the fire to the dead body) does the yearly funeral rites every year.

If a child within one year dies, then the barber bores the ear of the child with the thorn of karuvai (a thorn tree) and bury it. They do "punniyadanam" on 10th or 13th day.

Isai Velalar

At the moment of dying one has to give basil plant's water, milk etc. to the dying person. They clear the way to the dead person like the above caste people. They tie the thumb of the hand, leg and close the mouth. These people give bath to the dead body only when taking to the graveyard. It is in custom to cremate and bury the dead body in this caste. These people believe if one's body is burnt they will go to heaven, if one's body is buried they will go to hell. Placing the cowdung with nine grains on the hands of the dead body is done only if the dead person is a lady or married lady. They place the cowdung on the leg of that lady and place it on the wall. If male persons die, than the new cloth has to come from his brother-in-law.

Next day (or) on the 3rd day they do "paal teli" (If the day is unauspicious they do it even next day also). On 8th day they mourn for the dead person. On 11th or 16th day they do "karumati". On 30th day (i.e. on the 29th day) they offer three varieties of tiffen to the dead person, cook meals and offer it also to the dead person (They do this in the belief that they invite the dead persons again to the house "kaattukku poonavarkalai tirumpa viittukku azhaittal"). The clothes at the time of death of a person are kept and it is worshiped during Deepawali (termed as "Deepawali dukkam") 5 or 7 or 9 days before Deepawali and also during pongal (termed as "pongal dukkam") these people mourn for the dead person.

First year they do funeral rites and give offerings to their household God. Then they give yearly rites for every year. These people do not do any ceremonies if a child died within a year. The other customs regarding death resemble the Patayacci caste people.

Patayacci

At the moment of death of a person, the relatives give basil plant's water, milk etc. If the person does not die easily but the person is lingering, the relatives thought that, that dying person has some wish in his mind and so they dissolve the sand liked by that dying person in water and pour it drop by drop in his mouth. Immediately after death they give the dead body a bath and place holy ash or *kumkum* on that person's forehead. After this they do "vazhi kuutti vitutal" ceremony. The male persons in that house go with betel leaf, nut etc. to the end of the street and break coconut and light camphor and prepare the way to the dying person. Then they bring the camphor, coconut, betel leaf, nut etc. and place them in a measuring pot full of paddy which is kept on the forehead of the dead body. They light bathi above the dead body. Only after this ceremony, they send the death news outside and begins to weep.

This caste people bury as well as cremate the body. They beat all kind of drums to announce the death of a person. Relatives bring paddy, oil, Sikakkaay, new cloth, tender coconut etc. as the "vaaykkarisi" things for the dead person.

If the dead person is a lady then the new cloth come from her parent's house. Before taking the dead body, bath is given to it and this new cloth is put on the body. Relatives put rice in the dead person's mouth (vaaykkarisi) in the bathing place itself.

Then the eldest son and his wife go round the dead body thrice, taking measuring pot full of paddy in which a lamp is burning. Relatives also go round thrice with the nine kind of grains pressed in the cow-dung of a cow and it is placed at the foot of dead person and later paste it on the wall (This is done in the belief that "the dead person's good luck has to stay in the house itself"). Dead person's grand-son, grand-daughter hold the ghee torch (ney pandam). All the close relatives for 16 days do not attend any auspicious austericities. For these 16 days they won't comb the hair, never smear oil, take oil bath, they do not place *tilak* on their forehead etc. To put "vaykkarisi" to the dead person they take the flour mixed with ghee and jaggery, ("maa vilakku maavu") to the graveyard. Then the dead body is placed on the bier and all the relatives go round the bier and bow down to the body and they begin to weep.

When the dead body is in the house they never sprinkle cowdung water, or clean the house. Only after the dead body is carried away, that place is cleaned with water etc. The persons after taking bath while returning from the graveyard enter the house after washing their legs, hands etc. and bow down to the lamp (which is placed where the body is placed) and place the holy ash on their forehead and then only take food.

Next day they celebrate "paal teli". The paddy used for vakkarisi will not be kept in the house. It has to be cooked before "karumati". On the day of "paal tali" rice is made from this paddy and food is cooked. On this day they take milk and do some ceremonies in the graveyard. Before taking the milk to the graveyard that milk is kept in a vessel and the relatives put coins without making any noise in that milk. On the 8th day they mourn for the dead person (8th day dukkam). On that day tiffens, plantain etc. are placed in the dead persons place (where the lamp is always burning) and offered to him. On 16th day they do "karumati". On the 15th day evening relatives make tiffens, place a stone on that day night and offer thrice to that stone. After offering thrice and the offering on the third time are given to those who attend that ceremony. That whole night they lament and weep. In the early morning gents go to the river bank to finish the funeral rites. After finishing funeral rites new dresses are given and ring is put in the finger. Till the funeral rites are finished they will not use oil on the hair. Only after finishing the funeral rites they take oil bath next day and in the evening they comb and tie their hair. Next day again the relatives take oil bath and give a feast. On 30th day, the things which are liked by the dead person are prepared and offered to him. Mourning is done on Deepawali and Pongal days.

Only yearly funeral rites are done every year and on that day it is in practice to give alms to a brahmin priest. If a child within a year dies then they bore the ear of the child and then bury it.

Sengunta Mutaliyar

At the moment of death of a person first the son gives water or milk to the dying person (If there is no son, then that person's daughter or relatives give water etc. to that dying person). When the person is dead they break a coconut and worship in the house itself and clear the way to the dead person (These people do not go to the street end). This is also done by the son only. Then only they send the news to others and begin to weep. These people either cremate the body or bury the body. They keep the body in a chair and bury it and build a mode of interment. If the corpse is taken in the bier then it is burnt. They give bath to the dead body only once, i.e. while taking the body. That person's son has to take new cloth for the dead body and also two new clothes whether the dead person is a lady or male.

This new cloth is put one from the parent's house, another from the married house.

After giving bath, putting this new cloth to the corpse, they go round the bier thrice (It is not in custom of "Navadaaniyam araital" in this caste). Then they scatter fried rice, gingely etc. throughout the way by which the corpse is taken (If one died on Saturday these people tie a chicken on the head side of the bier and put it along with the corpse in the pit). Reason, it is believed that the person dying on saturday will search for two more persons as a companion. Then after placing and doing the ceremonies in the graveyard, they take bath and return to the house and clean their legs, hands and bow down to the lamp which is lit where the dead body is placed. Only after this they take the food.

Next day they do "paal teli". On the 3rd day they do "karumati". On that day a new *dhoti* is given to uncle, brother-in-law etc. Next day they take oil bath. On that day all the expenditure belong to that person's uncle or brother-in-law. On the 8th day they do 8th day mourning (8th day dukkam). That day they invite relatives and prepare three kind of tiffens, the other edibles liked by the dead person and offer to him. On the 16th day only the person in that person's (they do not invite anybody from outside) house offer by keeping meals in a plantain leaf. This is termed as *"nallali vaittu pataiattal"*. Only on that day the ceremonial impurity due to the death of a person is removed. They do funeral rites every year. This caste people do not perform any ceremonies if a child dies within a year.

Asari (Pattar, Kammalar, Goldsmith, Taccar-carpenter)

The customs like giving water etc. "vazhi kuutti vitutal" in the corner of the street, sending the news to others, weeping etc. resemble other caste people. They give bath to the corpse before "vazhi kuutti vitutal". They seated the dead body in a chair and bury it. They do not burn the corpse. These people do not put rice in the mouth of the dead body. They tie the legs, hands, mouth with a cloth and tie this cloth to a nail in the wall in the back of the dead body where it is placed. There they press the nine grains in the cow-dung and place it in the hands of a dead body, remove the nail in the wall and place this cow-dung in place of the nail.

Placing a "kalasa" with water in which mango leaves, coconut etc. are kept, the corpse is given bath second time with this water. Then keeping this "kalasam" in hand the eldest son and his wife go round the corpse. Following the two, others go round the corpse only after this the nine grains (navadaaniyam) is placed on the wall. After burying the corpse, taking bath, they return to the house and before entering into the house they wash the hands, legs etc. and bow down to the lamp which is placed where the dead body was laid, place the holy ash on their forehead and then only they take food.

They do "paal teli" next day. These people also do this like "Patayacci" caste people. They celebrate 8th day mourning for the dead person. They prepare tiffens, plantain, sugar etc. and offer it to the dead person. On 16th day they celebrate "Karumati". The tiffens given by the relatives, tiffen prepared in the house are placed and offered to the dead person and they give a feast to the relatives. On 16th day the sons of the dead person go to the graveyard, take the sand from there, made a shape of Lord Siva (Linga shape) and anoint it with milk, curd etc. and the brahmin priest (of this caste itself), come and do the "punniyadanam'. This is done to remove the ceremonial impurity due to the death of a person. On that day they do punniyadanam by sprinkling (cow's urine) "Koomiyam" throughout the house, sprinkle milk, curd etc. Till the "karumati" is finished they do not smear oil, do not take oil bath, never comb the hair etc. Only after that ceremony they take oil bath, comb the hair etc. and tie the hair. Only after this ceremony they smear oil on their hair. On this day the expenditure of meals belong to the son-in-law's house. These people do only funeral rites every year. If a child within a year dies they do not perform any ceremonies.

Chettiyar (Vysya)

If a male is going to die then his wife, son, daughter etc. put basil plant and milk in his mouth. Immediately after death they tie the thumbs of the two legs, hands etc. and light the lamp. Then a coconut is broken, the camphor is shown. Only after this they send the news to the relatives. After all persons come, the corpse is given bath. Then a brahmin priest with the help of dharbai makes a string and puts it on the bier and kindles the fire and do some ceremonies.

Then the new cloth is worn to the corpse, flowers are put and it is kept on the bier and tied by the string made up of dharbai grass. Then four persons carry the bier. The first son carry the fire pot in the front and the bier goes in the back. Before that in the graveyard, they place the firewood in a bundle to set fire. Then the bier is taken round thrice around the fire sticks and then it is placed on the ground. After doing some related ceremonies, it is placed on the fire sticks and relatives put rice in the mouth of the dead body. Then it is covered with the sticks. The first son kindle fire. In the fire pot three sandalwood sticks are placed. When the fire is kindled, he place the sandalwood sticks one by one for each round. Then with a pot of water first son goes round that place thrice and a brahmin priest recite mantras and for each round they put one hole in the pot and the water filtering out of that holes are sprinkled on the corpse. Then that pot is thrown away and without looking back, they return to the house after taking bath.

If one's wife is dead the same customs are followed but instead of first son last son puts the fire to his mother. Next day "paal teli". At the time of this ceremony a widow put rice, three type of vegetables, turmeric powder in a vessel and cooks it, places it in a bamboo plate on which a yellow cloth is spread. On that cloth this food is spharad and it is covered with a yellow cloth. Then with this plate and the things used for "abhishegam" (for anointing), tender coconut etc. they go to a tank. The person who lights fire for the dead body has to take the plate etc. to the graveyard. They go to the graveyard and the relatives pick up the bones of the leg, hand, chest etc. skull and ash and put them in a plate. Then the remaining ash is put in a pot and closed with a cover. Then they clean that place and make a shape of a man. Then they put three stones on the chest portion of the man and take water in a pot. After this they sprinkle milk in the pot in which ash is kept.

Small holes are made in that pot using the nail. Then the water squeezing through those holes is sprinkled on the stones and anointed with the water. Then in a plantain leaf they place the edibles liked very much by the dead person, coconut, plantain, the cooked food in the bamboo plate etc. and offer them to the stone. From among the stone placed on the chest of the man, a stone is taken to the house. Then the pot in which the ash is put is taken by the person who puts the fire to the corpse and with another person he goes to the river and dissolve the holy ash (asthi). Then they give rice, vegetables etc. to a brahmin priest. He recites some mantras and then only the ash is dissolved in the river. Then after taking bath they return to the house.

On the 16th day they do "karumati" ceremony. For all the 15 days the person who puts the fire to the corpse goes to the graveyard with a brahmin priest. While going to the graveyard they take a brass vessel, place plantain, small amount of rice, greengram dhall (Payattam paruppu), milk, ghee etc. Then they place five cowdung cakes and erect the stone (which was taken back to the house on the day of "paal teli") and anoint the stone with that of cooked rice. Then he puts the cooked rice to a crow. The person who puts the fire to the corpse does not go out during these fifteen days. If he goes, he has to come back before the dawn.

For these fifteen days his relatives give feast to him. He does not take the "rice" cooked on the previous day. He has to take tiffen only in the morning and evening and in the noon time he can take meals. All the relatives will go to the "karumatit turai" on 16th day (karumatit tuari—bank of a river where the funeral rites are done). They shave their faces and then they anoint that stone and leave it in the tank of the river. Then they return back to the house. Next-day they give alms containing nine grains to a brahmin priest. Rice, vegetables, salt, tamarind, all kind of dhalls are placed in six leaves and offered to the dead person. Then a brahmin is invited and they give rice, white pumpkin, vegetables, all kind of dhalls, a brass pot, tumbler, umbrella, chappel, *dhoti*, towel etc. to him. Then they wash and clean the house. On the 16th day itself all the members in the house take oil bath. The brahmin priest kindles the holy fire and from that day onwards the ceremonial impurity is removed. Next day relatives take oil bath. They give presents to the person who put fire to the corpse. Then a feast is given to all. Then the brass pot, tumbler, brass vessel etc. used in the "Karumatit turai" are given to a brahmin priest.

Wife of the dead person till the 16th day is not considered as a widow. For all the 15 days she wear flower, turmeric, *kumkum* etc. Only after finishing the worship to the stone on the 16th day, they weep and then untie the marriage badge and cut and put it in the milk. For 15 days a widow keeps company with the lady. After cutting the marriage string she takes full bath. Then her uncle gives her a new saree and taking that saree she go to a temple in a cart with the widowed lady. Then she return to the house where in a big plate milk is placed. Then the newly widowed lady sees her face by putting cloth on her head in the milk and the other married woman see her face in the milk. If her face is not seen by others in the milk then she does not come outside for one year. She has to remain in the house. Nobody can meet her.

If the wife dies

On 16th day in the river bank 16 (or) 32 new winnows are brought and in each winnow a saree, blouse, turmeric, *kumkum*, flower etc. are placed and it is given to 16 (or) 32 married woman. In the morning, oil is sent to a brahmin priest's wife and she takes oil bath. Then rice, tamarind, chilly, salt, vegetables etc. are sent. She cook food with these things and takes it to the dead person's house and a new saree, *kumkum*, flower, turmeric, plantain etc. are placed in a new winnow are given to her.

Then "masiyam" is done for each month. For this, each month 12 plantain leaves are placed and in each leaf a litre of rice, and other things like vegetables etc. are placed and this is given as an alm to a brahmin priest. Yearly funeral rites are done. If a person's wife is dead then after one year on the same "*tithi*", they give the offerings offered to the dead person to a brahmin preist's wife. Like this every year in the same day they offer a new saree, vegetables, *kumkum*, plantain, flower, turmeric etc. and these are given to a brahmin priest's wife. This caste people do not do any ceremonies if a child died within a year.

Chettiyar (Sozhiya)

At the moment of death of a person it is a habit to pour basil plant's water, milk etc. drop by drop into the mouth of that person. Immediately after death, these people do not give bath to the dead body. They never go to the street corner for "vazhi kuutti vitutal", like the other caste people. They go to the front of the house and do that ceremony and clear the way to the dead person. Then they send the news to the others and weep. Then they tie together the two thumbs of the hands, toes etc. These people both cremate and bury. The new cloth comes from both the uncle's and parent's house. They bring rice for putting in the mouth of the corpse. They keep measuring pot full of paddy and light a lamp on the head side of the corpse. Then the corpse is given bath and placed in a bier and after that the son, daughter-in-law and relatives go round the bier. At that time, the son and his wife hold the measuring pot full of paddy. The dead person's grandson holds the ghee torch. At the time of going round the bier they press the nine grains in the cow-dung, place it on the hand of the dead person and then place it on the wall. Then after burying or cremating the body in the graveyard they return to the house after taking bath.

On 2nd day they do "paal teli". That day they worship the dead person. For sixteen days, in the place where the dead body is kept, a lamp is lit and water is kept in a brass pot. On 8th day they mourn for the dead person. On 16th day "karumati" is done. On that day no tiffen is done but the edibles like vadai etc. are done and offered to the dead person. On that day night quarter litre rice, plantain, lamp, a stylus, cooked tiffens etc. are taken to the place where the funeral rite is to be done in the early morning. On that day night, three offerings with unhusked rice, dhall etc. are offered. Next day they take oil bath. After taking oil bath they take meals with vadai and payasam etc. On 30th day (i.e. on 29th day) they mourn 30th day mourning. On that day they do three kind of tiffens, grand meals etc. and take new cloth and offer to the dead person.

First year they do the funeral rites. They do "tarppanam" (a kind of rite) on every new moon day for each month. If a child dies within a year they do "punniyadanam" on 13th day.

Chettiyar (Vaniya)

These people do the same ceremonies as sozhiya chettiyar. When they clear the way to the dead person they break the coconut and light the lamp. This is also done by sozhiya chettiyar people. They celebrate "paal teli" on the 3rd day. They take tiffens, unhusked rice, dhall, milk etc. to the graveyard and offer them there itself. On 8th day they keep 8th day mourning. They celebrate "karumati" on 16th day (This is done on 15th day night and 16th day early morning). After the funeral rites they do "talaikattu" (talaikattu—This is a practice when a person is dead, new saree, *dhoti* etc. are given to the dead person's son from the son's father-in-law's house. Before giving these things a towel is tied round the head and after that the presentations are given to his. This is termed as "talaikattu" in all castes). This is done by the father-in-law's house. On 30th day they mourn for the dead person (This mourning is done in a belief that "kaattukku poonavarkalai viittukku azhaittal—i.e., the dead persons are invited to the house again"). Then they perform monthly funeral rites for one year. Yearly funeral rites for every year, are given, on that day rice is given as alm to a "pandaaram" or to a cow. If a child dies within a year, these people do punniyadanam on 7th or 9th or 11th day by inviting a brahmin priest.

Pillai (Tuluva Vellalar)

When a person is dying these people administer milk, basil plant's water etc. to that person. Then they break coconut, place betel leaf, nut, light the lamp and camphor and show them around the dead person and do the ceremony "vazhi kuutti vitutal". They do this in the street corner. They give bath to the dead person before taking to graveyard. Only after doing "vazhi kuutti vitutal" ceremony they inform others and then only they weep. These people cremate the dead body. They tie the hands, toe, and mouth of the dead person. These people put "vaykkarisi" to the dead person. All relatives, daughters etc. put the rice in the house and gents put the rice in the graveyard. These people beat drums for the death. After placing the dead body in the bier son (holds the paddy in the measuring pot), daughter-in-law, daughter, son-in-law and others go round the bier thrice and bow down to the dead person.

They place paddy in the measuring pot, broken coconut, betel leaf, nut, lamp etc. on the head side of the dead body. They put nine grains in the cow-dung, place it at the leg of the dead person and then they place it on the wall. This is done on the belief that the family will be fertile. At that time, the grand-daughter and grand-son hold the ghee torch. Usually, the first son sets fire and the relatives carry the bier to the graveyard.

Usually, the uncle (relative to the mother) put the new cloth to the dead body and if a male dies than to his widow, her parents put the new cloth. After going to the graveyard they place the bier, put rice to the dead person and do a ceremony "niir kudamudaittal". After doing funeral ceremonies they take bath, come back, wash the legs and hands, enter the house, bow down to the lamp and then only they take food. Till the "karumati' day a lamp is lit in the place where the dead body laid. These people use the paddy brought by the relatives house as "vaykkarisi" before the "karumati" day. Next day, they celebrate "paal tali". On that day they keep milk in a pot and if a male dies his widow puts coin without making any noise in that vessel.

Then tender coconut, milk etc. are taken to the graveyard for "paal teli" and the vessels are brought back to the house. These people mourn for the dead person on the 8th day and they offer tiffens liked by the dead person. These people do "karumati" on 16th day, they do some ceremonies in the river bank to a stone and leave it in the river. On that day itself they do "talaikattu". These people give monthly *tithi* for one year and then yearly *tithi*. If one dies then on the 16th day these people give cow, bamboo stick, lands, cloth etc. as alms to a brahmin priest. If a lady dies with married status then yearly they give saree, blouse, turmeric, *kumkum*, betel leaf, nut, flowers etc. to a brahmin priest's wife.

These people put red colour new cloth if a married woman dies, to a widow white new cloth and if a lady becomes widow it is in custom that she is to wear white or red saree. If a child within one year dies these people bury the child by boring the ear, do "punniyadanam" on 11th day. If an unmarried person dies then they decorate a plantain and perform marriage with it and then only they do the death ceremonies.

Reddiar

At the time of death of a person these people pour milk, basil plant's water etc. in the mouth of the dying person. These people do not tie the hand, toe, mouth etc. They do not perform the ceremony of placing cow-dung in the leg or hand of the dead person and place it on the wall. These people bury as well as cremate the dead body. Usually, if father dies first son does the funeral ceremonies and if mother dies last son does the funeral ceremonies. Usually relatives carry the bier to the graveyard. These people put new cloth to the dead person.

"Dead person's" elder brother puts new cloth ("kooti") to him if the dead person is male and for his widow, her relatives put new cloth. The "paddy" brought for "vaykkarisi" is taken back immediately.

These people celebrate "paal teli" next day and they give the vessels taken to the graveyard as alms to somebody else. These people mourn for the dead person on 7th day. After 13 days these people do "karumati", to the dead person. For this ceremony, they erect three stones in the house, anoint them and take them to the river bank and do some ceremonies and leave it in the river. On the same day they do "talaikattu" and for this they give money, cloth etc. to the person who does the funeral ceremonies to the dead person. On 30th day these people mourn for the dead person.

These people give monthly *tithi* for one year and yearly *tithi* to the dead person. On the day of "karumati" these people give vessel, money, rice, cloth etc. as alms to a brahmin priest. If a lady dies with married status then on the day of yearly *tithi* these people give a new saree, blouse, flower, turmeric, *kumkum* etc. to a brahmin priest's wife. If a lady dies with married status these people put red new cloth, if a widow dies people put white new cloth and in this caste it is compulsory for a widow to wear white saree. The other customs regarding death resemble the above caste people.

Naidu

These people seat the dead person (before this they give bath to the dead body) in a chair, put garland, show the camphor by breaking coconut and do "vazhi kuutti vitutal" ceremony.

These people give bath immediately after the death of the person and before taking to the graveyard. They either cremate or bury the body, both these are in vogue. These people blow the "taadar" conch only when a person dies. After giving bath to the body, it is placed in the bier and all the relatives go round the bier thrice. Only sandal wood is placed on the head side of the dead person. Dead person's first son sets fire to the dead person. They place cowdung only on the wall where a nail is driven into the wall. They seat the dead person in a chair, tie his leg, hand, mouth etc. and tie that in a nail in the back of his chair. When the mouth, leg, hand tying are untied they pluck the nail also and to fill up that hole they put the cowdung on that place. This is done on the belief that the persons who have no child at all will give birth to a child because of this action. Relatives carry the bier to the graveyard. They put "kooti" from the parent's house to the dead person. After burying or cremating the dead person they come back after taking bath. They do not put "vaykkarisi" etc. to the dead person. They do "paal teli" only on the 5th day and prepare tiffens, buy aval (unhusked rice), kadalai (groundnut), milk etc. and worship the dead person by informing all the members close to that person and take all the things to the graveyard. They mourn for the dead person on 7th day, prepare tiffens etc. like by the dead person, inform the news to the relatives only and worship the dead person.

They erect two stones on 10th day night and do "karumati" on 11th day. They give three offerings to the dead person on this day. First offering is given by the relatives, second offerings is by preparing sweet cooked rice (pongal) and the 3rd offering is by placing aval, pottukkatalai (a kind of pulse) etc. and they worship in the early morning. After all ceremonies are over they leave the stones in the river. Next day they do "talaikattu" and the relatives come to this ceremony. On that day according to the economic situation they take new clothes or they give only money.

Next day after "talai kattu", relatives take oil bath "sammandhi" do the "talai kattu". They mourn on 30th day, for Deepawali and for Pongal. They give "cow" as alm to the brahmin priest and they give white metal bowl, wooden plague (palagai), clothes as alms to a brahmin priest. They give only yearly *tithi* for dead person (not monthly *tithi* for one year). On the yearly *tithi* day brahmin priest comes, kindles holy fire, recites mantras, places various types of food in three plantain leaf and offers it to the dead person. If a married woman dies they can put any colour of "kooti", if a widow dies they put "naar muti" cloth, i.e. light yellow colour cloth as "kooti", if a male dies they put *dhoti* as "kooti". If a child within a year dies they bury the child after boring the ear, and do "punniyadanam", on 11th day. They cremate, if the child dies. If the first child dies immediately after the birth they bury it inside their compound. Then they take it on 30th day or 3rd month and put it in "gangas" or "kaveri". These people do not perform any ceremony if a unmarried person dies. The other customs resemble the other caste people. If the persons have "muttirai" in their hands (i.e. some persons went to a Vishnu temple and draw the conch and chakara in their hands), it is to be removed when they die and only after this they take the dead body to the graveyard. While removing the "muttirai" only those people who have right to be with him will be present. "Vashttumar" comes, kindles holy fire, ties dharbai grass, thread etc. and show the wooden mortor in the holy fire and place that mortor on the "muttirai" and take it from the dead body. Only after this ceremony they take the body to the graveyard. This is done only by Naidu caste people and Iyangar caste people. The other customs regarding death resemble the other caste people.

Thondaimandala Mutaliyar

At the time of death of a person they pour milk, basil plant's water, water from rubbing the coin, the sand water etc. immediately after death these people do "vazhi kuutti vitutal" ceremony. It is in custom to cremate the body. They keep broken coconut, betel leaf, nut, plantain, lamp etc. on the head side of the dead person. The other customs regarding death resemble the above caste people. If a male dies, for his widow, her parents give new cloth. The other customs regarding death resemble the Sengunta Mutaliyar caste people.

Nadar

They place the camphor shown to the dead body at the

time of "vazhi kuutti vitutal" in the street corner. Dead body is given bath only before taking to the graveyard. They either cremate or bury the dead body. After placing the dead body in the bier, son, son-in-law, daughter, daughter-in-law and relatives go round the bier thrice without taking anything in the hand or on their heads. They place broken coconut, betel leaf, nut, plantain, lamp, vaykkarisi etc. on the head side of the dead body. It is not in custom to place cow-dung with nine grains on the leg or hand of the dead person and place it on the wall. Funeral ceremonies are done by the last son to the father and by the first son to the mother. Relatives carry the bier. If a male dies, then his brother gives new cloth to dead person's widow. They do "paal teli" on 3rd day. These people mourn for the dead person on 8th day and prepare tiffens liked by the dead person. The other death customs resemble the above caste people.

On 16th day they perform "karumati", offer three times, relatives bring various tiffens, erect one stone in the house and anoint it and take it to the river bank and do ceremonies for the stone and leave it in the river. On the same day they do "talaikattu" ceremony. They mourn for the dead person on 30th day and after that they give only yearly *tithi*. On the day of "karumati" they give cow, bamboo stick, land, cloth etc. as alms to a brahmin priest. It is not in custom to give new saree, blouse etc. on the day of yearly "*tithi*" to a brahmin priest's wife if a married lady dies with that status.

They put red new cloth to the ladies with married status, white new cloth to the widows, and it is compulsory to wear white cloth for widows. If a child within a year dies they bury the child after boring the ear and on 8th day they celebrate "punniyadanam". If an unmarried person dies then they decorate a plantain and do marriage with the dead person and then only they do all the other death customs. The other customs regarding death resemble the other caste people.

Nayakkar (Canar)

These people put "vaykkarisi" to the dead person. Dead person's relatives, grand-son, grand-daughter, son, daughter put "vaykkarisi". After this other customs resemble the "pattar" caste people. They go round the bier, the dead person's son places a cloth around the head, dead person's daughter, relatives go round the bier thrice. The new cloth to the dead person is to be provided from the parent's house. They do "paal teli" on the 3rd day. They mourn on 8th day for the dead person and they prepare tiffens and offer them to the dead person. On the 15th day night they do the "karumati", put three offerings, erect two stones in the house and anoint it. After performing all the ceremonies to the stone they leave the stone in the river. After "Karumati" day they do "talaikattu" and this is done by the "sammandhi". This "talaikattu" is done only after taking oil bath. On the same day the relatives take oil bath. After "karumati" day the ceremonial impurities due to death of a person are removed.

These people mourn on 30th day, on Deepawali day and on Pongal day for the dead person. They give only yearly *tithi* and give alms to the brahmin priest. If a married woman dies they put red saree, for widow and male put white cloth as "kooti". A widow wears red saree. If a child dies these people bury the child and do "punniyadanam" on 9th or 11th day to remove the ceremonial impurities due to death. Other customs more or less resemble the other caste people.

Nayakkar (Tatar)

They put only the garland made up of basil plant and also put the rose flower garland to the dead person. Dead body can be seated or laid down and they bury the body. They also do not put "vaykkarisi". Immediately after death they give bath to the dead body. Then breaking a coconut, place this coconut, plantain etc. in front of the dead body, show camphor and place all these on the head side of the dead body. They place a small (kai vilakku) lamp on the head side of the dead body. These people also use drums. Before taking the body to the graveyard again they give bath to the dead body and put new cloth. If the dead is a female then her sister-in-law will put the "kooti", if it is a male his brother-in-law will put the "kooti". On the 3rd day these people do "paal teli" and they keep the milk in a vessel and the ladies put coins in the vessel. On 8th day these people mourn for the dead person. On 15th day night these people celebrate "karumati" and erect one stone and offer various tiffens (Mainly if the dead person has no father and mother these people erect the stone). On this day brahmin priest does "punniyadanam". Then washerman, barber etc. do the thing. These people give three offerings. First is tiffen, 2nd is varieties of fruits and 3rd is betel leaf, nut etc. After this the gents take the stone to the river bank.

In a white metal pot brahmin priest places mango leaves, coconut, flowers etc., kindles holy fire, recite holy mantras and gives it to the gents who go to the river bank. They take this to the house. In the house the ladies show camphor, alms etc. to this pot, hang a cloth around the pot and get this pot in the front portion of the saree (mundaani) and go inside. Next day "talaikattu". On this day they give "aattu viruntu" (Samandi ceytal). On 16th day the ceremonial impurities due to the death of a person are removed. These people mourn for the dead person on 30th day, for Deepawali and for Pongal. They put red colour saree for married woman, red colour saree without flower (termed as "Santirali") for widow as "kooti". Widowed ladies do not wear flowered saree. These people give yearly *tithi* to the dead person. If a child within one year dies they bury the child in the graveyard and on 8th or 9th day they keep mourning for the child. If the first child dies then they bury the child in their house itself and on the 9th month they take it out and put it in the graveyard. To remove the ceremonial impurities they do "punniyadanam". These people also get the nine grains put in the cowdung from the hands of the dead person and place it in the wall. They exchange leaf and coconut with each other. Other customs regarding death resemble the other caste people.

When a person is in dying stage these people give only milk and water to that person. These people do the "vazhi kuutti vitutal" ceremony in the street corner. These people give bath to the dead body only before taking to the graveyard. These people place measuring pot full of paddy and light a lamp on the head side of the dead body. They bury the dead body. These people put "vaykkarisi" to the dead person's mouth, after placing the dead person in the bier, first son (who is going to do funeral ceremonies) carry a cloth on his head goes around the bier thrice, others like sons, daughters, daughter-in-law, other relatives follows him. These people put nine grains in the cowdung and place it on the leg or hand of the dead person and then place it on the wall. This is done on the belief that "the family will be more fertile". Anybody can help in carrying the bier. If a male dies his parent's house people is to put "kooti" to him and if a lady dies her brother-in-law is to put the "kooti" to her. The other customs resemble the "Patayacci" caste people. On the 3rd day they do "paal teli".

On 7th day these people mourn for the dead person. These people do "karumati" on 16th day. They do this in the night. These people give only one offering and erect a stone and anoint it. Then they leave it in the river. These people do "talaikattu" next day after "karumati" and this is done after taking oil bath and done by the "Samandi". The other customs resemble the other caste people. They mourn for the dead person on 3rd month, for Deepawali and for Pongal. On these days they prepare tiffens etc. and offer to the dead person. These people give monthly *tithi* for one year, they give alms to the brahmin priest. They give "cow" as alms to the brahmin priest on "karumati" day. They also give "yearly *tithi*" and give rice, plantain, coins etc. as alms to the brahmin priest. If a married women dies they put red colour saree, if a widow dies they put white, if a male dies they put *dhoti* as "kooti". Widows can wear any colour saree, there is no restriction in this matter. If a child dies within one year they bury or cremate the child and do "punniyadanam" on 10th or 16th day. If a first child dies they bury the child inside the house and after some months they take the bones and burn them and put the ash in the river. These people's other custom are similar to the other caste people. These people do all the death customs even if the dead person is unmarried.

Devar

These people give bath to the dead both times. These people place "summaadu" to the head of the dead person, place tender coconut, lamp on the head side of the dead person. These people also place "batti' above the head-side of the dead person. Ladies put "vaykkarisi" in the house and the gents put "vaaykkarisi" in the graveyard. On 3rd day they do "paal teli", celebrate dukkam on 8th day, do 'karumati' on the 16th day. These people erect one stone and offerings are made three times. On 15th day night and 16th day early morning they celebrate "karumati" ceremony. First son lights the fire to the dead person. They put the nine grains in the cowdung, place that in the dead person's hand and then place it on the wall. Grand-son, grand-daughter etc. hold the ghee torch. They put parent's house "kooti" to the dead person. If husband dies that lady's brother-in-law puts the "kooti". These people mourn for the dead person on 30th day, Deepawali day and for Pongal day. If a lady dies with the married status these people give saree, blouse, flower, turmeric, *kumkum* etc. as alms to a brahmin priest's wife. These people do "yearly *tithi*" to the dead person. If a married lady dies they put flowered saree as "kooti", if a widowed lady dies they put white and red colour "kooti", if a male dies they put white cloth as "kooti". If a child within a year dies, these people bury the child, if the child dies later they cremate the child on 9th day they give offerings to the dead child. All the other customs regarding death resemble the barber caste people.

Udayar

This caste people bury the dead person. The other customs regarding death resemble the patayacci caste people. It is not in custom to put "vaykkarisi" to the dead person. They place only broken coconut, nut, betel leaf, nut, plantain, lamp on the head side of the dead person. After placing the dead body in the bier, son, daughter, son-in-law, daughter-in-law go round the bier thrice (without carrying anything in the hand or head) and bow down to the dead person. Only first son does the funeral ceremonies to the dead person. On the 3rd day they do "paal teli" Only on 8th day they mourn for the dead person and offer tiffens liked by the dead person. The other customs regarding death resemble the "patayacci" caste people.

On 10th day they do "karumati", offer three times, relatives bring tiffens liked by the dead person. It is not in custom to erect stone in the house, only they do ceremonies in the river bank and leave it in the river. Next day only they do "talaikattu". On 30th day they mourn for the dead person and do only yearly "*tithi*". If a lady dies with marriage status then they put "red" new cloth, put white new cloth to the widows and there is no compulsion for widows to wear a particular colour saree.

If a child within a year dies then they bury the child after boring the ear, do "punniyadanam" on 10th day. In this caste also these people do not marry the dead person with a decorated plantain. They do all the death customs without doing this.

Kallar (Devar)

While dying milk, basil plant's water etc. are poured in the mouth of the dead person. Regarding "vazhi kuutti vitutal" etc. these are done as usual in the front of the house. The dead body is given bath twice immediately after death and before taking it to the graveyard. These people place measuring pot full of paddy, betel leaf, nut, plantain, lamp etc. on the head side of the dead person. These people tie the hands, toes and mouth of the dead person. The dead body is cremated in this caste, "vaykkarisi" is put by the son, daughter, relatives and grand-son and grand-daughters. Gents put this only in the graveyard. After placing the dead body in the bier son, daughter-in-law, relatives go round the bier thrice, the son holds the measuring pot full of paddy in the hand while going round the bier. After going round the bier all bow down the dead body. After placing the body in the bier they place nine grains in cow-dung and place it in the hand (or) leg of the dead person and it is done on the belief that the luck will not go out with the dead person.

Grand-son, grand-daughter hold the ghee torch. First son does the funeral ceremonies to his father and last son does the funeral ceremonies to his mother. Relatives, friends, sons etc. carry the bier to the graveyard and while carrying the bier to the graveyard they scatter fried rice, flowers, coins etc. all the way to the graveyard. They put new cloth to the dead person from their parent's house. On the 3rd day "paal teli" is done. The other customs regarding death resemble the above caste people.

On 8th day they mourn for the dead person. On 15th day they celebrate "karumati", they offer three times, relatives bring tiffens, erect two stones in the house and anoint them, take the stones to the river bank and do ceremonies there and leave them in the river. On the same day they celebrate "talaikattu". On 30th day they mourn for the dead person. These people give only yearly *"tithi"* to the dead person. They put flowered new cloth if the dead person is a married lady, white new cloth for widows and there is no restriction for widows to wear particular colour saree. If a child within a year dies it is buried after boring the ear and they mourn for the child on 7th or 9th day. It is not mentioned if they do or do not perform death ceremonies to them, if unmarried person dies. The other customs regarding death resemble the "patayacci" caste people.

Tuluva Naickar

At the time of death of a person, these people pour milk, basil plant's water etc. in the mouth of the dying person. These people do the "vaahi kuutti vitutal" ceremony like other caste people but place the camphor in the street corner. The dead person is given bath only before taking to the graveyard. The dead body is buried and they tie hands, toe, mouth etc. of the dead person. All the persons put "vaykkarisi" to the dead person in the house itself. The beat drums in the dead person's house. They place measuring pot full of paddy, broken coconut, betel leaf, nut, lamp etc. on the head side of the dead person. After placing the dead body in the bier, son carries the measuring pot full of paddy and behind him daughter-in-law, relatives go round the bier and bow down to the dead person. After placing the dead body in the bier nine grains are placed in cowdung and placed in the leg or hand of the dead person and then placed on the well. This is done on the belief that the family will be fertile more and more. Grand son and grand-daughter hold the ghee torch. First son does the funeral ceremonies to the father and the last son does the funeral ceremonies to the mother. Relatives carry the bier to the graveyard. Regarding putting new cloth to the dead body they resemble the other caste people.

Next day they celebrate "paal teli", and the other ceremonies regarding "paal teli" resemble the other caste people. They mourn for the dead person on 3rd and 8th day, they offer tiffens liked by the dead person on these days. On 16th day they do "karumati", offer three times, relatives bring tiffens etc. After doing funeral ceremonies in the river they leave the stone in the river and next day "talaikattu" is done. On 30th day they mourn for dead person. Only yearly titi is given by this people to the dead person and they give clothes as alms to a brahmin priest on "karumati" day.

They put red colour new cloth to the married woman if she dies with married status, if a widow dies they put white cloth, and white cloth is to be worn by the widow compulsorily. If a child within a year dies they bury the child (even without boring the ear) and on 9th day they celebrate "punniyadanam". If an unmarried person dies these people do not perform "marriage" ceremony to him and do the funeral ceremonies. Without doing this ceremony they do the death customs.

Jankamar

These people bury the dead body. Immediately after death these people tie the hands, toes and mouth with a cloth. They blow conch and beat "seemankalam" for the dead person. They place a measuring pot full of paddy, broken coconut, betel leaf, nut, plantain and lamp on the head side of the dead person. After placing the dead body in the bier son (carrying the measuring pot in the hand), daughter, son-in-law, daughter-in-law, relatives go round the bier thrice and bow down to the dead body.

There is no custom of placing cowdung on the hand or leg of the dead person and place it on the wall in this caste. If a male dies, then for his widow, her brother-in-law puts new cloth (kozhundan kooti) to her. They do "paal teli", ceremony on the 3rd day. The vessels taken to the graveyard on that day are taken back to the house. The other customs regarding death resemble the other caste people.

On 7th day they mourn for the dead person and prepare tiffens liked by him and offer them to him. On 11th day these people celebrate "karumati" and offer three times. On that day relatives bring tiffens. These people do ceremonies on this day for a stone in the river bank and leave it in the river. On the same day they do "talaikattu". On 30th day these people mourn for the dead person. They give "yearly *tithi*" to the dead person. If a lady with married status dies then these people put red, yellow, green colour new cloth and if a widow dies they put white cloth and there is no restriction for the widows to wear a particular saree. The other customs regarding death resemble the above caste people.

Konar (Yadhavappillai)

At the moment of dying one has to give basil plant's water, milk etc. to the dead person's mouth. They both bury and cremate the dead body. They give bath to the dead body immediately after death and do the ceremony of clearing the way only in the street corner. Then when taking to the graveyard they again give bath to the dead body. All the other customs resemble the Patayacci caste people regarding death. The new cloth comes from his brother-in-law's house. If the dead person is a lady then the new cloth has to come from her parent's house.

Next day "paal teli". On 8th day they mourn (on 7th day, i.e. in odd numbered days) for the dead person. This can be done on the 5th day. On 16th day they do the funeral rites. This is done on 15th day night. In that night a stone is erected, oil is smeared, water is kept in a brass pot, putting thread in it, coconut, camphor are shown in five leaves and offered to it. They give offerings three times. First offering is given to the people who are weeping for the death in that house. Second offering is given to the washerman, barber etc. Third offering is done and the stone is put in the river. These who put new cloth to the dead body have to take bath 108 times. If the person is not able to do it, the dead person's son has to do it. If a woman become widow she has to cross the pestle, new cloth and the fire by putting fire in the straw. The person after taking 108 baths has to come inside and bow down to the lamp and sit facing northern side and take the curd, tender coconut, milk etc. given by others. They mourn for the dead person on 30th day. They do the rites for each month on new moon day. They give yearly "*tithi*" once in a year. If a child within a year dies they do "punniyadanam" on 11th day.

Kuravar (Ramajooki)

These people pour milk, water etc. into the mouth of the dying person. It is in custom to bury the dead body in this caste. They give bath to the dead body only before taking the body to the graveyard. They clear the way to the dead person like other caste people and do it in the road corner. They place measuring pot full of paddy and light the lamp on the head side of the dead body. Then the body is given bath and the relatives put rice in the mouth of the dead person. If a lady dies then the new cloth comes from her parents's house. If it is a male, brother brings the new cloth. Grandson and grand-daughter hold the ghee torch. Then the son, sister-in-law etc. hold the measuring pot full of paddy and go round the bier thrice. At the time of going round they place, the nine grains pressed in the cowdung in the hands of the dead person and then place it in the wall. Then after burying, they take bath, return to the arrack shop and then only, these people come to the house and take food.

Next day they celebrate "paal teli". First they do some offerings in the house and then take milk, tender coconut, camphor batti, unhusked rice, dhall etc. and place it in the graveyard and offer it. On 8th day they mourn for the dead person. On that day they prepare tiffens and offer them. On 16th day "karumati" is done. On that day relatives come with tiffens, offer to the dead person and do all the funeral rites. Next day "talaikattu" is done. On 30th day they mourn for the dead person (This is done on the belief that "the dead persons are invited again to the house"). It is not in custom to give yearly funeral rites to the dead person in this caste. If a child within a year dies these people do "punniyadanam" on 8th or 9th day.

Vannan (Cakkili)

At the moment of dying the relatives of that person give water, water mixed in the sand, rubbing the coin and mixed in water, basil plant's water, milk etc. to that person. These people do the "vazhi kuutti vitutal" ceremony like other caste people. This caste people both bury and cremate the corpse. Only after "vazhi kuutti vitutal" ceremony, they send the news outside and then only they weep. They place a coin on the forehead of the corpse and put garland on the corpse. The dead body is kept on a bench under which sand is spread. Then they tie the leg, hand and mouth. The new cloth for the dead body comes from the parent's house. After this the customs resemble the "Patayacci" caste people. Moreover, they press the nine grains in the cowdung and place it on the legs, hands of the dead person and then place it on the well.

Putting rice in the mouth of the dead person is also in practice. Then they go round the bier thrice and bow down thrice in three places. If one dies then three types of drum (viz., tappattai—small kind of tabrat, urumpusettu—a kind of drum, kooyil meelam-drums of the temple) are beat in that house. Then the corpse is taken to the graveyard and the cremations are done. While returning to the house they take bath, and before entering into the house they wash their hands, legs etc. and place the holy ash, *kumkum* etc. on their forehead and then only they take food.

Next day "paal teli", on that day after this ceremony and taking food, they do "talaikattu" to the dead person's son. Dead person's is made to sit in the son-in-law's house and a towel is placed on his head, sandal paste is smeared and he is given betel leaf and nut. These people do the same thing to the person in the son-in-law's house. On 3rd or 7th day they do tiffens and offer it to the dead person. After this they do "punniyadanam" and wear new dress,. On 16th day they do "karumati", on that day erecting a stone ("kal patittal") is done. On 15th day night and 16th day very early morning this is done.

On 15th day evening, on 15th day mid-night and on 16th day early morning they make offerings to dead person. When offerings are given third time, two bricks are placed in a laid position and both these pair tied with red cloth and the daughter of the dead person, smear oil and smear ground stuff and wash them. Then she puts sandal paste, *kumkum,* flower etc. on it. Before doing these things all the things to be taken to the "karumati turai" (river bank) are placed in the side. Then this brick is taken to the river bank and "karumati" is done there. New cloth is given to the persons who do "karumati" only after finishing the "karumati". After finishing "karumati", they take the "kalasam" and go to a Lord Ganesh's temple and break a coconut and then only they return to the house. The wife of the person who holds the "kalasam" show camphor and aalam and gets the "kalasam" from him and keeps it inside the house "paanagam" (Jaggery cardamom etc. dissolved in water), buttermilk etc. are given to the relatives and meals are arranged for them. After the meals these who want to present things give presentations. These people do funeral rites every year to the dead person. If a child within a year died then they do the "punniyadanam" on the 11th day.

Navitar (Barber)

The customs in this caste people resemble more or less the washerman caste people with slight differences. Immediately after the death they give bath to the dead body, place the holy ash on its forehead, place a twenty-five paise coin on its forehead and place the dead body on the bench in which sand is spread and dharbai (a kind of holy grass) is kept on the sand and on that the dead body is placed.

After cremating the corpse, they return after taking bath. Then the "pindam" (the boiled rice in lumps for the manes, rice cooked with plantain) is cooked by the relatives and it is placed in the shape of the number thirty two on the dharbai grass according to the sayings of the brahmin priest. Then they light the camphor and leave those "pindams" in the river. Then rice, jaggery, plantain, gingely, blackgram flour etc. are mixed and the "pindam" is placed. On this the person who lights the fire on the corpse puts gingely and pure water and this pindam is again left into the water. The other customs resemble the washerman caste people regarding death. More or less all the customs resemble the same as washerman caste people. These people do not do "talaikattu" immediately after "paal teli". But they do this only after "karumati", on the 8th day, they mourn for the dead person. These people do funeral rites for the dead person every year. If a child within a year dies then they do "punniyadanam" on the 11th day.

Cakkili

These people give the same kind of things in the mouth of a dying person like other caste people. They cremate the corpse and also do "vazhi kuutti vitutal". They go to the street corner (termed as "mandakkarai"), break a coconut, light the lamp and camphor and then they clear the way to the dead person. Immediately after death they give bath to the dead body. All kinds of drum are beaten, turmeric, rice, nine kind of grains, wooden mortor etc. are brought and these things are powdered and this powder is kept on the head side of the dead body and they worship. Then after the relatives come, again the dead body is given bath, the relatives both male and female put the rice in the mouth of the corpse. Males again put the rice in the graveyard also. Then new cloth is put on the body, and the powder which was offered first to the dead body, is tied in the lap by that person's sons, daughters-in-law and then they go round thrice the dead body and then they put the powder on the dead body. They termed this as "antaratchai ceytal". At that time priest (pandaram) recites holy mantras. Then the body is taken to the graveyard and it is cremated.

On the 3rd day they do "paal teli". They go to the graveyard, clean the place and offer cooked grains, milk, plantain etc. Only after worshiping, that person's uncle has to give these things to others. On 8th day they mourn for the dead person. On that day they do a ceremony "pazham parampputal". Only on the 16th day they do "karumati" which is done like other caste people. Immediately after finishing "karumati" they do "talaikattu" on the bank itself. On 30th day they invite the dead person's father-in-law and prepare tiffens and worship the dead person. This is termed as "muppatu kumpitutal". These people do funeral rites every year to the dead person. If a child within a year dies some people do "punniyadanam" on 8th day (or) some people do on 16th day.

Harijan (Aadi Dravidiar)

While a person is about to die, the relatives pour milk into his mouth. Only burying is in custom in this caste. They give bath two times to the dead body. One immediately after death and the other while taking the body to the graveyard. They put rice in the dead person's mouth. They clear the way to the dead person in the street corner. These people beats drum when a person is dead, oil, Sikakkaay, tender coconut etc. are brought by the relatives as "vaykkarisi siir" and using these things, they give bath to the dead body and smear the holy ash or *kumkum* on the forehead. They place paddy full of measuring pot, knife, stick, pestle etc. on the head side of the dead body the grand son holds the pot in which flour is kept, the son holds the measuring pot full of paddy and the others holds the other things and all go round the bier thrice. Then nine grains are pressed in cowdung and placed in the hands of the dying person and then placed it in the wall. These people with nine grains pressed in cowdung, add margosa leaves and place it in the wall. Then the body is removed to the graveyard and after taking bath they return to the house and take food.

Next day "paal teli". They do this ceremony like "Patayacci" caste people, on that day they cook meals, pulse, unhusked rice, a kind of pulse etc. take bath and offer these things to the dead person and take food only after this. On 16th day they do funeral rites. For all the sixteen days a lamp is lit and water is kept in the brass pot. If the dead person is a male then they mourn on 6th day, if it is a female then they mourn on 7th day. Same as for males they do the funeral rites on 16th day and for female on 15th day. These people mourn for the dead person on 30th day also.

These people give yearly funeral rites for every year. On that day they give rice as alms to a priest (Pandaaram) or to a cow. If a child dies within a year they do "punniyadanam" on the odd numbered days.

Sample of Questionnaire

1. Informant's Name :
2. Caste Name :
3. Age :
4. Sex :
5. Native Place :
6. Present Residence :
7. Educational qualifications :
8. Address :

1. Child Birth

1. Have you given bath to the child as soon as it born?

   Yes, No

2. Do you follow the custom of putting the child in the leaf?

   Yes, No

3. Do you give donkey's milk (or) donkey's blood to the newly born baby to avoid skin diseases like "karappaan" etc.?

   Yes, No

4. For how many days you give 'diet food' to the mother?

   ....to.............

5. What kind of food are included in the diet food?

6. After the child birth do you put kappu? Yes, No

   1. in which house? 2. on what date?

   1. .... 2. ....

7. What kind of "kappu" is tied to the child first?

   1. margosa fibre

   2. Then what kind of "kappu" are put to the child?

   3. Five metal bangle; silver bangle; golden bangle.

8. On the day of kappu :

   1. Do you take new dresses to the child?

   2. Do you prepare rice mixed with jaggery?

   3. Do you invite relatives?

   1. Yes, No 2. Yes, No
   3. Yes, No.

9. 1. When will you put the child in the cloth cradle (or) cradle?

   2. Which cloth do you use for tying the cloth cradle?

   1. New cloth; 2. Mother's marriage saree.

   1. .... 2.
   1. 2.

10. 1. When will you celebrate "Naming ceremony"?

    2. Do you invite relatives at the time of "Naming ceremony"?

1. .... 2. Yes, No

11. Do you have any other customs at the time of "Naming ceremony"?

    Yes, No

12. Do you celebrate "punniyadanam" 1. on what day? 2. For what purpose? Yes, No

    1. .... 2. ....

13. The lady who gave birth to a child takes margosa leaves (or) iron things in her hands.

    1.Is it in custom? 2. For what purpose?

    1. Yes, No; 2. To avoid the seizure of ghosts.

14. 1.When 2. where will you take the child outside first?

    1. .... 2. ....

15. 1. Do you remove the hair of the child?

    2. Then at what time?

    1. Yes, No 2. ....

16. When will you celebrate "Ear boring ceremony"?

17. At that time do you take new dress to the parents, child etc.?

    Yes, No, Only for the child

18. At the time of boring the ear 1. in whose lap the child is to be sit. 2. Who bore the ear. 3. Do you put the golden ear ring in the ear. 4. Where i.e. in house or temple will you celebrate the ceremony. 5. Who has to spend money for this?

    1. .... lap 2. .... bore the ear

    3. Yes, No 4. House, Temple

    5. .... expenditure

19. 1. In what age you admit the child in the school?

    2. At that time do you give money to the teacher in the school?

    3. Do you prepare rice mixed with jaggery at that time?

4. Do you give sweets to the children in the school?

5. Do you take new clothes to the child?

1. ....age, 2. Yes, No

3. Yes, No 4. Yes, No;

5. Yes, No.

20. Do you celebrate "sacred thread ceremony"?

    Yes, No

21. If so then at what age?

    .... age

22. What type of threads you put?

    1. thread, 2. silver
    3. gold

23. First what a type of thread do you put?

    1. thread

24. 1. Do you invite friends, relatives for the sacred thread ceremony?

    2. Do you give feast? On that day whether presentations are given to the boy?

    1. Yes, No; 2. Yes, No
    3. Yes, No.

25. Do you change the "sacred thread" ever year on the day of "avittam" star in the month of "aavani".

Puberty Rituals

1. When a girl attains her age whether she can tell the news first to her mother?

    1. Yes 2. Only through somebody else.

2. Immediately "after attaining age" what do you do?

3. 1. Do you pour water (give full bath) on the first day?

    2. Do you prepare "puttu"?

    3. Do you leave her in a separate room?

4. Do you build a separate room with green coconut leaves?

5. Do you pour water, decorate her hair with flower on that day?

1. Yes, No; 2. Yes, No;
3. Yes, No; 4. Yes, No;
5. Yes, No

4. On the first day immediately after giving bath what are the things given first to eat?

   1. dhall rice, 2. egg, blackgram flour, sugar; 3. sugar rice, 4. gingely oil, 5. plantain.

5. 1. On what days do you pour water?

   2. On what days do you prepare "puttu"?

   1. .... 2. ....

6. Do you prepare horoscope of the girl at the time of attaining age?

   1. Yes, No

7. 1. Do you hold sieve above the head of the girl while pouring water on the first day?

   2. If so who holds the sieve,

   3. What are the things you put into the sieve.

   4. Who pours water first in the sieve?

   1. Yes, No; 2. ....; 3. turmeric, margosa leaves, coin; 4. ....

8. When will you invite the girl inside the house?

9. 1. When will you celebrate "puberty rituals"?

   2. Who has to do "siir" for this celebration?

10. Is it in custom to take new saree at the time of puberty rituals?

    Yes, No

11. Is it in custom to do "nalungu" on the first day?

    Yes, No

12. At the time of doing "nalungu", is it in custom to smear sandal paste, place *kumkum*, put garland to the girl?

    Yes, No

13. 1. Whether relatives come, prepare food and serve it to the girl in odd numbered days?

    2. Is it in custom to prepare "puttu" on those days?

    1. Yes, No 2. Yes, No

14. 1. On the day of celebrating "puberty rituals", is it custom to wear new saree, put garland and give coconut in the hands, of the girl? 2. At that time is it a custom to place, stone mortor, roller etc?

    3. Is it a custom to decorate the roller etc. with sandal paste and *kumkum*?

    4. Is it a custom to give and get back the decorated roller thrice in the hands of the girl?

    5. Whether presentations are given to the girl?

    1. Yes, No; 2. Yes, No; 3. Yes, No; 4. Yes, No; 5. Yes, No.

15. 1. Do you send the girl out without celebrating "puberty rituals"? 2. If it is not possible to celebrate "puberty rituals", then is it a custom to show "puttu" around the girl and allow her to go out?

    1. Yes, No; 2. Yes, No

16. 1. If a girl at the time of menstruating period goes out then she has to take margosa leaves (or) iron made things with her? Is it on the belief that ghosts will not seize her?

    1. Yes, No; 2. Yes, No

17. 1. Is it a custom to give the dress of the girl on the day of attaining age of washer-woman?

    2. Is it a custom whether the washerwoman is to give the change of dress till the girl is invited inside the house?

    1. Yes, No 2. Yes, No

Marriage customs

1. 1. Do you compare horoscope?

   2. First from whose house they ask for the horoscope?

   3. After go and see the place and only if you like the place is it a custom to compare the horoscope?

   4. Or if the horoscope agree then only they go and meet the party?

   1. Yes, No; 2. Yes, No; 3. Yes, No; 4. Yes, No.

2. For the purpose of comparison bride's birth horoscope (or) the age attaining horoscope is used?

   1. Birth horoscope.

   2. Age attaining horoscope.

   3. If the birth horoscope is not available then they use age attaining horoscope,

   4. Both.

3. 1. If the horoscopes do not agree is it in custom to place flower before Deity?

   2. This is done in the house (or) in the temple?

   1. Yes, No; 2. House, Temple

4. If the horoscopes agree whether the bride and bridegroom meet each other?

   Yes, No

5. 1. If they approve of each other then is it a custom to celebrate engagement (or) muhuurtha oolai?

   2. Do you put the ornaments, give the dowry etc. to bride?

   3. Only if the marriage is fixed then is it a custom to take food in each other's house?

   4. Or if both the parties are relatives then they take food even if the marriage is not fixed?

   1. Yes, No; 2. Yes, No; 3. Yes, No; 4. Yes, No.

6. At the time of engagement is it a custom : 1. to get the written document, 2. to exchange the plates.

   1. Yes, No; 2. Yes, No.

7. For the engagement do you invite 1. relatives, friends, 2. give feast etc?

   1. Yes, No; 2. Yes, No.

8. 1. How many days before marriage you celebrate "nalungu" to the bride?

   2. Who celebrate the "nalungu" first to the bride?

   3. Whether relatives also do the "nalungu"?

   4. Only "uncle" does the "nalungu"?

   1. ....days; 2. ....; 3. Yes, No; 4. Yes, No.

9. 1. How many days before marriage do you soak nine grains?

   2. Whether they soak it in bridegroom's house?

   3. Whether they soak it in bride's house?

   4. If so how many days before marriage do you soak the nine grains?

   1. ....days; 2. Yes, No; 3. Yes, No; 4. They do it only in the place where the marriage is celebrated; certain days .... before marriage in bride's house; certain days .... before marriage in bridegroom's house.

10. 1. How many days before marriage do you build pandar for marriage? 2. In which direction you erect the first pillar for pandar? 3. Who erects the first pillar for pandar? 4. Is there any compulsion to erect certain number of pillars? 5. If so how many? 6. Do you decorate the pandar with any other things? 7. Is it a custom that the bride and bridegroom have to show the camphor to pillars in the pandar? 8. What things are tied in the first pillar for pandar.

    1. .... days before; 2. Eastern side, Northern east

side (isaniya muulai); 3. ....; 4. Yes, No; 5. ....pillars; 6. Washerman ties white cloth; 7. Yes, No; 8. turmeric, mango leaves, red cloth; sandal paste, *kumkum*.

11. Where do you celebrate marriage?

    Bridegroom's house; bride's house; temple.

12. 1. When will the bridegroom's party come to invite the bride?

    2. What are the things they bring at that time?

    3. Is it a custom to put "parisam"?

    4. After taking the girl to the (bridegroom's) house, is it a custom to offer for their family Deity by placing the things used on marriage day?

    1. Day before marriage; Two days before marriage; Three days before marriage; 2. siir; 3. Yes, No; 4. Yes, No.

13. Is it a custom to celebrate "nalungu" before marriage day (to the bride in bride's house; to the bridegroom in bridegroom's house)?

    Yes, No

14. 1. On the marriage day morning is it a custom that the bride and bridegroom keep fasting?

    2. Is it a custom to tie yellow string in each other's hand?

    3. Or anybody else tie the yellow string in their hands?

    1. Yes, No; 2. Yes, No; 3. For the bridegroom .... ties; For the bride .... ties.

15. 1. Do you decorate a separate marriage platform?

    2. What are the things placed in the marriage platform?

    3. Do you pour water in the "saalungaravam" pot before it is placed in the marriage platform?

    4. What are the things put inside that pot?

    5. Do you place "pantamuttiakal panai" (row of pot) in the marriage platform?

6. How many rows are to be there?

7. How many pots are there in one row?

8. Do you brought the pots newly from the potter's house?

9. Do you tie the peepul tree's bough with this pot?

10. or Do you erect it separately?

11. How many standing lamps are placed in the marriage platform?

1. Yes, No; 2. Saalungaravam; big pot; kutavilakku; 3. Yes, No; 4. milk ladle, knife, stylus for writing, palm leaf, lemon; 5. Yes, No; 6. ....rows; 7. ....pots; 8. Yes, No; 9. Yes, No; 20. Yes, No; 11. two, four.

16. Do you have any other custom before tying marriage badge?

....

17. While tying marriage badge which saree do you wear?

1. Cotton saree? or Silk saree?

1. Cotton saree; 2. Silk saree.

18. Do you wear nine yards saree?

Yes, No

19. 1. Do you put "punul" before tying marriage badge to the bridegroom?

2. Who puts it?

3. What kind of "punul" are put?

4. What type of "punul" do you put first?

1. Yes, No; 2. Relatives; married ladies; brahmin priest; 3. thread, silver, gold; 4. thread.

20. 1. Is it in custom that the brahmin priest places marriage badge, coconut, betel leaf, nut, plantain, flower etc. in a plate and get the blessings of elderly people?

2. Is it a custom to give yellow rice to the elderly people at that time?

3. Is it a custom, while tying marriage badge the elderly people put the flower, yellow rice on the newly married couple and bless them?

4. Is it a custom that the brahmin priest recites holy mantras and kindles holy fire?

1. Yes, No; 2. Yes, No; 3. Yes, No; 4. Yes, No.

21. 1. While tying marriage badge : 1. Is it a custom that the first knot is tied by the bridegroom, and the other two are tied by the sister-in-law?

2. All the three knots are tied by the bridegroom?

3. Is it a custom that the sister-in-law hold the lamp in the back of the bride while tying marriages badge?

4. Is it in custom to put coins in that lamp?

1. Yes, No; 2. Yes, No; 3. Yes, No; 4. Yes, No.

22. 1. Immediately after tying marriage badge is it a custom to go round the marriage platform thrice?

2. Who go round it?

1. Yes, No; 2. bride, bridegroom, bride's sister-in-law, bridegroom's brother-in-law.

23. 1. When will the brother-in-law puts fried rice in the hands of the newly married couple?

2. At that time is it a custom to put ring in the finger of the bridegroom (by the brother-in-law)?

3. In return is it a custom to put ring to his brother-in-law?

1. After going round the marriage platform—thrice.

2. Yes, No; 3. Yes, No.

24. 1. Who puts ring in the toe of the bride?

2. Is it a custom to put ring even before marriage to the bride?

3. For Deepawali :
Yes, No

4. For Karthikai :
Yes, No

5. For Pongal :
Yes, No

6. For Navarattiri :
Yes, No

7. For Krishna Jayanti :
Yes, No

First Pregnancy

1. When you come to know if a lady is pregnant, is it in custom to celebrate anything in the 3rd month?

   Taking black saree; go and meet the girl; prepare three kind of edibles; decorating her hair with flowers.

2. Do you celebrate any function on the 5th month?

   Preparing five kind of meals, take it and give it to the girl; If they do not take black saree in the 3rd month then take black saree in the 5th month; Preparing five kind of tiffens, celebrating "nalungu".

3. 1. When will you celebrate "valaikappu" to the lady?

   2. What kind of "kappu" do you put first?

   3. What kind of "kappu" are put?

   4. On the day of "valaikappu" whether the bridegroom is there with the lady?

   5. Is it a custom to put bangles to those married ladies who attend the function?

   6. In which house do they celebrate "valaikappu"?

   7. Is it in custom to do "siimandam"?

   8. If so in which house?

   9. Do you bring the girl to the house immediately after the "valaikappu"?

10. When will you take the girl to the house for delivery?

11. When will you send back the girl to her husband's house after delivery?

12. Do you do any "siir" to the lady while she is sending back to her husband's house?

1. ....; 2. margosa fibre; 3. five metal bangle, silver, black bead bangle, golden bangle; 4. Yes, No; 5. Yes, No; 6. .... house; 7. Yes, No; 8. ....house; 9. Yes, No; 10. 7th month, 9th month; 11th .... month; 12. Yes, No.

60th birthday

1. Is it in custom to celebrate 60th birthday (sashtiyapthapurtti) in your caste?

   Yes, No

2. 1. On that day is it a custom to invite brahmin priest, he recites holy mantras, kindles holy fire, place kalasas and anoint the couple?

   2. Do you place "kalasas", if so how many?

   3. Is it a custom to tie marriage badge at that time also?

   4. On that occasion is it a custom to take new dresses to the couple?

   5. Who celebrate this function?

   1. Yes, No; 2. ....kalasas; 3. Yes, No; 4. Yes, No; 5. Son, daughter, daughter-in-law, son-in-law.

3. Do you celebrate this in the house (or) temple?

   House, temple

70th or 80th birthday

1. Is it in custom to celebrate "sadhabhishegam"?

   Yes, No

2. Do you celebrate this like 60th birthday?

   Yes, No

Death Customs

1. At the moment of death what are the things you pour in the mouth of the dying person?

   Milk, basil plant water, coin water, sand mixed water.

2. 1. Immediately after the death of the person what do you do?

   2. Where do you perform the "vazhu kuutti vitutal" ceremony, i.e. whether in front of the house or in the street corner?

   1. By breaking coconut, placing betel leaf, nut, etc. lighting the lamp and showing the camphor—do the "vazhi kuutti vitutal" ceremony. 2. In front of the house, in the street corner.

3. 1. Do you give bath to the dead body immediately after death?

   2. Or do you give bath to the dead body before taking to the graveyard?

   3. Otherwise do you give bath both times?

   1. Yes, No; 2. Yes, No; 3. Yes, No.

4. 1. Do you send the news only after doing the "vazhi kuutti vitutal" ceremony?

   2. Then only do you weep?

   1. Yes, No; 2. Yes, No.

5. Do you cremate, bury or do both the things?

   Cremate, bury, both are in custom

6. Is it a custom to tie the leg, hand, mouth of dead person immediately after death?

   Yes, No

7. 1. Is it in custom to put rice in the mouth of the dead person?

   2. Who puts it?

   3. Whether ladies also put it?

4. Whether ladies put it in the house?

5. Whether getns put it in the house.

6. On the graveyard?

1. Yes, No; 2. relatives, son, daughter; 3. Yes, No; 4. Yes, No; 5. Yes, No; 6. Yes, No.

8. Do you beat drums?

   Yes, No

9. After placing the dead body in the bier

   1. how many times, 2. who?

   3. Eldest son hold corn-measure full of paddy (or) carry a cloth on the head and go round the bier?

   4. Is it a custom to bow down the dead body?

   1. ....times; 2. son, daughter-in-law, relatives,

   3. Corn-measure full of paddy, carry the cloth on the head;

   4. Yes, No.

10. What are the things you place on the head-side of the dead-body?

    Corn-measure full of paddy; broken coconut; betel leaf, nut, plantain, lamp.

11. 1. After placing the dead body in the bier is it in custom to place cow-dung with nine grains on the foot (or) hand of the dead body and place it on the wall?

    2. On what belief do you do this?

    1. Yes, No; foot; hand; both in the foot and hand.

    2. Family will be fertile; the luck of the dead person will not go along with him.

12. Is it a custom that the grand-son, grand-daughter hold the ghee torch?

    Yes, No

13. Who lights the funeral fire? eldest son; eldest son for the father; youngest son for the mother; relatives.

14. While taking the dead body to the graveyard who carry the bier?

    Relatives; Friends; Sons.

15. 1. Is it in custom to put new cloth (kooti) to the dead body?

    2. Who put it?

    3. Who puts the (from who's house) new cloth from the dead person?

    4. If the dead person is male then who puts new cloth to his widow?

    1. Yes, No; 2. From parents house, relatives; 3. parent's house; 4. parents.

16. Is it a custom to scatter fried rice, flower, coins etc. throughout the way to the graveyard?

    Yes, No; If the death is on astami, navami *tithi.*

17. Do you do any ceremony after placing the dead body in the graveyard?

    Yes, No

18. After cremating (or) burying the body, taking bath and after coming to the house, wash the leg, hand etc. is it a custom to bow down the lamp placed, where the dead body was placed and than take food?

    Yes, No

19. Is it a custom to place a lamp where the dead body is placed till the day of funeral rites celebrated?

    Yes, No

20. Is it compulsory to spend the paddy brought by the relatives to put "vaykkarisi" (rice) to the dead person before funeral day?

    Yes, No

21. 1. When do you celebrate "paalteli"?

    2. On that day is it a custom to place milk in a vessel

and the ladies has to put coins into it without making noise?

3. On that day is it a custom to take milk, tender coconut etc. to the graveyard, pick up the bones there, put them in a pot and dissolve them in the river?

4. Do you give vessels to the brahmin priest? or take them back to the house?

1. Next day, 3rd day; 2. Yes, No; 3. Yes, No;

4. Give the vessels to the brahmin priest so alms; take them back to the house.

22. 1. Do you mourn for the dead person on 3rd day, 8th day, 11th day?

2. On that day do you offer the edibles liked by the dead person?

1. 3rd day Yes, No; 8th day Yes, No; 11th day, Yes, No;

2. Yes, No.

23. 1. When do you celebrate "funeral rites"?

2. For that how many times do you offer?

3. Is it a custom that the relatives bring tiffens on that day?

4. Is it a custom to erect stones in the house and anoint it?

5. How many stones do you erect?

6. After doing funeral rites to the stone is it a custom to leave the stones in the river?

7. Is it a custom that gents only go to the river bank to do funeral rites?

8. Do you do "talaikattu" on the same day?

1. ....day; 2. three offerings; 3. Yes, No; 4. Yes, No; 5. two, one; 6. Yes, No; 7. Yes, No, Ladies also come; 8. on the same day, next day.

24. Do you mourn for the dead person on 30th day, 3rd, month?

    Yes, No; Yes, No.

25. Do you give monthly *tithi*, yearly *tithi* to the dead person?

    Yes, No; Yes, No.

26. If a person dies then is it a custom to give cow, bamboo, land, cloth as alms to a brahmin priest on the day of funeral rites?

Cow	Bamboo	Land	Cloth
Yes, No	Yes, No	Yes, No	Yes, No.

27. Do you give new saree, blouse, turmeric, *kumkum*, flower etc. to a married lady on the day of yearly *tithi*, if a lady dies with married status?

    Yes, No

28. 1. Lady with married status.

    2. for widows what colour of new cloth do you put?

    3. Is it compulsory for a widow to wear particular colour saree?

    1. red, flowered saree; 2. white, sandal colour;

    3. Yes, No; .... colour.

29. 1. If a child within a year dies then what do you do? Do you cremate? or bury?

    2. Do you celebrate "punniyadanam" for the dead child?

    3. If so on what day?

    4. Do you bury the child only after boring the ear?

    1. Cremate, bury; 2. Yes, No; 3. ....day; 4. Yes, No.

30. If an unmarried person dies then is it a custom to decorate a plantain and get it married to the dead

person, before the funeral rites to the dead person are done is it so in your caste also?

Yes, No

I have included Festivals, Fastings, Superstitions etc. in the questionnaire, but I have not included them in my report to delimit the page. I got answers for these things also from various caste people and various regional people.

17. Russel Reevar and Boswell, W. George : Fundamentals of Folk Literature
18. Sachadeva, D.R. and Vidya Bhusan : An Introduction to Sociology
19. Sakthivel, S. : Folklore Literature in India
20. Sankar Sengupta : Folklore and Folklife in India
21. Sankar Sengupta & Upadhyaya, K.D. : Studies in India Folk Culture
22. Shanmuga-sundaram, S. : Nattuppura Iyal
23. Singh, K. : Social and Cultural Anthropology
24. Singh, K.P. : The Principles of Sociology
25. Thurston : Caste and Tribe of Southern India, vol. I
26. Thurston : Caste and Tribes of Southern India, vol. II
27. Vatsyayan : Indian Society and Social Institutions

Index